Middletown Families
Fifty Years of Change and Continuity

Theodore Caplow
  and
Howard M. Bahr
Bruce A. Chadwick
Reuben Hill
Margaret Holmes Williamson

UNIVERSITY OF MINNESOTA PRESS

Minneapolis

Based on the research
of the Middletown III Project, 1976-1981,
under a grant from
the National Science Foundation

Published by the University of Minnesota Press,
2037 University Avenue Southeast, Minneapolis, MN 55414
Printed in the United States of America.
First published, 1982
Second printing, 1982
University of Minnesota paperback edition published 1985

Library of Congress Cataloging in Publication Data

Caplow, Theodore.
    Middletown families.
    "Based on the research of the Middletown III project, 1976-1981,
under a grant from the National Science Foundation."
    Bibliography: p.
    Includes index.
    1. Family – United States – Longitudinal studies. 2. Cities and
towns – United States – Longitudinal studies – Case studies.
3. Community life – United States – Longitudinal studies – Case
studies. I. Title.
HQ 535.C25   306.8   81-14757
ISBN 0-8166-1073-8   AACR2
ISBN 0-8166-1435-0   (pbk.)

Table of Contents

Preface

This is the first installment in paying a debt that all of us owe to Robert and Helen Lynd who studied the small industrial city they called Middletown in 1924 and 1925 and again in 1935 and published their findings in *Middletown* (1929) and *Middletown in Transition* (1937). Forty years later, Howard Bahr, Bruce Chadwick, and I went back to Middletown to repeat their studies and opened a field office in a little house near the river at the edge of downtown. The Lynds had been the first people to describe the total culture of an American community with scientific detachment. They were also the first to replicate a community study in order to trace the velocity and direction of social change. We proposed to follow their good example in both ways.

From the spring of 1976 until the fall of 1978, we took turns living in Middletown with our families and working on the study. Like the Lynds and their assistants, we read everything of local interest we could find, attended every public or private occasion to which we could gain access, interviewed the movers and shakers in business and politics and conducted cross-sectional surveys of carefully selected samples of the population: adolescents and adults, individuals and families, employed men, employed women with and without children, people in and out of churches, voluntary associations and government agencies. In all, we did 13 major surveys in Middletown, not counting some minor ones undertaken for special purposes. In three of these surveys—and they were the most informative—our questionnaires were largely copied from those used by the Lynds and we repeated many of their questions verbatim. As the study progressed, we became increasingly aware of how important it was to copy the original procedures closely in order to facilitate comparison between the Middletown of 1924 or 1935 and the Middletown of today. This effort was not entirely successful. We do not think we ever came to know the place as intimately as our predecessors; it is much larger now than it was in their time, and all of us were older than they were when they went to Middletown and more distracted by family responsibilities. Among us we brought 14 children to settle temporarily in Middletown and to attend the local schools. Their presence placed us firmly within Middletown's predominant life-style, which is intensely familial, but at the same time set constraints on our movements through the diverse social worlds that compose the community. But, if our experience of the rich tapestry of community life seems somehow less intense than the Lynds', our surveys were more thorough and more numerous and they were linked to a computer technology that permits extensive analysis. We are not at all sure that we understand the community as well as the Lynds did, but we have more information about it. Thus, we cannot fit our report into a single volume, as they did for each of their studies. As of this writing, 20 papers have been published to report the findings of the Middletown III study, and this book covers only one of the study's six major topics, leaving the rest for later volumes. Two and a half years after leaving the research site, our files still contain entire completed surveys on which analysis has not begun.

More books are projected, if Heaven gives us strength and our universities allow us the time to finish them. After *Middletown Families* comes *All Faithful People*, a report on religion in Middletown scheduled for publication next year and after that *Happily Ever After*, then a final report pulling all the pieces together and summarizing what has happened in Middletown as the adolescents observed by the Lynds grew into the elderly people we observed in recent years.

Whether or not this entire program is eventually completed, other writings are sure to issue from the Middletown III project. The papers already written bear the names of many authors besides those contributing to *Middletown Families*. Among them, we count proudly Dwight Hoover, Joseph Tamney, John Hewitt, Otis D.

Duncan, C. Bradford Chappell, Geoffrey K. Leigh, Penelope C. Austin, Alexander E. Bracken, William S Johnson, Thomas M. Guterbock, Lawrence A. Young, David M. Margolick, and Kathleen Bateman Several of these people were volunteers, from Middletown and elsewhere, who pooled their professional interests with those of the original investigators for our mutual benefit. Professors Hoover, Hewitt, Tamney, and Bracken linked the project firmly with Ball State University.

We are enormously indebted to the advisory council of distinguished scholars that guided the Middletown III project from its inception and marked out the directions to be followed by the project at two notable meetings held in Middletown in March 1977 and in Charlottesville in October 1978. Otis D. Duncan chaired the group whose other members were Jeffrey K. Hadden, Reuben Hill, Charles Hyneman (in 1977 only), Alex Inkeles, Sheldon Stryker, and Wilbert E. Moore. Besides relying on them collectively, we called upon them individually as often as we had need of their wisdom and expertise. Professor Hill's participation in the present volume grew out of such a request.

We cannot hope to name all of the people in Muncie and Delaware County, Indiana, for whose help and hospitality we are permanently indebted, but Whitney Gordon, Dr. Philip Ball, Hurley Goodall, Lester Hewitt, Alexander Bracken, Sr., John Pruis, and Mayor Robert Cunningham have done us special kindnesses that must be acknowledged here.

It goes without saying that the present report and any others we produce rest largely on the efforts of the research associates who directed parts of the field work: Geoffrey K. Leigh, C. Bradford Chappell, Penelope C. Austin, and Alice-Lynn Ryssman; and on our zealous and talented research assistants and interviewers: Daniel Hayden, Judy Wright, Debra Martin, Ellen Casky, Julie Hourclé, Mark Boarman, Linda Kessler, Debra Ensch, Thomas Wolforth, Cindy Stanley, Linda Holm, Esther Ball, Jan Hendrix, Linda Horton, and Dottie Murk in Muncie; Lawrence Young from Provo; and Carmen Matarazza, Robert Kelleher, John Mahoney, Calvin Stover, Donna Jost, John Albright, Bruce Morrow, Carl Pascale, Jr., and Patricia Passuth in Charlottesville.

We have had the support of an especially able secretarial staff headed, from the earliest days of the project, by Cleva G. Maggio and including Ruth Poll Barlow, Ellen Casky, Debra Ensch, and Lorraine Cote.

In November of 1980, most of us had the privilege of attending the ceremonies establishing the Center for Middletown Studies in the Bracken Library of Ball State University. It will be a permanent repository for the files and records of the Middletown III project, along with those from other studies of the community. We are already indebted to David C. Tambo, the curator of the center Dwight Hoover, the chairman of its advisory committee; and Ray R. Suput, the university librarian, and our indebtedness only increases with time.

Other scholars have played unscheduled but highly significant roles in this project. Jesse Pitts, editor of the *Tocqueville Review*, has provided us with an international forum for the examination of issues raised by Middletown III. With Henri Mendras and Jacques Lautman, the directors of a parallel study of social change in France, we have enjoyed a valuable exchange of results and ideas.

The National Science Foundation generously supported this work with a grant to the University of Virginia (NSF SOC 75-13580) in 1976 that was renewed or supplemented six times before it expired in 1981 and with another grant (NSF SES 79-18528) that enabled us to retabulate information about Middletown's population from the original enumerations of the seven decennial censuses from 1910 to 1970 in a form that facilitates comparison over time and constitutes a permanent resource for the study of Middletown. Three successive directors of the National Science Foundation's sociology program. Donald R. Ploch, Roland J. Liebert, and James J. Zuiches, have shown an affectionate interest in the project and given us much useful advice along with administrative support.

We are greatly indebted to Martin B. Hickman, dean of the College of Family, Home, and Social Sciences at Brigham Young University, who provided supplemental research support at various times throughout the project. Thanks to his enthusiasm for the study of Middletown, it was possible to conduct much of the computer analysis at Brigham Young University. Some supplemental funding and time for analysis and writing were also provided by Brigham Young University's Family and Demographic Research Institute.

We are most grateful to Dr. Helen Merrell Lynd, still lively and lovely after all these years, who gave us access to the files of the first two Middletown studies and thereby made our project possible. It could not have been properly carried out with only the published materials.

Middletown Families is a jointly authored book and not a collection of contributed papers and, because all of us have reviewed and corrected the contributions of the others, we have not separately attributed the chapters to their original authors. But, for the convenience of those who may want to address inquiries or remonstrances to the authors of particular chapters, I list them here: I am primarily responsible for Chapters 1 and 13; Bahr for Chapters 2, 3, 7, and 9; Chadwick for Chapters 4, 5, and 6; Bahr and Chadwick jointly for Chapter 8; Chadwick and Caplow jointly for Chapter 11; Williamson for Chapter 10. Those who know anything about the sociology of the family will recognize the style of Reuben Hill in Chapter 12.

Sociology is not a very old science. Middletown I, as far as we can tell, was the first large-scale sociological study sufficiently modern in design to permit serious replication. Such earlier studies as Booth's *Life and Labor of the People of London* and even Thomas and Znaniecki's magnificent work on *The Polish Peasant in Europe and America* are too archaic in form to be replicable in the vernacular of contemporary social science. The interval of time between Middletown I and Middletown III, some 53 years, is so far the longest interval that can be stretched between two contemporary empirical studies of a social system larger than a tribal village. But in the coming years, of course, there will be more such opportunities to cover longer and longer intervals. In this volume, we hope to demonstrate the extraordinary usefulness of replicative sociology in the study of social change and, in a narrower compass, to leave orderly archives for those who will come after us one day to do a study called Middletown IV.

Theodore Caplow

Charlottesville, Virginia
Thanksgiving Day, 1981

PART I Change and Continuity

Chapter 1

The Community Context

This is a book about continuity and change in the family life of one American Community during two generations, with a few flashbacks to earlier times and some modest attempts at visualizing the future. The community is Middletown, the place that our illustrious predecessors Robert and Helen Lynd selected for study in 1924 because it was not extraordinary in any way and so could be taken as a good specimen of American culture, at least of its midwestern variant. Then as now, Middletown[1] was a small city in eastern Indiana on the White River, 54 miles northeast of Indianapolis. It had numerous factories producing engine parts, glass bottles, steel wire, building blocks, and lawn furniture, and it was a trading center for 22 mostly rural counties in eastern Indiana and western Ohio. Between then and now, its teachers' college grew into a state university, a multitude of commercial enterprises appeared and disappeared, and the population doubled, from about 40,000 in 1924 to 80,000 in 1979. This increase in population, although considerable, did not outpace the increase in the country as a whole, and the spectacular expansion of the college did not obliterate Middletown's character as an industrial city. A Middletown Rip van Winkle, awaking in the 1970s from a 50-year-long sleep, would have noticed innumerable changes but would not have had any trouble finding his way around town. We must keep this in mind later on when we try to guess whether the elements of change and continuity we observe in Middletown families tell us anything about what has been happening in the larger society to which Middletown belongs.

The length of a generation in Middletown may be fairly taken at 26.5 years, the time elapsed from the birth of the median child in a cross section of families to the birth of the median grandchild of the sample couples. The distance of time that separates the Lynds' original surveys from our replications of them is just twice that long. The high school students who answered our questionnaires about their activities and attitudes in 1977 could easily have been the grandchildren of the adolescents who filled out questionnaires for the Lynds in 1924; about a third of them actually were. In the eyes of our adolescent subjects, born around 1960, 1924 belongs to remote history, along with Valley Forge and the Gettysburg Address, and they have no mental picture at all of their grandparents as adolescents necking in rumble seats. They—and their parents—have been taught by the mass media that they live in a uniquely wicked, uniquely troubled, uniquely unique era. Change is everywhere. Continuity escapes their notice.

Robert Lynd went back to Middletown in 1935 to study the changes wrought by the Great Depression, which, between 1929 and 1933, reduced the value of wages earned in Middletown's industrial sector by 46 percent, the value of what they produced by 57 percent, and the wages they earned by 67 percent. The effects of this catastrophe were apparent in every corner of Middletown's institutions, but the wholesale transformation that Robert Lynd had expected to find somehow eluded him.

As one walked Middletown's residential streets in 1935 one felt overpoweringly the continuities with 1925 that these homes represent. Whatever changes may have occurred elsewhere in the city's life—in business, education, or charity—here in these big and little, clean and cluttered houses in their green yards one gained that sense, always a bit startling to the returning visitor, of life's having gone on unaltered in one's absence (Lynd and Lynd 1937, 144).

Since then, 45 more years have rolled on. The Great Depression is almost forgotten in Middletown; innumerable social shocks and tremors emanating from outside have shaken these quiet streets in the meantime. Robert Lynd is long gone, but we, walking the same streets half a century later, feel the same continuity while noting the changes.

"Happy are the people who have no history," says the old Chinese proverb. Middletown has almost no history of its own. In

1977, at the sesquicentennial celebration of its founding, nothing was commemorated except the original land purchase, and almost nobody showed up. There has never been a great fire or a great epidemic or a great discovery in Middletown. But the community has no insulation against the wars and scandals, the cycles and fashions, the surpluses and shortages originating elsewhere.

External Change and Internal Continuity

Middletown does not make its own history but patiently suffers the history made outside. After the Great Depression came the threat of fascism, World War II, the Cold War, the Korean War, the Eisenhower years, the violent sixties, and the disappointing seventies.

Change, for Middletown, is something flowing irresistibly from the outside world. Continuity is furnished locally. The outside world continuously proposes new ways of living and thinking. The local community steadfastly resists most of these suggestions and modifies those it adopts into conformity with its own customs. This city in the American heartland bears a strange resemblance to a tribal society in New Guinea or Central Africa; the distant but irresistible influence of industrial society forces the tribespeople to give up polygamy or to take up contraception for reasons inscrutable to them. Middletown is part of industrial society, but it does not operate the engines of change by which industrial societies induce the continuous transformation of social institutions, both internally and externally. The decision to live in Middletown, a voluntary one for most of its adult residents, is a vote for custom and against innovation, and it is not surprising that a population recruited in that way should be able to resist innovation with considerable success.

In Middletown, as in a tribal society, custom has considerable inertia, and people continue to pursue activities, arrange relationships, and celebrate great occasions according to the same formulas so long as they are not forced by authority or by altered circumstances to abandon them. In their original study, the Lynds noted that some of Middletown's institutions were less resistant to change and some elements of its population more acceptant of innovation than others.

The Class System

New cultural traits appeared first in the business class and filtered down slowly to the working class, so that the working class in 1925 appeared relatively old-fashioned, closer to the semirural world of 1885 than to their business-class neighbors. The young were more receptive to innovations than their parents; and women more than men. The balance between continuity and change varied also among the six categories the Lynds used to classify Middletown's activities. There was least resistance to change in economics, followed by leisure, education, and politics. The church and the family were more committed to continuity. The tension between continuity and change was Middletown's principal problem, as the Lynds saw it in the 1920s.

Middletown's life exhibits at almost every point either some change or some stress arising from failure to change. A citizen has one foot on the relatively solid ground of established institutional habits and the other fast to an escalator erratically moving in several directions at a bewildering variety of speeds. Living under such circumstances consists first of all in maintaining some sort of equilibrium (Lynd and Lynd 1929, 498).

The business class, since it was more exposed to the winds of change, was more uneasy than the working class in 1925. In the business class the Lynds placed all those families—about a quarter of the population—whose husbands and fathers wore coats and ties to work, worked at desks with people and symbols, and kept their hands clean. Business-class wives stayed at home and kept house, often with some paid help. Working-class men wore overalls, worked at benches with tools and materials, and got their hands dirty. Their wives kept house, too, but about half of them held jobs outside the home. The burden was heavy, and their homes and children usually showed signs of neglect. The business-class homes of 1925 were not very different from today's. Central heating, indoor plumbing, and efficient kitchens were universal, and the average amounts of space and privacy were just about the same then as now. The working-class home of the same era was only partly modernized. Coal stoves in the parlor and wood stoves in the kitchen were still common. Many had outdoor privies, and some families still drew their water from outside wells.

Life in the working-class family of 1925 was harsh in other ways. The factory whistles blew to mark the beginning of the day's work at seven o'clock, long before sunrise in the winter. In working class neighborhoods, all the lights were on by six. A few streets away, the business class slumbered on until full daylight. For the working class there were not always jobs to go to. In the prosperous year of 1923, 28 percent of the men were unemployed at one time or another. Unemployment was a much more serious blow then than it is now. There was no such thing as unemployment insurance, and the loss of a job marked the start of a cruel race with time. Prolonged unemployment took the family savings, the house, and eventually the furniture. The wife went out looking for a job; that was nearly the sole reason why married women worked in those days. A little later, the children dropped out of school and went looking for jobs, too.

The business class was much less vulnerable to unemployment. The Lynds found only a single case among the business-class families they studied, and that involved unusual circumstances. Salaried persons were seldom discharged, and almost never fired summarily. For a clerk or a salesman, finding a new job was easy and dignified. Middletown's proprietors and professionals enjoyed varying fortunes, but few of them, during the 1920s, encountered economic disasters.

These differences of fortune were reflected by differences in what people could do for their children. Business-class parents, as a matter of course, expected to send their children to college. The completion of high school was as much as most working-class parents could aspire to for their children, and it was more than most of them could manage.

Thus, these two groups lived side by side under conditions that seemed as distant as though they belonged to different nations at different stages of development or as though they were the colonizers and the colonized. But, curiously, no differences in speech or religion or physiognomy set them apart. Ethnically, Middletown's business and working classes were indistinguishable, descended mostly from English, Scotch-Irish, and German immigrants of an earlier day who settled, mixed, and resettled along the East Coast and in the Appalachians before they moved to the Midwest. The evangelistic Christianity they brought with them was fairly uniform;

if the Presbyterian church was mostly business-class and the Holy Roller church mostly working-class, their creeds were closely related. The children of both classes went to the same high school and emerged from it speaking the same language with the same accent.

Social stratification is the most commonplace feature of modern societies, large and small. About the time the Lynds were doing their second Middletown study, Lloyd Warner was discovering and describing six well-defined social classes in the old New England seaport he called Yankee City (Warner and Lunt 1942), and John Dollard was finding both a class system and a caste system in a small Georgia community (Dollard 1937). In Yankee City, family history and ethnic origin were largely responsible for the assignment of people to classes. The descendants of old settlers, for example, were concentrated in the upper-upper and lower-lower classes, while the Irish, French-Canadians, Jews, Italians, Armenians, Greeks, Poles, and Russians each had their prescribed niche in between. In Georgia, the caste system classified all persons with any trace of African ancestry as Negro and treated them as social inferiors to all whites. Within the white caste, class position was largely determined by family history, and, within the black class, it was strongly affected by skin color.

The class system the Lynds identified in Middletown took no particular account of people's origins. Being an old settler never earned many points there. Even today, no particular prestige is attached to a family for having lived in Middletown longer than its neighbors. Race, religion, and national origin could not be expected to account for class status in a community where the overwhelming majority were white Protestants of native parentage. Middletown's class system bore a superficial resemblance to the Yankee City system and the Georgia system, but those other systems needed to be enforced while Middletown's just seemed to happen. The upper-class dowagers of Yankee City devoted a large part of their time and energy to rituals of inclusion or exclusion, deciding whose call to return and whose to overlook and who should not be invited to Jane's wedding and who, for that matter, should not be allowed to wed Jane. Their middle-class counterparts engaged in a constant struggle to draw closer to the people immediately above them on the status ladder and to repel the advances of those immediately below. In Georgia, a vast number of laws, ordinances, customs and contracts were barely sufficient to enforce the rules of color-caste. By contrast, snobbery in the Middletown of the 1920s was a weak and flickering force. Rituals of inclusion and exclusion were limited to a few places, like the high school and the country club, where they were practiced without much fanaticism. The few groups that attempted to be exclusive considered candidates on their merits and shrank from deliberate cruelty. For the most part, Middletown's class system seemed to operate without human intervention and with the barest minimum of class consciousness.

The Gradual Progress of Equality

The ubiquity of class division in American communities was the most notable discovery of the social sciences between the two world wars. The United States had been founded, it was taught in the schools, to establish a new kind of society based on the proposition that all people are created free and equal. Negro slavery had been the only admitted exception, but a great war was fought to expunge that exception. Jeffersonian equality does not imply equality of wealth, education, or influence, but it does imply that people having more of these desirable things are not intrinsically better than those having less and that no one ought to be prevented from getting them on the ground of being unworthy to enjoy them. The passion for equality, according to Alexis de Tocqueville, was stronger in America than the desire for freedom. "The social state of America," he wrote in 1823, "is a very strange phenomenon. Men there are nearer equality in wealth and mental endowments, or in other words, more nearly equally powerful, than in any other country of the world in any other age of recorded history" (Tocqueville 1823, 56). The last trace of hereditary ranks and distinctions had been destroyed, he thought, and he described Middletown's region as displaying the passion for equality in its most extreme form.

At the end of the last century a few bold adventurers began to penetrate into the Mississippi valley. It was like a new discovery of America; soon most of those who were immigrating went there; previously unheard of communities suddenly sprang up in the wilderness. States that had not even been names a few years before took their places in the American Union. It is in the West that one can see democracy in its most extreme form. In these states, in some sense improvisations of fortune, the inhabitants have arrived only yesterday in the land where they dwell. They hardly know one another, and each man is ignorant of his nearest neighbor's history. So in that part of the American continent the population escapes the influence not only of great names and great wealth but also of the natural aristocracy of education and probity. No man there enjoys the influence and respect due to a whole life spent publicly in doing good (Tocqueville 1823, 55).

That was written during the decade of Middletown's founding.

Tocqueville supposed the gradual progress of equality to be universal, permanent, and irresistible. "Does anyone imagine," he wrote in the introduction to the first edition of *Democracy in America*, "that democracy, which has destroyed the feudal system and vanquished kings, will fall back before the middle classes and the rich?" But in *Middletown* the Lynds informed the world that democracy *had* fallen back before the middle classes.

. . . It is after all this division into working class and business class that constitutes the outstanding cleavage in Middletown. The mere fact of being born upon one or the other side of the watershed roughly formed by these two groups is the most significant single cultural factor tending to influence what one does all day long throughout one's life; whom one marries; when one gets up in the morning; whether one belongs to the Holy Roller or Presbyterian church; or drives a Ford or a Buick . . . and so on indefinitely through the daily comings and goings of the Middletown man, woman, or child (Lynd and Lynd 1929, 24).

In *Middletown in Transition*, the Lynds told the tale of the X family and pronounced democracy to be helpless before the rich. Tocqueville may have been right about the inevitable progress of inequality in the long run, but the trend has been anything but even. On his evidence and that of his contemporaries, the high point of social equality in the United States was probably achieved in the 1820s. The manuscript censuses of Middletown from 1850 to 1880 show us the outlines of a society that still looked very much like Tocqueville's America (Bracken 1978). Nearly every family had some property; none were very rich. Literacy was almost universal and advanced education almost unknown. Wealth circulated rapidly and people even more rapidly, moving from place to place with goods and children and livestock to recoup their losses or to look for new opportunities. Only 8 percent of the Middletown residents recorded by the census of 1850 were still around for the census of 1880. Indeed, most of them had moved on within the first 10 years, and thousands more arrived and departed between censuses, leaving no trace. And once the War between the States had settled the question of slavery, the few black families of Middletown lived side by side with their white neighbors, following the same occupations, sending their children to the same schools, working and voting with everyone else.

All of this changed soon after 1880, when, for a variety of reasons, the gradual progress of equality reversed itself. The natural gas boom that began in 1887 changed Middletown from a placid county seat to a manufacturing city. The population doubled within ten years, and more than 40 new factories were started, including the X family's original glassworks, which was started on a $7,000 investment in a workshop perched on log piers. Electric lights and telephones came into use during that same decade.

The first national trusts were founded. A great wave of immigrants poured into the country, and the United States Congress passed its first laws restricting immigration and its first laws regulating industry. Giant corporations and mass unions appeared in the 1880s and went to war with each other. The federal courts nullified the Fourteenth Amendment on the separate-but-equal principle, and a new kind of slavery was imposed on the black population by a thicket of state and local legislation designed to keep blacks in legal subjection to whites. The small colleges of the land became universities, and their graduates began to monopolize the most lucrative occupations. Great wealth and abject poverty appeared together on the American scene. In the larger cities, the great stone palaces of the rich and the back-alley tenements of the poor presented contrasts that suggested European feudalism more than American democracy. The new rich toyed unashamed with feudal images, flaunting their wealth in imitation baronial halls attended by liveried footmen.

In Middletown, this aberrant phase of social development began with the gas boom of 1887 and lasted until World War II, reaching its apogee around 1935, the year the research for *Middletown in Transition* was being conducted. What the Lynds observed was the outcome of nearly 50 years of modernization and increasing inequality. The ethnically and culturally homogeneous population of Middletown was cleanly divided into privileged and unprivileged strata marked for separate destinies. The Great Depression had only made matters worse. It struck the working class much harder than the business class. Within the business class, it squeezed those who lived on earned income much more than the few families with substantial assets. The depression enabled one of these families to increase its control of the local banks, acquire the largest department store, and preside over the expansion of the state college and the city hospital. The feudal image hardly seemed misplaced in the wake of those triumphs, although the ubiquitous Xs never came close to controlling Middletown's industry or politics (Frank 1974).

Not long after the depression, the gradual progress of equality was resumed. the higher education that had raised the business class so high above the working class was offered to all the returning veterans of World War II and thereafter to the whole population. Middletown's little teachers' college grew into a vast, bustling university with generous admission standards, modest charges, and abundant financial aid. The children of the working class attended in droves.

In the celebrated case of *Brown* v. *Topeka*, the Supreme Court ruled that separate but equal was not equal at all. Martin Luther King led a bus boycott in Alabama. A brigade of federal troops made good the enrollment of a black student at the University of Mississippi. The voting rights of blacks were fully restored, and the resulting political influence guaranteed the government's support for racial equalization in Middletown as elsewhere.

Labor unions, still effectively excluded from Middletown's factories in 1935, were accepted soon after, grew, ramified, became respectable and bureaucratic, and won progressively better contracts as the years rolled on. By the 1970s, Middletown's factory workers were no longer at the bottom but nearly at the middle of the occupational distribution. They had job security, health insurance, paid vacations, and higher average incomes than the white-collar workers in the factory office.

The local dominance of a handful of rich families that looked so threatening in 1935 quietly faded away during the decades of prosperity that followed World War II. Hundreds of fortunes were made in old ways and new — building subdivisions and shopping centers; trading in real estate; selling insurance, advertising, farm machinery, building materials, fuel oil, trucks and automobiles, furniture and oriental rugs; speculating on the stock market; lending money; practicing medicine; introducing new products; dealing in franchises. Some money was even made in manufacturing, although industry, still the mainspring of the local economy, was no longer the principal source of private wealth. Middletown's new rich did not act nouveau riche. In proportion to their means, they lived much less ostentatiously than their industrial predecessors, and much of their money was spent away from Middletown (for yachts in Florida, condominiums in Colorado, boarding schools for their children, and luxury tours to everywhere for themselves). At home they lived like their neighbors, in slightly bigger and better versions of the same houses but with no full-time servants and no feudal pretensions. The handful of families whose wealth antedated World War II adopted the same style. The imitation castles of the X, Y, and Z families were torn down or converted for institutional uses. The distinctive upper class that the Lynds saw emerging in Middletown in the 1930s had vanished by the 1970s.

Meanwhile, at the lower end of the socioeconomic scale, lifestyles were becoming more homogeneous. The residential building boom that began after World War II continued, year after year, to submerge the flat, rich farmlands at the edge of town under curved subdivision streets bordered by neat subdivision houses with various exteriors but nearly identical interiors. They all had central heating, indoor plumbing, telephones, automatic stoves, refrigerators, and washing machines. As time went on, the machinery of such houses expanded and improved much more than the structural fabric, which hardly improved at all. By the 1970s, a comparatively inexpensive subdivision house in Middletown might have central air conditioning, two full bathrooms, a trash compactor, a separate freezer, a self-cleaning oven, an automatic dishwasher, a washer and a dryer, a water softener, an intercom, a built-in stereo system, and remotely controlled garage doors. The floor space of the median Middletown home in 1975 was about the same as in 1925, but the average power consumption had more than quadrupled.

A series of federal programs made home ownership easily accessible to working-class families. The special mortgage terms first offered to returning veterans of World War II were eventually extended to all comers. Since the federal agency guaranteed repayment, banks and other private lenders, freed of risk, were able to make long-term loans on new houses for almost their total value. With favorable interest rates, the buyers' single monthly payment for interest, principal, taxes, and insurance did not significantly exceed what they would have paid to rent a similar house; often it was less. Constant inflation made these loans quite safe. Few buyers ever paid off their mortgages in full. Most of them sold their houses at a profit within a few years and started the cycle over again in a better house, bearing the perpetual debt lightly. The average value of outstanding mortgage loans in Middletown rose from $2,000 in 1945 to more than $17,000 in 1975.

Compared with most other urban areas in the United States, Middletown's postwar housing boom was relatively mild. Its population was not increasing rapidly, and it ceased to grow at all after 1960. In larger cities during that period, a large proportion of the family population moved from multiple dwellings in the inner city to single-family homes in the suburbs, but most of Middletown's families had lived in free-standing houses with lawns and backyards all along. More than 80 percent of them were housed that way in 1935, the earliest year for which we have information, and most of the rest lived in row houses or duplexes or in flats over stores. There were very few apartment buildings. About half of the families living in single-family houses in 1935 were renters.

By 1979, the proportion of intact white families in single-family houses had increased to about 95 percent, and nearly all of them were owners. Several hundred more families were permanently settled in trailer parks, economy models of residential subdivisions. The remaining households, many of them composed of persons living alone, lived in apartment and housing complexes of various kinds. Of Middletown's 2,000 black families, those with adequate incomes were scattered throughout the community in houses indistinguishable from their white neighbors', while those at or near the poverty level were concentrated in several slum areas close to the center of the city and in two public housing projects. Even in 1979, there was some definitely bad housing in Middletown and thousands of citizens whose living arrangements differed, for one reason or another, from the single-family norm. But a significant majority of the population conformed to the norm by living in a family household composed of a married pair and their unmarried off-spring, in a house they owned, on a residential street surrounded on all sides by houses of similar size and value.

Home ownership, although nearly universal in these neighbor-hoods, did not discourage mobility. About a third of the families turned over each year; most of those who left went to similar houses and neighborhoods elsewhere in Middletown, while a few migrated out of the city or out of the state.

Within this dominant life-style, most of the differences that the Lynds observed between business-class families and working-class families half a century ago have by now been eroded away. Work-ing-class people play golf and tennis, travel in Europe for pleasure, and send their children to college. Business-class people do their own laundry and mow their own lawns. Business-class wives with children at home are as likely to hold full-time jobs as working-class wives. There is more decorum in the working-class churches and more fervor in the business-class churches than there used to be, and many congregations are thoroughly mixed.

Where there was one high school in 1925, there are now four; all of them are integrated by class as well as by race. The Lynds des-cribed at length the greater religiosity of the working class, but our 1977 studies of adolescent attitudes show almost identical patterns of religious belief among the children of the two classes. Their so-cial and political beliefs are similar, too, with the sole and interest-ing exception that many more working-class adolescents think that "the fact that some people have so much more money than others shows that there is an unjust condition in this country which ought to be changed."[2] The same survey *does* show a few significant dif-ferences in religious beliefs between white and black adolescents, the blacks being more in agreement with the tenets of fundamental Christianity and less likely to perceive the United States as the best country in the world. In other respects, the social values of black and white respondents are nearly indistinguishable.

The Perennial Crisis

The Lynds thought Middletown was facing a crisis in 1925. Seeing it divided by the "watershed" between the business class and the working class and strained by the tensions between change and continuity, they feared for the future of the community and its institutions. They were especially apprehensive about the family, which, it seemed to them, had lost the emotional harmony that prevailed in earlier generations and was being riven in one place by a generation gap and in another by marital instability.

The question of marital stability in Middletown presents us with a statistical puzzle. The records of marriages and divorces in Middletown's county are complete and unbroken from 1890 to the present. In 1890, there were 12 divorces for every 100 marriages. By 1925, there were 43 divorces per 100 marriages. The divorce rate remained at about that level until 1945, when it jumped to its all-time high of 64. Thereafter, it fell below the level of the 1920s until 1970, when it rose again to 48, remaining near that level for the rest of the decade. The Census Bureau's estimates of the divorce rate for the entire country since 1950 are roughly similar to the Middletown figures. (See Table 1-1.)

Table 1-1
Divorces per 100 Marriages

Year	Middletown	U.S.
1910	26	9
1920	33	5
1930	47	17
1945	64	29
1950	34	32
1955	28	25
1960	41	26
1965	32	28
1970	48	33
1975	51	49

Source: U.S. Bureau of the Census 1978, Table 74.

Census Bureau figures on divorce are also available for the 1920s. Between 1932 and 1950, divorce statistics were not collected by the bureau, but retrospective estimates for those years have been published by other federal agencies.[3] If the government figures are correct, Middletown's divorce rates during this earlier period were far out of line with the national averages. (See Table 1-1.)

Of the scores of social and economic trends we have measured for Middletown, the divorce rate is the only one that seems to deviate markedly from the national trend. In changes in family size, marriage rates, and rates of female employment, for example, Middletown's trends are indistinguishable from those for the United States. The remarkable match between patterns of social change in Middletown and in the country as a whole is what makes the place so useful as a sociological laboratory. But Table 1-1 seems to say that Middletown marriages were peculiarly unstable during the period covered by the Lynds' two studies, although their stability is now average. To put this another way, if the figures can be trusted, the stability of marriage in Middletown has not changed appreciably over the past two generations, while in the United States as a whole marriages have become much less stable.

By this interpretation, Middletown was a half a century ahead of the rest of the country in arriving at the modern style of marriage. If this were so, it might account for the continuity we find between the Middletown family of the 1920s and the Middletown family of the 1970s, but somehow such an interpretation does not ring true. It strains belief to imagine that Middletown had an avant-garde family system during the 1920s. The Lynds and all other observers were impressed by its traditional character.

The alternative explanation is that there is something wrong with the numbers. The Middletown figures can be given a fairly clean bill of health since they are based on actual counts of cases made in each local court from year to year. Moreover, at the Lynds' request, the tally of divorces in Middletown's county for the years 1929 to 1935 was rechecked in 1936 by the statistician for the responsible state department, who confirmed their accuracy (Lynd and Lynd 1937, 546). On the other hand, the Census Bureau's collection of divorce statistics for the 1920s is known from other sources to have been incomplete and slipshod (Cahen 1932). The Lynds, moreover, were aware of a discrepancy between federal and local counts of divorces in Middletown.

For the three years, 1925, 1928, and 1929, federal Census Bureau totals of divorce in Middletown's county fall 17, 8, and 19, respectively, below those published in the statistical report of the clerk of the circuit, superior, and criminal court issued by the state legislative bureau. This problem is here resolved . . . by assuming, on the advice of the state official in charge of compiling these statistics, that the federal figures may not include the returns from both the circuit and superior court of the counties for which their respective clerks made separate reports (lynd and Lynd 1937, 544-45).

It is conceivable, although not provable, that the national figures for the 1920s and 1930s understate the actual number of divorces by 50 percent or more and that the widely lamented increase in the American divorce rate in the past half of a century is partly a myth. We do not have enough information to resolve the issue for the whole country, but it is quite clear that the general level of marriage and divorce in Middletown has remained about the same since World War I, although it oscillates in response to historical events; for example, both the number of marriages and divorces dropped sharply at the onset of the depression and rose sharply in the aftermath of World War II.

Whether this tells us anything about psychological solidarity is another question. Looking at Middletown couples of 1925, the Lynds were impressed by the dreariness and weariness of working-class marriages and the lack of communication between business-class husbands and wives. Ten years later, the Lynds were swept into partial acceptance of Middletown's own belief that the depression had been good for family life, bringing husbands and wives and children closer together under the stress of adversity. They were also much more aware of the changing female role, set against the relative fixity of the male role. The world of the two sexes, then saw, constituted something like separate subcultures governed by different rules and expectations; the men public, practical, responsible, and logical; the women private, delicate, sensitive, affectionate, and emotionally more competent. The subcultures enjoined men and women not only to do different things but to be different kinds of people. But all that was changing, as the Lynds saw clearly in 1935.

Careers for women have opened an alternative path diverging sharply—in its demands for male traits of drive, single-mindedness, the qualities associated with power—from the traditional woman's path in the home with its emphasis upon the feminine traits of gentleness, willingness to be led, and affection. Not only has the alternative path of independence, career, and power beckoned harder, but the traditional world of the affections has become more demanding as the franker, modern world has emphasized more openly extreme femininity, including less passivity, more positive allurement, and a richly toned sexual response (Lynd and Lynd 1937, 178).

These lines, so applicable to today's situation, illustrate the paradox we encounter in trying to get a firm grip on continuity and change in the Middletown family. The changes that were taking place 45 years ago are *still* taking place, but, nevertheless, the changes were real then and are real now. Women's roles have changed much more than men's during the interim. We have only to compare the photographs of groups of Middletown people that Margaret Bourke-White made for *Life* magazine in 1936[4] with similar photographs taken recently. The clothes, haircuts, and facial expressions of the 1935 men would not attract any notice at all in Middletown today. But the 1935 women display the costumes and the postures of a vanished era.

The changes in women's roles have been real and continuous but slower than the Lynds expected and much slower than popular sociology of the "future shock" variety would lead us to expect. There seem to be several explanations for this gradualness. First, the family, with its complex of attitudes and practices for regulating the relationships between the sexes and between the generations, is too massive and deep-rooted an institution to be rapidly transformed under any circumstances. Second, the structural features of family life in Middletown have been remarkably constant in this century; constant have been the average age at marriage, the rate of marriage, the size and composition of households, the predominant type of family housing, and the connection of family life to churches and schools. Third, changes in patterns of intimate human relationship are necessarily much slower than technological changes, if only because the new form of relationship is seldom indisputably superior to the old, as new machines are to old. Even the introduction of technology into the family is relatively slow. Contraception was in nearly universal use in Middletown's business class by 1925 and had just begun to be adopted by working-class couples at that time, but that adoption is still not quite complete today. It took nearly a hundred years for central heating to become nearly universal in Middletown's homes.

The Lynds give us a full description of the disagreements between parents and their adolescent children in the Middletown of 1925 (the same adolescents who, as we noted before, became the grandparents of today's adolescents). The description has a strangely modern tone. Child rearing, said the Lynds, was traditionally viewed by Middletown parents in terms of making children conform to social norms, but

today [1925] the swiftly-moving environment and multiplied occasions for contact outside the home are making it more difficult to secure adherence to established group sanctions, and Middletown's parents are wont to speak of many of their "problems" as new to this generation, situations for which the formulae of their parents are inadequate (Lynd and Lynd 1929, 132-33).

They mentioned the lack of continuity between occupations of fathers and sons, employment of mothers outside the home, extensive extracurricular activities in the schools, precocious sophistication, late hours, pairing off at an early age, and more sexual activity than parents could deal with. One of their informants remarked that "the parents are wise to a lot that goes on, but they just don't know what to do, and try to turn their backs on it" (Lynd and Lynd 1929, 152). Changes in family life are not events that occur once and for all. Many of them have a recurrent character that stems from the similar responses of successive generations to similar responses of successive generations to similar conditions.

Looking at the situation ten years later, the Lynds concluded that "the gap between the purposes and mutual understanding of parents and children noted in 1925 has apparently widened still further. One gets the impression in 1935 of a more self-conscious subculture of the young in Middletown." Again, we glimpse the curious *continuity of change* in Middletown's families, the ever-widening generation gap that never manages to change the relationships between parents and children. In 1977, we administered to all of Middletown's high school students questionnaires about adolescent behavior that duplicated the questionnaires administered to them by the Lynds 53 years before. We found among other things that boys in 1977 spent the same number of evenings away from home as boys in 1924 and that a somewhat higher proportion received allowances but that more of them held part-time jobs. The proportion who obtained most of their sex information from their parents had declined from a third to a fifth. The proportion who quarreled with their parents about the time they got home at night was about the same in 1977 as it had been in 1924, and that was again the most frequent source of disagreement. Disagreements about home duties, dress and grooming, and unchaperoned parties were slightly more important in 1977; and those about use of the family automobile, the adolescent's choice of friends, and church attendance were slightly less important. In 1924, about two-thirds of the Middletown students mentioned "spending time with his children" as a desirable trait in a father; the same proportion selected that trait in 1977, and it was again the most important. "Respecting his children's opinion" came next in 1924 and was as important as "spending time" in 1977. No other paternal quality approached these two in importance. On the other hand, the qualities wanted in mothers showed an interesting shift. In 1924 being a good cook and housekeeper was what both boys and girls most wanted in their mothers. In 1977 they wanted their mothers, like their fathers, to spend time with them and to respect their opinions. In all matters concerning their relationships with parents, the girls of 1977 were more like their brothers than they were like the girls of 1924. The total amount of disagreement was about the same in 1977 as in 1924. The actual time that parents spent with their children was considerably greater in 1977. The generation gap, although perceived by today's parents to be widening, seems, on the evidence, to have narrowed slightly from 1924 to 1977.

It would be a gross misreading of this information to conclude that the relationship between parents and adolescent children is always and everywhere the same. What the Lynds told us about Middletown in 1890 suggests quite a different pattern. The boys of that era were much closer to their fathers and the girls to their mothers. In both sets of relationships, the transmission of skills was much more important and recreation much less important than it became later. In this and many other ways, the changes that occurred between 1890 and 1925 were much more extensive and important than those that took place between 1925 and 1977. The decisive transition from a traditional to a modern family configuration, from child labor to prolonged education, from the hand-powered to the machine-powered home, and from an enclosed to an open community had been accomplished by 1925, although many details remained to be filled in (Lynd and Lynd 1929, 87). Today, Middletown has become, for the first time in its history, a place where the experience of the present generation resembles the experience of the past generation and prefigures the probable experience of the next generation. The frontier is quite gone.

The Intrusion of the Media

The conversion of Middletown from an enclosed to an open place was well under way in 1924. Nineteenth-century Middletown was enclosed in the sense that most of the events that preoccupied its inhabitants were local events and most of the communications to which they responded emanated from local sources. Although the population was somewhat more mobile then than it is now, the people who moved in resembled the people who moved out in their origins, habits, customs, and values. They resembled each other, too. Important vestiges of this uniformity remained in 1925, but the community was bombarded—through newspapers, magazines, popular books, radio broadcasts, traveling preachers, salesmen, and promoters—by a continuous barrage of exotic ideas and projects. A large proportion of the events that preoccupied Middletown's inhabitants in 1925 took place at great distances and involved people they never saw or expected to see face to face. By 1935, in response to the depression, at least a dozen new federal agencies created by the New Deal were actively involved in Middletown's local affairs, finding jobs for the unemployed, cleaning up the river, supervising the banks, regulating labor relations, and devising all sorts of social improvements. The distant national government whose local functions had been confined to the operation of the post office and the collection of a few modest taxes emerged on the local scene like a genie from a bottle and grew into a towering presence that nobody in Middletown could ignore. During the years that followed, these two great streams of external influence, the mass media and the federal presence, expanded in an astonishing way.

Television broadcasting was introduced in 1946; a single station at first presented two hours of programming a day. By 1975, a local station, four stations in Indianapolis, and a cable service carrying four additional stations offered programming around the clock every day of the year. The programs were of variable quality (to put it as kindly as possible) and were interrupted every few minutes for clusters of commercial advertisements. Ninety-eight percent of Middletown's households owned at least one television set; nearly half had more than one set. Many had three or four.

The amount of time Middletown's residents devoted to viewing television staggers the imagination. According to one estimate, the median for the entire population was 28 hours per week in 1976. Elderly women (35 hours), elderly men and middle-aged women (32 hours), and preschool children (29 hours) had the highest viewing rates. Adolescents, at 21 hours, had the lowest rate, a mere 3 hours per day! The phenomenon is unprecedented in human history. No large population anywhere had ever spent so much of their time being entertained. We could try to explain away these staggering statistics by supposing that people keep their sets turned on without actually watching them, but viewers in Middletown, at any rate, are able to recall the programs they claim to have watched, even though most of them have developed the trick of doing housework or homework at the same time and intermittent family conversation accompanies television viewing more often than not.

The whole commonplace phenomenon is steeped in mystery, and the mystery deepens as we investigate some of the obvious questions. Where did all the time come from? What other activities were replaced? What are the moral and cultural effects of incessant exposure to other people's fantasies?

It is hard to believe, but the older mass media have not been displaced at all. Middletown had a single morning newspaper in 1925. It was still being published in 1975 under the same name and with much the same editorial tone, and its circulation increased in exact proportion to the increase of Middletown's population during the interim. The Sunday edition of the same paper and Middletown's evening newspaper did considerably better; the growth of their circulation between 1925 and 1975 outpaced the growth of the population. The circulation of out-of-town newspapers increased enormously more. All these newspapers contained many more pages in 1975 than in 1925, the division of space between editorial and advertising matter remained about the same, and there was no evidence that readership was more thinly spaced.

Radio broadcasting did equally well. Middletown had two AM and two FM stations of its own in 1977, and there were dozens, or hundreds, of other stations within reception range, depending on the weather, the time of day, and the receiving set. Virtually all Middletown households had several radios, in cars and trucks, on bedside tables, in combination with television sets, record players, recorders, and clocks; the radios were fixed and portable, of all shapes and sizes. Most of the programming consisted of music and news. The music was divided between rock and country western. The news was boiled down into hourly summaries of a few minutes each. But from 1925 to 1975 the radio audience never ceased to grow.

Motion picture theaters were at first hard hit by the advent of television; their weekly audiences declined by about 75 percent between 1950 and 1970. Thereafter, there was a significant recovery. By 1977, Middletown had a larger array of movie theaters than ever before: three theaters with multiple halls in shopping centers, three drive-ins outside the city limits, and two surviving downtown movie palaces. Collectively, they offered a wide mix of domestic and foreign, old and new films. One of the drive-ins specialized in pornographic films; such were also offered intermittently at the shopping-center theaters. All this still left room for two well-attended film series at the university and a number of semiprivate film clubs. In one of our surveys, a third of Middletown's married couples said that they went to the movies together ten or more times per year, and they reported considerably higher attendance by their children.

We might expect that reading would have been swamped by this audiovisual deluge, but the reverse seems to have occurred. At Middletown's public library, the number of card holders declined from 48 percent of the population in 1925 to 31 percent in 1975, but the average number of books drawn out annually by each cardholder increased from 15 to 22, leaving the per capita circulation almost unchanged. Although we lack exact figures, it is clear that the public library accounted for a much smaller part of all book reading than it formerly did. "Bookreading in Middletown today," the Lynds wrote of 1925, "means overwhelmingly, if we exclude schoolbooks and Bibles, the reading of public library books" (Lynd and Lynd 1929, 229-30). They repeated the same observation 10 years later (Lynd and Lynd 1937, 252) with the comment that

"Middletown is not a book-buying city." By 1977, Middletown was emphatically a book-buying city. Besides the bookstores serving the university, it had 13 retail bookstores; 2 specialized in religious literature and 2 in pornography, but the rest covered a broad range of materials. Paperback books were available at innumerable retail outlets—drugstores, supermarkets, department stores, discount houses, and convenience stores. There is much more recreational reading in Middletown today than in 1925, and its content is not noticeably less serious. Nearly half the books drawn from the public library during the 1970s were nonfiction compared to only about one-sixth of those drawn out in the 1930s. Many of the paperback books and most of the hardcover books sold during the 1970s were solid and serious works that express contemporary high culture (history, criticism, biography, science, and the arts), while many others were practical manuals for the learning of every conceivable skill (child raising, public speaking, accounting, xerography, seduction, beekeeping, waterskiing, auto repair, animal training, preparing omelets—the list is endless). To round off the inventory, the circulation of national magazines has also increased, and the high school students of 1977 reported reading more magazines than those of 1924.[5]

The increase of audiovisual experience was not acquired at the sacrifice of more active forms of entertainment either. Every type of participant sport about which we have any information, with the exception of billiards, showed spectacular growth. In 1977, there were seven bowling centers in Middletown, where there had been one in 1925; five golf courses, where there had been one in 1925 and two in 1935; more than a hundred private planes in place of the "several" owned by wealthy young men in 1935; and more than a thousand home swimming pools, where there were none in 1935. The list is nearly endless. Add to this the fact that attendance at high school basketball games, the principal spectator sport in Middletown, is perhaps proportionately higher now than then, that the number of miles driven in motor vehicles has tripled in relation to Middletown's population since 1925, and that the average workweek in Middletown's factories was longer in 1978 than in 1935, and the question of where Middletowners found so much time to watch television becomes even more intriguing.

The Federal Presence

If the numbers associated with television in Middletown are as-
tounding, so are the numbers associated with the other great intrusion—the federal presence. From its beginnings in the New Deal,
the presence burgeoned until, by the late 1970s, federal agencies
were spending about $1,200 a year in Middletown for every man,
woman, and child in the population. This was more than $4,000
per household, even though Middletown contains no important
federal installation and its share of military contracting is modest
for a manufacturing city. Between 1968 and 1979, more than 30
governmental agencies operating scores of separate programs spent
nearly a billion dollars in Middletown.[6] About one-third of all the
income received by Middletown families in 1979 came out of the
federal treasury, and a clear majority of Middletown's families depended on federal dollars for a significant part of their support
during that year.

Contrary to the opinion held by most Middletowners, the bulk
of this largesse does not go to the poor, and it does not result in
any important redistribution of income. The workings of the system are extremely complicated and are not clearly understood by
anyone, including the officials in charge, but their net effect is to
subsidize persons at every income level more or less in proportion
to their nonsubsidy income. Physicians receive much larger payments from the Medicaid program than their indigent patients receive from any of the programs that offer assistance to the poor.
Landlords receive much larger dollar payments from the Department of Housing and Urban Development's rent-subsidy program
for low-income families than those families obtain from all the assistance programs combined. University professors draw larger
sums from their federal research grants than graduate students are
paid under their federal fellowships. The fees of legal-aid lawyers
greatly exceed the wages of their clients.

The workings of this curious and totally unplanned system can
be seen with special clarity in two programs that sooner or later
touch nearly every Middletown family: housing assistance (through
the Veterans' Administration, the Department of Housing and
Urban Development and the Federal Home Loan Bank Board) and
retirement pensions (through the Social Security Administration,

the Railroad Retirement Board, the Veterans' Administration, the Civil Service Commission, and the Treasury Department).

Aside from the builders, developers, mortgage lenders, and realtors who receive the greatest cash benefits from the federal housing programs, nearly all of Middletown's home-owning families receive assistance in the purchase of their homes from one or another of the federal programs, and the cash value of that assistance is generally proportional to the size of the mortgage, which in turn is proportional to the value of the house. The assistance given to home owners is much greater than the benefits offered to low-income renters in publicly assisted housing or subsidized private housing; subsidized housing benefits landlords more than tenants.

Social Security retirement benefits are intended to have a redistributive effect inasmuch as the amount received bears little relation to the amount paid in or to the level of the recipient's preretirement earnings, so that elderly millionaires in Middletown receive —and cash—Social Security checks for about the same amounts as elderly factory workers. But there are several jokers in this egalitarian arrangement. The amount of earned income a pensioner can receive is severly limited, but there are no limits at all on unearned income. As of 1980, an elderly person who earns $5,000 a year as a part-time carpenter forfeited his entire pension, while another elderly person, with an income of $50,000 a year from stocks and bonds, forfeited nothing. Moreover, persons retired from high-income occupations enjoy other pensions proportionate to their preretirement incomes without losing their Social Security benefits. Salaried federal employees, most of them at middle-income levels, receive unusually generous pensions scaled to the highest level they reached in the government service, as do the permanent employees of states, counties, and cities.

In 1925 nearly all of Middletown's families earned their livings in the private sector. In 1934, at the depths of the Great Depression, 10 percent of Middletown's labor force held emergency jobs paid for by federal funds and one in four families were assisted by relief payments of various kinds from local public agencies, to which the federal government was a significant minor contributor (Lynd and Lynd 1937, Chapter 4 and Appendix 3, Table 10). In 1977, after 30 years of nearly uninterrupted prosperity, at least 50 percent of Middletown's families received public assistance in one form or another, either directly from federal agencies or from local agencies to which the federal government was the major contributor.

By 1979 the federal government was also the major contributor to the annual budget of Middletown's city government. The city's normal operations, financed almost entirely out of local resources as recently as 1945, had become dependent on federal and state subsidies transmitted through a tangle of direct and indirect conduits. The formal transition between local autonomy and local dependence was marked symbolically in 1972 when the Chamber of Commerce, long fanatically opposed to outside intervention in Middletown's affairs, hired a "grantsman" to assist the city in soliciting grants from federal agencies.

Other aspects of the federal presence in the 1970s reflected the peaceful but sweeping transformation of the American form of government that took place after 1964 as the executive and judicial branches of the government began to develop large and far-reaching legislative programs of their own that were only tenuously related to those of the Congress. Thus, the long arm of the Department of Health, Education, and Welfare reached into Middletown's schools to ensure racial integration, to insist on interscholastic competition in girls' basketball, and to forbid the posting of examination grades in the halls. The Department of Transportation told used-car dealers what blandishments they might use in their advertising. The Occupational Safety and Health Administration went through the local factories and ordered guardrails to be installed here and there. The courts at all levels have refined judicial procedures until the average interval between arrest and conviction for a property crime in Middletown, which was about a week in 1925, is now more than a year; and they have continuously broadened their own jurisdictions so that a woman excluded from a neighborhood tavern or a doctor who wishes to continue treating a reluctant patient now go to the law as a matter of course.

By the end of the 1970s, there were very few moral situations for which Middletowners still wrote their own rules. The distribution of social rewards and of punishments was closely monitored from outside in the pursuit of ideals that they themselves did not always share.

When, in 1978, we asked a cross section of Middletown citizens for their opinions on these matters, the majority of them, at all income levels, expressed some degree of resentment at the federal presence and a preference for the local management of their affairs. The images of the distant government held by welfare clients and by business executives were virtually identical; they perceived it as bureaucratic, wasteful, corrupt, and ineffective. Nearly every category of the population—physicians, truck drivers, students, postal workers, blacks, shopkeepers—felt that they had been singled out for special maltreatment. Middletown's numerous federal employees shared these views. For them, too, the government was "them," not "us." Although 30 federal agencies have full-time employees in or near Middletown, no common bond unites these people and there is no occasion on which they acknowledge a shared identity. For them, as for other Middletowners, the government is a source of constant complaint, like the winter weather and just about as difficult to reform.

The sheer scale of these outside intrusions into the quiet, small-town life of Middletown makes us look for massive consequences. If we did not have the Middletown I and Middletown II studies to depend on, it would be easy to imagine such consequences as a widening of the generation gap, a disintegration of religion, a spread of political apathy, a breakdown of local authority, or a vast increase in anomie. But, when we look at the data, most of these effects are unaccountably missing. The general style of family life has hardly changed at all since 1925. The number of churches has risen more than the population, and their average attendance is greater now than then. The relationships among employers and employees, although elaborately regulated today, are not conspicuously more cordial or more hostile than they used to be. The level of political participation in the presidential election of 1976 was almost identical with the level of participation in 1924 (40 percent and 41 percent of the total population, respectively). Moreover, close analysis of the precinct-by-precinct vote shows that the choice between the Republican and Democratic candidates was more affected by occupational position in the election of 1976 than in the election of 1936 (Guterbock 1980), for which the Lynds did a similar analysis. The reverse of that would be expected from a trend toward political apathy. The suicide rate, the classic indicator of anomie, was 0.32 per thousand of the population in Middletown in 1925 and 0.17 in 1975. The "social indicators" seem to be indicating either that Middletown's institutions have shown a remarkable capacity to resist outside pressure or that they have somehow been reinforced by television and federal intervention. Indeed, both interpretations may be valid.

We have already examined the reasons why the family in Middletown is so resistant to change; similar considerations apply to religion. The roots of both institutions go very deep. The habits associated with them are learned in childhood and never completely forgotten. Alternative practices, such as open marriage and militant atheism, offer little attraction to the people who live in Middletown. In addition to the resistance these traditional institutions pose to innovation, they may actually be reinforced by the influences emanating from the metropolitan centers. Even a cursory review of the content of television programs and federal programs shows how this might happen. By incessant repetition, television series and commercials portray and idealize a normal family that is indistinguishable from the standard family in Middletown; the middle-income, complete nuclear family occupying a single-family house in a homogeneous residential neighborhood. The role models most commonly displayed for fathers, mothers, sons, daughters, and other kin tend to reinforce, not subvert, the indigenous images of these roles. Moreover, the television networks have responded to external pressures by developing affirmative action policies that stress the inclusion of blacks and other excluded groups in the standard family style much more than the realistic depiction of deviant family styles. That is done, too, of course, but only occasionally and exceptionally; the standard style is reiterated day and night.

Federal programs may have the effect of reinforcing traditional institutions. By subsidizing home ownership, higher education, and care of the aged, the government makes it possible for a larger proportion of Middletown's families to practice and exemplify the standard family style.

The Paradoxes of Social Change

These reassuring findings may leave us uneasy. The sense of calamitous change is so pervasive in contemporary American society that it seems perverse to suggest that Middletown's fundamental institutions are changing very slowly and not for the worse. Are we perhaps overlooking the more subtle changes of behavior and consciousness that do not show up in gross indicators like voting patterns and suicide rates? That question is too important to dismiss and too difficult to answer casually. Subtle changes are by definition difficult to detect, especially with the crude instruments we have for measuring social change. It is conceivable, for example, that, although people in Middletown today hold much the same values as their grandparents held two generations ago, they hold them in a different way. Indeed, some of our own data suggest this possibility.

The religious, political, and social beliefs of Middletown adolescents, as we noted above, changed remarkably little from 1924 to 1977, so that, for example, the proportion agreeing that "Jesus Christ was different from every man who ever lived in being entirely perfect" declined by only 15 percent over that long interval of time and the proportion saying that the United States is unquestionably the "best country in the world" declined by only 14 percent; both statements are still accepted by a large majority of Middletown adolescents. The traditional precepts of religion and patriotism persist with amazing strength. Nevertheless, other responses to the same questionnaire show that they are held in a different fashion nowadays. The Middletown adolescents of 1924 were not only religious and patriotic, they were intolerant. Nearly all of them believed that, since Christianity is the one true religion, "all people should be converted to it." By 1977, only a third were still of that opinion. Similarly, the proportion of them favoring unlimited free speech on political issues had greatly increased. Similarly, although the majority of Middletown adults are churchgoers and favor the teaching of religion in the public schools, only 18 percent of them maintained in 1978 that Christianity alone should be taught there; 65 percent thought that all the major religions ought to be included—a degree of ecumenism that would have been unthinkable in 1925 or 1935.

In sum, although contemporary Middletowners adhere to the same values as their predecessors, they are much less eager to impose them on other people and much more tolerant of beliefs and life-styles that differ from their own. Like nearly everything else in

Middletown, the shift toward increased tolerance is not entirely new. Speaking of 1935, the Lynds wrote, "The growth of the city and its increased communication with the outside culture have brought it into contact with a greater variety of ways of living differing from its own, and thus have encouraged more tolerance of certain types of unfamiliar people and manners" (Lynd and Lynd 1937, 426).

Many people in Middletown, especially those charged with the management of many people in schools and factories, describe this attitude as "permissiveness" and hold it responsible for various problems of discipline and social control. They see themselves as living in a society in which nearly everything is permitted and even those few things that are prohibited can be attempted with impunity. How accurate is such a picture?

The measurement of permissiveness is full of paradoxes. In 1925 the Prohibition amendment was in force, but liquor was available locally at speakeasies. Since they were illegal anyway, the speakeasies asked no questions about their customers' ages and served adults and minors without discrimination. Adolescent drinking was commonplace but not widely perceived as a social problem. In 1935, after the repeal of the Prohibition amendment, drinking was legal for persons over 21 but illegal for juveniles. As a result, drunkenness was conspicuous at high school dances and juvenile drinking *was* identified as a social problem. By the 1970s, the drinking age had been lowered to 18, and, since the local pattern of control favored retail distribution over public drinking places, liquor was freely available to persons of all ages. Middletown, which had 40 saloons as far back as 1891, had only 12 public bars in 1976, most of which were in restaurants; but it had 23 "carryout" liquor stores, some of which stayed open until 2 AM on Saturday nights. There were fewer arrests for liquor offenses in 1975 than in the Prohibition year of 1931. Despite extensive drinking among adolescents, the control of alcohol in general and of juvenile drinking in particular was no longer much of a public issue in Middletown. In that direction there has surely been an increase in permissiveness.

With respect to drugs, the trend toward permissiveness has gone the other way. There are no references to drugs or drug addiction in the Lynds' two reports, but we estimate from other sources that there was relatively more addiction to narcotics in the Middletown of 1925 than there is today. It was mostly confined to elderly persons of the business class and was not a subject of public concern. A certain amount of experimentation with milder drugs seems to have occurred as well, but the amount is impossible to estimate. There were no arrests at all in 1925 for drug-connected offenses. Today, recreational drug use is highly illegal and widely practiced by adolescents. In Middletown in 1975, there were nearly 400 arrests for the sale or the possession of marijuana, and the smell of the stuff pervaded every large informal gathering of adolescents. "The drug problem in our schools" was high on the list of local concerns; there were even some rumors of heroin use.

Similar shifts back and forth make it difficult to strike any firm balance. With respect to sexual activity, Middletown is infinitely more permissive now than in 1925. With respect to driving, it has become much less permissive. Children of any age could drive the family automobile in 1925, at any feasible speed. There were no parking fines or compulsory inspections and no special penalties for drunken driving.

The scope and weight of parental authority in Middletown do not seem to have changed very much since 1925. By that date, corporal punishment for adolescents was virtually unknown — as it still is today — but parents held sufficient disciplinary sanctions at their disposal because of the prolonged economic dependence of their children. The degree of dependence has been somewhat diminished because more of today's adolescents hold part-time jobs and more of today's college students receive financial aid from public sources. On the other hand, the period of dependence now lasts considerably longer. In 1925 and in 1935, as today, most children past the age of 13 or 14 did not accept parental dictation in choosing their friends or setting limits on their sexual experiments, and they were not really expected to.

If Middletown's children and adolescents are not conspicuously freer or more constrained than their predecessors, the situation of Middletown's adults has evolved in a more complex way. As the long arm of government regulation has reached into local institutions, the balances of power in them have shifted in various ways that can be roughly summarized as follows. (1) Citizens generally have less freedom vis-à-vis public authority. In the Middletown of 1935, only about half of the population paid direct taxes of any kind (the property taxes paid by the minority who were home owners and the federal income taxes paid by some fraction of the 10 or 15 percent of employed persons who filed returns in that year). By 1975 a large majority of the population paid both income and property taxes, all employers and employees paid social security taxes, and anyone who spent any money at all paid sales taxes, all collected with unforgiving efficiency. (2) Persons exercising private authority outside the family (school principals, factory managers, physicians, priests, landlords) typically have less freedom of action now than such persons had in 1925, with their decisions being constrained by innumerable statutes, regulations, and judicial rulings as well as by unions, insurance companies, and protest groups capable of marshaling public opinion in defense of mistreated subordinates. (3) The freedom of action of Middletown's black citizens in all relationships with whites has been vastly increased by the eradication of the whole body of formal and informal regulations that, in this midwestern community oriented toward the South, subordinated all blacks to all whites as recently as 1935. The lesser and more informal constraints imposed on other minorities have, for the most part, been eliminated, also. (4) Middletown has become less permissive with respect to the expression of bigotry by the dominant majority; the darkie jokes, the anti-Semitic jokes, and the racial and religious epithets that used to be a large part of the local folklore are now uttered furtively.

It is tempting to add to this list that women now have more freedom of action with respect to men and men correspondingly less with respect to women, but the facts do not entirely support such an interpretation. As later chapters of this book will show, "women's liberation" has had mixed effects on the relationship between the sexes in Middletown. Some of these effects favor women, as intended, but others clearly favor men, and some are difficult to decipher in terms of relative advantage. A Middletown woman now has an enforceable legal right to be paid at the same rate as a man doing similar work. In a hierarchical organization, she cannot be barred from promotion, and, once promoted, her authority is not resisted by male subordinates as it would have been in the past. She has at least a theoretical right to enter most of the occupations that used to be exclusively male (for example, the armed services, the ministry, police work, airline piloting, truck driving, the building trades), and a few of Middletown's young women have actually entered these male preserves. In the learned professions (medicine, law, college teaching) in which women used to be a small minority confined to specialized women's work, there has been significant progress toward equal representation. In other professions in which women used to be very rare (such as engineering, architecture, and dentistry), their numbers have been rising fast. Throughout the occupational sphere, men are now under some obligation to treat women as equals, and the obligation is generally respected.

What this does to their informal relationships nobody really knows. The sexual exploitation of cringing and dependent female employees by brutal employers was never much of a problem in Middletown. It is perhaps more likely to occur now than formerly since the protection of women's virtue has ceased to be one of the community's goals. The establishment of unmarried liaisons between co-workers is much easier than it used to be. The parties can no longer be punished by a disapproving supervisor or turned out into the snow by a censorious landlady. On the other hand, there is no evidence at all that Middletown is more tolerant of extramarital affairs than before. Now, as in 1925, divorce often follows the discovery of a clandestine affair.

The net effect of recent developments has probably been to decrease the bargaining power of nonworking women while increasing that of working women. The woman who wants to be supported by a man can no longer use pregnancy as a means of ensnaring him, given the availability of reliable contraception and legal abortion. The dependent wife with a reluctant husband can no longer threaten him with the burden of lifelong alimony. Today's working woman has more to bring to the marital partnership in the first place and more to take away from it if the marriage dissolves. It is no wonder that large numbers of business-class women have forsaken their traditional life at home for the occupational marketplace. But, on balance, it is hard to find any decisive shift of relative advantage, as the general stability of Middletown's marriage and divorce rates might have already suggested to us.

It remains for us to consider the kind of future that Middletown families face together. The Lynds thought that one of the best ways to grasp the essence of any culture was to examine its orientation toward the future compared to its orientation toward the past and the present.

The concept of the future, the Lynds remarked, had two compartments in Middletown; one contained the large symbols that defined the collective future of the community and the nation, and the other held the network of small plans and hope that defined the future for families and individuals. During the boom years of the 1920s, the Lynds thought, the two kinds of future had moved closer together, and then during the depression years of the 1930s they had floated rapidly apart, so far apart as to challenge the validity of the doctrine of opportunity that loomed so large among Middletown's collective beliefs. Ignoring some of the nuances patiently traced out by the Lynds, we can summarize what they reported as follows: during the 1920s, Middletown people were optimistic about both the collective future and their individual futures. In both eras, the community's picture of the collective future was announced with missionary zeal by the business class and grudgingly accepted by the working class.

By the late 1970s, as far as we can determine, Middletown's orientation to the future was nearly the reverse of the pattern the Lynds observed in the 1930s. In the compartment of personal hopes and plans, most people in Middletown were confident and optimistic. The great majority of those who worked for a living regarded their jobs as secure and satisfactory; the great majority of younger workers looked forward with confidence to promotion, wider responsibilities, and higher incomes, while older workers generally took satisfaction in the stability and security of their jobs and the prospect of comfortable retirement. About the futures of their children, they expressed no anxiety at all. Most of them would go to college and get married without encountering any notable obstacles, and those who abstained would do so at their own choice without causing their parents much disappointment. With the slowing of modernization, the proportion of Middletown parents who fix their hopes on having their children rise far above their own level is much smaller than it used to be. With the erosion of cultural differences between the business class and the working class, the allurement of rising from the working class to the business class is much diminished, as is the fear of falling in the other direction.

But about the collective future contemporary Middletowners are more pessimistic than any of their predecessors, back to the first settlers. Their pessimism is focused on the national society, rather than on their own community. The local future of Middletown is hardly ever discussed these days. The "booster spirit" that the Lynds viewed with such misgiving has disappeared. What Middletown's contemporary citizens value most about the place is that it is not a big city and is not likely to become one. Although an earlier generation beat the drum for civic growth and industrial expansion, the present generation talks of controlling growth and improving urban services and takes it for granted that any major change in the community is likely to be for the worse.

With respect to the larger society, Middletown is gloomy indeed. What people of all ages see as they look into the future is nuclear war, environmental pollution, inflation, exhaustion of resources, and a general deterioration of the quality of life. Faced with these discouraging prospects, they avert their eyes and return to the felicities of family life, the comforts of religion, and the wide range of private pleasures available to them. The alternative to catastrophe that they desire is not continued progress but a prolongation of the status quo. They are not at all sure that the world will last, but they are reasonably sure that Middletown will endure if the world does. So, in the here and now, between an unremembered past and an unimagined future, they persevere.

Chapter 2

Changes in the Setting

The organized booster spirit and bristling civic loyalty that the Lynds described as "various mass boostings of the 'Magic Middletown'" (Lynd and Lynd 1929, 484 and 486) is little in evidence today, but its absence does not necessarily denote community decline. Modern Middletowners speak less favorably about their community than their grandparents did, and the Chamber of Commerce is only a vestige of its former vibrant and powerful self, but most residents still believe that Middletown is a pretty good place to live.

Just as Middletowners are less likely today to say that everyone ought to be converted to their particular brand of Christianity, they are less likely to prescribe residence in Middletown, or in a community like it, as the cure for everyone's ills. The parochial spirit that led a woman from one of Middletown's leading families to say, upon returning from a middepression European trip, that "Europe is all right, but I can have a better time in Middletown" and her husband to agree by asking "What can anybody see in them old masters? We got better pictures in our Middletown liberry" is little in evidence today. If anything, the norm is mild disparagement, of the "why would anyone spend a summer in Middletown if they could be elsewhere?" variety. But the spirit of increased toleration does not signify that modern Middletowners are unhappy about their place in the world. The collective self-image, though less provincial and self-righteous, is still positive. The dominant attitude seems to be that some places are better than Middletown but most places are much worse.

Members of our research staff were repeatedly told that Middletown's disadvantages were compensated by its being such a good place to raise a family. In the family role survey, we asked respondents to rate the community as a family environment. About half of them rated it above average, including 37 percent as "better than most places" and 9 percent as "outstanding." The two mildly negative categories drew only 6 percent of the respondents between them. In the roster of family environments Middletown may not earn high honors, but nearly everyone grades it as average or better. Incidentally, there were no sex differences in the ratings of Middletown as a place to raise a family; the women were no more and no less enchanted with it than the men were.

We also inquired about whether the community had improved or deteriorated as a family environment. Here opinions were less certain. But of those who did have ideas on the subject, the majority thought that contemporary Middletown was as good or better a family environment as it had been in the 1930s.

The conventional advantages of that environment were spelled out by the wife of a local physician.

Middletown people are honest and neighborly. People who come here from out of town, when they get into the retirement period of their lives, this is the town they want to retire in. They think it is a balanced community; they don't talk about California or Florida, they talk about Middletown. They enjoy the variety of seasons here.

People care about others here. You don't find what you'd find in big cities, people seeing an event or someone in trouble and just sailing by. . . . If there is someone who has had a tragedy, Middletown people are generous.

A less one-sided view was given by another woman who repeated the question "Why do I think Middletown's a good place to raise kids?" and then answered herself with a recital of some of Middletown's defects and how they were counterbalanced by its simplicity.

I think this is one of the reddest areas I've ever been in, and I think the Ku Klux Klan is alive and well. I was just at a place where a guy is dealing in coke. . . . Our school system here in Middletown is run by a bunch of WASPies, people who are living back in the days when a Sock Hop was the answer to all the problems. The Middletown Community School people would not allow the State Police drug abuse survey to be taken in our school system, which is anonymous, because the illusion is that Middletown has no drug problem among its teenage population. Sure. Who are they kidding? Nobody.

Industry leaves this area very quickly because of the labor problems. We've got a redneck organizer here in town who uses Mafia-type tactics, burning and injuring people, breaking their bones. We've got a group down in the southeast end of town that flies gamblers in from Chicago, picks them up at the airport, and has big-name games.

We've got prosecutors who deal, . . . city services stink, . . . our ambulance service here in town in corrupt. Our mayor is a hillbilly who cannot speak English. . . .

But through Middletown we have grown to know our children, and it would not have occurred at any place, . . . and I feel good about it because it happened here. And it is quiet. . . . The quietness appeals to me, the lack of all this pressure that comes with a big city, four-lane roads with everybody going. . . . A person in this area has to develop real communications because the diversions such as bars and social things are few.

And that's why I think it's a good place, not because of what it is, not because those things are happening. Maybe because of the negatives, . . . the negatives I can stand.

Population and Family Milieu

The prospects and problems of a community are affected by the kind of people who live there. Family life in a community dominated by older people is apt to be different than it is in a younger population. A city of large families has different neighborhood, educational, and recreational challenges than one in which most couples are childless or have only one or two children.

The distribution of a population by sex and among the various categories of age, marital status, education, and occupation provides the background against which people can be seen playing out their family roles. It also determines the attributes and attitudes family members bring to their family relationships. Where divorce is common, people who marry usually have had some direct contact with it, either in their own experience or through that of friends and relatives. That experience affects their attitudes on the divorce process and whether they view it as a realistic option in their own lives.

The family patterns of the community reflect the population structure of the region and the nation as well. If Middletown were in any way typical of the country, we would expect to find national trends mirrored in local trends. Indeed, several recent changes in the national population appear in bolder relief in Middletown than in the country at large. Among the more important of these are the aging and the "feminization" of the population, the fluctuating propensity to marry, and some interesting trends in family size and marital stability. We must also consider some other changes that do not mirror national trends but are peculiar to this one community (for example, recent increases in the number of blacks and the number of college students).

The Maturing of Middletown

Nineteenth-century Middletown was a city of young people. In 1880 the median age was 22.1 and more than a third of the residents were under age 15. Elderly people were scarce; only 123 of the city's 5,028 residents were 65 or older. Even so, Middletown's population was somewhat older than the national population, which had a median age of only 20.9. A generation later, Middletown had become middle-aged. Its median age in 1920 was 28.5 (compared to a national median of 25.3), and the population was quite evenly distributed by age: about half of them were between ages 15 and 44; the other half were evenly divided between children and persons over 45.

Until about 1950, Middletown's age pyramid continued to resemble the nation's. In that census year, for the first time, the majority of the U.S. population was over 30. In the subsequent decades, despite the increasing proportion of elderly people, the nation's birth rate was high enough to reverse the long-term aging trend, and the median age of the population fell below 30 again, to 29.6 in 1960 and 28.1 in 1970.

The decline was more dramatic in Middletown, where the increased proportion of young persons brought into the population by the high birth rates of the 1950s and early 1960s was augmented by a growing body of college students. Between 1950 and 1960, the local university's enrollment more than doubled, from 3,144 students to 7,036; by 1970, it had doubled again, reaching 15, 824 in the fall of 1970. Since 1970, the university's enrollment has remained fairly stable at about 17,000.

The growth of the university has made Middletown "mature" as a cultural center. Asked about the city's best features, the things she was proud of, the wife of one of Middletown's influential professional men responded, "The university has just been tremendous. I would not be happy here, even though it is my home town, if it weren't for the university."

Today's Middletown population is both older and younger than the population of the 1920s. It is older in having nearly twice as many persons of retirement age. In 1970, for the first time, there were more Middletown residents over 65 years old than under 5 years old, and the city's declining birth rate during the 1970s portends a much higher ratio of old people to young children in the next census. (See Appendix A, Table 2-1.)

The Feminization of Middletown

Before 1940, there were more males than females in the United States population, as there had been since the founding of the republic. According to the Census Bureau's annual estimates, there were more males than females until 1946; since that time, there has been a slight majority of females—51.1 percent of the national population in 1970.

The relative number of males and females is sometimes expressed by the sex ratio, defined as the number of males per 100 females in a specified population. Until 1946, the sex ratio for the national population was always over 100. Since then, it has been under 100. In 1970, it was 96 (i.e., there were 96 males for every 100 females). The sex ratio of each age cohort tends to decline with increasing age, so that, by the time persons reach marriageable age, there are considerably more females than males in their age-group. The sex ratio for persons 14 years of age and over was 92 in 1970.

If we call the increasing proportion of females a "feminization" of the general population, the term can be applied with somewhat more assurance to Middletown, where the rise in the female proportion of the population has been more rapid than for the country as a whole. Middletown's sex ratio was 103 in 1920, 102 in 1930, and 99 in 1940. The decline has continued since then, with sex ratios of 95, 93, and 90 for 1950, 1960, and 1970, respectively. Among persons of marriageable age, the decline has been more precipitous, from 104 in 1920 to 86 in 1970.

This trend cannot be directly attributed to the growth of the university, for (1) it is more pronounced among the married or formerly married than among single persons, and (2) the sex ratio of the nonstudent population is much lower than that of the university students. For the Middletown population aged 14 and over in 1970, the sex ratio for single (never-married) persons was 97; for students, it was 92; and, for all persons married, divorced, or widowed, it was 82. In summary, then, when the Lynds studied Middletown it was a predominantly male town; in our times, it has many more women than men.

The Propensity to Marry

To the Lynds Middletown seemed a "marrying city." Apparently, the unmarried research assistants who accompanied them to Middletown from New York City experienced considerable "pressure of pairwise activity" in Middletown. The city was not oriented toward meeting the needs of single men and women; adults were expected to "pair off" with members of the opposite sex, and most social life was organized around couples or families. "One felt it all the way from such simple matters as the dearth of pleasant places to eat if one did not have a home, through the customary activities that constitute 'spending the evening' in Middletown" (Lynd and Lynd 1937, 147). The Lynds cited the 1930 census figures showed Middletown's proportion of single people to be substantially lower than that for the urban United States[1] and they almost seem to suggest that Middletown's obsession with marriage is a symptom of social retardation.

Although Middletown may not have been in step with the investigators, it was not behind the times but rather was in the vanguard, for the entire United States was experiencing a gradual decline in the proportion of single adults, a trend that would continue until 1960. The United States was becoming a "marrying nation," and Middletown and communities like it were leading the way.

Both in Middletown and in the country as a whole, men have

been, and continue to be, more likely to remain single than women, but the upward trend in marriage affected both sexes. In 1920, more than a third of American men had never married; by 1960, fewer than a quarter were bachelors. Between 1960 and 1970, there was a reversal of the trend, and the proportionate size of the single population increased to the level of the 1940s. Again, the trend of marriage in Middletown prefigured the national trend, for the upturn in the proportion of single people occurred in Middletown a decade earlier.

Between 1950 and 1960, the proportion of single adults in Middletown rose about 2 percent, and, in the following decade, it rose by more than 10 percent, far outstripping the trend for the country as a whole. In 1970, 34 percent of Middletown's adult males and 30 percent of its females were single; the corresponding figures for the United States as a whole were 29 and 23 percent.

A large part of the increase in the percentage of single adults in Middletown is attributable to the growth of the university and the inclusion of its students in the local population for census purposes. We might also suggest that it reflected a possible decline in the appeal of marriage, were it not for the fact that marriage rates in the country seem to be rising. In 1975 there were 10.1 marriages per 1,000 population, and by 1979 the national figure had risen to 10.5 per 1,000. On balance, we cannot conclude that marriage is any less popular now than it was before.

Family Size

To the Middletowners of 1935, a family meant "a nice marriage with children," and there were subtle sanctions against couples who chose to remain childless. The Lynds found that "a marriage without children is regarded, according to the traditions of the culture, as incomplete, and healthy couples who choose to remain childless are alternately sympathized with, gently coerced, or condemned as 'selfish.' " Nevertheless, they reported, the economic reality was that children were increasingly defined as mouths to feed and decreasingly as hands to work. The high standard of living of the predepression era, followed by the economic hazards of the Great Depression, were deterrents to fertility, and "the resulting failure of parental nerve is, in part, registered in the continued decline in the average size of Middletown's families during the 1920's" (Lynd and Lynd 1937, 164).

The Lynds cited census figures that showed that the average size of Middletown's families dropped from 4.6 persons in 1890 to 3.7 in 1930.

The Lynds' attribution of declining family size to conditions specific to the 1920s and 1930s loses much of its force when we observe (1) that the decline in the percentage of young children during those years was very small (there was actually a slight increase between 1920 and 1930) and (2) that what decline there was continued a trend going back to 1860. If it were attributable to "failure of parental nerve," that failure would have been more characteristic of the 1890s than of the 1920s and 1930s.

An examination of the crude birth rates and of the fertility rates shown in Table 2-2 (in Appendix A) confirms that the decline in fertility between 1920 and 1940 was very modest compared to the substantial increase of fertility during the postwar "baby boom" Middletown's 1950 birth rate of 28.2 births per 1,000 population was higher than that of 1900, when there were 25.0 births per 1,000 population. The rapid decline that eventually followed the baby boom outpaced any earlier change; in just half a decade, between 1970 and 1975, the crude birth rate dropped almost seven points to the lowest point in the city's history. If the decline continues at anywhere near the same rate, the decade of the 1970s will have witnessed a change in Middletown's fertility without precedent.

The percentage of young children in the city's population may be a better indicator of fertility in Middletown than either the crude birth rate, with its familiar defects, or the average family size. Until 1940, one-person households were counted as families, so variations in the proportion of unattached persons in the city produced variations in family size unrelated to fertility. A 120-year series, based on the manuscript censuses of Middletown for 1850 through 1880 and on published census reports thereafter, is given in Table 2-3. It shows that younger children made up a larger percentage of Middletown's population in the 1850s, 1860s, 1870s, and 1880s than they have ever been since. It also documents the decline in fertility during the second half of the nineteenth century that had run its course by about 1910.

Table 2-3
Percentages of Middletown's Population under
Five Years Old, from 1850-1970

Year	Under Age 5	Year	Under Age 5
1850	16.2	1920	8.7
1860	19.0	1930	9.2
1870	13.2	1940	8.3
1880	11.7	1950	10.7
1890	10.5	1960	11.1
1900	9.5	1970	8.3
1910	9.2		

Source: U.S. Bureau of the Census, Manuscript Census Reports 1890 estimate based on the assumption that the population of females under five years old would equal the population of males, U.S. Department of the Interior 1896, part 1, pp. 547, 817; U.S. Bureau of the Census 1901, vol. 1, part 1, p. 616; U.S. Bureau of the Census 1913, vol. 1, p. 493; U.S. Bureau of the Census 1922b, vol. 2, p. 317; U.S. Bureau of the Census 1932, Vol. 3, part 1, p. 702; U.S. Bureau of the Census 1943, vol. 2, part 2, p. 790; U.S. Bureau of the Census 1952, vol. 2, part 14, p. 14-56; U.S. Bureau of the Census 1963, vol. 1, part 16, p. 16-61; U.S. Bureau of the Census 1973a, vol. 1, part 16, p. 16-100.

Despite the violent oscillation of birth rates since 1920 (Appendix A, Table 2-2), the proportion of young children in the Middletown population has remained fairly constant during the past 50 years. Between 1920 and 1970, the proportion of the population under age 5 ranged from 8.3 to 11.1 percent, and the 1970 percentage was very close to the percentages of 1920 and 1940. The proportion of older children (5 to 14) in the population was also fairly constant, remaining between 15 and 19 percent.

During the period between 1929 and 1935, the economic depression had adverse effects on both marriage and childbearing, but the Lynds found that fertility was less affected than the propensity to marry. "It is significant," they wrote, "that the birth rate had fallen off in the depression by only 16 percent, whereas the marriage rate had dropped by 41 percent. In other words, 'having a baby' was less vulnerable to the prolonged economic pressure than 'getting married' " (Lynd and Lynd 1937, 166).

The figures on family size given by the Lynds (1937, 164-65) were, as they noted, only roughly representative of the size of biological families. They were obtained by dividing the total population by the total number of households without excluding single persons living alone, inmates of institutions, and persons living in group quarters. The two measures of family size given in Table 2-4, though approximate also, are somewhat more accurate since (1) persons living alone are excluded and (2) the top row refers specifically to children.

Table 2-4
Two Measures of Family Size in Middletown, 1920-1970

	1920	1930	1940	1950	1960	1970
Mean number of children aged 0 to 17 per family	1.27	1.21	1.04	1.07	1.35	1.21
Mean number of persons per family	4.02	3.91	3.59	3.27	3.52	3.37

Source: U.S. Bureau of the Census 1922b, Vol. 2, p. 121, vol. 3, p. 297; U.S. Bureau of the Census 1932, vol. 3, part 1, p. 702; U.S. Bureau of the Census 1943, vol. 2, part 2, p. 790; U.S. Bureau of the Census 1952, vol. 2, part 14, pp. 14-56, 14-61; U.S. Bureau of the Census 1963, vol. 1, part 16, pp. 16-61, 16-205; U.S. Bureau of the Census, 1973, vol. 1, part 16, pp. 16-100, 16-301, 16-336.

Table 2-4 supports the conclusion that in 1970 Middletown families had about the same number of minor children at home as they had in the 1920s and early 1930s. The irregular decline in the average number of persons per family between 1920 and 1970 apparently represents a decrease in the number of grown children living with their parents and of other relatives or boarders sharing the family household.

The Lynds' description of Middletown as "a city of small families" (Lynd and Lynd 1937, 165) continues to be appropriate. Our review of birth rates and age distributions indicates that the small-family pattern was well established by 1920 and that it has prevailed ever since, except during the postwar baby boom, which temporarily returned the proportion of young children to the levels of 1880 and 1890. The more recent decline of fertility to the lowest levels in the city's history may presage an eventual change to even smaller families, although such a change has not yet occurred. On the basis of national trends, a stabilization of family size at about the present level may be the probable pattern in Middletown's near future.

Divorce

By 1923, the Lynds noted, divorce in Middletown was taken for granted, and, to a certain extent, it fed upon itself. "One factor in the increasing frequency of divorce," they observed, "is probably the growing habituation to it" (1929, 122). In 1895 there had been only 18 divorces for every 100 marriages, but between 1920 and 1924 the annual ratios ranged between 33 and 55. In the 1890s, divorce was still officially abhorrent. The Indiana State Statistician, presenting his annual table of divorces by counties, described it as "the repulsive exhibit." By the 1920s, divorce was deplored without much fervor. The Lynds commented that married women who worked or had opportunities to work outside the home were "less willing to continue an unsatisfactory marital arrangement." They described Middletown's younger generation as "less content with . . . maladjustment today when spending money is more in demand, jobs for women common, and divorce easy" (1929, 127-28). They referred to the "increased lifting of the taboo upon the dissolution of marriage" (1929, 121).

A decade later, a local high school teacher remarked to Robert Lynd that "our children aren't any longer regarding divorce as a thing to be feared particularly, and in the same way they are breaking with their parents' ideas that marriage is to be regarded as permanent." Nevertheless, Middletown in the midthirties was still a place where marriage was described as a "sacred institution" (Lynd and Lynd 1937, 152 and 162). Its attitudes toward divorce were ambivalent, with much wringing of hands and viewing with alarm on one side and much official facilitation and private noninterference on the other.

The institution of divorce, like sickness, has largely settled down in Middletown to the status of a means of livelihood for a profession, with the public officials supplying seemly rituals and the official seal. . . .

Thus the official responsibility of the community to sift, and in doubtful cases to check, divorces has been largely given up in response to the pressure of the interested parties for easy divorce with no questions asked and the pressure of the lawmen to make more income out of legal cases. . . .

The truth of the matter appears to be that God-fearing Middletown is afraid of sex as a force in its midst, afraid it might break loose and run wild, and afraid to recognize too openly that those "whom God hath joined together" can be mismated (Lynd and Lynd 1937, 161-62).

Middletown in the late 1970s seems to have come to terms with sex and with mismating. Even the ministers now maintain that there are many justifiable grounds for divorce, and many ascribe no responsibility to divine providence for the matching of marriage partners. If marriage is still regarded as sacred, it is as a primary social institution and not as an indissoluble bonding of souls. The marital contract is now viewed by those who solemnize marriages as a matter of "interpersonal adjustment" and "mutual benefit."

We were repeatedly told by Middletowners that almost everyone was getting or thinking of divorce, that marital infidelity was commonplace, and that marriage itself was dying out. There is no evidence for trends of this kind in Middletown, but these perceptions are part of the contemporary culture, and they define the norms against which people evaluate the success of their own marriages. Comments like the following are typical.

All my friends are getting a divorce. I guess that means my marriage is better than my friends'. . . . My sister wants a divorce, not for any reasons; she just wants one. I've thought about it, but we've stuck it out. Some of my friends who were thinking about getting a divorce are getting back together now, so I don't know. . . . Hardly anyone stays together now. I hope we do. But then a lot of people just don't get married anymore.

I don't associate with people having marital troubles—it makes me nervous. I will help if I can, but not unless the two people try to help themselves. I try to be understanding if a divorce is not their fault, but, if there's no reason for it, it's catching like an epidemic in Middletown. I really think that many of my friends become divorced for no reason and that in future years they'll see it's not a picnic.

A middle-aged college professor expressed this pattern succinctly when he described his marriage as ". . . better than most; most of my friends are divorced."

The variations in family stability in Middletown can be measured by following the fraction of the population shown by census reports to have experienced a broken marriage. The advantage of this procedure is that it omits the single population and, hence, excludes the distorting influence of Middletown's growing student population in recent years.

In 1920 only 3.3 percent of the ever-married population of Middletown reported their current status as "divorced"; the proportion was the same for both sexes. The incidence of divorce increased consistently over the next five decades, rising to 6.4 percent of the ever-married men and 8.4 percent of the ever-married women by 1970. If we consider both types of marital termination (divorce and widowhood), the male proportion remains fairly stable; 10.4 percent of the ever-married men were divorced or widowed at the 1920 census. Females show an increase; 16.6 percent of the ever-married women were divorced or widowed in the 1920 census, and 25.6 percent were in 1970. Thus, 1 out of every 4 Middletown women who had ever married was a widow or a divorcee in 1970, compared to 1 out of 10 of the men.

These figures are informative as far as they go, but they tell us nothing about the majority of divorced persons who have entered another marriage. The measurement of changes in the propensity to divorce is a surprisingly difficult matter. The Lynds' discussion of divorce rates compared the annual number of divorces in Middletown's county to the county's total population (the crude divorce rate) and also to the number of marriages.

The major defect of the crude divorce rate is that its base includes many persons who, because they are not married, have absolutely no chance to be divorced. Yet, variations in the proportion of such persons (for example, significant increases in the number of formerly married persons or in the number of single adults or children) produce changes in the divorce rate that are unrelated to changes in the probability that married persons will divorce. In Middletown's case, after 1950 there was an increasingly large proportion of single college students in the population. If the propensity to divorce had remained precisely the same from 1950 to 1960, the increase in the number of students in the population would have produced a spurious decrease in the crude divorce rate.

The other measure of divorce trends has equally serious defects. One problem in comparing annual frequencies of divorces and marriages is that the people married in a given year amount to only a small part of the total pool of married persons, all of whom risk divorce each year. Moreover, the factors that cause the number of marriages to vary from year to year may be quite different from those that affect divorce, although a high marriage rate is a factor in the divorce rate.

Trends in crude divorce rates and in the ratio of divorces to marriages must, therefore, be interpreted with great caution. A better base population for a divorce rate is the population at risk, namely married persons. Furthermore, because one divorce separates two married persons, the base population should consist of either married men or married women, but not both. Figures for the number of divorces per 1,000 married women in Middletown's county, as well as the other, less preferable rates, are given in Table 2-5 (Appendix A). They are derived from the Lynds' work (1937, 544-45), from the available county records, and from census reports.

On the basis of these numbers, it appears that the propensity to divorce in Middletown's county increased to a peak of about 21 divorces per 1,000 married women in 1920 and then declined somewhat and leveled off for about 40 years at roughly 16 divorces per 1,000 married women per year, except during the brief, high-divorce period following World War II. In 1945 the county recorded 27 divorces per 1,000 married women, a higher rate than ever before or since. The 1975 level of divorce was lower than the 1970 level and roughly comparable to the 1920 rate.

Again, the propensity to divorce in Middletown increased from 1890 to a peak in 1920, then receded to a slightly lower level, reached its highest peak after World War II, receded again, and then moved in the 1970s to a level between the two postwar highs. But, contrary to general opinion, it has not risen dramatically since the 1920s and it currently is not rising at all. (See Appendix A, Table 2-5.)

Divorce in Regional Perspective

The Lynds claimed that it was local pressure, rather than state or regional pressures, that influenced the Middletown divorce rate.

Middletown cannot comfort itself by blaming these broken homes upon its neighbors; its divorces are overwhelmingly a local product, with a year's residence in the state and six month's in the county required before filing suit for divorce, and with only about three percent of its divorces coming from outside its county on a change of venue (Lynd and Lynd 1937, 154).

If Middletown's divorces are largely of local origin, then the conditions that foster them must be common to neighboring communities, for in recent years the proportion of divorced persons in Middletown has not significantly exceeded the proportion in other Indiana cities. Since 1950, as can be seen in Appendix A, Table 2-6, Middletown's proportion of divorced persons has been comparable to that for the five Indiana cities in the same size category.

Incidence Estimates from Sample Surveys

The incidence of marital instability in the Middletown population is higher than the national census data suggest because the "percent divorced" category in the census reports includes only those persons who have not remarried following divorce or widowhood. The published census data on marital status do not distinguish between first marriages and subsequent marriages.

We were able to make such distinctions in our own surveys, and the findings suggest that there are at least as many previously divorced persons who have remarried as there are persons presently identified as divorced. Among the adults who responded to our kinship survey, 8 percent listed their marital status as divorced and 12 percent as remarried following divorce. Among married respondents in our family role survey, 14 percent reported a prior marriage ending in divorce. Of the adults who responded to our neighboring survey, 11 percent were divorced and the same percentage gave their marital status as remarried following divorce.

Additional data from two of our surveys permit us to estimate the change in family stability during the past generation. The 1977 high school survey included a question about whether the student was living with both parents, a parent and stepparent, a single parent, or someone else. The kinship survey contained a similar item about persons that the respondents had lived with when they were 16 years old (their median age at the time of the survey was 39).

In the Middletown high schools of 1977, a third of the students came from broken homes (that is, they were not living with both parents) compared to a fourth in the previous generation. Most of these were living either with their mother alone (14 percent of all students) or with their mother and stepfather (9 percent). Both in the contemporary generation and in the immediately preceding one, the children of broken homes were more likely to live with their mothers than with their fathers. If anything, the probability that children from divorced couples will live with their mothers (whether married or not) is somewhat greater for the present generation. (See Appendix Table 2-7.)

The slightly higher risk of a broken home that Middletown's contemporary adolescents experience, compared to adolescents of the previous generation, presumably reflects the somewhat higher level of divorce in the 1970s compared to the fairly stable (although high) levels of the preceding decades.

If the divorce rate per 1,000 population has changed but little over the last 50 years, that is not true of the direct experience of divorce. In the Lynds' Middletown, the high divorce rate was a recent trend. Some of a Middletowner's friends, or even a brother or a sister, might have been divorced, but the odds were greatly against his or her parents having been divorced. In 1890 Middletown's county had recorded only one divorce for every eight marriages, compared to one for every two or three marriages in 1925 and subsequent years. By 1975, Middletown had experienced 60 years of high marital instability, with the annual number of divorces ranging between a third and a half of the number of marriages. And, by 1975, a majority of the adult population (59 percent according to our family roles survey) had experienced one or more divorces in their immediate family, either their own or those of their parents or siblings.

Attitudes about Divorce

Over this long period of time, people have become accustomed to marital breakups. The dismay about the numerous Middletown divorces noted by the Lynds is not much in evidence anymore. Divorce, like marriage, is a normal part of life, and most people do not expect marriages to last forever.

Our family dynamics survey included a question about whether it is realistic to expect people to stay married for a lifetime. Over half of the respondents said no or gave equivocal answers like "It depends on who the people are and how well they get along together." The minority who said that marriage ought to be a lifetime commitment—about 4 out of every 10—referred either to their religious convictions or to the "lesson of experience." A divorced and remarried glass-factory worker affirmed the sanctity of marriage in these words:

I think there are enough of the people that put integrity above having fun that the value of marriage is not going to be done away with. I think it will stay just like it is, that there are enough people around that respect the marriage vows that they're going to keep it intact. People that do not respect them are just fooling themselves. They're going to beat their shirt on the rocks. They'll never destroy it. . . . We're all born with a sense of these values. There's no doubt about it. God didn't leave that to people.

We did not detect any sense of crisis in Middletown with respect to marital instability. People may deplore the divorces they know about, but they are not actively concerned or indignant about them. The pervasive philosophy of live and let live was as commonly expressed by those who said marriage should be a lifetime commitment as by those who opted for more temporary relationships. Today's Middletowners are much less sure of what is right and wrong than were people of their grandparents' generation. They are reluctant to judge others' situations, and they hesitate to apply moral sanctions to the actions of their relatives and friends.

Nevertheless, a majority, including those who said marriage should be for life as well as those to whom such expectations seemed unrealistic, believe that society does not demand enough marital commitment and that couples in difficulty turn too quickly to divorce. A Protestant minister who argued that it was frequently unrealistic to expect a marriage commitment to last a lifetime because people change at different rates and in unpredictable directions was, nevertheless, concerned that the expectations of Middletown—and today's society generally—are so low.

. . . in some ways people are not expecting enough from marriage now. When I say that, I think a lot of the young couples that I relate to in terms of marriage, really don't expect too much and, if not very much happens, they say "so what, we just dissolve it and go on." And I think that marriage still does demand a commitment and give and take to make it, and I know of no better state of life than a happily—than a well-married man and woman. . . .

There's a lot of marriages that would go on and be fulfilled . . . if it weren't so easy for them to dissolve. The old structure of social expectations did carry a lot of couples through. And it was worth getting carried through, with that period of difficulties. I think also it carried some people through to hell. I don't defend. I'm just saying that it did help. We're not very supportive today, either. The whole moral structure is—we just don't have very many expectations, and yet people are judged by what they do, by a society that isn't really very expecting of them.

The most common themes in responses to a question about the feasibility of lifetime marriages were that couples today do not take marriage seriously enough and that divorces are too easy to obtain. Young women in their first marriages were particularly emphatic on these points.

If you ever truly love someone, it never dies. Nothing would ever go wrong with our marriage. Most people don't work hard enough at marriage.

I think they make divorce too easy to get. That's the wrong attitude to take. For me, marriage is once in a lifetime.

If two people knew each other well enough before getting married, it should work out. Each of you has to change a little, or else one of you changes completely.

But the prevalent opinion that people should try harder to make their marriages work is counterbalanced by the equally prevalent opinion that couples should not continue unrewarding relationships. Most people were not willing to tell others how long they ought to try to hold a marriage together, but there was widespread agreement that getting a divorce might be preferable to continuing a hollow or harmful marriage. There are many nuances.

I used to say that after my children got grown, if I really wasn't satisfied, I'd probably leave my husband. I think if you're not satisfied I don't think that you should just stay. You should probably try to live life to the fullest. . . .

I wouldn't hurt my husband. I wouldn't do anything to hurt him. But also I wouldn't stay with him if I was very unhappy.

Feelings can change. If you're going to get married, you might love somebody very much, but feelings can change; even though you don't want them to, they can. And then I don't think you should stay together for a lifetime. I think life is too short. I think you should do what you feel like you want to do.

If they're not suited or compatible, they shouldn't stay together. Marriage today is overestimated. You can get by without it. Couples living together are just as good as those married as long as they're getting along okay. . . . The values aren't there that were there 30 years ago. It's the disposable trend today, whether it's furniture, wife, or house. . . . In general I think the attitudes toward marriage have changed quite a bit, the stigmatism of divorce and that type of thing. It doesn't exist like it did 20 years ago. Now you can just call it quits, and you start off again.

A more systematic review of people's attitudes about divorce is available from our housewife survey, which included the question, "In your opinion, what is the cause of the increasing divorce in America?" The answers to this question were recorded as given, coded into categories, and tabulated by social class (business or working class) according to husband's occupation. According to these respondents, the principal causes of the increasing divorce rate in America are a lack of commitment to marriage, the influence of the "new morality," the modern woman's independence, inadequate preparation for marriage, and poor communication between married couples. To the business-class wives, the first three— lack of commitment, the "new morality," and the modern woman's independence—were by far the most important. Working-class wives emphasized poor communication and inadequate preparation for marriage, but the lack of commitment and the influence of the "new morality" were also mentioned by them. (See Appendix Table 2-8.)

The Growth of the Black Population

Another trend affecting Middletown's families is the growth of the city's black population, which comprised only 5.6 percent of the population in 1920. Fifty years later, according to the census, 9.5 percent of Middletown's residents were black, and, according to our high school survey, 11.3 percent of Middletown's adolescents in 1977 were black.

The trend toward feminization also appears in the black population. The sex ratio was 109.8 in 1920. It declined sharply over the next 20 years, to 96.6 in 1940, but only slightly thereafter. In 1970 the sex ratio of blacks was 94.9.

The trend toward a lower median age can be observed in the black population as well, not so much by an increase of young adults as by an increasing number of children. In 1920 the percentage of the black population under age 15 was less than the percentage for whites (i.e., there were proportionately more white children than black children). That situation continued until about 1940, when the declining rate of fertility for the whites during the depression years brought the two percentages together. Since 1950, the black population has included a much larger proportion of children than the white population, and the difference continues to increase.

The reverse trend may be observed among older adolescents and young adults. In these age-groups, whites have been relatively more numerous since 1940, as the census figures in Table 2-9 show.

Table 2-9
Percentages of Children and Young People in Middletown's Population,
by Race, 1920-1970

	1920	1930	1940	1950	1960	1970
Under age 15						
Blacks	23.4	24.9	23.2	30.2	35.3	34.2
Whites	26.0	25.6	23.5	25.8	29.6	23.9
Age 15-24						
Blacks	18.2	17.3	16.1	13.8	12.5	20.4
Whites	18.2	18.4	17.3	16.7	17.2	28.3

Source: U.S. Bureau of the Census 1922b, vol. 2, p. 317; U.S. Bureau of the Census 1932, vol. 3, part 1, p. 702; U.S. Bureau of the Census 1943, vol. 2, part 2, p. 790; U.S. Bureau of the Census 1952, vol. 2, part 14, p. 14-56; U.S. Bureau of the Census 1963, vol. 1, part 16, p. 16-61; U.S. Bureau of the Census 1973, vol. 1, part 16, p. 16-100.

During the 1920s, the major difference between the black and the white populations of Middletown was that the blacks were over-represented in the early middle-aged group (ages 25-44). Today, the characteristic black population is differentiated by a surplus of children and a deficit of young adults.

Over the years, a consistently lower proportion of black men than of white men have been married, and relatively more black men have been widowed or divorced. But the differences in marital status between black and white women have been much larger. Black women of any given age are less likely than white women to be single but much more likely to be widowed or divorced.

Sharp differences in family stability were apparent in the 1977 high school survey, which showed that fewer than half (48 percent) of the black students were living with both of their parents, compared to 71 percent of the white students. The percentages living with a stepparent were the same, but black students were more than twice as likely to live in a household headed by their mothers (29 percent compared to 12 percent) and also more than twice as likely to live with relatives (8 percent compared to 3 percent). Both in white and black families, children from broken homes were much more likely to live with their mothers, whether their mothers were remarried or not, than with their fathers.

The Academization of Middletown

The Middletown the Lynds studied in 1924 was not a college town. If it had been, it would not have been chosen for their study. Since one of their criteria for choosing a city that would be representative of contemporary American life was that it have "a substantial local artistic life to balance its industrial activity; also a largely self-contained artistic life, e.g., not that of a college town in which the college imparts the community's music and lectures" (Lynd and Lynd 1929, 7). The local teachers' college had grown noticeably by 1925, but, "Despite the rapid growth of the college, . . . even in the spring of 1925 its impact on the town, other than its increment to local trade, was practically nil. It was an inconspicuous institution out in the edge of the cornfields, on the margin of the city's consciousness" (Lynd and Lynd 1937, 215). The college's share of the local labor force was trivial. The 1920 census listed a total of 9 "college presidents and professors" in the labor force; the 1930 census showed 50 of them. Even if we include all the professional teachers serving the city's elementary and secondary schools, the total number of persons employed in education in 1920 amounted to only 236 persons in a labor force of 16,150 (less than 1.5 percent).

Business or trade (13.5 percent) and manufacturing/construction (56.5 percent), accounted for more than two-thirds of Middletown's largely blue-collar labor force in 1920. Less than 6 percent was found in any professional occupation.

During the intervening years, there has been a gradual decline in the proportion of the local labor force working in manufacturing and construction and a huge increase in the proportion of professionals, most of whom are employed by the university or by the city's schools. By 1970, the educational industry accounted for 17 percent of Middletown's labor force, manufacturing and construction for 38 percent, and retail trade for 16 percent.

The permanent staff of the university has become a substantial and influential part of the community, different in life-style and aspirations from the business and industrial parts. By 1960, Middletown was a three-sector town, and its new character was emphasized by the sharp segregation of college students and professors in the quarter of the city where the university is located, in contrast to the more even geographical distribution of families who drew their living from manufacturing, construction, and retail trade.

The "great divide" that separated Middletown's people used to be the barrier between the business class and the working class. By the late 1960s, the educators were as clearly separated from both of these groups as the two groups were from each other. To the degree that the homes of professional educators provided a different family environment from those of factory workers or businesspeople, a new dimension had been added to the family context of Middletown.

The changes that have come with the growth of the university are generally regarded by Middletowners as having improved the city as a family environment. There are the usual town-gown problems and renter-student conflicts, but the university's influence is widely regarded as beneficial. A real-estate developer was characteristically emphatic.

It's easy to tell you the best thing about Middletown. It's State University, by far. That is the major employer anymore. It's the biggest industry that this town has, the biggest asset. When we've got things like Z Auditorium going, they bring you the same things you can see in Chicago, New York, or San Francisco. Perhaps they are second-rate companies, but at least you're exposed to them.

Others echoed the same theme.

We think it's wonderful how recreation and leisure have changed. We have tennis courts—there were tennis courts in the thirties—tennis is coming back.

Golfing used to be just the Country Club, and the one little public course; . . . golfing has expanded.

We used to have to go to Indianapolis to see a good play. Now we have concerts, artists' series, right here in Middletown. We don't go to Indianapolis for anything in the way of theater anymore, . . . thanks to the university.

In sum, today's Middletown is still the same place the Lynds studied in the 1920s. Although its population has changed in some respects and some of its customs have been modified by the passage of time, continuity—not change—has been the keynote of its recent history.

People in Middletown are older than they were, but at the same time the sizable college-age population adds a "youth culture" to the city that was missing in previous generations. Supporting that emphasis is a fairly recent increase in the proportionate size of the single population. In the 1920s, almost two-thirds of the city's adults were married couples. In the 1970s, that figure was closer to one-half.

The proportion of children in Middletown was about the same in the 1970s as it was in the 1920s, although there are indications that there will soon be fewer children than the city has had before. Attitudes toward divorce are more liberal now. There are more divorced persons in the population, and the population has a longer and more extensive experience with divorce than it had in the 1920s. As a consequence, perhaps, Middletown's children are slightly more likely to be living with only one of their natural parents than was the case in the 1920s. Today, there are more black people and many more black children.

The city's industrial structure is now divided into three parts: manufacturing/construction, retail trade, and education. Along with the growth of education as a major industry has come a widely appreciated development of cultural and recreational facilities. In fact, the city's manufacturing and retail trade declined between 1960 and 1970, but the growth of the university during the same period more than compensated for the loss of population that would otherwise have occurred.

Most Middletowners see their city as a good place in which to raise children and to grow old, but the self-praising and myopic boosterism so evident in the 1920s is gone. It is as though the community, more tolerant of diverse beliefs and behavioral patterns, is also more apt to recognize the virtues of other places. Middletown is seen as a good place, but it is no longer puffed up as the best place.

PART II Who Does What and How Well?

PART II Will Democracies End Basketball?

Chapter 3

Family Roles

In the Middletown of 1924, there was a sharp division of sex roles in the family. The husband's responsibility was to be a good provider. The wife was responsible for keeping the house, raising the children, and, particularly in the business class, maintaining the family's social position. A successful marriage did not necessarily involve close companionship between husband and wife. When couples participated in activities outside the home, they customarily divided into same-sex groups in which they talked "men's talk" and "women's talk." Although there were some joint recreational pursuits (business-class husbands sometimes played a round of golf with their wives, couples played cards with friends, and families motored together), the joint activities were exceptions to the standard division of activity by sex.

That division reflected a widely held view of men and women as nearly different species. Women were seen as emotional, illogical, and incapable of sustained thought and as being morally superior to men. "Men are God's trees; women are His flowers" was the motto of one of the local women's clubs. As far as the Lynds could tell, since the 1890s there had been few changes in the accepted view of male and female natures. "The recent mottoes of two of the local federated women's clubs," they said, "suggest little change from the prevailing attitude reflected in a commencement essay in 1891, 'Woman Is Most Perfect When Most Womanly' " (Lynd and Lynd 1929, 118).

In 1935 the Lynds lamented that the time and resources available to them did not permit a detailed study of sex roles, "these subtle aspects of family life." As in 1924, they found a fairly strict division of activities by sex, with men still primarily responsible for providing and women for homemaking and child care. However, the depression had reduced some men's opportunities to provide and increased the need for women to work. Some husbands were even caring for home and children while their wives worked. The depression seemed to have had more devastating effects on men than on women. In many families, the husband's main responsibility had been to provide the income. To the degree that the depression curtailed that role, his self-esteem and the family's respect for him declined.

By contrast, the depression widened the opportunities available to women somewhat, but the new roles of women were seen as temporary. In the Middletown of 1935, said the Lynds, "The worlds of the two sexes constitute something akin to separate subcultures. Each involves an elaborate assignment of roles to its members and the developing of preferred personality types emphasizing various ones of the more significant role attributes" (Lynd and Lynd 1937, 176).

In 1935 men were still expected to earn the money, to pay the bills, and to formally represent the family in civic and professional matters. They were responsible for such practical things as auto repairs and encounters with representatives of the government. In contrast, women were expected to look after household affairs, to care for and discipline young children (with male authority in the background), to organize family social life, and to take part in aesthetic pursuits and "unpaid civic activities of a refined or charitable sort."

The Stability of Traditional Role Definitions

Sex differences in family roles in the United States do not seem to have changed much since the Lynds wrote about Middletown. Twenty-five years after the Lynds' last visit to Middletown, Robert Blood and Donald Wolfe studied the division of activities between husbands and wives in Detroit. Their main finding was that the division of labor in the family of the late 1950s fit the "traditional" pattern. Husbands and wives were specialists who complemented rather than duplicated each other's work, with the men doing "men's work" (providing for the family and doing heavy work and technical tasks) while the wives did "women's work" (running the household and doing nearly everything associated with child rearing) (Blood and Wolfe 1960, 73).

There were, however, indications of modest change. Blood and Wolfe could not fail to notice that more married women were working outside the home and that the husbands of employed wives bore a somewhat larger share of family responsibilities than those who were married to full-time housewives.

Fifteen years later, Stephen Bahr reviewed the effects of women's employment on family power and the division of family labor and concluded that, while women's employment often blurred the distinction between women's and men's work in families, women were still primarily responsible for housework and child care (Bahr 1974). A recent study of the division of labor by cohabiting and married couples found cohabiting couples to be as traditional as married couples in their attitudes on the traditional place of the woman as primary manager and producer of household labor. In short, the way husbands and wives (or even male and female "roommates") divide up household tasks has not changed very much since Middletown was first studied. "At least in terms of the division of household labor, the couples of the 'now' generation, whether cohabiting or married, are still dividing the work along traditional lines with the woman bearing the brunt of the labor" (Stafford, Backman, and Dibona 1977, 54).

Neither the Lynds nor any other investigators seem to have described the division of labor by sex in full detail for American families of the 1920s and 1930s. Without that information, we cannot speak very confidently about long-term changes in family roles. We can, however, set down in detail the family roles observed in Middletown in 1977 and compare them with those observed in similar studies conducted elsewhere.[1]

At least eight family roles have been identified. These eight are the provider, housekeeper, child care, child socialization, therapeutic, sexual, recreational, and kinship roles. To be considered roles, specific family activities had to have a normative aspect (a specification of what a person in a given position should or should not do) and they had to be supported by a sanction (reward or penalty) for nonperformance. The provider role includes those duties and responsibilities associated with obtaining the goods and services necessary to maintain the family. The duties and responsibilities of the housekeeper role include cooking, cleaning, marketing, caring for clothing, and other kinds of housework. The other roles are equally self-explanatory.

In designing the family role survey for Middletown, we emphasized four aspects of role behavior: (1) people's expectations about which spouse ought to be responsible for necessary activities, (2) how husbands and wives actually divide up role activities, (3) how they perceive their own and their spouses' competence in role enactment, and (4) the family conflict generated by role performance.[2] Respondents in the family role survey were married couples drawn from the 1977 Middletown City Directory. We requested that both husbands and wives fill out a questionnaire. We obtained completed questionnaires from both spouses for 199 couples. The 473 respondents in the family role survey included these 199 couples plus 75 individual husbands or wives whose spouses were not represented. For most of the analyses in this chapter, we will use the total sample of 473, which included 220 males and 253 females. However, for comparisons between social classes, the matched set of husband-wife pairs is a more appropriate sample,[3] and we will refer to this part of the total sample, representing 84 percent of it, as the matched set of husbands and wives.

Norms on Family Roles: Who Should Do What?

None of the family roles is normally the *sole* responsibility of either husbands or wives. People may believe that husbands should be the providers, that wives should take care of the babies, or that husbands should handle the home repairs, but behind each of these prescriptions is the unspoken reservation "under normal circumstances." They also believe that families should be more or less flexibly organized. Yes, fathers should bring home the paychecks, but even the most conservative traditionalists nowadays allow that, while Dad is at school improving his earning skills, Mom may have to support him temporarily. Yes, the husband should do the home repair work, but, if he is too busy or if he is sick or if he has a congenital incapacity to handle a hammer or a screwdriver, then it is certainly permissible for the wife to paint, paper, or plumb.

In Middletown, as in other settings in which family roles have been examined, most respondents were unwilling to say that any family role is entirely the responsibility of either spouse.[4] Only 23 percent of Middletown husbands said that husbands should be solely responsible for providing; only 20 percent said that wives should do all of the housekeeping; only 18 percent said that wives alone should care for preschool children; and only 29 percent said that husbands should do all home repairs. Among Middletown wives, the comparable percentages were 15, 20, 18, and 15. Only a handful (1 to 4 percent) assigned the kinship, recreational, or child discipline (socialization) roles to either husbands or wives exclusively. The overwhelming majority regarded each family role as a joint, if unequally shared, responsibility.

This is not to say that the roles are not sex-stereotyped; almost all of them are. But the stereotypes are flexible; one spouse is normally responsible for a given task, but there are circumstances in which it may be shared with or performed by the other.

There was remarkable agreement between the Middletown husbands and wives about which spouse should do what for the seven roles described. (See Appendix A, Table 3-1.) Only the kinship role showed less than overwhelming (70 percent or more) agreement about whether it ought to be done by the husband, the wife, or both.

Of the seven roles, four were clearly sex-stereotyped. Most husbands and wives agreed that earning the family income and making home repairs were husbands' responsibilities and that housekeeping and caring for preschool children were wives' responsibilities. There were two roles, disciplining older children and organizing family excursions, that almost everyone said could be shared equally or assigned according to preference. The least consensus appeared for the kinship role as it affected the husband's relatives. Between one-half and two-thirds of the respondents said that communication with husband's relatives was a responsibility to be equally shared; but, among those who did not agree, more assigned the responsibility to the husband.

In summary, our questions about which spouse ought to perform which activities revealed two male roles (provider and home repairs), two female roles (child care and housekeeping), and three shared roles (child socialization, kinship, and recreation).

There were no important differences between working-class and business-class husbands about assignment of marital roles, but two significant class differences showed up in the wives' responses. Business-class women were more than twice as likely as working-class women to say that housekeeping should be equally shared between spouses (31 percent versus 14 percent), while working-class wives were more likely to say that housekeeping was mainly a wife's responsibility (85 percent, versus 69 percent for business-class wives).

Thus, there is substantial sex-stereotyping in the perceptions of family roles held by Middletown adults, and the stereotyping does not vary much between the sexes. Wives are as likely as husbands to agree that husbands should be the main providers and home-repair experts and that wives ought to be the chief housekeepers and child-care specialists. Not only are there few sex differences in these perceptions, there are equally few class differences. Business-class men are almost indistinguishable from working-class men in their perceptions about family roles; business-class women are only a little more egalitarian than working-class women.

One young business-class mother described how she and her husband looked forward to moving out "in the country," where it would be easier for them to "get back to the basics." "We believe in distinct roles," she said. "I can teach the girls to sew and bake, and my husband can teach the boys to hunt, shoot, and fish." Another said complacently that "we've never really had problems; there have been few disagreements. I hate to sound conceited; I don't know, everything is fifty-fifty. I know what I'm supposed to do, he knows what he's supposed to do."

Role Enactment: Who Does What?

When we asked husbands and wives about who actually performed the various family roles, their answers revealed that the enactment of the sex-stereotyped roles was consistently less flexible than it was supposed to be. (See Appendix A, Table 3-2.) Although only 69 percent of the husbands said that wives should do most or all of the child care, 77 percent of them reported that their own wives did most or all of the child care; 74 percent of the husbands said that housekeeping was primarily a wife's responsibility, but 90 percent of them said their own wives took that responsibility. The actual behavior of Middletown families shows more division of roles by sex than their opinions call for.

The shared roles were less equally shared than people said they ought to be, and, in the usual case, it was the wife who ended up performing most of the roles that were supposed to be shared. For example, in about a third of the families, the wife was primarily responsible for keeping in touch with the *husband's* relatives, even though most of those husbands accepted that responsibility as their own.

This failure to achieve an egalitarian ideal in practice was even more apparent in the wives' responses. For *every* role, the portion of women reporting an egalitarian pattern of sharing was significantly smaller than the portion expressing support for such sharing. Although 86 percent of the wives said that older children should be equally disciplined by mothers and fathers, only 64 percent reported that there was such an arrangement in their families. Though 23 percent said that the provider role should be equally shared, only 13 percent said that it *was* equally shared in their own families.

Husbands and wives were fairly consistent in their reports about who performed the various roles. In each of the three instances in which there was a small but significant difference, the wives claimed a larger share of the role than was reported by the husbands. With respect to child care, 77 percent of the husbands said that in their families the wife did most of the child care, but 89 percent of the wives said they did most of it. Similarly, 8 percent of the husbands said that the wives did most or all of the disciplining of older children, but 21 percent of the wives reported that arrangement. And, while 88 percent of the husbands said that they did most or all of the home-repair tasks, only 76 percent of the wives saw things that way.

Although business-class wives were more likely to prefer an equal sharing of housekeeping chores, they were not much different from the working-class wives in actual performance (13 percent of them reported equal sharing of housekeeping tasks, compared to 6 percent of the working-class wives).

So who does what in Middletown families? In about 84 percent of them, the husband earns all or most of the family income, and in 90 percent the wife does all or most of the housekeeping. In almost 85 percent of the families with young children, the wife does all or most of the caring for them. These two roles, house-keeping and child care, are still "women's work" in Middletown. At least two other roles, disciplining older children and planning family excursions, are equally shared by more than half of the families; and two others, the therapeutic role and the kinship role, are more or less shared.

Thus Middletown families support role flexibility in principle at the same time they faithfully practice traditional roles. "There are no shoulds. If a husband and wife are both working, they should both help, but in my situation with all my time at home I do most everything. I don't *require* my husband to do anything." This woman also does most of the home repairs, a responsibility that most Middletowners ascribe to husbands. She explained her doing the home-repair work this way: "My husband can't do anything; he's all thumbs. Rather than trying to get him to fix things around here, I'd just rather do them myself, and if I can't I'll call someone who can."

When we apply the five-category scale for the division of labor by sex (ranging from the performance of a given role entirely by the husband to its performance entirely by the wife) to the roles of provider and housekeeper, there are 25 possible combinations (a 5-by-5 matrix). That is, in those couples in which husbands earn all of the family income, the division of housekeeping chores would include situations in which the husband does all of them, most of them, half of them, a few of them, or none of them. In couples in which the husband earns most of the income, the same five housekeeping arrangements are possible, and so on. However, we observed only 13 of the possible patterns in Middletown and, as it can be seen in Appendix A, Table 3-2, 5 of them account for 85 percent of the families studied and only 3 of them account for 70 percent.

In other words, although there are many different ways that Middletown couples *could* divide family roles, one of a few standard arrangements is usually adopted. More than three-fourths of Middletown couples arrange their rules so that the husband earns all or most of the income and the wife does all or most of the housekeeping.

Violated Expectations in Role Enactment

The actual division of family roles is not always in line with what the parties expect. Middletown men and women agree that husbands are wholly or primarily responsible for earning a living, that wives are mainly responsible for preschool children and housekeeping, and that disciplining older children, organizing family recreation, and communicating with kin should be shared.

To what extent does the division of labor in Middletown families match the expectations? One way to answer this question is to compare people's opinions about how activities ought to be divided with their reports about how they actually are divided. For seven roles, we computed a discrepancy score for each respondent, which shows how far the reported division of roles in the family departed from his or her expectations. For example, if a husband said that husbands ought to do all the providing but reported that all the income in his own family was earned by his wife, a maximum discrepancy score would result. Discrepancy scores do not show what the preferred or the actual division of labor is for a given couple; they show only the extent to which the couple's actual division of roles matches their expectations. The scores range from zero (total congruence) to four (total discrepancy). The five possible points in both expectations and enactments are "husband entirely," "husband more than wife," "husband and wife equally" (or "doesn't matter"), "wife more than husband," and "wife entirely."

Congruence, in which perceptions of "who should" are in line with "who does," can be viewed as a low-stress situation for that particular role. The highest congruence (a situation of no discrepancy, where "who should" corresponds to "who does") inferred from both husbands' and wives' responses was for the recreational role (74 percent for wives, 77 percent for husbands), and the lowest was for the provider role. (See Appendix A, Table 3-3.) For three roles, care of preschool children, discipline of older children, and recreation, over three-fourths of the husbands indicated that tasks were divided in their families as they thought they should be. The discrepancies reported by husbands and wives were significantly different only in the child-care role. That role, more than any other, seems to be one in which husbands' expectations are more frequently realized than wives'. It was the only role for which there was a significant difference in the percentages of husbands and wives who perceived that the wife was performing more than her share of the role.

The fairly close correspondence of husbands' and wives' assessments of what ought to be done and of how things are actually done in their own families suggests that Middletown couples have achieved a fair level of agreement about the division of labor by sex in the family. This does not mean that the same couples did not experience substantial stress along the way to their present adjustment. It stands to reason that their statements about how family roles ought to be divided and about how they are divided apply to the time our survey was being conducted; few of the couples in the sample were newlyweds. Since the sample was composed of presently married couples, some other couples who held highly discrepant views of their sex roles were presumably excluded because they had already been divorced. Both of these possibilities are illustrated by some of the interview responses we obtained in another survey.

According to a business-class husband, "I saw life as women being dependent on the man. When a man came home in the evening, a woman would turn cartwheels, greet him with a kiss and a martini." It did not take many weeks of marriage to destroy that illusion for him. A working-class wife sketched the other side of the picture when she said, "It seems to me that a lot of women have been catered to by their fathers and now they expect the same treatment from their husbands. And that makes it hard to adjust after marriage." An earlier marriage that ended in divorce was described by a wife in this way: "After we were married, he informed me that he wanted me up at four o'clock in the morning with my makeup on and serving breakfast and looking good. I said, '----off, fella.' That was it."

Women and Housework

Despite the attention given to "women's liberation," "alternative life-styles," and "househusbands" in the mass media, in Middletown husbands still earn most of the income and wives still do most of the housework. Many Middletown wives told us that people took housework more seriously in the past than they do today. Two characteristic statements were these. "My mother came home from work and cleaned house the rest of the night if she had to. No matter how clean I had it when I cleaned house for her, it wasn't clean enough. My mother was really picky." And "My husband's mother is very neat. She says her house is a mess when it's not, when there isn't a speck of dirt anywhere." We do not know how widespread this view of contemporary women as less skilled in housework may be since there are women who express other attitudes. For example:

Of course my housekeeping has improved. I took after my mother. We always figured our houses should be lived in and not show places, and I have times when I keep everything reasonably clean out here that can be seen, and I'll let our bedrooms—since it's back in the corner—pile until you can barely walk through it, you know, and it comes to the point where my husband says, "do this or else," and I'll finally get it done.

It is not fashionable in Middletown to appear to take housework too seriously. Wives and mothers receive public acclaim in the local press for accomplishments in the arts, in their jobs, and in church and community work but not for housework. Even those mothers who say that they do all of the housekeeping in their families do not manifest much of the "cleanliness is next to godliness" attitude. Asked how she felt about housework, one 35-year-old mother said, "If it gets done, it gets done; if it doesn't, it doesn't." She went on to say that the wife should be entirely responsible for the housework and that her own mother had the same relaxed attitude about it.

A few women see housework as something that is downright enjoyable.

I like it. I'd rather stay at home and clean than work eight hours a day and then come home and do it. I feel very fortunate. I enjoy doing it when I feel like doing it. I have a schedule of things I do every day. And I enjoy being at home. A lot of women don't. It *was* hard for me to adjust after I quit work, but after about two months I got used to it.

The same woman described the circumstances in which her husband might do housework. "My husband will do some housework if I get sick. He has done dishes and fixed dinner, but only if I'm not able to. I feel that the housework is my job just as my husband has his job."

Predictably, husbands seem much more willing to report that wives really like housework. According to one business-class husband:

She likes to do it. She won't let me help her. I could never quite figure it out. She feels that it's her duty. If I'm doing some of the housework, I'm bumping her out of her roles. . . . I'll do whatever is necessary to help and I enjoy when company's coming, I actually do, and she doesn't mind if there's an emergency. She does about everything around the house.

Most women seem to accept their responsibility for housework, but they do not like it. It is a duty, often a duty of love, but not a pleasure. Still, few are as negative as these.

I hate it. It's the most disgusting thing I've ever had to do in my life. Cleaning the toilet is not my idea of a good trip, you know. Unfortunately, I do most of it and bitching the whole time, really mad about it. Who should and who does are two different things. If everybody in the family were really responsible for their own little pile of dirt, it wouldn't be a problem. But that really doesn't happen.

And:

I hate it. I really hate it. I really do. I do it because, you know, I equally hate bugs, but I never figured out why anybody considers dust ugly. It really does save money on paper when you can write phone numbers using the dust on the table. I clean the house because it has to be somewhat presentable, and I like to keep the dishes picked up because the cat walks over and licks the bowl. That gets gunky. I don't just really run around with my little white gloves cleaning up the dirt. . . . I do most of the housework because of my husband's hours. When he was home more we shared almost completely. When I was working and he was going to school, he did all the housework.

This attitude is more typical.

I think it's a wasted life, to stay at home all the time, if you don't have to. . . . It's hard trying to keep your house in order when you're working all day. But you can do it. . . . Trying to take care of a house, coming in, trying to fix dinner after you've worked all day and you're tired. And the husbands may expect too much. . . . If they work all day, they come in, they don't have anything to do. Watch TV, read the paper. A woman has everything to do. And I think that's kind of hard. . . . I'm not crazy about housework. I think you have to do it. You can't live in a home and not do it. But it's not that important. It's important for me to have a clean house for my family, but it's not so important that it's my whole life. It's just a job that has to be done. I do most of the housework. If my husband's laid off, he will vacuum. He washes the clothes for me if I have to leave, . . . he's pretty good. . . . I just think that men expect too much out of women, sometimes, as far as the house. They'll go to work, and they'll come home, you know, and they think you've laid around all day. And there's quite a bit to do in a house. It's never really done; you just get it done and then do it over again. That's why I don't like it. And you don't get paid for it, in money, like they do.

As is this.

I'm not a person who likes the role of housewife as far as dusting everything and waiting for the dust to pile up again and again. I have never liked staying home and doing housework. That's just not me. I'd rather be out doing something and so I enjoy working and just having a chance to be with other people.

And this:

I love to be with people and to scream and holler and carry on, just to be away from home. I've enjoyed that. . . . How do I feel about housework? It's a necessary evil. I don't mind doing it and I enjoy cooking. I don't mind doing dishes at all, in fact, I'd rather wash them than see my children wash them and put them away dirty. But I still suffer through letting them do it. I really don't mind housework, I just don't get thrilled over it. . . . I can't stand to see ashtrays sitting around, that drives me crazy, I have to keep them emptied and that sort of thing, and I don't like to see dust piled up, but I'm definitely not one to be cleaning all the time. I take spells when I clean out closets and dresser drawers and cabinets, and that's about once a year and that's often enough, and I like to keep the dishes done up. It doesn't bother me to see them sitting around.

And this:

If your husband considers housekeeping important, *it's important*. It's a job just like everything else. Of course the wages are lousy. If it's important to the husband, then it's important. . . . I have always been home when he came home, his meal was on the table. . . . I try to keep the house the way he wants it to be.

One husband, who said that the wives had the primary responsibility for housekeeping but that husbands ought to help out, said that his own wife did *all* the housework, even though she got little praise for it. "Well, she gets kidded by some of our friends about being so spotless . . . because they just don't keep house like she does." He admitted that her style of housekeeping used to bother him, too.

Now that I'm accustomed to it, I'm happy with the way she keeps house. I thought she was a little bit finicky. If I leave a coat on the arm of the chair, I'm going to wear it the following morning. But she says it has to go in the closet. Do I do that all the time? No, rarely. But still, that's just something she's accepted. As far as housework goes, everything has a place and that's where it should be.

But another business-class husband was much less sympathetic.

I'll do it if I have to. I don't think anybody likes it. My wife has help with it. She thinks I should help her more. But I don't. I learned that a long time ago. Do the dishes the first year you're married, and you'll be doing them the last year. . . . I just bought a dishwasher. . . . In our particular situation, we have all the convenience advantages. How hard is it to run a vacuum cleaner?

Role Competence

We have no objective way of measuring how well the people in our survey performed their various roles. A subjective assessment was obtained in a series of questions that asked respondents to rate themselves and their spouses on their role performance for seven roles (the provider role was purposely excluded). Most Middletown adults rated their abilities to perform family roles fairly high. Except for the roles reserved for the other sex (most men did not claim much competence in child care and most women did not claim to be good at home repairs), almost everyone rated himself or herself as average or better. See Tables 3-4 and 3-5.

For none of the family roles did a majority of the men judge themselves to be above average. For one role activity, household repairs, almost half affirmed their high competence, and about 40 percent judged themselves to be above average in therapeutic and child socialization activities. In contrast, a majority of women rated themselves as above average in taking care of young children and in providing emotional support for their husbands, and almost half rated themselves above average in housekeeping and in maintaining contact with relatives.

Table 3-4
Husbands' Ratings of Themselves

Role	Percentage above Average	Percentage Average
Making household repairs	45	46
Being supportive when the other is upset, depressed, or unhappy (therapeutic)	39	51
Disciplining older children (child socialization)	38	55
Taking care of preschool children (child care)	35	48
Organizing family excursions (recreation)	28	55
Housekeeping	26	54
Keeping in touch with one's own relatives (kinship)	22	50

Source: Middletown III family role survey, 1977.

Table 3-5
Wives' Evaluations of Themselves

Role/Activity	Percentage above Average	Percentage Average
Taking care of preschool children (child care)	70	28
Being supportive when the other is upset, depressed, or unhappy (therapeutic)	54	41
Housekeeping	49	46
Keeping in touch with one's own relatives (kinship)	49	44
Disciplining older children (child socialization)	41	52
Organizing family excursions (recreation)	29	59
Making household repairs	17	49

Source: Middletown III family role survey, 1977.

Working-class couples rated themselves somewhat less favorably in their family roles than did business-class couples. (See Appendix A, Table 3-6). On three family roles (housekeeping, organizing family excursions, and disciplining older children), business-class wives rated themselves more favorably than working-class wives did, and the differences were significant. Husbands' responses revealed the same pattern. For two roles (organizing family excursions and being supportive to their wives), business-class husbands' self-ratings were significantly more favorable. As far as self-ratings of role performance can be taken at face value, these findings suggest that business-class couples may be somewhat more success-ful in performing roles involving housekeeping, family recreation, therapeutic support of spouses, and disciplining older children.

When we compared the respondents' ratings of their spouses' competence, we got essentially the same results. Husbands' ratings of their wives' competence in family roles were generally higher for business-class husbands than for working-class husbands. For example, 92 percent of the business-class husbands rated their wives as above average in caring for preschool children, compared to 67 percent of the working-class husbands.

Using the matched-couple subsample, we cross-tabulated each husband's self-rating of his competence in various family roles with his wife's estimate of her competence in the same roles. Three categories, above average, average, and below average, were used. The cross-tabulation produces a three-by-three matrix, with nine combinations of ratings for each role. (As an illustration, the table for the housekeeping role is reproduced in Appendix A, Table 3-7. Three of the nine possible patterns account for most of the cou-ples surveyed; the most common pattern is that both husband and wife rate themselves as average in housekeeping skills (55 cases), followed by the pattern in which the wife rates herself as above average but the husband rates himself as average (44 cases), and then by the pattern in which both the husband and the wife rate themselves as above average (32 cases). These three patterns ac-count for the 69 percent of the couples.

Similar matrices were prepared for the other roles. We then com-bined the couples into three categories of competence: high, with one spouse above average and neither below average; moderate, with both spouses average in the role or one above average and the other below; and low, with one spouse below average and neither above. The resulting summary of the competence of Middletown couples in each family role appears in Appendix A, Table 3-8.

According to their self-ratings, most Middletown couples are quite skillful in housekeeping, child care, child discipline, and mu-tual emotional support. They are somewhat less assured about their abilities to organize family recreation, to maintain adequate communication with kin, and to manage household repairs; but, even in these roles, more than a third rated themselves as highly competent. That few couples have low self-ratings in *any* role shows how favorable the prevailing view of family life is in Middle-town.

We were struck by the large proportion of couples with children who rated themselves as above average in child care and child social-ization. There is little evidence here for the "failure of parental nerve" (Lynd and Lynd 1937, 164) that troubled the Lynds in the 1920s. Instead, the "above-average" family is the statistical norm. The message these responses seem to convey is that Middletowners have a sense that in family role enactment "they know how to do it" and "they can handle it."

Similarity and Complementarity in Role Competence

The great French sociologist Emile Durkheim speculated that the division of labor between husband and wife made for a cohesive re-lationship. "Precisely because man and woman are different, they seek each other passionately." But differences alone, he argued, do not produce mutual attraction; the differences must be comple-mentary.

In short, man and woman isolated from each other are only different parts of the same concrete universal which they reform when they unite. In other words, the sexual division of labor is the source of conjugal solidarity. . . . It has made possible perhaps the strongest of all unselfish inclinations (Durkheim 1964, 56).

And, as with society in general, Durkheim maintained, the more developed the division of labor, the more cohesive the resulting so-cial unit.

This idea found a much later expression with Robert Winch's idea that "complementarity of needs" is one of the bases of the attraction that brings potential mates together (Winch 1958). Most of the recent research on complementarity and mate selection however, suggests that similarities are more important than com-plementarities in stimulating mutual attraction.[5]

The data from Middletown do not resolve the question. There is evidence of some complementarity. In any given role, between 6 and 19 percent of the couples reported that one of them was above average and the other below average in competence. But, in most cases, spouses differed only slightly or not at all in their self-rated competence in particular roles.

We have a strong impression that Middletown people believe there is much more sex complementarity in their families than their self-ratings of competence in role performance reveal. We did not include questions on the psychological or temperamental differences between men and women in any of our questionnaires, but the extended interviews of the family dynamics survey included some questions that bore tangentially on male-female differences. In the main, women continue to be characterized as sympathetic, sensitive, and emotional; and men, as hardheaded, pragmatic, and analytical. There are some dissenting opinions, but, just as the traditional norms about who should do housework and care for small children seem to have changed very slowly, the accepted ideas about the nature of men and women have not changed very much since the Lynds' time. The traditional views show up both in comments about people's personalities and in accounts of how couples cooperate.

"Women are more complicated," said one wife; and another explained, "I'm sympathetic; he's not. He feels for you but don't know what to say." A third said:

I listen a lot. I give a different perspective on his work. We are actually very different and he's much more analytical and I'm much much more emotional and so I look at things from a totally different perspective and I think that helps a lot. . . . I suppose I'm sort of a buffer. He says I do a lot of protecting.

Husbands described the differences between themselves and their wives in comparable terms. One said:

I'm an engineer and I try a rational approach, and my wife with her training has an emotional response. I'm trained to avoid the emotional problem. My wife says that sometimes she wishes I wasn't so damned rational. . . . She probably wishes I were more emotional and I wish that she was more rational. But the older I get, the more I realize that the differences may be the key— don't eliminate them.

Another said:

What appears to me to be a very practical thing, the way things ought to be, sometimes to her it's a gray area. To me it's just, you know, two and two makes four, and you don't spend five if you've only got four or whatever. But they are not plain to her. The insurance policy, the will, she gets lost in comprehension. She can't balance our checkbook, but is treasurer for two or three organizations. . . . And some things to her are second nature. . . . I can never second-think her. It's part of the mystique of being a woman.

The women's views often derived from the same stereotypes. For example:

He is the leader and he earns a living for us. . . . He is so glad I'm dumb and want to stay home and work with the children. . . . Through the giving, loving attitude of a wife, all men may be reached. All men can be reached through this way, that is, through admiration. Men have a fantastic ego. . . . I don't think most men really listen.

And:

Men are often emotional cripples, and so I am trying to raise my boys so they won't be. . . . Sometimes it's OK to play "weak," so the guy gets a chance to be strong.

Even in couples in which wives said that they were trying to share the household repair tasks, the traditional division of labor sometimes showed up in the accounts of who did what. Here are two examples, both from the working class. "Home repairs? We do them equally. He does the physical labor and I watch and hand him things. . . . He can do anything around the house, and does. I am learning." And "We help each other on home repairs. He actually does the work, I hold the hammer if he needs help." In a similar vein, some wives complained about too much complementarity. "Before we were married, he would pick out my outfits, but now he's not interested, although I would often like his opinions on different patterns and fabric. I worry about the wallpaper and bedspreads and he concerns himself with the heating and plumbing."

Involvement in Community Organizations

In the Middletown of the 1920s, it was part of a business-class wife's responsibility to participate in the charitable and cultural activities of voluntary associations. Reading Middletown newspapers in the 1970s, particularly feature stories in the life-style sections of the papers, one might infer that women still dominate the organizational life of Middletown. And in our interviews, several husbands did comment or complain about the amount of time their wives devoted to clubs and volunteer work. Nevertheless, an enumeration from the 1977 family role survey does not show wives to be more involved in voluntary associations than husbands. On the contrary, husbands were more likely than wives to belong to associations; 90 percent of the men had at least one organizational affiliation, compared to 82 percent of the women.

When we examined involvement in specific types of associations, we find that husbands were more likely to belong to veterans' organizations, labor unions, and civic organizations. Wives were more likely to belong to self-improvement groups ("such as Weight Watchers, great books clubs") and parent-teacher associations. For the other types of associations considered (country clubs and political committees, for example), men and women were about equally likely to belong and to participate.

Class, not sex, makes a substantial difference in organizational participation. Membership in a labor union is much more likely in the working class. Veterans' groups, farmers' organizations, and political committees show no class differences. In every other type of association, business-class people are more active than working-class people. It is startling how much of Middletown's organizational life involves only the business class. Most of the voluntary associations that receive attention in Middletown's daily newspapers have very few working-class members. Working-class women are less likely to belong to self-improvement organizations, hobby clubs, and parent-teacher associations and much less likely to join country clubs, athletic clubs or teams, voluntary service groups, cultural associations, and the YWCA.

Perceptions of Change

Our finding that traditional sex roles are still in force in Middletown does not mean that there has been no change in the way sex roles are perceived. Women continue to do most of the housework and men most of the providing, but people *think* that today's women are more liberated. That perception is itself a notable change. What people define as real is real in its consequences, and Middletown's men and women are convinced that there have been important recent changes in women's roles.

"What is it like to be a woman these days?" We asked this question during the course of the family dynamics interviews. This is how women answered.

We can do so many things that, say, my mother couldn't do. I think a woman is more complex than twenty years ago. She's got so many more things she can be involved in.

It's really harder on a man today. If a woman wants to work, the law is with her now. But I feel that some women's libbers are pushing it too far and may penalize the woman who stays at home.

I think it's the greatest time in the world to be a woman. And I have high hopes that it will get better. Clear back in 1962 I was in this advance guard of women's rights. But it was still a male-dominated society while I was working in it. And today, incredibly better.

I think it's a lot better than it used to be. As far as I'm concerned in the world that I grew up in, I haven't met up with a lot of discrimination. I have been allowed to do as I want, and I haven't been working where I've had to be in a position of not equal pay. I'm not sorry that I'm a woman, if that answers it. I'm perfectly satisfied being a woman.

Being a woman? Really, I think it's pretty great. If you've got the know-how and go out, you can get any job you want; you can do pretty much as you please. I am not what you call a woman's libber, but I think they have it pretty much made.

Being a woman today. Well it's better, much better, than it was for my mother. Definitely. Not as good as it will be for my daughter, hopefully. It's better for me now than it was for my first marriage, because I wasn't allowed to go anywhere and do anything and for some reason I took it. I've never yet figured that out. I was always very strong and independent, and I somehow allowed myself to be captured under somebody's thumb. That's probably one of my biggest regrets.

Their husbands' answers to a parallel question contained similar themes, but there was occasionally a tinge of bitterness about women being given advantages in competition for jobs or the good life.

What's it like being a man these days? Well, a white man to me is being discriminated against. To get ahead right now you have to be black, or a foreigner, or a woman.

Being a man these days? It's a two-sided coin, you know. Previously, a man enjoyed more power and respect, but was expected to be more masculine. Today it's sort of reversing. I feel more comfortable in this situation. I like to think of a man as masculine and feminine and not afraid to be weak. What's it like to be a woman these days? Wonderful! She needs and gets more respect now. She's not treated so bad and there's more opportunities. . . . Marriage adds security for a woman but ties her down. She pays the price of security by being tied down. Now Women's Lib is changing things. She feels jailed by a man unless he's careful to lessen that feeling of imprisonment.

When I was younger, I found nothing difficult for me to accept the fact that I'd be the breadwinner. And the wife feels nothing wrong with being the one that raises the children and takes care of the home. But if I talk to our daughter and the daughters-in-law, then I think I can see that the approach today is different. There is more of a feeling by the young women that they have a right to a career and an active married life other than just raising children or taking care of a home. I mean, I can't argue the point. And that's why I say, under those conditions, I would have to tell our children what I told them, that if you both work you both have to pitch in at home, that there's no other way. . . . I can understand that somewhere a male today might say as far as the male/female relationship is concerned, that maybe he's slightly threatened, I can understand that. There seems to be more of a balance. In other words, going back to history, a woman had an inferior sex whether it be intentional, accidental, or just what. That does not mean that the women did not get their way in their own manner. In other words, I think the difference is, you don't change a situation really. It either becomes overt or there's other ways. If it's a marriage in the old days I'm sure the women, either theoretically or actually, had a way of compensating to get what they wanted accomplished one way or the other. It's just that openly, and maybe legally, there is more equality today. Now there's some people feel what we need is male liberation, but getting off of that kick, I would think there's more acceptance today by the males of the rights of females.

Even though the general perception is that marked change has occurred, there is also a recognition that many of the traditional definitions, even some of those that women find irritating and offensive, are likely to remain. The same business-class woman who described the present situation as "incredibly better" than just 15 years ago remarked a little later in the interview that

we're beginning to understand each other as individuals rather than as stereotypes. Still I find even in my work, the residue of the pretty little lady who has the meals on time lingers with the male, and the residue of the gallant, decision-making, ever-sexual male. And I don't know that these things will ever be changed.

Chapter 4

Earning a Living

The daily existence of Middletown's families during the 1920s was dominated by the necessity of earning a living. The Lynds' awareness of the pervasive influence of work-related activities grew as they studied Middletown: ". . . it became more and more apparent that the money medium of exchange and the cluster of activities associated with its acquisition drastically condition the other activities of the people" (Lynd and Lynd 1929, 21). The type of work the husbands and fathers of Middletown's families performed affected the number of children they had, how their families spent their time, and many other subtle details of family life. A large part of the population was occupied in paid work. Of every 100 Middletown people in 1920, 43 were earning a living, 23 were keeping house, 19 were being trained, and 15 were very young or very old (Lynd and Lynd 1929, 21).

This distribution remained fairly stable during the next half of a century. Of every 100 Middletown people in 1970, 40 were earning a living, 10 were keeping house, 33 were being trained, and 17 were very young or very old (U.S. Bureau of the Census 1972a, Table 85). The importance of earning a living was still apparent. The proportion of the population engaged in paid work in 1970 was only slightly lower than it was in 1920, but the underlying trends were more complicated.

First, education has become available to a steadily larger segment of Middletown's population. In the 1920s, only the children of business-class families were likely to obtain higher education even though it was already regarded as the most effective way of improving one's chances in life. Today, nearly 90 percent of both business-class and working-class parents aspire to a college education for their children, and about 50 percent of the young people graduating from the local high schools actually go to college.

Second, a substantial fraction of Middletown's women have shifted from housekeeping to gainful employment over the years. In 1920, one out of every four women over age 14 was in the labor force; by 1978, it was one out of every two. The employment of women outside the home is thought by some observers to be the most important social change to have occurred in American society during the twentieth century (Bird 1979, xiii).

Work and Family Life

The men engaged in earning a living in 1924, according to the Lynds, fell into two separate groups, the working class and the business class. The working-class men were three times more numerous. These men used their hands and backs to make things and to provide services. They wore overalls to work and came home from work dirty and exhausted. The smaller group of business-class men made their livings by selling or promoting ideas and by arranging the goods and services produced by the working class. These men wore suits to their jobs in offices, banks, and shops. They returned home from work with no more dirt than a ring around the collar of their white shirts. Ten years later, in *Middletown in Transition*, the Lynds noted that subgroups had emerged within these two classes, but they contended that the differences of life-style *between* them had increased visibly.

The Workday

The day's activities started early for the working-class family during the 1920s; more than 90 percent of them arose by six o'clock. Almost all working-class men walked to work. The normal work week consisted of five, 10-hour weekdays plus a half-day on Saturday. When the factories were producing at capacity, many of their workers were required to work night shifts, which meant that they went to bed when their families were waking up and slept through most of the daylight hours. Shift work limited the association of husbands with their wives and children. Family activities were dislocated by this routine, with some adverse consequences. The Lynds (1929, 58) quoted a father appearing before a juvenile judge who blamed his night work and lack of daily contact for his son's wayward conduct.

Life for business-class families during the 1920s was considerably more comfortable than for working-class families, and, among other things, their days began significantly later. None of them got up before six and most lingered in bed until after seven. Their breadwinners arrived at work after eight o'clock, nearly two hours after the blue-collar workers. The latter were generally required to be at work by six-thirty, and they remained there until five, eating lunch at or near their machines. The business establishments of Middletown during the 1920s opened at eight or eight-thirty and closed at five.

During the intervening years, the daily schedules converged until they met, and by 1978 the difference between them had been reversed to some extent. The working class now sleeps in later, and the business class rises earlier. Today, stores and banks stay open later and work longer hours than factories. Professionals are commonly induced by the competition in their fields to spend extra hours at their offices, while unionization and collective bargaining have reduced the factory workday from 10 hours to 8 and the workweek from five and one-half days to five, and in some industries to four days. This change in work schedules encourages closer association among the members of working-class families. The general tendency for husbands to spend more time with their families in 1978, compared to 1920, will be described in detail in a later chapter.

Occupations

In 1920 the people of Middletown worked in more than 400 different occupations. About a third of the blue-collar workers were skilled craftspeople. They worked 10 hours a day blowing glass, designing molds, and shaping metal in factories and foundries. Some of them worked in the construction trades. All of the craft jobs involved a high level of skill and required some kind of apprenticeship that led to certification as a journeyman. The Lynds noted the decline of craftsmanship between 1890 and 1920 and lamented the fact that the "cunning hand of the master craftsman" was being supplanted by "batteries of tireless iron men." In 1890, 21 glassblowers assisted by two dozen boys produced 1,600 dozen quart jars per shift; in 1920, 8 men operating three machines turned out 6,600 dozen jars in the same amount time. The "batteries of iron men" made some of the old craft skills obsolete, but not all of them by any means.

Another third of the blue-collar workers of 1920 operated the machines that tirelessly produced goods. Adolescent boys could be trained in less than a week to run most of the machines in Middletown's factories. The more difficult operations could be mastered in a few weeks or months. But the work required the speed and endurance of youth. On most assembly lines, the machines set the pace and the workers had to keep up or lose their jobs.

The rest of Middletown's factory workers were laborers. They unloaded raw materials and supplies, wheeled or carried them to stations on the production line, and loaded the finished products. They also cleaned up after other workers. The lucky ones had reasonably stable employment. The less fortunate hired themselves out daily at whatever work was available.

The business-class men were proprietors, lawyers, bankers, public officials, engineers, teachers, shopkeepers, merchants, and clerks, among other things. One out of five were in the professions. Professionals earned relatively high incomes, and, within limits, most of them set their own working hours. A much smaller number managed factories, foundries, banks, and large stores, directing the manufacture and distribution of the industrialized products that sustained Middletown's economy during the 1920s. The business-class workers enjoyed the highest incomes and the widest influence in the community. The largest group of male white-collar workers were clerical and sales employees. They worked, for example, as tellers in banks, bookkeepers and clerks in factories, and salesmen in stores and shops.

The continued development of production machines and the introduction of computers has altered working-class occupations much more than business-class occupations over the intervening decades. The men and women who performed most of the dangerous and dirty jobs moved upward in the occupational hierarchy.

Between 1920 and 1970, the working class shrank from 70 percent of the male labor force to 54 percent. (See Table 4-1 in Appendix A.) Within the working class, the number of unskilled laborers was reduced by automation and other factors from 20 percent of the total in 1920 to less than 4 percent in 1970 and no more than 2 percent in 1980. The attrition of craftsmen noted by the Lynds has continued. They constituted 21 percent of the male labor force in 1920 but barely 9 percent in 1970. Meanwhile, the number of machine operators (semiskilled workers in conventional terminology) has risen sharply, and their proportion of the total labor force is about the same today as it was 50 or 60 years ago, despite the relative decline in the amount of blue-collar work.

Just as the contraction of the working class has not diminished the number of machine operators in factories, so the expansion of the business class has not increased the proportion of businessmen in the labor force. A large part of the expansion of the business class has been in the increased number of professionals. The proportion of the labor force in professional occupations more than tripled between 1920 and 1970. Clerical occupations also experienced considerable growth during the 50-year period, and the number of salesmen has declined sharply during the era of self-service stores and prepackaged merchandise.

Unemployment

The threat of unemployment hovered continuously over working-class families during the 1920s. Even during a year of economic prosperity like 1923, one out of every four men in the working class was laid off for a time. During bad years, unemployment mushroomed. The consequences of being out of work were more severe in the 1920s than now; there was no unemployment insurance, little public assistance, and no aid to dependent children, and the average family's cushion of savings was much smaller.

When questioned about unemployment and its consequences, 68 percent of 122 working-class wives interviewed by the Lynds reported that their husbands had been out of work for one or more periods during the previous five years. Four out of five of these families had changed their life-styles drastically. The father's being laid off forced the working-class family to curtail family expenditures in every way possible so that their meager reserves and what credit they could muster might carry them through the siege.

Surprisingly, the incidence of temporary unemployment has not changed appreciably since 1924. (See Table 4-2 in Appendix A.) The percentage of working-class men laid off at some time during 1977 (24 percent) was nearly the same as the percentage laid off during 1923 (25 percent). Although we expected to find much less change in spending patterns due to unemployment in 1978 because of present-day social-welfare programs, the reductions of spending in the late 1970s were almost the same as those of the early 1920s. During the 1920s, 76 percent of the unemployed reduced the amount spent on clothing; 73 percent cut amusements; 62 percent, food; 57 percent, gasoline; and 19 percent, life insurance; and 7 percent moved to less expensive housing. Despite social-welfare programs, the families whose principal breadwinners were unemployed in 1978 curtailed their spending patterns just as severely and in the same categories as their predecessors two generations before.

The other way of mitigating the devastating consequence of unemployment was for wives or children to seek work. As mentioned earlier, a third of the wives who reported in 1925 that their husbands had been out of work had gone to work themselves. Indeed, almost all the married women who then worked gave the present or past unemployment of their husbands as their principal reason for being in the labor market. Today, nearly half of the married women in Middletown have jobs outside the home, but the unemployment of husbands has ceased to be the precipitating factor. The modern wife works for other reasons as well. Today, business-class wives are as likely to hold jobs as working-class wives, even though the risk of unemployment is negligible for their husbands, as it was for business-class husbands back in 1924.

In 1924, older children frequently dropped out of school, or were taken out of school, and tried to find work to enable the family to survive until the father was providing again. Ten percent of the wives whose husbands had been unemployed reported that they had taken children out of school and sent them to work. The physical quickness of the young sometimes enabled them to find jobs when their fathers could not. Today, child-labor laws and compulsory-education laws prevent children from seeking serious employment until they are close to adulthood.

The business-class men of the 1920s entered the labor force two to five years later than their working-class counterparts because of their lengthier education. They continued to increase their status and earnings as they matured and had little concern about being laid off temporarily during hard times or let go permanently when they reached their late forties. Unemployment of any kind was not a serious threat to business-class families before the depression. Only 1 of 40 business-class wives interviewed in 1924 reported that her husband had been out of work any time during the previous five years.

The business-class wives of that era not only did not work, most of them refused to be concerned with financial matters. They were often unaware of their husbands' earnings and assets. In the Middletown of the 1920s, it was considered unfeminine for business-class wives to discuss money and demeaning for them to work outside the home. The lone business-class wife in the Lynds' sample whose husband had been unemployed was the only one who had worked during the preceding five years.

The most devastating type of unemployment in the 1920s affected blue-collar workers who reached the ripe old age of 40. Most factory jobs required the maintenance of a high rate of effort for a 10-hour shift, and years of working at this pace used men up by the time they reached early middle age. Retirement programs and pensions were then unknown for manual workers in industry. A few companies kept superannuated employees on as janitors or watchmen, but they were not obligated to do so. Most workers hoped to save for their old age, but few did. The despair they experienced in the face of premature retirement comes through poignantly in the comments made by employers and working-class wives interviewed by the Lynds in 1924 (1929, 33-34).

In production work forty to forty-five is the age limit because of the speed needed in the work. Men over forty are hired as sweepers and for similar jobs. We have no set age for discharging men [personnel manager of another outstanding machine shop].

The age deadline is creeping down on those men — I'd say that by forty-five they are through [superintendent of another major plant].

Whenever you get old they are done with you. The only thing a man can do is to keep as young as he can and save as much as he can [wife of a 40-year-old laborer].

I worry about what we'll do when he gets older and isn't wanted at the factories and I am unable to go to work. We can't expect our children to support us and we can't seem to save any money for that time [wife of a 46-year-old machinist].

Since that time, the obsolescence of many dangerous and exhausting jobs and the protection afforded to workers by the unions have virtually eliminated the threat of premature retirement for Middletown's factory workers. Recent legislation has extended the minimum age of compulsory retirement to 70. In addition, social security provides a basic retirement income that for most factory workers is supplemented by other retirement benefits from company and union plans, veterans. benefits, and insurance.

Responses to our question "What seems to be the future of your husband's job?" revealed the great strides Middletown's labor force has made in extending the age of retirement. Even in working-class families, a large majority (82 percent) of the wives reported that their husbands' jobs are secure and offer opportunities for advancement. Nearly all (94 percent) of the business-class wives in our survey report the same.

Job Satisfaction

The Lynds were much concerned that the changes associated with the increasing mechanization and rationalization of work in Middletown's factories were inadvertently destroying the satisfaction that had previously been associated with productive work. They never mentioned the Marxist notion of the alienation of workers from their work in *Middletown*, but they clearly had it in mind.

The shift from a system in which length of service, craftsmanship, and authority in the shop and social prestige among one's peers tended to go together to one which, in the main, demands little of a worker's personality save rapid, habitual reactions and an ability to submerge himself in the performance of a few routinized easily learned movements seems to have wiped out many of the satisfactions that formerly accompanied the job. Middletown's shops are full of men of whom it may be said that "there isn't 25 percent of them paying attention to the job." And as they leave the shop in the evening, "The work of a modern machine-tender leaves nothing tangible at the end of the day's work to which he can point with pride and say, 'I did that—it is the result of my own skill and my own effort' " (Lynd and Lynd 1929, 75-76).

We noticed a contemporary Middletown worker who was paying minimal attention to his job on a visit to an automotive plant in the spring of 1978. The worker whose task was bolting a part on a transmission had a paperback novel attached to a clipboard hung from a ceiling by a rope. His eyes never left the pages of the book as he accomplished his assigned work by touch. When a transmission approached on the assembly line, he felt it with his left hand and guided it into position against his work stand. The power wrench that had the part and five bolts attached to it was guided to the transmission by his right hand. His right foot then activated the power wrench that tightened the bolts. While waiting for the next transmission, he inserted the new part and bolts into the wrench with his right hand and turned the pages of the book with his left. Obviously, this man and many like him were performing their jobs with limited emotional involvement. But it does not follow that they were frustrated or dissatisfied. Blue-collar workers were significantly less satisfied with their jobs than white-collar workers were (60 percent versus 79 percent satisfied), but all were much more satisfied than dissatisfied. Only a small minority, 6 percent, of either business-class or working-class men in Middletown are dissatisfied with their occupations. (See Table 4-3 in Appendix A.) The Lynds were puzzled about why Middletown's people worked so hard when they *seemed* to derive so little satisfaction from their jobs. They concluded that working-class men, and at times their wives and children, worked hard because the money they earned allowed them to achieve a higher standard of living than their parents had ever known. Despite the hardships of the shop floor and the fear of unemployment, factory work offered them a better life than they could have found elsewhere.

The motivation of Middletown's present work force is more complex. When we asked a sample of employed men whether they worked primarily for money, three-fourths of the business-class respondents but fewer than half of the working-class respondents rejected the notion that their work was just a way to make money. The difference between the two classes is substantial and significant, but not overwhelming. Only a third of the working-class respondents hold with that "alienated" attitude, that work is just a way to get money. For the majority, such factors as pride in one's work and identification with an enterprise are part of the motivational pattern. (See Table 4-4 in Appendix A.)

There is no denying that earning a living is much easier for working-class men today than it was 50 years ago. Many of the dangerous, dirty, and routine tasks are now accomplished by machines. Labor unions and legislatures have forced employers to improve working conditions and to provide innumerable fringe benefits. Today, if we can trust the survey evidence, the majority of Middletown's blue-collar workers enjoy their work and feel secure in their ability to provide for themselves and their families.

Family life has been favorably affected by these changes. Fathers have more time to spend with their children. Paid vacations, health insurance, unemployment insurance, and retirement plans have improved the quality of life for Middletown families. Most working-class families now live in comfortable homes, drive reliable automobiles, travel to faraway places, and provide the education their children desire, in addition to covering the basic requirements for food, shelter, and clothing.

The Feminization of Middletown's Labor Force

The percentages of Middletown women gainfully employed in each decennial year from 1920 to 1970 evidences a gradual increase from 25 percent to 44 percent. (See Table 4-5 in Appendix A.) Even though compulsory-education laws are keeping young people in school longer today, the proportion of women working in Middletown rose from 25 percent in 1920 to 44 percent in 1978, and some observers estimate that 50 percent will be working in 1980. Obviously, working women are economically more independent than those supported by their fathers or husbands. That independence permits women to avoid marriage if they wish or to terminate an unsatisfactory marriage. But it would be a mistake to conclude that the feminization of the labor force is the consequence of single or divorced women working to support themselves. Married women have also moved out of the home and into the workplace. It has been estimated that in nearly half of all American marriages both spouses worked in 1979 (Scharff 1979). Our surveys show the same for Middletown. Some observers regard this trend as portentous. One,

Eli Ginzberg, the Columbia University specialist in human resources who has advised every president of the United States since Franklin Delano Roosevelt, believes that the employment of women outside the home is the most important social change of the twentieth century, more important than the rise of Communism or the European Common Market. "Its long-term inplications are absolutely unchartable," he adds. "It will affect women, men and children and the cumulative consequences of that will only be revealed in the 21st and 22nd Century." We may not have to wait that long (Bird 1979, xiii).

And, according to another observer, ". . . the increasing labor force participation of women is one of the most significant transformations of the American social structure to have occurred since the end of World War II" (Wright 1978, 301). A closer look at the situation of Middletown's working women may shed some light on the nature of this transformation.

Why Women Work

As we noted before, nearly half of the wives of working-class husbands held full-time outside jobs during the years 1920 to 1924. Most working-class families of that era had migrated to Middletown from rural places. Factory employment provided a higher standard of living than farming but was even more unpredictable. Factory workers could be laid off at any time for a variety of reasons, including oversupply of goods, weather (too hot to make glass jars), illness, injury, and machine breakdowns. There were very few buffers against unemployment; unions and unemployment insurance had not yet come to Middletown. The usual way for a working-class family to cope with the problems created by periodic unemployment was for the wife to go to work.

Although a significant proportion of working-class wives had been part of the labor force during the years 1920 to 1924, only one business-class wife in the Lynds' sample had worked outside the home during this five-year period, and, not surprisingly, her husband was the only business-class husband in that sample who had been unemployed. Since then, Middletown's business-class wives have adopted the employment pattern of working-class wives. Forty-two percent of them held full-time jobs outside the home during the five years 1973 to 1977, a dramatic shift that brought them very close to the situation of working-class wives, 48 percent of whom were employed during the same years.

Working-class wives in Middletown were almost as likely to be in the labor force during the early 1920s as they are today (44 percent then, 48 percent now). The recent entrance of business-class wives into the world of work has been the significant change. In the movement of married women out of the home and into the labor force, the working class was in the vanguard. Since the initial surge of working-class wives into the labor force at the turn of the century, their participation has remained fairly stable. If business-class women follow the same pattern, their participation in the labor force may not rise much above present levels.

On the other hand, the motivational pattern has changed considerably. In 1924 the need for an additional income to support the family when the husband was laid off, to supplement his income in order to keep the children in school, or to pay family debts was given as the reason why women worked. (See Table 4-6 in Appendix A.) The Lynds did not report what the "other" reasons of the remaining 24 percent of working women were, but it appears that very few, if any, talked about boredom at home or a desire for self-fulfillment as reasons for working. The need to work was perceived as a hardship by the married women who worked. It is not so perceived today, although economic pressures are still mentioned with significant frequency. But the reasons for working given by both working-class and business-class wives in 1978 reflect a popular consensus that paid work is more satisfying than housework, for some or all women.

Television, magazines, and other mass-media presentations proclaim that women have come a long way in the world of work and imply that the supporting values have appeared only recently. Although this may be true with respect to discrimination in hiring, pay, and promotion, it appears from the Lynds observations that the significant shift occurred between 1890 and 1924. In 1891 the editor of Middletown's daily newspaper lamented that "it is true that qualities inherent in the nature of women impede their progress as a wage-earner. . . . Women are uniformly timid and are under a disadvantage in the struggle for a livelihood" (Lynd and

Lynd 1929, 26). But, as more women were attracted to factory work, the focus of concern shifted as well. An Indiana factory inspector with a talent for prose wrote in 1900 that

it is a sad comment on our civilization when young women prefer to be employed where they are compelled to mingle with partially clad men, doing the work of men and boys, for little more than they would receive for doing the work usually allotted to women in the home. . . . [One fears] the loss of all maidenly modesty and those qualities which are so highly prized by the true man (Lynd and Lynd 1929, 25).

Twenty years later, the employment of women in factories was taken for granted in Middletown. Nearly all (97 percent) of the girls in the Middletown high school in 1924 said that they intended to work after they graduated. And a women's club flourished with the slogan, "Better business women for a better world."

The Lynds noted that some husbands felt psychologically threatened by their wives' working, which reflected on their ability to provide for their families, but they characterized such sentiments as eddies in a strong current heading in the opposite direction. Whether such emotional eddies have persisted to the present is difficult to assess. Husbands are, understandably, reluctant to admit that their wives' working threatens their feelings of self-worth. The majority of husbands reported that they approve of their wives' working, and the few objections that were voiced were couched in terms of neglected children or unfulfilled family responsibilities.

The psychological threat of a working wife is heightened when she earns more money than her husband. This situation is exemplified by a Middletown couple in their midtwenties who have a four-year-old son (Scharff 1979, 36-37). The husband earned $15,000 in 1979 as a car salesman, while his wife anticipated earning over $20,000 selling real estate. Even when the wife earns more, Middletown couples seem to accept the departure from the traditional role of the husband being the sole, or at least the primary, breadwinner. Perhaps the large number of contemporary wives who work for self-fulfillment mitigates against husbands' feelings of inadequacy. A wife working to avoid the boredom of housework does not challenge her husband's earning power. Thus, as in the case of the couple just mentioned, the husband "doesn't mind" that his wife works or that she makes more money. The overall impression is that a husband's self-esteem is not particularly influenced by a working wife, even when she is a better provider. If such anxieties exist, they are not voiced.

Occupations of Women

Up to this point, we have assigned working wives to a given social class on the basis of their husbands' occupations to permit the comparison of our results with those of the Lynds, who followed the same procedure. This is a regular practice in sociological research, but critics argue that it ignores the contribution a wife's employment makes to the family's social status. Although we have no means of resolving this controversy, it is informative to examine separately the changes in the occupations held by women in Middletown.

The data show, when compared with similar data on men's occupations presented earlier in this chapter, that there were relatively more women than men in white-collar occupations and correspondingly fewer women than men in blue-collar occupations throughout the years between the Lynds' original study and ours. (See Tables 4-1 and 4-7 in Appendix A.)

On the other hand, the employment of women has been concentrated toward the bottom of each major category and toward the bottom of particular occupational groups within each category. For example, most of the professional women are public school teachers rather than physicians or lawyers. In factories, they are much more likely to be machine operators than craftspeople.

The persisting difference in occupational distribution accounts for the fact that the median income of fully employed Middletown women in 1978 was $6,835 while the median income of fully employed men was $14,767. This situation exists even with the effective enforcement of the principle of equal pay for equal work within individual occupations.

Working Wives and Marital Satisfaction

The housewife's move from the home to the factory, bank, or restaurant presumably had important consequences for herself and her family. There has been considerable research done to determine whether housewives or working wives are happier with their lives in general and with their marriages in particular. After reviewing studies conducted during the 1950s and 1960s, Ronald Burke and Tamara Weir (1976) concluded that housewives were slightly more happy, satisfied, and adjusted in their marriages than were working wives. But they hinted that the employment of the wife affected working-class and business-class families differently; the advantage (in happiness) of working-class housewives over employed wives was significantly greater than the advantage of business-class housewives. Although the Lynds did not report that housewives were happier than employed wives, their descriptions of Middletown families in the 1920s seem consistent with that idea.

Several recent studies contradict the happy housewife hypothesis by finding that employed wives are happier. In a study of 189 married couples in Ontario, Canada, Burke and Weir (1976) reported that employed wives were more satisfied with their marriage and with their emotional and physical well-being than housewives. Myra Ferree (1976b) interviewed a sample of 135 working-class women in Massachusetts and obtained similar results. Starting from the theory that working-class housewives are better adjusted than their employed counterparts because of the unrewarding occupations open to them, she hypothesized that her subjects would find housework more enjoyable than routine factory jobs and similar positions. She found instead that the employed working-class women in her sample were happier than the full-time housewives. Interestingly, the women in her sample who worked part-time were happiest of all, seeming to have the best of being at home and having extra income. She concluded that "for most of these working class women, having a paid job is more a liberating than alienation experience" (Ferree 1976b, 440).

Susan Orden and Norman Bradburn (1960) identified an intervening variable that affected the relationship between a wife's working and her marital satisfaction. They analyzed data from a sample of couples drawn in several major cities. They found that when the wife was employed by mutual agreement with her husband, both were happier than when she had taken a job over her husband's objection. This is hardly an earthshaking discovery.

These studies reported that employed women are happier than housewives, but their samples were small and the differences found were modest. Other recent studies using large national samples have consistently found housewives and employed wives to be quite similar in their happiness and in other aspects of their lives. Angus Campbell (1976) studied a national sample of 736 married women and concluded that employment outside the home had no influence on satisfaction with marriage and life. James Wright (1978) analyzed six national surveys conducted between 1971 and 1976 and found similar results. There were no significant differences between housewives and working wives in their ratings of their marriage, family life, and life in general. Wright suggested that the image of the confused, isolated, and lonely housewife is just as much a myth as the image of the satisfied, fulfilled working wife. The evidence from these national surveys is that outside employment has surprisingly little effect on the happiness, satisfaction, and adjustment of married women.

The reactions of husbands to the employment of their wives have been studied also. Not surprisingly, most of these studies have found husbands with employed wives to be somewhat less satisfied than husbands with wives who stay home. Presumably, the wife who works outside the home cannot provide the same attention and services for her husband as a full-time housewife. And some husbands probably feel threatened in their position as head of the family by employed wives. Leland Axelson (1970), in a study of Florida families, found that husbands whose wives stayed at home were happier than those whose wives were in the labor force. Similar results were obtained by Burke and Weir (1976). They found that professional men with employed wives reported poorer health, lower marital happiness, and less satisfaction with life than those with wives at home.

An exception to these findings on neglected husbands was reported by Campbell (1976), who surveyed a national sample of married couples. He found no difference in marital happiness between husbands with employed wives and those with wives at home. We have already mentioned the earlier study of Orden and Bradburn (1969) that suggested that, when both husband and wife agreed about the wife's employment, they were as likely to be as happy as if she remained a housewife.

Comparable information was obtained from two of our Middletown surveys, and the results (for general happiness, marital satisfaction, and family satisfaction) revealed that, in every case, husbands of housewives were happier than husbands with employed wives. (See Tables 4-8, 4-9, and 4-10 in Appendix A.) The data suggest that men married to full-time housewives are more satisfied with life in general and derive greater satisfaction from their marriages and family life.

The differences in happiness were somewhat greater for the business-class husbands. It may be that they resent the deprivation of services and the implied challenge to their breadwinning ability more than do the working-class husbands because the employment of wives is a more novel experience for them. Working-class husbands may be better prepared to have their wives employed, as were their own mothers and grandmothers in their time.

The drastic effects of women's employment on family life predicted by some sociologists are not evident in contemporary Middletown. All things considered, the employment of married women has had only a modest influence on their own life satisfaction and that of their husbands. These findings are reasonably consistent with those of other studies and suggest that a good deal of anxiety about the consequences of married women's employment is unfounded. One reason the effects are so small may be that the movement of married women into the labor force began nearly 80 years ago; the family and other social institutions have had time to adjust.

The Two-Income Family

Very little is known about the spending patterns of two-income families compared to single-income families. The Lynds collected information about the amounts expended in 16 consumption categories by 100 working-class families, including 38 with employed wives. The categories included automobiles, housing, life insurance, contributions to church and charities, furniture, union dues, lodge and club dues, and vacations and recreation. Together with similar information we collected in 1978, these data permit a comparison to be made between the expenditures of two-income families and single-income families in 1923 and in 1978.

The relative contribution of employed wives to the family income has increased significantly during the past 50 years. Among the working-class families studied in 1924, an employed wife increased the family's income by an average of 20 percent, from $1,274 to $1,525. Among the working-class families studied in

1978, an employed wife increased the family income by an average of 36 percent, from $14,543 to $19,756. Among the business-class families studied, the average increase attributable to an employed wife's contribution was 38 percent, from $19,557 to $26,905 Access to higher-paying jobs, equal pay, and seniority benefits all tend to increase an employed wife's income in relationship to her husband's. Thus, the contribution of an employed wife to the family's income is greater today than it was 50 years ago.

The data on the expenditures of working-class families reveal only minor differences between single- and two-income families. If we were constructing the list of expenditures today, we would have deleted some of those included by the Lynds and added others. But, in order to assess changes in spending patterns, we duplicated the 1923 list. It should be noted that the percentage of family income spent on each category of goods and services was not very different in 1978 than it was in 1923. The nine categories included in the table accounted for about 35 percent of all family expenditures in both years. (See Table 4-11 in Appendix A.)

The percentages of family income spent in each category show that the proportionate differences between single- and two-income families in 1923 were relatively small. In 1923 the working-class family with two incomes spent a higher proportion of its income on housing and, oddly enough, on music lessons, while the single-income family spent somewhat more on life insurance, presumably to protect the family in case the lone breadwinner died. But, if the differences in spending patterns between single- and two-income working-class families were small in 1923, they were entirely trivial by 1978. Single-income and two-income families spent about the same percentage of their income on each category of goods and services.

The popular notion that the two-income family has a conspicuously luxurious life-style appears to be unfounded. What is left of the wife's earnings in two-income families after her work-related expenses are paid seems to be added to her husband's earnings and spent on the same things. That is how it is now and how it used to be when Grandma was a girl—and held a job outside the house.

Chapter 5

Trends in Housekeeping

When Robert and Helen Lynd observed the people of Middletown during the early 1920s, they saw them as people who divided their lives between the workplace and the home. Within the home, food and shelter were provided, social and occupational roles were learned, emotions were aroused and expressed. But it seemed to the Lynds that the home was gradually losing these functions to outside groups, which had begun to compete with the family in the provision of food, training, and emotional support. Schools, churches, clubs, professional associations, labor unions, and friendship groups all seemed to be encroaching on the family's territory.

These tendencies were checked by the Great Depression, which radically curtailed activities outside the family. The little money available during the depression was spent for basic needs within the family. Men and women out of work, children deprived of extracurricular school activities, and housewives whose club memberships had expired spent more time at home with their families. Many Middletown people saw this reinforcement of family solidarity as a silver lining in the dark cloud of the depression.

Today, we hear again in Middletown that the family and the home are dwindling in importance in the face of competition from day-care centers, nursery schools, public schools, singles' clubs, professional associations, country clubs, labor unions, fast-food restaurants, and other facilities that cater to the physical and emotional needs of Middletowners. The family, we are given to understand, has become obsolete. That opinion is supported by an abundance of anecdotal material. Reliable information on trends in family life is much harder to come by, and the scattered facts gathered by the Lynds during the 1920s are now an invaluable resource for measuring such trends.

Houses That Are Homes

The Lynds' description of the typical working-class home in the Middletown of 1924 is a classic of its kind.

The poorer working man, coming home after his nine and a half hours on the job, walks up the frequently unpaved street, turns in at a bare yard littered with a rusty velocipede or worn-out automobile tires, opens a sagging door and enters the living room of his home. From this room, the whole house is visible—the kitchen with table and floor swarming with flies and often strewn with bread crusts, orange skins, torn papers, and lumps of coal and wood; the bedrooms with soiled, heavy quilts falling off the beds. The worn green shades hanging down at a tipsy angle admit only a reflected half-light upon the ornate calendars or enlarged colored portraits of the children in heavy gilt frames tilted out at a precarious angle just below the ceiling. The whole interior is musty with stale odors of food, clothing, and tobacco. On the brown varnished shelf of the sideboard the wooden-backed family hairbrush, with the baby bottle, a worn purse, and yesterday's newspaper, may be half stuffed out of sight behind a bright blue glass cake dish. Rust spots the base-burner. A baby in wet, dirty clothes crawls about the bare floor among the odd pieces of furniture (Lynd and Lynd 1929, 99).

To this squalor the tired working man returned with obvious reluctance. His wife was glad to escape from it to a factory job of her own. Their children spent most of their time at school and at play and fled permanently as soon as they were able. At the other end of the Lynds' continuum were the wealthy business-class homes, the "fine old places" of brick or fieldstone on the banks of the White River, with ample space inside and out and all the material amenities for comfortable family life. In between were the modest but comfortable homes of the more prosperous working-class families and the less prosperous business-class families. Residential subdivisions were just starting to spring up in the cornfields around Middletown, and the houses in them had indoor plumbing, electric appliances, and central heating as a matter of course.

In 1924, the preferred type of housing in Middletown was a

single-family, two-story house. Only 34 percent of the working-class families surveyed in 1924 had achieved this ideal, but fully 80 percent of the business-class families had done so. (See Appendix A, Table 5-1.) In the long interval since, as subdivisions and suburbs have grown in all directions, the relative disadvantage of working-class families with respect to housing has diminished dramatically. By 1978, the single-family, two-story home was no longer preferred by either social class. Most of the houses built in Middletown after World War II were single-family, one-story "ranch" houses. Today, the majority of business- and working-class families occupy houses of this type. Those of the business class are larger and more lavishly furnished, but they are clearly of the same type. The vast majority of contemporary working-class homes are clean and well kept and have tidy yards. The major laborsaving and convenience appliances (dishwasher, washing machine, clothes dryer, vacuum cleaner, range, and refrigerator are found in virtually every single-family house of the standard type.

The frequency with which families moved during the early 1920s contributed to the Lynds' impression that the nation was ". . . in one of the eras of greatest rapidity of change in the history of human institutions" (1929, 5). They showed that the rate of residential mobility had risen substantially over that for the period between 1893 and 1898. During those five years, 35 percent of Middletown's families had moved; 57 percent of Middletown's families moved at least once between 1920 and 1924. (See Appendix A, Table 5-2.) Increased mobility is also revealed in the *number* of moves reported. The average was 0.7 moves during a five-year period in the 1890s and 1.1 moves during a five-year period in the 1920s.

The Lynds expected that residential mobility would continue to increase because of forces set in motion by industrialization. In fact, it significantly decreased during the following 50 years. Only 27 percent of Middletown's families moved during a five-year period in the 1970s; the average number of moves was 0.6, slightly lower than in the 1890s. Middletown's rate of residential mobility at first glance appears to be somewhat less than that of the nation as a whole. A study of the geographical mobility of Americans concluded that in a five-year period around 1970 43 percent of the American population moved at least once (Long and Boertlein

1980). Most of this difference, if not all of it, can be accounted for by the fact that the Middletown data, both in the 1920s and 1970s, included everyone over the age of 15. Older, established families are less mobile than a population including younger people, especially those just starting their own families. With this in mind, the national data here again seem to confirm that what has occurred in Middletown is a part of trends that have affected the entire country.

The Lynds noted that working-class families moved more frequently and observed that ". . . the tendency is for the place-roots of the working class to be somewhat more shallow than those of the business class" (1929, 104). Working-class families in the 1890s had an average of 0.8 moves in five years, compared to 0.6 moves for business-class families. During a similar period in the 1920s, working-class families had an average of 1.2 moves, compared to 0.6 moves for business-class families.

Since then, Middletown's working-class families have achieved remarkable housing stability, averaging only 0.3 moves from 1973 to 1978. (See Appendix A, Table 5-3.) By contrast, the rate of residential mobility for business-class families remains substantially unchanged from what it was in the 1920s or even in the 1890s— 0.7 moves in five years in the 1970s compared to 0.6 moves in like periods 50 years ago and 80 years ago. It is the working-class families that now have deeper roots, an effect, presumably, of greater job security (which makes moving less necessary than before) and of home ownership (which makes it more difficult). Aside from the reversed differential between the two classes, it is interesting to note the lessened mobility of the population as a whole, another sign of slowing modernization in Middletown.

Habits of Housework

When the Lynds observed Middletown families in 1924, husbands were just beginning to share the housework with their working wives. The pattern was confined to the working class, however, since very few business-class wives held outside jobs. Earlier, housework had been performed almost exclusively by wives with whatever help they could elicit from their daughters. But the Lynds observed a number of working-class families in which the husband began to share the housework when the wife took an outside job.

Laundry and baking had largely been turned over to commercial establishments; vacuum cleaners, gas stoves, and refrigerators were lightening other household chores. When asked to compare the time they spent in housework with the time spent by their mothers a generation earlier, the majority of the Lynds' respondents said they worked less. In one of their less felicitous metaphors, the Lynds spoke of Middletown's families as being carried "along on the wave of material change toward a somewhat lighter sentence to household servitude" (1929, 169). In 1924, the majority of Middletown housewives spent more than four hours a day at household tasks and about a fourth of them more than seven hours a day. (See Appendix A, Table 5-4.) Business-class wives did significantly less housework than working-class wives, partly because they could afford domestic help and outside services and partly because they owned superior household equipment. By 1978, the class difference had disappeared, and a majority of the wives in both classes devoted less than four hours a day to housework. Thus, the reduction of drudgery has proceeded in a very satisfactory way. But some surprising details are concealed by the general trend.

In spite of having automatic washing machines, clothes dryers, and wash-and-wear clothing, the working-class housewife spent somewhat more time doing laundry in 1978 than her grandmother did in 1924. (See Appendix A, Table 5-5.) The great majority still wash and iron more than five hours a week; more than a third are so occupied for nine or more hours. The commercial laundries that seemed to be displacing home laundries in 1924 have been displaced in turn by more efficient home laundry equipment. But the increased efficiency of home washers and dryers is offset by more family clothing and by the custom of washing it more frequently. At any rate, the work is lighter now than it was then. Washing clothes at home in 1924 meant filling the washer and rinse tubs, running the clothes through the wringer as they moved from wash to rinse, and hanging the wet clothes on the line. Ironing meant heating a heavy iron on the stove and dampening the things to be ironed one by one. Hanging clothes on the line to dry and taking them down again was strenuous outdoor exercise.

In 1890, when the washtub and the flat iron sufficed for laundry machinery, the labor was arduous indeed. At that time, 61 percent of working-class wives spent nine or more hours a week at that heavy toil, while only 23 percent of business-class wives did so. Indeed, more than half of the business-class wives of 1890 were virtually free of laundry duties, compared to a mere 2 perc it of the business-class wives of 1978 (Lynd and Lynd 1929, 174). Plainly, this means that Middletown's working-class wives of 1978 devoted considerably less time to doing laundry than their great-grandmothers in 1890 but business-class wives devoted considerably more, an unmistakable reduction of social inequality.

Today, clothes are dropped in a washer, removed semidry, and tossed in the dryer, from which most of them emerge ready to wear. Equivalent laundry time involves much less effort today; much of the time is spent waiting for the machines to complete their cycles.

The business-class wives of 1978 spent more time washing and ironing than those of 1924. The extent of the increase is surprising—67 percent devoted five or more hours a week to washing and ironing, compared to only 25 percent in 1924. It becomes even more surprising when we remember that nearly half of the business-class wives interviewed in 1978 held outside jobs while nearly all of the 1924 respondents were full-time housewives. It appears that in 1924 most business-class families had their laundry done by hired help or by commercial laundries; today's business-class wives have the same laundry responsibilities as their working-class sisters.

The trends in home baking are surprising, too. In 1924 the practice of home baking was disappearing. Home-baked bread had been replaced by bakery bread on the tables of two out of three business-class families and four out of five working-class families. The Lynds made several interesting comments on that trend. Nearly all of the mothers of their working-class respondents had baked their own bread and rolls around 1890, and about half of the mothers of their business-class respondents had done so. According to one respectable estimate, not over 25 percent of the bread eaten in the city in 1890 had been commercially baked (Lynd and Lynd 1929, 155). Most of that was eaten in working-class homes. The apparent contradiction resolves itself when we remember that many business-class housewives of 1890 had paid help who did their baking for them and that many working-class housewives of 1890 held full-time outside jobs that did not allow them time for daily baking. " 'The people who lived in the better homes and kept help in 1890 never thought of buying bread unless to fill in when the home-baked bread ran short,' according to an old time baker. 'They regarded baker's bread as poor folksy; it was the working class who bought baker's bread. It was in the factory district that groceries first began about 1890 to keep baker's bread for the accommodation of their customers'." (Lynd and Lynd 929, 155). The diffusion of baker's bread from the working class to the business class, the Lynds remarked, was a trend opposite to most of those they had observed in Middletown. They would probably be surprised to discover how many habits, like the employment of married women and early rising on weekdays, have more recently diffused from the working class to the business class. Since 1924, the trend has reversed. (See Appendix A, Table 5-6.) Four out of five Middletown housewives of both classes regularly baked bread in 1978, although most of them also seem to have made use of bakery bread and other commercially baked products.

Sewing and mending have followed a different course. In 1924 most of the men's clothing worn in Middletown was purchased, but most of the women's and children's clothing was made at home. This was especially true of working-class families; 78 percent of working-class wives sewed and mended three or more hours a week, compared to 49 percent of the business-class wives. (See Appendix A, Table 5-7.) The Lynds reported that the mothers of the women they interviewed had done much more sewing and mending in the 1890s than their daughters were doing in the 1920s. Before the turn of the century, 94 percent of the mothers of working-class women had sewed more than two hours per week, while 70 percent of the mothers of business-class women had done so. The merchants of 1924 lamented that the demand for piece goods had declined drastically and that even special sales could not revive it. In 1978 about four-fifths of all wives reported doing two hours a week or less of sewing and mending. Both groups have greatly decreased the amount of needlework they perform, but the working class so much more that no class difference remains.

One important advantage the business-class family enjoyed in the 1920s was employing domestic help. Ninety percent of the business-class wives had some paid help; one out of three had full-time servants. (See Appendix A, Table 5-8.) Young girls from the country or older women from town were hired for cleaning, laundry, and dishwashing. In a few affluent families, servants did all of the housework, including the preparation of meals and the care of small children, thus freeing the wife to participate in social and civic activities. Paid help was uncommon in working-class homes and appeared only in special circumstances.

In 1978 fewer than 1 percent of Middletown's families had a full-time servant; fewer than 20 percent of business-class families had any paid help at all. Working-class families employed somewhat more part-time help than they had in 1924, but the total in both years was small. Business-class wives no longer count on hired help to get the housework done, even when they could easily afford the cost.

Men and Housework

As we mentioned earlier, the traditional roles of the husband as provider and of the wife as homemaker were beginning to change in the 1920s. One out of four working-class wives worked full-time outside the home in 1920. Although the Lynds did not collect systematic information on the subject, they observed that some of the husbands of these wives were beginning to help them clean the house, cook the meals, shop for groceries, do the laundry, and care for the children.

Given the continued movement of married women into the labor force and the women's liberation movement, we expected to find extensive sharing of household tasks by husbands in 1978. But the expected shift in the division of home labor has not occurred, either in practice or in theory. In 1978 a majority (two-thirds) of Middletown's husbands and wives still believed that the wife should be primarily responsible for the housekeeping. (See Appendix A, Table 5-9.) Only about a fifth favored an egalitarian family style in which housekeeping tasks would be evenly shared. Despite the wide media coverage of husbands who have opted to stay home and keep house while their wives work as providers, almost no one in Middletown admires that pattern. Working-class people hold more strongly to the traditional wife-as-housekeeper pattern than business-class people. Although both husband and wife work in nearly half of the families in our sample, it is still preferred that the wife do most of the housework.

The wife actually did *all* of the housework in nearly half of the families in the sample. (See Appendix A, Table 5-10.) In four out of five of the remaining families, the wife was responsible for most of the cooking, cleaning, and child care, but the husband made a recognized contribution. Only 7 percent of the business-class families and 9 percent of the working-class families reported an egalitarian arrangement whereby housekeeping was shared equally. Popular culture identifies the egalitarian arrangement as the "modern" family style, but relatively few Middletown families have taken it up. Only 2 families out of the 400 surveyed in 1978 reported that the husband did all or most of the housekeeping while the wife provided most of the income. Twenty couples in the same sample hired someone else to do the housekeeping; as many, by the way, were in the working class as in the business class.

The literature of the women's movement suggests that many modern wives should try to compel their reluctant husbands to do more of the housework. When asked how often they argued about standards of housekeeping or about who should do it, most of the husbands and wives in the sample said *never*. About a third reported occasional arguments about household chores and who should do them. Fewer than 5 percent reported frequent disagreements over these issues. Most of Middletown's husbands and wives seem to feel comfortable with a more or less traditional assignment of housework. There is no sign of a war between the sexes over the division of domestic labor.

Most married persons in Middletown are fairly complacent about their own performance of housekeeping tasks, and they are even more pleased by their spouses' performances. Fewer than 15 percent rated themselves or their spouses as below average. Whoever does the laundry, mops the floor, makes the beds, or cooks dinner is likely to be applauded for the way he or she does it.

Time with Children

One of the supposed trends in contemporary family life is that family members are spending more time outside the home and less with each other. Parents are said to have abdicated the care of their children to day-care centers, schools, friends, and other outside organizations. Indeed, the Lynds saw this trend as early as 1924.

Even from the earliest years of the child's life the former dominance of the home is challenged; the small child spends less time in the home than in the ample days of the nineties (Lynd and Lynd 1929, 133).

And with entry into high school, the agencies drawing the child away from home multiply (Lynd and Lynd 1929, 134).

But a comparison of our survey data with theirs shows no further reduction of parent-child contact or of time spent at home since 1924. In that year, one-fourth of the working-class mothers were with their children an hour or less a day. (See Appendix A, Table 5-11.) About a tenth of the fathers (both business and working class) were reported to spend no time at all with their children, although the survey sample was limited to intact families (husbands and wives and their children under 18 living in the same home).

By 1978, the incidence of parental neglect was much diminished. Only 7 percent of the mothers in the 1978 sample spent an hour or less a day with their children; two-thirds spent more than 2 hours a day (over 16 hours per week) with them—a significant increase over 1924. The frequent neglect of children by working-class mothers reported in 1924 (24 percent spent an hour or less a day with their children) had almost disappeared by 1978, when only 7 percent of working-class mothers fell into this category, as did the same proportion of business-class mothers. Fewer than 2 percent of the fathers were reported to have neglected their children in 1978, compared to the 10 percent who did so in 1924. (See Appendix A, Table 5-12.) The time spent with children is the same for business-class and working-class fathers (as it was in 1924), but it is appreciably greater now than then.

The Influence of Feminism

The winds of feminism have swept through Middletown, needless to say. The most obvious result has been the demand for an end to economic discrimination against women. Access to male-dominated occupations (such as skilled crafts, management, and major professions) has been increasingly open to women. Equal pay for equal work is now enforceable at law, and the income gap between men and women in the same occupations has narrowed. Middletown women now have their own credit cards and their own mortgages.

Among Middletown's married women, at any rate, the seminal ideas of feminism fall on barren ground. In Middletown, and perhaps in other places like it, the married state is considered more favorable for both sexes than single living, and the unmarried working women defers to the working wife. The woman who remains at home doing housework and caring for children can no longer lord it over the woman who leaves the children with a babysitter and goes out to work. But she is not considered to be deficient in ambition or self-esteem. The role of full-time wife and mother is still highly respectable, while the more demanding role of working wife and mother is performed with every appearance of ease and comfort by the majority of Middletown's married women.

Chapter 6

The Quality of Marriage

In recent years, considerable media attention has been devoted to claims that the traditional family is losing favor in American society. Some of the more ardent critics have contended that the traditional family has not adapted to the changing society and has become obsolete. It has been argued that the obsolete traditional family stifles, rather than fosters, the happiness of married people. This chapter will assess the validity of such claims by exploring the quality of Middletown marriages in the 1920s, 1930s, and 1970s and by noting changes in levels of marital happiness.

Marriage in the 1920s

The Lynds' portrait of the average marriage in the Middletown of the 1920s was a dreary one, especially for the working class. Marriage for many husbands meant weariness from trying to provide for their families, numerous children, and wives weary from doing other people's washing (Lynd and Lynd 1929, 129). For many wives, marriage meant poverty, cruelty, adultery, and abandonment. The Lynds did observe a few happy marriages. "There are some homes in Middletown among both working and business class families which one cannot enter without being aware of a constant undercurrent of sheer delight of fresh, spontaneous interest between husband and wife (Lynd and Lynd 1929, 130). But they noted that such marriages stood out because of their rarity and that the majority of Middletown's couples seemed to lead a depressing existence. Though disappointment and depression did not

116

dominate the family's daily life, they lurked in the background, occasionally resulting in a domestic fight or a drinking spree. It appeared to the Lynds that most families, although less than happy, were held together by community values discouraging divorce and by the husband and wife's focusing on "the plans for today and tomorrow," "the pleasures of this half-hour," and their "share in the joint undertaking of children, paying off the mortgage, and generally 'getting on' " (1929, 130). Married life was disappointing, but the prospect of a divorce was even more painful. They forgot their discouragement by focusing on day-to-day living and by ignoring the question of whether it was worth the effort.

Companionship

Observations of husbands and wives revealed that most of them developed a relationship with limited companionship. In the social and recreational activities of the 1920s, the sexes were separated more often than not. At dinners, parties, and other social gatherings, men and women seemed to form separate groups so that the men could talk about business, sports and politics and the women could discuss children, dress styles, and local gossip. Men's leisure activities generally excluded women. Business-class husbands played golf or cards at their clubs without their wives, while no self-respecting working-class wife would join her husband for an evening in the local cigar store. The one recreational activity that husbands and wives shared was card playing with friends in their homes.

Because of the harsh demands of work in the factories, working-class families had less time, energy, and money to spend on family leisure. According to the Lynds, "Not infrequently, husband and wife would meet each other at the end of a day's work too tired or inert to play or go anywhere together" (1929, 119). Compounding the problem was the economic pressure of the times that left few dollars to spend on entertainment.

The time couples did spend at home does not appear to have been filled with pleasant or stimulating conversation. Decisions about the children, the house payment, and the food budget were quickly dealt with in a bickering fashion, and, with those problems disposed of, couples often lapsed into "apathetic silence." The Lynds reported that many times during their survey of wives, the interviewer had a difficult time terminating the interview. The women seemed hungry for someone to talk to.

"I wish you could come often. I never have anyone to talk to," or "My husband never goes anyplace and never does anything. In the evenings he comes home and sits down and says nothing. I like to talk and be sociable, but I can hardly ever get anything out of him" (Lynd and Lynd 1929, 120).

The limited communication between husbands and wives and the trivial nature of their conversation left many of them isolated in their separate worlds, his pertaining to work and friends and hers to the children and the home. In many marriages, they shared a house, each other's bodies, and little else.

Even their sexual relations seemed troubled. Lack of information about birth control and the prejudice against its use made babies the inevitable consequence of physical intimacy for most working-class couples. The uncertainty of employment often made another child an unwanted burden. The conflict between not wanting more children and needing the physical pleasures of marriage, and the resulting stress placed on the marriage, were evident in the comments of Middletown wives.

One wife hopes to heaven she'll have no more children. She said that people talked to her about contraceptives sometimes, and she told "him" what they said, but he said it was none of their business. She had never dared ask him what he thought about birth control, but thought he disapproved of it. She would "die" if she had any more children, but is doing nothing to prevent it (Lynd and Lynd 1929, 124).

A wife of twenty-two replied to the question about number of children: "We haven't any. Gracious, no! We mustn't have any till we get steady work. No, we don't use anything to prevent children. I just keep away from my husband. He don't care—only at times. He's discouraged because he's out of work. I went to work but had to quit because I was so nervous" (Lynd and Lynd 1929, 125).

Such comments provide considerable insight into Middletown's working-class marriages of the 1920s. The fact that a wife might not dare ask her husband what he thought about birth control, let alone what he felt about practicing it, shows how shallow some of the relationships were. In some cases, the threat of unwanted children made wives resentful; they felt that their husbands were insensitive and selfish to expose them to the risk of conception. In other cases, the fear of an unwanted pregnancy forced a wife to "keep away" from her husband, which certainly did not strengthen their marital relationship. On the other hand, husbands felt rejected by their wives' avoidance of physical contact.

It may have been that limited marital sex contributed to the flourishing prostitution in Middletown during the 1920s. Husbands whose wives were sexually unresponsive, perhaps because of their fear of pregnancy, may have sought sexual satisfaction outside of marriage. Although a husband's visits to prostitutes probably did not strengthen his marriage, they were not a sure indicator of marital dissatisfaction. Some men sought commercial sex out of consideration for their wives' fear of unwanted pregnancy. And, of course, we do not know what proportion of the clients of Middletown's brothels were unmarried. Moreover, the effects of changing laws and policies on prostitution make its prevalence a very unsure indicator of marital happiness. The number of whorehouses in Middletown fluctuated dramatically over the years, before beginning a permanent decline in the 1940s.

Another glimpse of the shallowness of husband-wife relationships in the 1920s is provided by the responses of 69 working-class wives to the question "What are the thoughts and plans that give you courage to go on when thoroughly discouraged?" Not one of them mentioned her husband as a source of emotional support!

Divorce

The trend in divorce was discussed in detail in *Middletown*. Divorce rates increased significantly in Middletown from 1890 to 1920. Whether there were significantly more unhappy marriages during the 1920s than there had been at the turn of the century is a question neither the Lynds nor we could answer with the available data. The legal grounds for divorce in force at a particular time and contemporary public attitudes toward it greatly influence the likelihood that a marriage will end in divorce. When divorce laws are stringent and public sentiment strongly opposed, unhappy marriages endure. Between 1890 and 1920, Indiana's divorce laws were conspicuously liberalized and prevailing attitudes toward divorce became much less censorious. Nevertheless, the high divorce rate observed during the 1920s does suggest that more marriages were experiencing unresolvable stresses and strains than had been the case 30 years earlier.

Marriage in the 1930s

The Great Depression was thought by Middletown people to have mixed effects on marital happiness. On the one hand, they spoke of how married couples spent more time together and became more dependent on each other, and this enforced togetherness was perceived as strengthening the quality of Middletown's marriages. The Lynds quoted an editorial in a local newspaper in the spring of 1933 that remarked that

All of us are hoping for a quick return of the prosperity we once knew, or thought we knew, but in the meantime, some millions of Americans already have a kind of prosperity that includes the strengthening of family ties, better health, and the luxury of simple pleasures and quiet surroundings, although of this they may not be aware (Lynd and Lynd 1937, 147).

On the other hand, the economic chaos of the depression created problems in many marriages, including those of the business class. *Middletown in Transition* suggests that the depression did increase the amount of time husbands and wives spent together by making outside activities unaffordable. Although couples spent more time together, they often reacted to economic pressures by mutual recrimination. The wives were quick to reproach their husbands for failing to provide for the family's needs, and the husbands were equally quick to defend their wounded egos by lashing out at wives and children. Despite these mounting tensions, the typical marital relationship during the depression was similar to that of the 1920s. According to the Lynds, in the 1930s Middletown's homes still housed

somewhat impersonal, tolerant couples, in the same rooms, with the same pictures looking down on them, planning together the big and little immensities of personal living by which people in families in this culture seek to ameliorate the essential loneliness and confusion of life. These homes seem to give the lie to the ricocheting process of social change outside (Lynd and Lynd 1937, 145).

Divorce

The divorce rate decreased in Middletown between 1920 and 1940, a fact that might be taken as evidence for the positive effects of the depression on the quality of marriage. But conversations with divorce lawyers and judges revealed that one very important reason that fewer divorces were being filed in the 1930s was that many couples could not afford the $60 necessary to obtain one. The standard attorney's fee was $50, and court costs were $10. During the depression, the sum was hard to raise, and some bad marriages that would have ended in divorce during more prosperous times seem to have survived for no other reason.

On the other hand, husbands failing to provide for their families, wives entering the labor force, homes being lost by foreclosure, and other adversities placed extreme stress on many marriages, particularly working-class marriages. The Lynds reviewed 90 divorce cases handled by an attorney between 1931 and 1935 and concluded that a large number of them were directly attributable to the depression. The following cases were fairly typical.

Case 5. Husband and wife middle-aged. Married about twenty years. Three children. Husband out of work most of Depression, though willing to work. She grew irritable and quarrelsome and made home life unbearable. He sought other female company (Lynd and Lynd 1937, 159).

Case 22. Both in early thirties, though wife three years older than husband. Married a little more than five years. Three children. Husband has had a streak of hard luck, having been out of work for several years. Her relatives kept them until the relatives tired and urged her to get a divorce. (Lawyer's comment: "This is a real depression case.") (Lynd and Lynd 1937, 160.)

Case 49. Well along in thirties. Married about eight years. One child. Husband had a prosperous business until the Depression hit him. Fine home and family life up to then. Husband began drinking after Depression hit him. Business failed and wife went to work to support the family. (Lawyer's comment: "This is a real Depression case.") (Lynd and Lynd 1937, 160.)

The economic upheaval of the 1930s hit the working class harder than it hit the business class, and this fact was reflected in the divorce rates for the two groups. The majority of the 90 divorces that the Lynds reviewed involved working-class couples, with a smaller group of couples from the lower range of the business class included, as well as a "thin sprinkling of wealthier business class representatives" (Lynd and Lynd 1937, 157).

Marriage in the 1970s

During the years between 1920 and the late 1970s, the family institution faced a great deal of criticism. It has been argued by some that the family has not changed as rapidly as other social institutions and thus it has become obsolete. The death of the nuclear family has also been widely heralded.

Depending upon whether one regards oneself as an attacker or defender of the institution, the final death scene may be viewed in different terms. The attackers seem to see the family's death as being hastened by natural causes—that is, hardening of the institutional arteries or something akin to inability to make the evolutionary adjustment to a changed social and economic climate. In this latter view, something has caused the family, like some ancient dinosaur, to breathe its last. Some ardent defenders regard the family's demise as having been engineered by a devilish army of debauched sociologists, radical psychiatrists, "Commie perverts," bra-burning feminists, "knee-jerk liberals," and assorted libertines of predictable intent (Pickett 1975, 7).

Those who would celebrate the death of the family feel that, because the family is not in step with modern society, it stifles human potential, creativity, and freedom. Their conclusion is that most people would be happier free of family ties (Crosby 1975, 12). On the other hand, some claim that many of society's current problems—crime, alcoholism, and drug abuse, for instance —stem from the weakening of the family and that a return to the "old-fashioned family" would alleviate such problems.

Some writers (Libby and Whitehurst 1975) contend that, as American society has adjusted to rapid technological development, new forms of the family have emerged even though they have not been accepted by the vast majority of the population. Some of the alternative forms of the family that have appeared are *cohabitation*, in which couples live together without being married; *group marriage*, which involves the marriage of three or more people; *part-time marriage*, in which the couple is married only for certain family activities for a specified time period; *open marriage*, which allows each partner to establish relationships, including sexual relationships, with other people; and *mate swapping*, or *swinging*, which organizes extramarital sexual behavior. The more radical family forms have usually appeared in some type of communal setting, since they require extensive group support to endure.

Except for a few cases of discretely practiced cohabitation and mate swapping, alternative forms of the family are rare in Middletown. This situation is not a function of ignorance about alternative family styles. Middletown people are very much aware of family innovations because of their exposure to the mass media. Middletown's newspapers showed an interest when the members of Synanon began dissolving their marriages and entering into three-year love matches (Middletown's evening newspaper, January 2, 1978). Synanon is an organization of approximately 1,600 individuals that was founded in 1958 to rehabilitate "drug addicts, alcoholics and other social misfits." When the wife of Chuck Dederich, the 65-year-old founder and leader of Synanon, died, he married a much younger woman, and the experience started him thinking about how other people would react to a similar experience. He decided that most would enjoy it as much as he had. Besides, according to Dederich, "Most of these people [members of Synanon] were going to divorce anyway, eventually." He persuaded nearly all the married couples in Synanon to divorce and enter into three-year love matches with other people. Husbands and wives helped each other draw up lists of potential love-match partners, and, within a few weeks, 230 couples had made love matches. Dederich felt that he had demonstrated a viable alternative to the traditional family. He concluded that "what happened is what I thought would happen. People fell madly in love with their new partners." Although the love matches were only for three years, Dederich predicted that many would last much longer. Although this experiment in family style occurred within a mini-society isolated in the mountains of northern California, it was noted and discussed in Middletown. But there was no rush of Middletown couples to involve themselves in love matches.

The consequences, both good and bad, of couples living together before marriage have been continually debated in the mass media. Some social scientists have been reported as favoring cohabitation as a way of determining a couple's compatibility before marriage. This practice, according to them, should reduce the frequency of divorce, " . . . since the subtleties of a marriage relationship are not taught in school and not learned in courtship living together provides the only proving ground" (Snider 1975, 12). Other "behavior experts" take up the opposing position and claim that trial marriages place too much pressure on the partners and make it more difficult to develop a close, stable relationship.

. . . a truly successful marriage and sexual relationship need time to grow and to mature and must be measured in years rather than weeks or months.

To be successful . . . marriage needs the security of an unconditional future. Living together doesn't provide sufficient time for thought about the future. Partners in a trial marriage do not live in a marriage environment while each must be on guard to pass the examinations of the other (Snider 1975, 12).

Contradicting both positions, research has indicated that cohabitation has little effect on the quality of subsequent marriage. A recent study of a sample of college students in a southern state reported that "persons with a history of premarital cohabitation do not describe their marriages differently from persons without a history of cohabitation" (Jacques and Chason 1979, 36). Although living together has received considerable media coverage, very few Middletown couples have adopted this family style. Less than 2 percent of the adult respondents in the various surveys indicated that they were living together.

In spite of the proclamations that the traditional family has not kept pace with modern society and that it is "dead," Americans continue to marry at a very high rate and seem to be happiest and healthiest when married, as Chapter 12 will show in detail.

Companionship

The last 15 years have witnessed a major change in the style of communication between husbands and wives. Numerous books and magazine articles have appeared, encouraging wives to make their needs and preferences known to their husbands (and vice versa to a lesser degree). Assertiveness-training programs have blossomed across the country. They attempt to teach people, primarily women, to communicate their feelings and opinions to others and, as the term "assertiveness" implies, to do so forcefully. Marriage-enrichment programs, including recorded lessons, weekend training sessions, and month-long retreats, have purported to teach thousands of American couples how to communicate with each other more effectively. The women's rights movement, as well as other forces in American society, have fostered a more equal marriage relationship in which the needs and wishes of the wife are considered to be at least as important as those of the husband.

It is difficult to imagine many contemporary wives who would be afraid to discuss birth control with their husbands, particularly after the couple has had several children. The taboo on discussing financial matters observed in the 1920s has almost disappeared, and today nearly all wives play an active role in the management of family finances, especially when they work and contribute to the family income. The open communication between spouses in most Middletown families today was evident in some of the comments housewives made during our interviews. A typical example from one wife who emphasized the openness between her husband and herself was this: "I feel there is nothing I couldn't go to him and ask. . . . I mostly talk to one of my best friends, but I feel that you should look to your own husband for basic communication."

Free communication between spouses apparently has permitted many contemporary couples to increase the happiness they derive from their marriages; at the same time, it has helped other couples to identify their irreconcilable differences. The process of identifying and solving a marital crisis has occasionally been reported in Middletown newspapers and probably has encouraged couples to improve family communication. An example is an account of a working wife who had been married eight years and who resented the fact that her husband did not do a greater share of the housekeeping chores (Middletown's evening newspaper, January 17, 1978). She attacked the problem by using a communication technique called the "contract method," whereby she negotiated the assignment of household tasks with her husband. She remarked after the initial session that, "for the first time, I could see his side. I didn't agree, but I did [at least] understand how he felt." This couple then drew up a list of housekeeping chores and "listened, negotiated, and compromised" about who would do what. The young wife credited improved communication with resolving a serious marital problem and preserving an otherwise good marriage.

This does not mean that all couples in Middletown communicate openly. Interviews with both husbands and wives about their marriages revealed cases of lack of communication, too. An example was one husband, who admitted, "She tries to tell me what she does all day but I don't like to hear it. . . . We don't really talk a lot. She talks about things at work. But I don't really like to talk about it. . . . We eat together every night, but don't spend much time together." A working class wife said, "I would try to talk to him about the other women he was seeing or money problems we were having, but whatever it was he would refuse to talk about it." She reported that, when she persisted in her complaints, her husband shouted and cursed at her until she stopped. Occasionally, her insistence angered her husband to the point that he "shut her up" with a severe beating. But such cases were relatively uncommon, and the evidence is overwhelming that husband-wife communication has improved during the past 50 years.

Not only are contemporary husbands and wives talking to each other, they are engaging in a great deal of leisure activity together. Shopping; eating out; going for drives and to movies, sporting events, fairs, and musical presentations; and taking part in physical fitness activities are frequently shared by husbands and wives. This conclusion is based on the observations of married couples in the malls, shops, theaters, parks, and playing fields of Middletown made by the research staff over a three-year period. The people we interviewed referred again and again to the voluntary activities and interests they shared with their spouses.

In contemporary American society, television has become an integral part of daily life, a source of news as well as of recreation. The sample of wives interviewed in 1978 was asked how often they watched television with their husbands alone. (See Appendix A, Table 6-1.) The majority of both business- and working-class couples spent an average of more than five hours each week watching television together. The time spent watching television may not involve much direct interaction between husband and wife when the attention of both is focused on the screen, but they *are* together and can comment on the program or share a snack. It is interesting that both working- and business-class couples report almost identical patterns of joint television viewing. The pervasive class differences in marital behavior observed during the early part of this century are not apparent in this contemporary behavior.

So that we could assess marital satisfaction, the married respondents in the samples of men and women were asked to describe how they felt about their marital relationships. (See Appendix A, Table 6-2.) Our results indicate a high level of satisfaction; 57 percent were "very satisfied" with their relationships, and another 38 percent were "satisfied." Barely 5 percent said they felt "neutral" or were "dissatisfied." Many couples said that their relationships had been satisfactory since their honeymoon, and others reported that they had had to work out an agreeable arrangement. One working-class wife told us that the adjustment was harder than she had expected but that a meaningful relationship eventually developed. "In marriage, there is always an adjustment period. During this time you learn your mate's strengths and weaknesses which you must understand. I expected it would be easier than it was." She said that, although it took them six years to achieve, she and her husband "have a total marriage, . . . [we have] really adjusted to each other."

Although there were some slight differences between the average satisfaction reported by working- and business-class couples, none was statistically significant. Working-class couples were as satisfied with their marital relationships as business-class couples. Husbands in both social classes felt somewhat more satisfied with marriage than wives, although the differences were not extreme.

These results do not hinge on the exact wording of the question. When we asked about "happiness" rather than "satisfaction," a similar pattern of response emerged. Again, a majority of the husbands and half of the wives perceived their marriages as "very happy," while very few reported "so-so," "unhappy," or "very unhappy" marriages. (See Appendix A, Table 6-3.)

As was the case with satisfaction, the small differences in marital happiness between business- and working-class couples were not significant. Husbands, once again, seemed to find marriage somewhat more pleasant than wives did. The claims in the mass media that modern marriage is an oppressive yoke borne by many because they do not know how to unburden themselves appear absurd in Middletown, where a happy marriage is the common experience. These findings are consistent with recent studies of other communities and of the nation as a whole (Chadwick, Albrecht, and Kunz, 1976; *The Playboy Report on American Men* 1979).

There is additional evidence suggesting that the quality of the average marital relationship has improved over the past 50 years—the number of wives who mentioned their husbands as a source of strength during difficult times. As noted earlier, when a 1924 sample of Middletown housewives was asked the question "What are the thoughts and plans that give you courage to go on when thoroughly discouraged?" not a single wife mentioned her husband as a source of reassurance. In response to the same question in the

1978 survey, 7 percent of the wives mentioned their husbands as a source of strength and comfort, and another 16 percent referred to their families, which, in most cases, included husbands as well as children. The question was asked in the context of religious beliefs, and most responded in such terms; if it had been set in a different context (in terms of "who" rather than "what"), the number of responses mentioning husbands might have been even higher. The data suggest again that the marital relationship has deepened since the 1920s and that husbands and wives share each other's burdens and provide emotional support to a greater degree now than then. Despair about the family is as fashionable in Middletown as it is elsewhere in the United States, so it comes as something of a surprise to learn that 95 percent of Middletown's husbands and wives are satisfied with their marital relationships.

The influence of the media's portrayal of marital conflict is apparent in people's evaluations of their marriages compared to those of their friends. Almost *all* respondents rated their own marriages as happier than those of their friends ("I wish everyone got along as well as we have"). One business-class woman described her third and current marriage as "incredibly better" than those of her friends. Even those who confessed to having problems were likely to describe their marriages as "better than most." Many couples compare their marriages to what they see of their friends' marriages, what their friends tell them about their marriages, and what they observe of marriages in the media, and they are pleasantly surprised that their own marriages seem so satisfying.

We often heard in the in-depth interviews that a satisfying marriage takes time, even years, to develop. "It took us a long time to kind of get things worked out so that we can work together. . . . We now have things worked out and have a good marriage." "It's lasted four years and gotten better each year." This finding is not inconsistent with studies of marital happiness over the life cycle (Rollins and Feldman 1970; Burr 1970). Such studies have discovered that, on the average, marriages are the happiest during the early years but not necessarily at the very outset.

Divorce

Divorce increased significantly after the turn of the century and peaked during the early 1920s. The divorce rate then declined during the 1930s and early 1940s but shot up in the post-World War II period, when the wartime separations of husbands and wives put millions of marriages under great stress. During the prosperous and placid 1950s, the divorce rate dropped back to the level of the 1930s. In the late 1960s and early 1970s, the number of divorces began to increase again, and it eventually surpassed the level of the 1920s, although it remained well below the post-World War II peak. The divorce rate has increased during the past 15 years, but the popular belief that it has "skyrocketed" is as unfounded in Middletown as it is elsewhere.

Our interviews of housewives revealed considerable ambivalence about divorce. On the hand, many respondents deplored what they perceived as rampant divorce and blamed it on moral decay, by which they meant sexual freedom and irresponsibility in marriage. They often lamented that the religious and spiritual foundations of marriage have been eroded. One housewife said, "Regardless of how agnostic I am, I feel marriage is a sacrament and it can't be undone. People today don't have any moral aspect to it—it's just legal. I don't think divorce is a solution, you can work out your problems." And another held a similar opinion. "There is a total absence of religion. People focus too much on materialism; it detracts from home life and then it falls apart."

A number of women complained that young people are more selfish, individualistic, and hedonistic than they were in the past. The Vietnam war, the student rebellions, the sexual revolution, and the emergence of a drug culture are variously blamed. Young people dropped out of the "establishment" and insisted on doing "their own thing." The women interviewed think the insistence on personal freedom has carried over into marriage and interfered with the willingness of husbands and wives to make the sacrifices necessary for a successful marriage. There was an undertone of pessimism in these complaints. The prevailing sentiment seemed to be that nothing could be done to remedy the situation.

Some respondents insisted that divorce is contagious. As more couples divorce, their children, relatives, and friends may be induced to do the same. The mass media were blamed by a significant number of respondents for disseminating the idea that marriage is impermanent. Others attributed the same effect to the letdown in the moral code . . . . Sure, there are numerous reasons for it. I'm concerned about the answers to it. It's accepted more than it used to be and they're more willing to divorce because of it. It's easy to obtain a divorce. When divorce was difficult to get people stayed together because of that difficulty.

Another housewife said, "It's awfully easy to get a divorce, and I think a lot of young kids go into marriage thinking if it doesn't work out I can always get a divorce."

The major deterrent to divorce for the few unhappy couples we identified was their concern about the effect a divorce would have on their children. This anxiety persists in spite of considerable propaganda to the contrary from various licensed sages. The local newspaper carried a report on research conducted by a university psychologist showing that children are harmed more by living in a family with marital discord than by their parents' divorce. "Parents who hold a troubled marriage together because of their children may do them more psychological harm than if they divorce, according to a research team" (Middletown's morning newspaper, May 22, 1978). Although this finding was based on a very small sample of children and was somewhat speculative, it represents the consensus of at least one school of family counselors. It is resisted by Middletown's parents until, for one reason or another, they decide to divorce and need to be assured that they are not acting irresponsibly. Distress about the contemporary acceptance of divorce and yearning to revert back to the era when divorce was less acceptable and couples worked harder to make a marriage endure were expressed not only by older people who had never been divorced, but also by those who had been married recently and by a fair number of those who had been divorced recently.

In sum, divorce in the abstract is still detested. The erosion of the spiritual foundations of marriage, the emphasis on the right to pursue personal pleasure, and the community's approval of divorce are said to undermine the commitment to marriage and to encourage divorce. And there is widespread nostalgia for the values of an earlier day, when divorce was rare, difficult, and scandalous.

But, even though divorce is condemned in the abstract, there is little disapproval of those who dissolve their marriages. They are excused on various grounds, the gist of which is that it is better to end a bad marriage than to suffer through it. The operative term is "bad marriage." In the words of one respondent, "People are more honest when they end a bad marriage and give themselves the opportunity to find a more satisfying one." A syndicated columnist in Middletown's evening newspaper gave a succinct justification for a divorce as a lesser evil than a bad marriage. "It is true that the divorce rate is rising rapidly, and true that both children and adults suffer when a family breaks up. But the suffering caused by a divorce cannot compare to that of two people trapped in a destructive relationship, one from which escape is impossible" (Middletown's evening newspaper, March 9, 1978).

In relation to particular marriages—a friend's or a daughter's, for example—the ease with which a divorce can now be obtained and the absence of scandal are perceived as social improvements by the same people who condemn divorce in general. It is appropriate, if not virtuous, to end a sincerely unsatisfactory marriage, and this evaluation is not shaken by the presence of children.

Another curious aspect of easy divorce is that it is often perceived as part of a bundle of women's rights associated with economic independence. These quotations are examples of this opinion.

Women don't have to put up with their [husbands'] crap—they can support themselves. They are free to end an unhappy marriage.

A lot of it has to do with the freedom women are gaining. Now a woman has rights. A woman is a person, not chattel.

Girls nowadays are more independent. They can have jobs that provide them with enough money to live alone if they want to. There was a time when a lot of women married to have someone take care of them.

Women no longer feel they've got to be married to be accepted. Women aren't staying in a miserable situation just to say they have a husband.

As is apparent from these comments, the women's rights movement is thought to increase divorce but also, in many cases, to justify it. Middletown's contented wives strongly resent the possibility that a woman might be forced to endure a cruel husband or a miserable marriage because she had no other means of support.

A few women recognized the potentially deleterious effect of a wife's emancipation on her husband. A young policeman's wife remarked thoughtfully:

I think a lot of it is that women are getting out and working and I think the men feel threatened. They feel threatened that they are no longer the heads of the household and they are worried that while the women are out working they may find a better man. They've become insecure and suspicious.

Middletown housewives are much less likely to perceive the various ways in which women's liberation has also liberated men, especially concerning divorce. Alimony is less frequently awarded today; and, when awarded, it is generally for smaller amounts and for limited periods of time. Current legal doctrine calls for awarding alimony sufficient to allow a wife time to find employment and become self-supporting, not enough to support her indefinitely. The liberation of men is even more apparent in cases in which husbands have sued their wives for alimony. The Supreme Court's ruling that state laws forbidding awards of alimony to men were unconstitutional spurred a flurry of legal activity as men began to ask for support from their former wives.

Not long ago, the custody of children was routinely granted to the mother in cases of divorce. For custody to be granted to the father, the mother had to be proved conspicuously unfit to maintain a home for the children. About the only way a father could gain custody of his children after a divorce was to kidnap them. According to one dubious estimate, some 100,000 children are still kidnapped each year by their desperate fathers (*Marriage and Divorce Today* 1980, 1). But very recently the courts have begun to grant the custody of small children to fathers and to set the two parents on an equal footing with respect to the initial determination of custody rights.

Fathers in Middletown appear to be part of this national trend. Divorced Equality for All is an organization in Middletown that is engaged in educating "men presently going through a dissolution of marriage as to their rights in terms of child custody and visitation and payment of child support" (Middletown's morning newspaper, April 26, 1978). Divorced Equality for All urges the courts to consider whether the father or the mother "is the most suitable person to have custody of the children" and assists divorced fathers who have grievances about custody in pursuing legal remedies.

Several other local organizations and programs have offered help for people dealing with the trauma of divorce. Counseling for children and parents, workshops on single-parent family life, and social activities for the recently unmarried are widely advertised. The community mental health association offers psychological counseling on how to cope with feelings of rejection and failure resulting from divorce. Middletown's university sponsored a one-day Creative Divorce Workshop in 1978, in which the social, emotional, legal, and economic effects of divorce on parents and children were discussed and suggestions were offered on how to establish a new life independent of a former spouse. During the summer months, the local chapter of Parents without Partners sponsors weekly volleyball games for single parents and their children. During June of 1978, a three-day workshop with the theme Happy Days '78 was offered by the same organization. The workshop included a seminar on assertiveness training, primarily for divorced women, to help them become more forceful in their interpersonal relationships. Drug and alcohol use was discussed in a session to which both parents and children were invited. There was a skating party, a dance, and an awards banquet on the final evening. The existence of such programs is evidence that the community has managed to normalize the status of divorced persons and their children.

Thus, Middletown both condemns and facilitates divorce. Although such attitudes and actions appear inconsistent at first glance, upon closer inspection, they seem much less so. Middletown people are thoroughly committed to marriage as a way of life, and they consider it essential for the well-being of the individual, the community, and the nation. Most of them are satisfied with their own marriages. On the other hand, they believe that, when partners are mismatched in one way or another, the marriage will be hopelessly and permanently miserable. In such cases, divorce is construed as the removal of a destructive relationship with the expectation that a more satisfactory one will be substituted. Divorce under such conditions is applauded, although there is some anxiety that too many couples use it to escape minor or solvable problems.

Family Violence

During the past four or five years, wife abuse has become a recognized social problem in the United States, complete with all the institutional paraphernalia—government programs, academic experts, journals, conferences, lobbyists—associated with other established social problems, such as drug abuse and water pollution. The attention given to the problem by journalists, officials, police officers, social workers, and activists has been interpreted by the unworldly to mean that the phenomenon is new or increasing and that it represents a further deterioration in the quality of married life. The frequency of wife abuse (or, more rarely, husband abuse) is unknown. Current estimates vary widely and appear to be based on surmise. The residents of Middletown could have found in a column by Jack Anderson an estimate that there were 3 million cases a year (Middletown's evening newspaper, February 15, 1979) or in one of the new books at the public library a more generous estimate that there were 28 million battered wives in the county (Middletown's morning newspaper, August 25, 1977). Whatever the actual number of cases, the number receiving public attention has certainly increased.

The emergence of the battered wife movement, for want of a better name, is probably not symptomatic of a decline in the quality of marriage. It seems to be another step toward the improvement of marital happiness. Conversations with police officers and social workers in Middletown suggest that wife beating has been going on for as long as they can remember but that only recently have wives called it to public attention. The women's rights movement has made women less willing to endure physical abuse from their husbands, and their growing economic independence has made it less necessary for them to do so. In some cases in which the wife obtains outside assistance, the husband accepts psychological help in controlling his emotions, and the problem disappears or is at least reduced. In other cases, abused wives are helped to escape from a physically punishing relationship.

The national trends are evident in Middletown. There are no reasonable estimates of how much wife abuse occurs in Middletown, but there was enough to justify the creation in 1977 of the Middletown County Task Force on Battered Wives, which was to make recommendations to the appropriate city and county social service agencies. A number of public meetings were held, and in 1978 a shelter for battered wives was established. The shelter was named A Better Way to emphasize that there are alternatives to enduring physical abuse from a husband. In 1979 the shelter received approximately 1,900 calls from women with abusive husbands. If the current rate continues through this year, the shelter will receive over 3,500 calls for assistance in 1980.

All things considered, the quality of marriage seems to have improved substantially in Middletown during the past half a century. Such dismal marriages as the Lynds described as typical in the 1920s are now relatively rare. The overwhelming majority of contemporary husbands and wives say that their marriages are happy and fulfilling.

We do not mean to imply that all marriages in Middletown are happy. The data indicate that most are, but the divorce rate is a reminder that many unhappy marriages occur. Indeed, the high divorce rate is one important reason why contemporary marriages are so happy; most of the unhappy ones have been terminated. Women's employment has freed many wives from economic dependence on their husbands. The public acceptance of divorce, embodied in no-fault divorce statutes, has made divorce a viable option for many people who might formerly have been trapped in unhappy marriages. With respect to divorce, both spouses have been liberated in various ways. Alimony awards have declined; divorced wives are now expected to support themselves eventually. More fathers are claiming the opportunity to raise their children alone or with a new wife.

Divorce not only terminates the unsatisfactory marriage, it allows each unhappy partner to attempt a more satisfying marriage with someone else. The number of happily remarried persons encountered in our various surveys suggests that this procedure often works. It is not the best of all possible worlds, but it compares very nicely with the Middletown of 1935 or 1924 or 1890.

Chapter 7

Parents and Children

The preceding chapters have introduced the reader to the two major themes of the original *Middletown* study: the modernization[1] of the community with the resulting disruption of traditional social patterns and the sharp division of the population into a business class and a working class. Either of these themes could dominate this chapter. We could, for example, begin by asking whether the trends in family life that accompanied modernization in Middletown between 1890 and 1924 persisted from 1924 until 1980. Or we could try to discover how today's business-class and working-class families are different in their patterns of child care and child socialization.

We are, however, going to take a slightly different approach. Instead of discussing modernization and stratification separately, we will treat them as different aspects of the same process. For each topic taken up, the order of discussion will be the same. First, we will ask whether Middletown's ways have continued in the direction the Lynds described or changed as the Lynds anticipated. Then, we will ask whether the effects on business-class and working-class families were the same or different. In sum, this chapter is centered around two questions about parents and children and the relationship between them: (1) how have things changed? and (2) what have these changes done to Middletown's class system?

It appeared in the 1920s that the role of the family in the socialization of the young was declining. "Even from the earliest years of the child's life the former dominance of the home is challenged" (Lynd and Lynd 1929, 133). The lessening importance of home showed up in the smaller size of yards, the construction of community playgrounds, and the diminution of parental responsibility for occupational and religious training. The attrition of family functions was especially noticeable with respect to adolescents. The Lynds noted increasing generational conflict over "early sophistication" and precocious independence, and they expected that the gap between generations would widen farther as "the agencies drawing the child away from the home multiply" (1929, 134-37).

The Lynds' view of the influence of modernization on the Middletown family is consistent with a theory about the gradual loss of family functions under the pressure of modernization that William Fielding Ogburn presented four years after *Middletown* was published (1933). Sociologists have since revised that theory, and they now refer to the "expansion and spatial separation" (Adams 1975, 77) of functions formerly concentrated in the nuclear family. The family is said to have lost many of its former functions but to have become more competent "in gratifying people's psychological needs—for understanding, affection, and happiness" (Adams 1975, 95).

If these notions of family attenuation—the idea that families have declined in the range of needs or functions that they serve—are generally correct, we might expect to find Middletown adolescents less involved in their families now than they were in 1924. Let us see what the evidence shows.

Trends in Adolescents' Involvement in Their Families

The questionnaire administered to all of Middletown's high school students in 1924 included questions about occupational and educational aspirations, high school activities, leisure pursuits, church attendance, extracurricular reading, part-time jobs, spending patterns, and home life. Our 1977 survey repeated the same questions. The topics for which statistical comparisons can be made between the Lynds' findings and our own[2] include evenings out, sources of spending money, sex education, parent-child disagreements, and qualities in parents admired by adolescents.

The items most relevant to the presumed decline in family influence are the number of evenings per week young people are away from home, the sources of their spending money, and the sources of their sex education. We will also look at the hours per week they spend with one or both parents, but, because the Lynds did not publish the data they obtained on hours spent with parents, no detailed comparison between 1924 and 1977 is possible on this point.

Evenings Out

If activities formerly performed within the family are increasingly centered in other organizations, the 1977 respondents should have been away from home significantly more than their 1924 counterparts, but the data are equivocal. High school boys in 1977 were no more likely to spend their evenings away from home than boys in 1924. For girls, however, the difference is in the predicted direction, with twice as many of the 1977 girls away from home six or seven evenings a week and a correspondingly smaller proportion staying home five or more evenings. (See Appendix A, Table 7-1.)

It appears that by 1924 the boys had achieved about the same degree of independence from home that they enjoy now. If some family functions are less centered in the nuclear family now than in 1924, they do not affect the boys' physical presence at home. In contrast, the girls of 1924 were much more homebound than their brothers; there was a significant difference between the sexes in this regard. By 1977, the difference had disappeared, so that both boys and girls were out about as many evenings as the boys of 1924.

Time with Parents

There is further evidence on this point from another question in the same survey. The 1977 respondents were asked to "estimate carefully the total number of hours, aside from meal times and when you are sleeping, that you have spent *in the past seven days* at home or elsewhere in the company of both your father and mother, your father alone, and your mother alone." To separate the possible effects of social class from those of gender in the tabulation of these hours of contact, the 1977 high school sample was divided into business- and working-class groups according to father's occupation.[3] There is indeed a difference by social class: working-class adolescents of both sexes spend much less time with their parents. But there are no important differences between boys and girls in this regard. (See Appendix A, Table 7-2.)

Sources of Spending Money

According to family attenuation theories, the adolescents of 1977 should have been less dependent on their families for spending money than their predecessors in 1924. In fact, the 1977 boys were significantly *more* likely to get their spending money from their families (either as allowances or as handouts): 32 percent of them, compared to 18 percent in 1924. Slightly more of the 1977 boys also reported earnings from part-time jobs (45 percent, compared to 37 percent in 1924). Although these findings are somewhat ambiguous, they do not suggest reduced dependence. In contrast, the 1977 girls were much less likely to receive money from their families and more than four times as likely to be earning their own spending money (40 percent versus 9 percent in 1924).

In 1924 the female pattern was strikingly different from the male pattern, a situation the Lynds summarized.

. . . while over three-fourths of these Middletown boys are thus learning habits of independence as regards money matters by earning and managing at least part of their money, over half of the girls are busily acquiring the habits of money dependence that characterize Middletown wives by being entirely dependent upon their parents for their spending money without even a regular allowance (Lynd and Lynd 1929, 142).

By 1977, the difference had quite disappeared: 12 percent of the girls received a fixed allowance but so did 14 percent of the boys, and about as many girls as boys earned their own money (40 percent and 45 percent, respectively).

Sex Education

The part of the family in the transmission of sex information to young people has clearly declined over the past 50 years. In 1924 a third of the boys and two-thirds of the girls gave their parents as their major source of sex information. By 1977, each of these proportions had declined by about half. Friends were the most important source of sex information for boys in both 1924 and 1977. The number of boys who mentioned YMCA workers dwindled from 11 percent in 1924 to none in 1977; books and films had replaced the YMCA. The trend was slightly different for girls, for whom parents had been the main source of sex information in 1924. In 1977 friends were as important a source as parents (each 35 percent), followed by teachers and books or films (each 9 percent).

Once again, we see the girls becoming more like the boys. By 1977, the proportion of girls identifying friends as their primary source of sex information was almost the same as the proportion of boys who did so (35 percent versus 38 percent), and, in all the other categories, the two distributions were much closer in 1977 than they had been in 1924.

Class Differences in Parental Influence

The Lynds, perhaps revealing a bias in favor of their own social class, repeatedly suggested that business-class parents were better parents than working-class parents. For example:

It is the mother who has the chief responsibility in child-rearing, and many Middletown mothers, *particularly among the business class*, are devoting a part of their increasing leisure to their children (Lynd and Lynd 1929, 146). [Emphasis added.]

At the opposite pole from the most-leisured mothers of the business group are a considerable group of the working class wives for whom the pressure of outside work or of housework never done prevents the giving of much time and thought to the day-to-day lives of their children . . . (Lynd and Lynd 1929, 147).

But fathers of the business group seem somewhat more aware of the concern over parenthood being diffused to the city through civic clubs and other channels, and *one meets less often among them than among the working class the attitude*, "My husband never pays any attention to the children." There is a busy, wistful uneasiness about not being a better parent among many of the city's leaders (Lynd and Lynd 1929, 148-49). [Emphasis added.]

The growing tendency for working class mothers to work outside the home has accelerated the assumption by the group of even some of the more intangible functions of parents (Lynd and Lynd 1929, 134).

The appointment of a dean of women in the Middletown high school around that time was justified on the grounds that working mothers did not have time for their children.

It was found impossible for mothers who worked during the day and were busy with household duties during the evening to give proper time to the boy and girl in school. . . . It was deemed necessary to have women in the schools who were sufficiently interested in boys and girls . . . to devote their entire time to working with and for them. . . . It is the dean's business to help solve their problems along every line — social, religious, and educational (Lynd and Lynd 1929, 134, quoting a local newspaper).

More than a decade later, in a lengthy report on the needs of youths and services for them in Middletown, Raymond Fuller reached similar conclusions about the inadequacies of home life in the working class and recommended community programs to supplement parental efforts.[4] His survey of "local experts," who comprised the Middletown Youth Study Group and provided much of the direction and support for his study of Middletown, generally revealed an impression that working-class parents were unable to rear their children properly and needed help from community agencies. Here are two statements made by knowledgeable people: "So-called character-building agencies have not broadened their activities to adequately reach the under-privileged group" and "All kinds of educational and character building work should be broadened and intensified due to the apparent decrease of control and guidance in the homes" (Fuller 1937, 123 and 125). The areas of the city that were inadequately served included the black neighborhoods as well as most or all of the South Side. Said the experts:

. . . the Northeast, Southeast, deep South and Southwest sections of the city are inadequately served with recreational and social facilities.

There is a line of cleavage at the railroad. The area south of the railroads should be served in such a manner that it will lose its inferiority complex.

The geographical areas that are most inadequately served are the south part of town, which might be termed the industrial districts. . . . In these districts the household income is small, homes are poorly equipped, families are large, and living conditions very poor. If they are to have a happy outlook on life, the influences must come from elsewhere than the home (Fuller 1937, 127, 128).

Among the other influences mentioned were "low level of home life in some areas," "lack of parental responsibility," "divided homes," and "breakdown of the home as a family center" (Fuller 1937, 133).

Some of the forces that were breaking down the home were seen to affect both working- and business-class families.

Organizations, clubs, etc. in too great numbers that cause one or both parents to be away from home many nights during the week. We are all "joiners" and carry out our obligations to clubs, etc. at the expense of the home. This takes place in the best and typical American homes (Fuller 1937, 134).

But most of the family problems were more commonly ascribed to working-class families. Among the problems named were:

Unemployment, causing several families to live together with no proper family life.

The inability of parents to understand the effect of the insecure and unstable economic situation on their children. Conditions today make it impossible for a youth of 16 or 18 to go out and make his own living without help from anyone. Parents must support children several years longer than formerly, and they are often unsympathetic and resentful of the burden.

Lack of parental responsibility and unwillingness to face our youth problems in the spirit of working at the job is, of course, at the root of most of our youth problems. As long as parents are not willing to spend time and effort to interest themselves in their children's problems, any work by "agencies" will probably be in the nature of a hopeless task. At best they can only reach a few, and for a comparatively short time or small part of their time, and then after years of observation of poor examples from careless parents and older brothers and sisters.

Middletown is lacking in health and mental clinics. We cannot expect equal efficiency from our youth when they do not have equal health opportunities. For instance, our schools are full of boys and girls with defective teeth, tonsils, ears, and eyes. The families are too poor or indifferent to take care of these, yet the families are not on relief. . . . This is a big stumbling stone that must be eradicated if the youth of poor families are expected to go forward with the same strides as the youth of the more fortunate families (Fuller 1937, 134, 135, 136, and 139).

Said a teacher-interviewer who worked in the follow-up survey of high school graduates and withdrawals:

I am more convinced than ever of how ridiculous and absurd it is to try to teach technical English to the types of children who live in a dirty hovel with ignorant parents and many brothers and sisters, none of whom have had proper food or care. How much more valuable to them would have been some beautiful and inspirational literature, which would have permitted them to get away, in imagination at least, from the sordid conditions at home (Fuller 1937, 219).

Despite the absence of statistical detail about business-class and working-class parental care in the 1920s and 1930s, it can be assumed, we think, that there was some difference between the social classes at that time. It remains to be determined whether that difference persisted into the 1970s.

Using data from our 1977 high school surveys,[5] we examined the indicators of parental influence used above—evenings out, spending money, and sex information—to see whether working-class parents still have less influence on their children than business-class parents have. For business-class boys and for girls in both classes, the distributions of evenings out are similar; about a fourth of them are home no more than one evening a week; a slightly larger number are at home most (five to seven) evenings. But, 37 percent of the working-class boys are home no more than one evening a week.

As for time spent with parents, the findings summarized in Table 7-2 reveal two patterns. (1) Business-class boys spend more time with both parents together than do working-class boys or girls of either social class. (2) Working-class boys spend the least amount of time with their mothers, and the differences between them and working-class girls in this respect are greater than those that separate them from business-class respondents of either sex. Nevertheless it appears that the class difference in parental contact has largely disappeared. To the slight extent that a difference persists, it is the working-class boy who is least attached to his parents. The sex differences are typically as large or larger than the class differences. The class difference in time spent with fathers was especially small.

The differences among the four categories of adolescents in sources of spending money were not very large. The young people in working-class homes somewhat more frequently ask their parents for money, but they are just as likely to work at part-time jobs and/or to have fixed allowances. Whatever class differences in adolescents' sources of spending money there were in the 1920s had largely disappeared by the 1970s.

Similarly, in sources of sex information, there were no significant differences by social class among the 1977 respondents.

The foregoing indicators do not provide much support for the presumption that Middletown's business-class parents are closer to their adolescent children than their working-class neighbors. Other indicators might tell a different story, of course, but these are the ones we have to work with.

The Generation Gap

The Lynds suggested at several points in their report that social change was widening the gap between parents and young people, thus foreshadowing the modern concept of the "generation gap." They may even be said to have invented the term. However, they also recognized some countertrends. "Despite the difficulty of holding children to established sanctions and the shifting of the sanctions themselves, not all of the currents in the community are set in the direction of widening the gap between parents and children" (Lynd and Lynd 1929, 146). A decade later, they affirmed that "the gap between the purposes and mutual understanding of parents and children noted in 1925 had apparently widened still further. One got the impression in 1935 of a more self-conscious subculture of the young in Middletown (Lynd and Lynd 1937, 168).

We do not have enough data to trace the history of the generation gap between 1924 and the present, but our 1977 high school survey makes some long-term comparisons possible.

Disagreement with Parents

The Lynds presented their respondents with a list of 13 possible subjects of disagreement between parents and children. The respondents were encouraged to mark as many of the items on the list as fit their situations. There was no attempt to measure the intensity of disagreement but only the matters disagreed about. Comparing the incidence of disagreements on given matters, however, may provide some clues about changes in the relationship between Middletown adolescents and their parents over this long period. The distributions of responses are given in Appendix A, Table 7-3. For reasons we can no longer remember or defend, slight changes of wording were introduced in our 1977 replication of the original survey.

In 1924 the most frequent subject of disagreement with parents, reported by more than 40 percent of both boys and girls, was the number of times they went out on school nights and the hours they got in. In 1977 this was again the issue most frequently reported by the boys (and the second most frequent for the girls), and the proportion of respondents reporting it was about the same as in 1924. Issues that were slightly less important in 1977 than in 1924 were the use of the family car, the people they chose as friends, and Sunday (or Sabbath) observance. The 1977 boys reported much more disagreement than the 1924 boys about home duties, dress, and grooming, and unchaperoned parties. Friendship choices and home duties were somewhat more frequently mentioned by the 1977 girls. The amount of reported disagreement about grades, spending money, student organizations, and hours of getting in at night were about the same in 1977 as in 1924.

The trend toward greater similarity of male and female responses appeared again in this analysis. Going to unchaperoned parties was a more important issue for girls than for boys in 1924; by 1977 the percentages were nearly identical. The girls of 1924 reported more disagreements about their home duties than the boys of 1924; by 1977 the difference had disappeared.

These findings do not at all suggest that the generation gap was wider in 1977 than in 1924. There has been some minor shifting of issues, but the levels of disagreement in 1977 are comparable and, on many issues, remarkably similar to those of 1924.

Identification with Parents

The 1977 high school survey provided some other evidence about the generation gap by means of this series of questions: "How close would you say you are (or were) in your feelings toward your father?" "Do you and your father agree in your ideas about the things you consider really important in life?" "Would you like to be the kind of person your father is?" The questions were repeated for mothers. The responses can be interpreted as indicators of parent-child solidarity.

The same questions were put to a sample of adults in our surveys of Middletown kinship patterns.[6] Although most of the adults who responded to that survey, which was also administered in 1977, were not literally parents of the students involved in the high school survey, they were a cross section of the city's adults. It is meaningful to compare their attitudes toward *their* parents with those of the high school students toward theirs. If we found, for instance, that the adolescents' responses closely resembled those of the adults, it would count against the hypothesis of a widening generation gap. On the other hand, if the young people identified less with their parents than the adults did with their parents, the finding would be harder to interpret. For as young people undergo the stresses of adolescence and search for identities of their own, they may temporarily reject their parents and their parents' values. Conceivably, the adult respondents, long past the identity crises of adolescence, may have regained some of the closeness to their parents that they lost as teenagers.

Indeed, this cycle of partial rejection of parents and their values followed by a subsequent acceptance and reidentification seems to be demonstrated by the adults' responses to the question "Would you say you feel closer to your parents now than you did when growing up, or not as close?" Fifty-one percent said they felt closer to one or both of their parents now, compared to only 13 percent who felt less close. When asked to account for these sentiments, many of the adult respondents referred to a new appreciation of their parents achieved through their own experience as parents. For example: "We understand each other better—especially since I've experienced raising children and their problems . . . " and "I'm older and I have children of my own. I appreciate what they did for me. I understand better."

Having made the point that adults might have shown more solidarity with their parents because of this life-cycle effect, we were disconcerted to find that they did not. In fact, the similarity between these two generations of Middletown people in their feelings about their parents is remarkable. (See Appendix A, Table 7-4.) In none of the response categories is there any significant difference between the samples. More than half of the respondents claimed to be "quite close" or "extremely close" to their fathers, and almost two-thirds to their mothers. Again, the findings provide no support for the supposed widening of the generation gap. Indeed, when we take into account the temporary alienation from parents that often occurs in adolescence, the similarity between adolescents and adults raises the possibility that the generation gap has been *narrowing*.

Both samples reported only moderate agreement with their parents about the "important things in life," and here the adolescents put somewhat more distance between themselves and their parents than the adults did, but not very much more. (See Appendix A, Table 7-5.) In neither group was there much outright rejection of parental standards. Although adults are more likely to report agreement with their parents "to a great extent," more than three-fourths of both samples expressed at least moderate agreement with parental values. The proportion would have been even higher if persons with little or no contact with their parents had been excluded from the tabulation. Plainly, Middletown successfully transmits parental values from one generation to the next.

Adolescent and adult respondents were much farther apart in their acceptance of parents as role models. (See Appendix A, Table 7-6.) Most of the adults wanted to be like their fathers and mothers. Half of the adolescents rejected their parents as role models, saying either that they did not want to be like them at all or that they wanted to be like them in just a few ways. Thus, many adolescents are in the curious situation of feeling close to their parents and accepting their values without wanting to be like them. We are not sure that we understand this phenomenon.

Is the Generation Gap Wider in the Working Class?

If the children of working-class families reported more disagreement and less identification with their parents than the children of business-class families, we might infer that working-class families are less effective in maintaining family solidarity and, perhaps, in socializing the young. The comparisons shown in Appendix A, Table 7-7, suggest that this may indeed be the case. Working-class adolescents of both sexes reported significantly more disagreement with their parents over the people they chose as friends, their style of dress (boys only), and their home duties (girls only). Also, working-class adolescents of both sexes identified less with their fathers. Forty-seven percent of the working-class boys and 62 percent of the girls did not want to be like their fathers, compared to 35 percent and 44 percent, respectively, of the business-class boys and girls. Furthermore, the working-class students were less likely to agree with their fathers about the important things in life or to feel close to them.

The class differences were smaller in the questions about mothers. There is little class difference in feelings of closeness or in the sharing of values and none at all among girls in accepting their mothers as role models. But business-class boys were more inclined to accept their mothers as role models than working-class boys were.

These various indicators of parent-child solidarity suggest that the gap between adolescent children and their fathers is somewhat wider in Middletown's working-class families than in business-class families. Alienation, if we may call it that, seems most pronounced for working-class boys, who also tend to reject their mothers as role models.

Another indicator of parent-child solidarity reinforces this finding. A question in the high school survey read "Do you have someone you can confide in and tell your troubles to, someone who understands you?" Those who said yes were asked to say who their confidant was, "a girl friend, uncle, brother, minister, etc." We intentionally omitted parents. Nevertheless, many respondents mentioned one or both parents as their confidants.

Of the 1,647 students who answered the question, 14 percent said they had no one to confide in. Among those who listed one or more confidants, 8 percent said mother, 5 percent said parents or mother and father, and only 1 percent mentioned father. If we assume that all those who said parents did mean to include their fathers as well as their mothers as confidants, then 13 percent of the Middletown adolescents have a confidant relationship with their mothers and 6 percent have such a relationship with their fathers.

When the sample is divided into sex and class categories, we see that fewer working-class adolescents mention their parents as confidants: 19 percent of the business-class boys, 13 percent of the business-class girls, 12 percent of the working-class boys, and 8 percent of the working-class girls. However, there were no class differences in the frequency that mothers were mentioned as confidantes. In both the business class and the working class, 4 percent of the boys and 8 percent of the girls mentioned their mothers but not their fathers as confidants. Confidant relationships between daughters and fathers are very rare in Middletown. Only 1 of the 671 girls who specified a confidant mentioned her father separately, and only 2 percent mentioned their parents together.

Let us add one other scrap of evidence. The high school questionnaire included the statement "Students of high school age are as well able to decide their problems as are their parents to decide for them." This expression of adolescent independence was one of the attitude items used by the Lynds, but no data on it were published in *Middletown*. However, in the responses of the 1977 students, there were significant class differences. Seventy-six percent of the working-class boys "agreed" or "strongly agreed" with this statement, compared to 60 percent of the business-class boys, and there was an equal difference among the girls (78 percent and 62 percent, respectively). Working-class adolescents are readier to reject parental influence.

The Qualities of Good Parents

Two questions in the 1924 high school survey, one referring to mothers and the other to fathers, called on respondents to identify from a list the two parental qualities they considered most desirable. The questions were repeated verbatim in the 1977 survey. The qualities listed for fathers included "being a college graduate," "spending time with his children . . . ," "making plenty of money," "being an active church member," "owning a good-looking car," "being prominent in social life," "never nagging his children about what they do," "being well-dressed," "having a love of music and poetry," and "respecting his children's opinions." The qualities listed for mothers were very similar, except that "being a good cook and housekeeper" was substituted for "owning a good-looking car."

If there had been a major shift in Middletown's family pattern between 1924 and 1977, we would expect the qualities of good parents to have been transformed accordingly. The responses did reveal some interesting changes, but the continuities were more striking. (See Appendix A, Table 7-8.) About two-thirds of the 1924 adolescents selected "spending time with his children" as one of the two qualities most wanted in a father, and no other quality was nearly as popular. In 1977 nearly the same proportion again selected that quality. What they wanted from their fathers then and now was their company.

In 1924, 34 percent of the boys and 42 percent of the girls selected "respecting his children's opinions" as a desirable paternal quality. Although it was second in importance, it was mentioned far less frequently than "spending time." By 1977, the perceived importance of this quality was on a par with "spending time." The 1977 students overwhelmingly chose these two qualities as the most desirable in fathers. The next-most important qualities of fathers in 1924 were being an active church member and being a college graduate. The 1977 respondents did not consider either of these to be important.

There was more change, during the same interval, in the qualities wanted in mothers. The 1977 respondents were much less interested in cooking and housekeeping skills, active church participation, and "never nagging." In 1924 both boys and girls put being a good cook and housekeeper first on the list of desirable maternal qualities. In 1977 that quality was placed in third place, well behind spending time with children and respecting their opinions, the same qualities most desired in fathers.

There were fex sex differences in these listings. The qualities chosen by boys and girls were roughly the same in 1924 and again in 1977, except that girls in 1977 were less inclined than boys to consider being a good cook and housekeeper important (24 percent, compared to 41 percent) and more insistent about having their opinions respected.

On qualities desired in a father, there were no social class differences. On qualities desired in a mother, working-class students, both boys and girls, were somewhat more interested in her cooking and housekeeping.

Incidentally, there was much more consensus about the desirable parental qualities in 1977 than in 1924, particularly among girls, almost three-fourths of whom mentioned having their opinions respected as a quality desired in both parents in 1977. These findings must be interpreted cautiously because we were limited to using the 10 qualities included in the Lynds' list, but it seems that the range of desired parental characteristics has narrowed somewhat and is more directly linked to the parent-child relationship.

Child Care and Discipline

As the Lynds described Middletown's normal family pattern, the men were providers, represented the family in public, and handled certain practical matters. The women's role was to "look after affairs within the household; they care for the small children, and rear and teach the children, always with male authority in the background. . . ." These traditional family roles were undergoing change, especially in 1935 under the stress of the depression, but most of the change was on the female side of the pattern. The men continued to follow "the traditional single path of gainful employment." In fact, if anything, the economic pressures of the depression had pushed the father farther out of the family circle. "He may have been narrowing his role in the home as a parent, leaving child rearing more and more to his wife" (Lynd and Lynd 1937, 176).

Writing of Middletown family roles in 1925, the Lynds observed that many Middletown mothers, "particularly among the business class, are devoting a part of their increasing leisure to their children" (1929, 146). Elsewhere in *Middletown*, they explain how some working-class mothers were forced by circumstances to neglect their children.

The Lynds had very little to say about small children in Middletown. Their chapters on "Child-rearing" and "Training the Young" were mostly about school-age children, particularly the high school students from whom they collected questionnaire data and whom they visualized as presenting "problems" to their parents. About younger children, the Lynds had hardly more to say than that they were kept at home until age 5 or 6 and that the home remained the dominant influence in their lives until they were 12 or 13 (Lynd and Lynd 1929, 132).

Lacking any statistical data from the earlier Middletown studies about the care and discipline of younger children, we can only repeat that in the midthirties, as it had been a decade before, women looked after the household, cared for the small children, and were generally in charge of children until they reached adolescence (Lynd and Lynd 1937, 176). Now, let us discover how things are managed in Middletown today.

In 1977 we conducted a survey of the family roles and activities of married people in Middletown. The findings of this survey were discussed in an earlier chapter, but the information it provided about child care and discipline are relevant here. Husbands and wives were asked which of them ought to be responsible for each type of parental activity and which of them actually was. The majority of Middletown's husbands and wives agreed that pre-school children ought to be taken care of by women. About three-fourths of them thought so and the rest maintained that child care should be equally shared. The similarity of male and female opinions on this point was a little surprising to us.

This congruity diminished, however, when we asked who actually cared for small children. The husbands' collective description of what actually happened parallels their statements of the norm; a fifth of them said their wives did all of the child care, about half said their wives did most of it, and about a fifth said that child care was shared equally in their families. The wives' responses, however, differed both from their own view of what is normal and from their husbands' reports of what happens: 37 percent of the wives said they did *all* of the child care, and 52 percent said that they did more than their husbands. Only one wife in nine reported sharing child care equally with her husband, although as many more would prefer that arrangement.

There was less discrepancy between norm and reality in the answers to questions about disciplining older children. Almost no one ascribed the primary responsibility for this to mothers. The majority (69 percent of husbands, 74 percent of wives) said that the responsibility should be shared by both parents equally, and an additional 11 percent or so thought that either one might do it as occasion demanded. According to the husbands' reports, three-fourths of them shared the responsibility of disciplining older children with their wives; in the wives' responses, that figure was slightly lower.

Class Differences in Child Care and Discipline

There are some class differences in norms about child care. Working-class respondents were more likely to see child care as entirely the wife's responsibility (for husbands, 23 percent versus 15 percent; for wives, 23 percent versus 9 percent), but business-class husbands and wives were no more likely than their working-class counterparts to prescribe an equal sharing of child care.

Apparently, there are also some class differences in the actual division of labor between parents. Working-class wives are much more likely to be *exclusively* responsible for their preschool children. This situation occurs, according to husbands, in 33 percent of the working-class families in contrast to 7 percent of the business-class families (according to the wives, the percentages are 35 and 24, respectively). In business-class families, the typical pattern of child care is for the wife to handle most of it, but not all.

Perceived Competence in Child Care and Discipline

We asked the same respondents to estimate how well they and their husbands or wives performed the tasks associated with various family roles. Each of them was asked to rate each type of performance on a five-point scale from "much above average" to "much below average." In general, the ratings were consistent. Few people gave themselves or their spouses low ratings in child care. About half of the husbands set their own competence in caring for preschoolers at "average," and about a third rated themselves "above average" or "much above average." The wives' ratings of their husbands' competence in child care matched the husbands' ratings almost perfectly, deviating no more than 3 percent in any of the five categories. Most wives rated themselves above average in caring for young children, and most of their husbands agreed: 70 percent of the wives and 80 percent of the husbands said that the wives' performance was above average, and only 2 percent of the wives and 1 percent of the husbands rated wives "below average."

A similar pattern appeared with respect to child discipline in the home, except that no greater proficiency was ascribed to wives. About half of the respondents estimated their own and their spouses' competence in discipline about average, about a third above average, and most of the rest as "much above average." Middletown parents have a high opinion of themselves as disciplinarians. These confident—even complacent—ratings hardly square with the "failure of parental nerve" that the Lynds discerned in Middletown two generations ago. Today's parents are confident of their ability to raise their children, and average parents think that they and their spouses are doing a superior job.

We checked for social class differences in these ratings,[7] but only trifling differences appeared. Business-class husbands rated their wives' competence in child care somewhat more favorably than working-class husbands did, and business-class wives rated their husbands' performance in the same duties somewhat more favorably. However, there were no class differences in the same respondents' ratings of their *own* competence in child care.

There was more differentiation by social class in the ratings of competence in child discipline rather than child care. About half of the business-class husbands rated themselves as above average in child discipline, compared to a third of the working-class husbands. And the business-class husbands rated their wives' competence higher than did the working-class husbands. A similar pattern appeared in the wives' responses.

In sum, Middletown parents generally rated themselves as competent in child care and discipline, but business-class parents rated themselves and their spouses a bit more favorably than did working-class parents.

Attitudes about Day Care

Forty percent of the wives who responded to the 1977 family role survey were employed at that time. Of those, 55 percent had children under 18 years old, and 12 percent had children under 6. Because of the considerable number of young mothers employed outside the home, we included a question about day care in the schedule. It asked "Where do you think is the best place for the preschool children whose mother works?" The 461 responses were distributed as follows.

At home with a babysitter	26%
At a babysitter's home	2
In a licensed day-care center	33
None of the above (mothers of preschool children should not work)	39
	100%

There were no differences between men and women in the distribution of these responses, and only a slight difference by social class. Licensed day-care centers were slightly more acceptable to business-class people than to working-class people (36 percent versus 30 percent), and the "mothers should not work" position was more frequently taken by the working-class people (45 percent versus 33 percent).

Sixty-nine percent "strongly agreed" and an additional 29 percent "agreed" with the statement that "parents should assume the responsibility for molding the character of their children rather than expecting the schools to do it." Also 49 percent "strongly agreed" and another 49 percent "agreed" that "children should assume significant housekeeping tasks beyond just taking care of their own belongings." Middletown parents' opinions on these points were virtually unanimous.

Organized Assistance for Parents

The organized assistance available to parents during the 1920s in Middletown was quite limited. For instruction in the Montessori method of child training a mother had to travel to a nearby city. Some of the churches occasionally sponsored "mothers' training classes" under the direction of the minister's wife. There were occasional demonstrations organized by the State Division of Infant and Child Hygiene. The domestic science department of the high school sometimes offered evening classes in cooking, sewing, and nutrition. There was a short-lived Mothers' Club. The Visiting Nurses' Association gave some assistance to working-class mothers (Lynd and Lynd 1929, 150). (We are not sure at this distance of time what it consisted of.)

The Lynds depicted Middletown parents as eager to "lay hold of every available resource for help in training their children." Yet, despite the classes they took and the pamphlets, books, and women's magazines they read, the prevalent mood among Middletown's parents was one of bewilderment. They were afraid of mistakes and confused about advice, and they sensed that their difficulties with children were outrunning their efforts to cope (Lynd and Lynd 1929, 149-51).

In *A Study of Youth Needs and Services in Middletown* (1937), Raymond Fuller commented on the absence of agencies specifically devoted to children's needs. Except for a day nursery, he said, there were no private agencies especially concerned with children.

We refer to special agencies in the fields of child health, child welfare, and child protection, not to group-work or so-called "character-building" agencies; and we do not refer to such organizations as the Junior Red Cross, the Junior Humane Society, or the Junior Garden Club. In the city (or the town) government, there is no child health or child welfare bureau. School health, though coordinated to some extent through administrative and faculty committees, has no centralized organization under an executive director. In the county there are the juvenile court and probation officer, the county department of public welfare with children's services, and the County Children's Home for dependent and neglected children. The fact that there are no special child health, child welfare or child protective agencies among the private agencies does not mean that services they would naturally render are neglected, as the general health and welfare agences affect children both directly and indirectly. An apparent exception is in the field of child protection, where few of the functions of a juvenile protective society seem to be performed at all (Fuller 1937, 53-54).

Since that time, Middletown has experienced a proliferation of agencies, both private and public, devoted to family services. Most of them focus on the problems of parents, but some deal directly with children. For example, in 1977, Catholic Charities offered premarital counseling, foster-care referrals, marriage counseling, and family-life education, as well as information for persons needing welfare or food stamps. The state university's Counseling and Psychological Services Center offered academic, vocational, and personal counseling to the university's faculty, staff, and students. The Counseling Practicum Clinic, operated as a training center for graduate students in counseling, provided free counseling in cases of parent-child conflict and for marital problems. Family Counseling Service, Inc., an organization founded in 1898 as the Associated Charities of Middletown, advertised a crisis intervention center, community planning, professional education for social work students, and general counseling. Travellers' Aid, mysteriously, also provided family-life education. Comprehensive Mental Health Services, a tri-county publicly funded agency, was staffed for crisis intervention, treatment of chronic behavioral disabilities, and follow-up care for patients released from state mental hospitals. Big Brothers and Big Sisters worked on the adjustment problems of children aged from 7 to 17. Psychiatric Clinics of Indiana operated a clinic to provide supportive therapy for a mostly working-class clientele, who were said to be "depressed all the time"; the Middletown Psychiatric Clinic offered psychiatric treatment to permanent residents, and a sizable fraction of its case load involved family problems. Community Social Service, an extension of the state mental hospital, evaluated candidates for admission and followed local patients after their release. Church-related volunteer agencies, such as Concern, offered newcomers' assistance, marital and parental counseling, and emergency babysitting. Planned Parenthood, which began on a volunteer basis in Middletown about 1966, was in 1977 subsidized by federal and state funds to provide "contraceptive, infertility and/or genetic counseling" to clients "on the poverty level," as well as contraceptive counseling to "sexually active adolescents."

Parents with preschool children could choose from more than 25 day-care facilities, including a Montessori school, the Huffer Memorial Children's Center, United Day Care Center, Jack and Jill Day Nursery, Kandy-Kane House, The Learning Tree, Nanny's Nursery, Pla-n-Stuff, Campus Day Care, First Presbyterian Junior Kindergarten, the Friends School, Heritage Hall, the Isanogel Center, the Playtime Nursery, St. Andrews Nursery School, St. Paul's United Methodist Preschool, Step-n-Grow, Wee Wisdom, the YMCA Kindergarten Readiness School, the University Living Learning Lab, Head Start, the Children's World (Lutheran), the Pre-School Mobile Lab (federally funded), the Readiness School (Nazarene), the Language Enrichment Laboratory for Toddlers, the Scheidler Parent-Child Center, and many more.

Summary

In Middletown 45 years ago, the Lynds discerned an unprecedented generation gap. "It is our impression that no two generations of Americans have ever faced each other across as wide a gap in their customary attitudes and behavior as have American parents and children since the World War. And this disjunction, we believe, has been increased by the depression" (Lynd and Lynd 1937, 168). Nothing in our findings about contemporary Middletown suggests that the generation gap of the 1970s is wider than that described by the Lynds. Indeed, if we may be permitted to state an impression only partly buttressed by statistical data, the generation gap of the late 1970s seemed considerably narrower than that of the 1920s. The slowing of modernization has meant, among other things, that the world of today's Middletown adolescents is much closer to the world of their parents than it was for the two or three preceding generations.

Some aspects of the generation gap of the 1920s seem to have persisted. Describing the "Middletown spirit," the Lynds included the belief that "fathers do not understand children as well as mothers do" (1937, 411). The reports of the 1977 high school students about closeness to their parents suggest that this is still the way things are.

And, if the parents are often complacent about their child-raising efforts, the children are not free of anxieties, and the anxieties are more prevalent in the working class. When our adolescent respondents were asked whether they agreed or disagreed with the statement "It's hardly fair to bring children into the world with the way things look for the future," 40 percent of the working-class boys and 46 percent of the working-class girls agreed, compared to 24 percent and 25 percent of the business-class boys and girls, respectively.

All this should not be taken to say there are no class generational subcultures in today's Middletown. The old class differences are muted, but they are there, as a stroll from the northwest corner to the southeast corner of the city would easily reveal. But the barrier between the business and the working class is much lower today than it was in the 1920s and 1930s. In many family attributes, it has disappeared. The differences between males and females have lessened also, and, as we said before, so has the generation gap. Our findings seem to confirm the recently published work of Joseph Adelson, who characterized the generation gap as "the reigning slogan of the late 1960s" and concluded that

there was, in fact, no generation gap, at least no more so than in any other historical period, so far as one can tell from the evidence. What was happening . . . is that we were in the midst of a number of significant changes in politics and values, changes that affected all strata of the American population. Those changes were put into generational terms . . . (Adelson 1979, 33).

PART III Ties That Bind

Chapter 8

Sex in Middletown

Acccording to Robert and Helen Lynd, Middletown suffered from sexual repression as well as economic depression during the mid-1930s. The main theme of their observations on sexual attitudes and behaviors was that the community was afraid of sex.

The truth of the matter appears to be that God-fearing Middletown is afraid of sex as a force in its midst, afraid it might break loose and run wild. . . .

Sex is one of the things Middletown has long been taught to fear. Its institutions—with the important exception of the movies and some of the periodicals it reads, both imported from the outside culture—operate to keep the subject out of sight and out of mind as much as possible (Lynd and Lynd 1937, 169).

In 1979 evidence that Middletown was no longer afraid of sex was readily apparent, even to a casual observer. Driving into Middletown on the main highway from the north, one encountered a drive-in theater that specialized in X-rated films, usually triple features (XXX). On weekends, the films ran from "dusk till dawn," presenting "five XXX features." Among the titles displayed in 1979 were *Love in Strange Places*, *Inside Babysister*, *Hungry Mouth*, *Long Jean Silver*, *Sweet Wet Lips*, *My Sex-Rated Wife*, *Helena* ("A Film about a Woman's Ultimate Passion"), *Candy Lips*, *Violation of Claudia*, *Jail Bait*, *Honey Buns*, *Hot Nasties*, and *Wet Rainbow*.

When one drove on into the heart of the city's central business district and walked the sidewalks of the downtown shopping mall, one encountered an adult bookstore just a block away from the county courthouse. Its offerings included hard pornography in peep-show movies shown in darkened booths; obscene books, magazines, and rental movies; and various sexual "novelties" and "aids" fashioned of rubber and plastic. According to the proprietor, a new competitor had just opened, making a total of seven such establishments, "plus two places that sell the stuff used." Six drugstores, including the large drug/department stores in the shopping malls, sold an array of soft pornographic publications, including *Playboy, Penthouse, Sensual Women, Hustler,* and *Oui.* Such magazines were also available in almost every neighborhood at convenience stores, as well as at "the best source of soft pornography in the city," the student bookstore at the university.

The telephone company's yellow pages directory for Middletown, on the same page as the advertisements for marriage and family counselors, listed the category massage, followed by a large ad for the local "modeling service center," which invited prospective patrons to come "Look — No Tipping Required — New Low Prices" and offered extraordinary hours of business, from 10 AM to 3 AM weekdays and from 5 PM to 3 AM on Sunday. There were also advertisements for two massage parlors in nearby towns, one of them a "rubdown palace" open ".24 hours, 7 days," which advertised female attendants and "complete privacy."

Not all of the available publications about sex were secular. The local "Christian supply center," an outlet for books and teaching aids serving conservative Protestants, had a home and marriage section, which offered a selection of marriage manuals and publications on marital adjustment. Among the titles stocked in the winter of 1979-1980 were *The Act of Marriage, The Beauty of Sexual Love, At Home with Sex, The Mirages of Marriage* ("A profoundly original look at the marital relationship with no-nonsense procedures to help solve its problems"), *Becoming Woman, The Quest for Wholeness in Female Experience, Forever My Love* ("For husbands and wives who want more . . . more pleasure, more loving, more respect"), *Sexual Maturity for Women,* and *Sexual Happiness in Marriage.*

In 1979 more than a third of the county's total population of teenage females were "patients" of the local planned parenthood clinic. Here is a description of activity at the local planned parent-hood clinic that appeared in the state university newspaper in 1976.

A rush of girls begins at 3:30 p.m., all laughing and talking as they enter. Each holds a stack of books, obviously stopping in from the local high school. Each checks in with the nurse who juggles a mountain of record folders like a professional. As the room grows more crowded, the nurse tries to organize the situation, shouting, "Who's here for pill pick-up? All pill pick-ups here!" This is the scene on a Friday afternoon at Planned Parenthood. . . .

What has happened to beliefs about human sexuality and sexual practices in Middletown may not amount to a revolution, but, by comparison to the Middletown of 50 years ago or even of 20 years ago, there have been some dramatic, highly visible changes.

The National Context

We have been informed by the mass media for many years now that American society has recently experienced a sexual revolution. The exact timing is usually unspecified, but it is generally under-stood to have begun in the 1960s. Among the component elements of this revolution are said to be "an explosion in the creative ex-ploration of new life-styles," including coed college dormitories, cohabitation among young people, open marriages, and gay liber-ation. Its roots include improved contraceptive technology, especi-ally the contraceptive pill, and the women's liberation movement (Francoeur 1980, 3).

There has been a fair amount of empirical research on these matters. Although much of it has covered atypical localities or populations, there have been some representative surveys of the national population.[1] The results exhibit some consistent patterns. On the national scene, there is evidence for the following general-izations. (1) The association between sexual expression and pro-creation and the correlation between sexual activity and fertility are weaker than they were formerly. (2) There is greater accep-tance of nonmarital forms of sexual expression than there used to be, in particular an increased tolerance of premarital sexual activ-ity and homosexual activity. (3) There has been a vast increase in the availability of vicarious sexual experience through sexually ex-plicit material in the printed and visual media. (4) People are beginning sexual activity at an earlier age. (5) The frequency of sexual activity, both within marriage and outside of it, seems to have increased slightly during the past two decades.

Premarital Sex

In describing apparent changes in Middletown's sexual behavior, it is easy to compare today's Middletown with the Middletown of the 1950s, before the sexual revolution. Most of the information communicated to us by local people relates to changes that have occurred during the past two decades. It is much harder to make comparisons with the Middletown of the 1920s, as described by the Lynds; we are hampered by the sketchiness of their material on sex. Their only reliable data about sexual activity came from the high school survey. Paradoxically, we found the schools less permissive in the 1970s and were unable to replicate their surveys; we were warned by school officials that questions about sexual behavior would be defined as invasions of privacy and would present difficulties to the legal counsel and school administrators who had to approve our questionnaires before they could be used.

The Middletown studied by the Lynds during the 1920s was in the throes of sexual revolution as far-reaching as the one we have experienced during the past two decades. The earlier revolution's components were the change from courtship to dating that came with the advent of the automobile; the initiation of dating by girls; the use of feminine clothing for erotic display instead of erotic concealment; and the development of sex, especially illicit sex, as the dominant theme in popular literature and movies.

The automobile freed young people from adult surveillance and greatly enhanced their opportunities for intimacy. Before the era of the automobile, courting had been home-centered. Dating in automobiles meant that teenagers and young adults selected their own partners and spent their evenings outside the range of parental disapproval, often in the backseats of parked cars. The circulation among high school students of magazines like *True Story*, which told tales of sexual adventure, and the "constant witnessing of 'sex films'" also heightened young people's interest in sex, according to the Lynds (1929, 138).

As for changing fashions in clothing and in the initiation of dates, Middletown mothers in the 1920s had these comments to make.

It's the girls' clothing; we can't keep our boys decent when girls dress that way. Girls have more nerve nowadays—look at their clothes!

Girls are far more aggressive today. They call the boys up to try to make dates with them as they never would have when I was a girl.

Last summer six girls organized a party and invited six boys and they never got home until three in the morning. Girls are always calling my boys up trying to make dates with them (Lynd and Lynd 1929, 140).

There was also some corroboration from the young people themselves. Half of the junior and senior high school students the Lynds interviewed agreed that "nine out of every ten boys and girls of high school age have 'petting parties,' " and, among the entire high school population, 44 percent of the boys and 34 percent of the girls indicated that they had taken part in a "petting party" (Lynd and Lynd 1929, 138-39).

We have only fragmentary evidence from which to reconstruct the patterns of sexual behavior common in the 1920s, since no general studies of American sexuality were undertaken until Kinsey's studies in the 1940s. According to Morton Hunt, who has pieced together a description of sexual change in America, the 1920s were the era when petting became popular. The dating pattern that emerged in the twenties provided the opportunity to engage in premarital intercourse. But traditional values proscribing such behavior were slow to fade, and Hunt argued that petting emerged as a compromise between new opportunities and old values. Although petting included most of the sexual activities that often precede intercourse, it stopped short of actual intercourse and allowed sexually active girls to preserve their virginity technically. In Hunt's words, petting was the compromise between "desire and purity."

In 20th-Century America, however, petting came to occupy a most significant position in terms not only of the number of persons involved but of the number of years involved. Even in its "game" aspect, it was serious business: The boy tried to see how much he could get—and the girl how little she could give—by way of recompense for the time and money he had spent on her, and the better he "made out," the higher was his status among his fellows, while the less she gave in, the more desirable she was deemed. But petting was also expressing erotic and emotional feelings before marriage. The more deeply a boy and girl cared about each other, the "further" they considered it all right to go. The standard enforced by the girls and grudgingly accepted by the boys held, in a general way, that kissing was all right if the two merely liked each other; "deep" or "French" kissing if they felt romantic about each other; breast touching through the clothing if they were halfway "serious" about each other, and with the bra off if they were somewhat more serious than that; and explorations "below the waist" . . . only if the couple considered themselves really in love (Hunt 1974, 132-33).

The emergence of petting as acceptable sexual expression between dating partners did not preclude entirely premarital intercourse. But the fragmentary evidence suggests that, although the incidence of premarital intercourse had increased between the turn of the century and the 1920s, it was much less common than petting.

Kinsey (Kinsey, Pomeroy, and Martin 1948 and 1953), writing 25 years after the Lynds, reported substantial differences in the incidence of premarital sexual behavior by sex and class. Twice as many young men as young women reported having premarital sexual intercourse. Working-class men reported having more premarital intercourse and less petting than business-class men. The double standard kept most young girls from having intercourse with their boyfriends, many of whom experienced their sexual initiation with prostitutes.

A pioneer study of premarital sexual behavior was conducted in the mid-1930s by Louis Terman. Although Terman's sample was not representative of the entire nation, his findings did suggest that some remarkable changes had occurred in sexual behavior during the first decades of the century. Of his male subjects born before 1890, 51 percent had been virgins when they married; the corresponding proportion for men born after 1910 was only 14 percent (Terman 1938, 321-23). Of his female subjects born before 1890, 87 percent said that they had been virgins when they married, compared to only 32 percent of those born after 1910. Terman predicted that premarital coitus would become increasingly common to the point that practically all men born after 1930 and all women born after 1940 would be sexually experienced at marriage.

Surprisingly, Terman's prediction was wrong. The petting pattern seems to have stabilized in the mid-1930s and persisted through the 1950s. Kinsey's studies, which collected information about sexual behavior from reasonably representative samples of the American population, revealed that Terman had overestimated the increase of premarital coitus and that it had leveled off after 1935. Kinsey saw the year 1900 as a turning point in premarital sexuality. Women born before 1900 consistently reported much lower rates of premarital intercourse than women born later. By their twenty-fifth birthdays, only 14 percent of the women born before 1900 had experienced premarital intercourse, compared to 36 percent of those born between 1900 and 1920. Women born after 1910 reported only slightly higher frequencies (Kinsey, Pomeroy, and Martin 1948, 339).

The stability of attitudes toward premarital sex between the 1930s and the 1950s is evident in two national surveys prepared by Roper reported by Hunt (1974, 115). Both surveys—they were conducted in 1937 and in 1959—included the question "Do you think it is all right for either or both parties to a marriage to have had previous sexual intercourse?" The 1937 and 1959 responses were virtually identical: 22 percent of the respondents answered "all right for both"; another 8 percent said "all right for men only"; and just over half (56 percent in 1937 and 54 percent in 1959) said "all right for neither."

Behavior, too, seems to have been relatively stable for several decades. Robert Bell, a keen observer of trends in sexual behavior, summarized the research up to 1970.

In general, the studies have shown that significant increase in premarital coital experience for unmarried girls occurred in the 1920s and since that time there have been no striking changes in their probabilities of having premarital coitus. . . . One of the authors, after an extensive look at past studies came to the conclusion that "there is no evidence to suggest that when women born after 1900 are compared by decades of birth, there are any significant differences in their rates of premarital coitus" (Bell and Chaskes 1970, 81).[2]

The incidence of premarital intercourse began to increase again in the late 1960s and continued to increase during the 1970s. Most studies agree that the change in male behavior has been rather modest, with the exception of a significant increase in the sexual activity of college men. Hunt surveyed a national sample of men over 18 years old in 1972 and found that by the age of 17 half of the college-bound young men had premarital coital experience, which is more than double the rate reported by Kinsey in the late 1940s. The increase for males not attending college was much smaller, only 5 or 6 percentage points (Hunt 1974, 149). Thus, for men as a group the increase in premarital sex during the past decades has not been particularly startling. Although unmarried men are having more premarital sex, the increase certainly does not warrant the term "revolution."

Much more change apparently has occurred in the sexual activities of young women. Appendix A, Table 8-1, illustrates changes in the percentage of women who reported that they had premarital coital experience during their teen years. The change from the Kinsey era (1938-1949) to 1971 is impressive. The rates of premarital sex in 1971 are more than double the 1940s rates for each age category. But the increase during the subsequent five years (1971-1976) was nearly as great. By 1976, over half of the unmarried 19-year-old girls in the United States had engaged in intercourse. The liberation of women and the consequent demise of the double standard brought men and women to virtual equality in premarital sexual experience.

That more than half of all men and women are sexually experienced when they marry for the first time does not mean that most young Americans are promiscuous. The premarital sexual experience of most of them is brief, infrequent, and limited to one partner (or a few) whom they hope to marry. One exhaustive analysis of the studies of premarital sexual behavior conducted since 1965 concluded that, while there has been a gradual liberalizing of premarital sexual behavior, "the available data suggest a gradual evolution in sexual behavior of adolescents; there is little support for the notion of a sexual revolution" (Diepold and Young 1979, 45).

We do not wish to minimize the changes in premarital sexual behavior that have occurred in the United States during recent decades, whether we call them an evolution or a revolution. They have been important, and often they have been startling. But surely the mass media have exaggerated the scope of the changes. Monogamic heterosexual marriage is still the nearly universal norm, and most nonmarital sexual behavior involves the possibility of eventual marriage.

The national trend toward increased tolerance of premarital sex and increased rates of sexual activity among the young is clearly evident in Middletown. Every indicator, from the perceptions of local observers to the statistics assembled by Planned Parenthood, from the percentage of out-of-wedlock births to teenagers to the percentage of abortions that involve pregnant teenagers, suggests that there has been a substantial increase in the amount of premarital sexual activity.

A campus clergyman and counselor made the point about both college and high school students.

Today's students are much more active sexually. In some of the high schools here it is almost to the point that there's a stigma attached to being a virgin. In a family we know, the girl became pregnant at age 16, parents are both working and the girl was babysitting at home with younger brothers and sisters, so she had lots of time at home. They took the traditional route of having the young people marry. . . . I can think of several cases where the grandparents are raising the children of their own children.

A high school teacher provided additional corroboration about the precocious sexuality of Middletown children when she considered the problems her own child would face as she grew up and entered the high school social milieu with which the teacher was familiar.

There's the problem of little girls and birth control. . . . I don't know what's going to happen in a few years. I don't really see myself as a mother who's going to run out and get birth control pills for my daughter as though I'm condoning what I think she may or may not be doing. . . . I know from girls that I've worked with in high school. I had a lot of them last year as freshmen and this year as sophomores, and the number of them who have not had intercourse was so small, it's just scary. Fifteen out of the 55 of them have not had sexual intercourse and that's kind of scary because you look around and you think, well, this one doesn't even know what a boy is, you know, so we can put her in the safety zone, but to really have to look at those kids and decide what 15 — it makes you wonder. And that was last year's statistic, when they were freshmen, not even this year's. Maybe there aren't even 15 of them left. And you wonder, why so young? . . . It doesn't bother me so much when girls are college age and they know how to be real mature by the time they're seniors in high school, and definitely into college, and they know what they're doing. . . . But these girls who are in junior high and barely into high school cannot possibly know what they're doing, and I worry about that a great deal. So I just hope I can get her through high school.

Planned Parenthood has come to play an increasingly important role as a provider of contraceptive information and supplies for teenagers in Middletown. In 1976, 6 percent of Middletown's teenage girls were clients of Planned Parenthood. By 1979, as previously noted, more than a third used that service. Planned Parenthood estimates that 42 percent of Middletown's teenage girls were sexually active in 1978. The abortion rate for teenage girls in Middletown's county increased from 29.5 per 1,000 in 1974 to 41.1 in 1977 and then declined to 36.5 in 1978. Figures from the National Center for Health Statistics show that in 1975 Middletown had an illegitimacy rate of 146 (i.e., 146 out-of-wedlock births per 1,000 live births), compared to 90 in 1970 and 58 in 1957. (See Appendix A, Table 8-2.)

Some of the change in the sexual attitudes and activity of teenagers may be attributable to a long-term decline in the age of sexual maturity. Today's youngsters achieve sexual maturity about two years earlier than their grandparents did. The average age for the onset of menstruation today is about 12 (Tanner 1973),[3] and 14-year-old high school girls can and do pass as full-grown women. This influence, however, is difficult to assess.

Attitudes toward Premarital Sex

Our 1978 survey of Middletown housewives included a question that the Lynds asked of a similar Middletown sample in 1924: "What is your opinion concerning the reported increase in petting, spooning and sexual freedom?" Although "spooning" is not in the contemporary lexicon of sexual terms, "petting" and "sexual freedom" are current enough to allow us to use the question in its original form. Like the Lynds' respondents in their time, most of our respondents took for granted the increased sexual activity of young people. (See Appendix A, Table 8-3.)

It's obvious there's an increase in sexual freedom. I don't feel it's right, morally or otherwise. I don't think it's bringing the young people happiness.

It has definitely increased. For example, at college kids now can find a place for necking and intercourse a lot easier than even 10 years ago. This is because more students live off campus and are no longer required to live in the dorms and also there are no more curfews. There is a dangerous lack of commitment in relationships. But we are better off with our freedom to talk about it than we have been. It's healthy.

The petting and the spooning's not bad, but the sexual freedom I don't like.

It's just like animals. I feel sexual freedom is too widely accepted.

I think sexual freedom has definitely increased among all age levels. I think in some ways it's good and some ways it's bad. I think young people are so exposed to sex through movies and television that it becomes a part of their attitudes.

Although most of the married women felt that today's young people are much more sexually liberated, a sizable minority (22 percent) thought that the only change in premarital sexual behavior has been the attention it has received. A number of them pointed out that the current generation of young people did not invent sex, and they insisted that the young people of earlier generations practiced premarital sex in the same ways but more discreetly. For example: "I am not sure that it's so much an increase as more publicity"; "I don't think it's any different. Kids are more open. People are out in the open. They used to sneak around"; and "I see no difference between now and when I was young, except openness."

Of the women who perceived a real increase in sexuality among the young, 86 percent were opposed to the current "permissive" standards. Erosion of family values, growing up too early, unwanted pregnancies, abortions, illegitimacy, and divorce were the adverse effects they mentioned. "Oh, I think it's terrible. I think it's awful that we have lost our morals. There is too much emphasis on sex and not enough on love." And "There is too much sexual freedom. I can't see them giving 12-year-old girls birth control pills and stuff."

In some cases, women who themselves had engaged in premarital sex were opposed to the sexual liberation of their children. They did not express regret or remorse for their own premarital sexual experience, but, nevertheless, they said that they felt it was wrong for their children. As one business-class mother stated, "Just because it was right for me doesn't make it okay for my kids."

A few of the mothers who perceived an increase in premarital sex were pleased with it, either because they viewed sex as normal and healthy or because they took it as part and parcel of women's liberation. Nearly every respondent who approved of sexual freedom added the qualification that contraceptive information and supplies should be readily available to young people.

In addition to well-organized programs of sex education in the schools, there is sexually explicit material available in books, magazines, and movies and on television. As a result, today's adolescents are likely to know more about sex than did most adults a generation ago. If any of the changes we have been discussing qualify as revolutions, it is perhaps the extraordinary public availability of sex information today. According to a Middletown physician of long experience:

There's been a revolution in sexual information. It's partly a matter of contraceptive information, beginning about 1963, and carried on in part by Planned Parenthood and the television. Public TV now has chapters on VD and birth control. . . . I feel the kids are much more liberal than they used to be. . . . Certainly they are more frank. Twenty-five years ago a young girl basically didn't have a vagina. . . .

When asked whether his patients asked many questions that called for "sexual counseling," the doctor said, "There was an increase in the frequency of queries until about 10 years ago. Twenty-five years ago people had no information. By 10 years ago, who needed to ask a doctor? You could buy the books, go to the movies, and learn all you needed."

One of the Lynds' high school questionnaires asked students to identify the source "from which you have received most of whatever knowledge you have on sex matters." None of the students surveyed in 1924 mentioned books or films as a primary source of knowledge about sex, but the Lynds (1929, 146) commented that, according to many parents, movies and "sex magazines" played an important part in the sex education of Middletown's young people. The 1977 high school survey included the categories books or films and television as possible answers to the same question about sources of knowledge about sex; 14 percent of the males and 9 percent of the females identified books or films as their primary source of the knowledge about "sex matters."

Some clues about young people's access to sexually explicit reading matter are available in the responses to a question about magazine reading. The high school questionnaire contained the item "What magazines other than assigned school magazines do you usually read every month?" Among both girls and boys, about one student in five said that they did not read any magazines. Among those who did, boys were most likely to mention *Sports*

Illustrated (26 percent), followed by *Playboy* (16 percent), and *Time* (16 percent). Six percent of the boys said that they regularly read *Penthouse*, a soft pornographic magazine. Similar magazines mentioned by at least 1 percent of the males as regular reading were *Oui* and *Hustler*.

High school girls in Middletown do not read the same magazines the boys do. Less than 1 percent of the girls said that they read *Playboy* regularly, versus 5 percent for *Sports Illustrated* and 8 percent for *Time*. The magazines most often mentioned by the girls as usually read each month were *Seventeen, Glamour, Teen,* and *Coed* (these magazines were mentioned, respectively, by 39, 17, 10, and 10 percent). Of the girls who read magazines 6 percent listed themselves as regular readers of *Cosmopolitan*.

Another indication of contemporary exposure to sex-oriented material is the number of R- and X-rated movies shown in Middletown. Movie advertisements in Middletown's newspapers during 1979 were sampled and the ratings of individual movies recorded. Out of nearly 1,500 advertisements, 25 percent were for R-rated films and 18 percent were for X-rated ones. Judging from the films' titles or from descriptive advertising about them, most of the R and all of the X films received their ratings for portraying explicit sexual activity and not violence. Many of the X-rated movies were shown at a drive-in theater, located in a neighboring county, that specialized in such films. But it was not uncommon for theaters in one of Middletown's shopping malls to have G- or PG-rated shown on Monday through Thursday and then an X-rated film for the weekend.

Middletown newspapers carry advertisements and features that suggest that a relaxed, permissive, nontraditional attitude toward sex is normal and desirable. In 1977 a series of feature stories included a piece called "Thoughts on Sex, Love, and Being Single," in which the columnist (Wilkes 1977) advised formerly married readers.

And there is nothing wrong with proving yourself or sharing physical pleasure with somebody else. Sure, old moralistic rules flash by, but for a growing number of us they can satisfactorily be put aside. For once, it's exhilarating to be the "bad" kid and also to find out who we are as mature individuals, not part of a family or half of a pair. Sometimes we know we are fooling ourselves, saying that we are more free than we are, but we can go on.

By having a variety of partners we learn there are interesting variations on the theme; we even judge that our former spouse was either good by comparison or lacking. For many of us, there had been little basis for comparison.

A more tolerant attitude toward sex is apparent in the following letter to the editor of one of Middletown's daily newspapers (Middletown's morning newspaper, July 3, 1978).

The real danger to our community is not pornography. The danger is the self-righteousness of people who are so impudent as to believe God has given them a right to dictate moral principles to others.

Some fanatics think that because of pornography our society will become another Sodom and Gomorrah. They are wrong. The decline of our society will come because of people who believe they can legislate morality to others. I submit that those people who call themselves protectors of the moral fabric of our society are more immoral than the sellers of pornography. They do not realize that it is the repression of sexual desires which contributes more to sexual promiscuity and perversion; it is the kind of repression which they and others are seeking to impose on the rest of the society. . . .

. . . That those who advocate legislation against pornography don't realize the immorality of what they are doing indicates that they are not really concerned about anyone. What they really want is to stop people from enjoying themselves.

In 1978 Middletown's Planned Parenthood organization gave 41 lectures in community settings (to a combined audience of 733 persons) and 115 presentations in the schools (attended by 3,527 students). In 1979 they increased their combined student audience by more than a thousand, giving 162 presentations to 4,600 students. Early in 1980, Planned Parenthood was designing a program for sex education discussions in a Middletown elementary school. Said a staff member in charge of establishing the program:

We have seen teenagers the whole time [throughout the past decade] without parental consent. . . . Kids are starting to take more responsibility for their own behavior.

I'm talking to a grade school principal at _____ School, to help develop a program for sexually active 5th and 6th graders. They have 10 kids who say they want the information. They have admitted they're sexually active. We're getting the parents involved in setting up the program.

Planned Parenthood's growing role as a source of contraceptive information and supplies for teenagers is explained by one of its local program administrators as an outcome of its substantial federal funding, which is justified on a "cost-effectiveness" basis. As a local Planned Parenthood administrator explained, "The reason Planned Parenthood is where it is today is that we went to HEW with a data system which proved cost-effectiveness. For every dollar they spend on family planning one year, they save $1.80 the next year on welfare."

One of the current objectives of Planned Parenthood is to get more information to students about contraception and pregnancy, as opposed to what the agency has defined as an overemphasis on the perils of venereal disease.

In most counties there are four times as many people involved in abortions as there are in venereal disease. The bigger problem is pregnancy; yet the abortions alone are the far greater problem. Yet in the high schools they almost never talk about abortions or pregnancy, but instead give a big VD scare.

Marital Sex

The change in the availability of knowledge about human sexuality and the gradual liberalization of the American public's attitudes toward sex during the twentieth century have been described by Hunt as "the liberation and legitimation of human sexual enjoyment." Hunt has suggested that the major effect of this sexual liberation upon American life may have been "to increase the freedom of husbands and, even more so, of wives to explore and enjoy a wide range of gratifying sexual practices within the marriage relationship" (Hunt 1974, 177-79). Marital sex has always been defined as acceptable behavior, but it was not necessarily supposed to be pleasurable, especially for the wife. A significant aspect of the "sexual renaissance" (Reiss 1966) of the twentieth century has been the legitimation of sexual pleasure for both married partners.

Sexual compatibility and enjoyment have become a more important part of marriage during the years since the Lynds studied Middletown. Part of this change has resulted from a gradually changing definition of the place of sexual relationships in marriage. In Hunt's words, "Marital intercourse began to be viewed as a positive and healthful activity rather than a shameful and somewhat debilitating indulgence" (Hunt 1974, 177).

The research on sexual satisfaction in marriage, much of it

consisting of comparisons between the findings of Kinsey (who collected his data in the 1930s and 1940s) and those of later researchers, consistently shows higher rates of enjoyment of marital sex reported by wives.

In the 1930s and 1940s, when Kinsey was doing his fieldwork, writers and social critics ranging from Sinclair Lewis to Philip Wylie were still scornfully portraying the typical American marital sex act as a crude, hasty, wordless Saturday-night grappling. But Kinsey's data partially gave them the lie; his figures proved that the early phase of sexual liberation had already had a considerable ameliorating effect. The younger married women in Kinsey's sample, for instance, were having somewhat less marital intercourse, at any given age, than older women had had at that same age, undoubtedly because wives' own wishes were beginning to count. . . . At almost every age, in almost every stage of marriage and in nearly every detail . . . the differences between the older and the younger generation, though not large, were consistently in the direction of greater freedom, pleasure and mutuality. The beginnings of sexual egalitarianism and the legitimation of pleasure were changing marital sex as nothing else had in nearly two millennia (Hunt 1974, 177-78).

Good quantitative data on marital sexual activity in Middletown or anywhere else in America more than 50 years ago is hard to find. In Middletown, as in the rest of the nation, the "sexual renaissance" seems to have brought about increased sexual adjustment in marriage and to have had a marked effect on wives' knowledge about and enjoyment of marital sex. Said the Middletown physician we quoted earlier:

Women . . . were the ones left in the dark; in fact, there were a lot of the older generation women who were really kept in the dark. . . . Twenty-five years ago, . . . the amount of knowledge about sexual matters that people had, particularly among women, was abominable. Almost everything except the "missionary position" was looked upon as dirty by a large section of the population. The problems that people present us with in marriage now are less often particularly sexual, but more often symptomatic of other problems in the marriage. The primary question when you see a sexual complaint is, is it primary or secondary? Nowadays, it is more [apt to be] secondary. . . . There is no doubt that the increased availability of information has liberated people. Sexual adjustment in marriage has increased. I can't tell you if there's more extramarital or premarital activity. . . . I have an idea that the frequency of sexual activity is greater now. Also, it isn't purely a man's world anymore. Especially the older woman had problems [back then] . Unless they had an empathetic, understanding husband, they were about as much in the dark at middle age as at age 20.

Respondents in our family dynamics survey sometimes commented on the relative sexual motivations of husbands and wives. Whenever some degree of sexual frustration was seen as characterizing a marriage, it was the husband who defined himself (or was defined by his wife) as being more amorous. Typically, if the topic came up at all, it surfaced when the respondent was talking about conflict or adjustment in marriage and volunteered information about sexual adjustment. Usually, the adjustment described was one of long standing, rather than a recent development, and was an arrangement that left the men feeling relatively deprived. Female respondents might say that their men were more interested in sex than they themselves were, usually with the implication that such a situation was normal and that there was little either spouse could do about it. For example, when we questioned a business-class husband about conflict in his marriage, he said, "There was a period sexually." Asked how the conflict was resolved, he replied, "with discussion. Not fighting, we never fight. It doesn't change, but we understand each other perfectly. It is one of those things you just learn to accept." And here is the statement of a local business man.

Sexually, we have had a pretty good adjustment, I think. I am a little more sexed than she is. That is, the need might be more. I am more, well, I am more attracted to the other sex and the other sex is more attracted to me than she is attracted or they are attracted to her. Does that come through? And this makes a little bit of a problem for a wife. I mean there are women who make some plays and so forth and that I enjoy. And this is hard for her. And I'm aware of that and try to be careful about it. . . . Although it's so much of a problem that we don't discuss that. It just comes out in the events.

Another business-class husband, asked about whether his marriage had turned out as he had expected or whether there had been an adjustment in his expectations, said he had scaled down his expectations about sex.

I thought sexually it'd be much greater. But then that brings up the old story, if you put a penny in for every time you have intercourse the first year, you can take a dime out every time you have intercourse every year after that, and there will always be money in the jar. Something like that. And I suppose that's true. I had a fraternity brother tell me that.

In following up on the man's story, the interviewer asked, "Are you happy with the change [the lowered expectation of sexual fulfillment] or are you frustrated?" The man's reply was:

I'm frustrated. Well, I mean it's accepted, if that's what you are saying. It's definitely accepted. That's how it is. None of us are perfect. As I've mentioned before, it [marriage] is give and take. I will say this. Before I got married I never imagined the importance of money and sex. Never dreamed the importance of it in a marriage.

Then, there was the working-class husband who worked the midnight-to-eight shift in a local factory. He said that he and his wife were having problems, that she did not respond to him as often as he would have liked. Asked whether it was hard for a woman to understand a man, he agreed, saying that he did not know whether his wife understood him or not, but he did not think she did. We asked whether their different work schedules, and especially his night work, interfered with their sex life. He answered, "Yes, but not just the working. She just doesn't care about it that much and I do. Oh, she called me a sex maniac or something like that." Later in the interview he said that, before they were married, his wife had been very cooperative sexually, "whenever I wanted it." But after marriage things changed.

A business-class wife commented that men had "more of an inclination" to want sex than women did. "If it was left up to us wives," she said, "there might not be much physical intimacy."

A working-class husband who had numerous marital adjustment problems answered the question on how easy it was for him to talk with his wife about sex this way: "We have a hard time talking about it because my wife doesn't like to talk about it. It upsets her. I try to talk about it. She wants to drop the subject." Later, discussing the conflicts in their marriage, he expanded on the topic.

My wife thought, well, all I want to do, well, that's all they [men] think about is sex. And a man, really, he does. He puts a lot of importance on that where a woman doesn't. Or a lot of women don't. Some do, some don't. My wife doesn't put a lot of importance on it. She don't think that's as important as other things.

A middle-aged business-class wife, responding to the same question, said:

We don't [discuss sex]. He may not get as much as he wants. The doctor says he doesn't *need* as much as he wants. It keeps him interested. In fact, we [she and the doctor] just discussed this recently, whether age is an important thing [in sexual activity]. It used to be the only thing in marriage. Today things are different, people's attitudes change.

Extramarital Sex

There is little evidence of any major national trend in extramarital sex, despite the sensational accounts of "wife swapping" and "swinging" that have received so much attention. National surveys conducted between 1971 and 1974 showed that about 70 percent of all respondents thought that such relationships are "always wrong" and an additional 15 percent said that they are "almost always wrong." The researchers did find that young people were more likely to be permissive about extramarital sex than older people, but they cautioned that "the data provide no basis for predicting a high degree of extramarital permissiveness in the foreseeable future, since more than three-fourths of the young adults reported restrictive attitudes in the mid-1970s." They also concluded that there seems to have been no revolution in the acceptability of extramarital sex. Whether there has been an increase in the frequency of extramarital sexual activity is another issue, and the evidence to resolve that question is not now available (Glenn and Weaver 1979, 114, 117-18).

The available behavioral evidence, though sketchy, suggests that there has been little, if any, increase in the incidence of extramarital affairs. Let us quote at some length Hunt's *Sexual Behavior in the 1970's* on this point.

The web of meaning and social structure surrounding sex has been stretched and reshaped, but not torn asunder.

The traditional sexual exclusivity of marriage is a case in point. In sharp contrast to most of our findings . . . our data in this area suggest that in the past generation there has been almost no measurable increase in the number of American husbands who ever have extramarital experience, and only a limited increase in the number of American wives who do so.

These findings will seem surprising if not unbelievable to many persons. In the last decade, and especially in the last four or five years, we have all been subjected to a barrage of propaganda to the effect that sexual exclusivity in marriage is obsolescent. An endless stream of books and articles and an endless parade of guests on TV talk shows have informed us that such exclusivity is archaic, or male-chauvinist, or unsuited to modern life, or unnecessary, or absurd, and that a number of alternatives are more workable, more sensible and more fun. Books advocating permissive marriage have outsold almost everything but diet books. . . .

In the present survey we did not explore attitudes toward extramarital sex in general, but several of our specific questions touched on the matter, and the answers to them suggest that things had not changed much. . . . The responses were remarkably traditional: Anywhere from 80 to 98 percent said they, or their mates, would object to each of these activities. Wives were no more accepting of husbands' extramarital actions than the other way around, and, most revealingly, the young in our sample were no readier to accept extramarital activity in their mates, even hypothetically, than were older persons.

All of which is very strange indeed. How is one to reconcile the public's current interest in the subject of extramarital sex with its continuing disapproval of it? . . . [A] thoughtful answer might be the the majority of people have always experienced extramarital desires, at least from time to time, and kept them hidden; in today's climate of open discussion those desires are being manifested in the form of discussion and of an unconcealed appetite for vicarious experience. At the same time most people continue to disapprove of such behavior because they believe that when it becomes a reality rather than a fantasy, it undermines and endangers the most important human relationship in their lives (Hunt 1974, 253-54, 256).

In that national context, the opinions of long-term residents of Middletown that there has been no apparent increase in extramarital affairs take on added credibility. For example, a university professor's wife said, "The infidelity, that's about normal. We have a fair amount of that here. We don't know many women who fool around on their husbands, but there's the traditional amount."

To the degree that Middletown family life is seen as being threatened, usually it is factors other than extramarital sex that are identified as the causes. A police administrator commented:

I think family life is deteriorating, but I don't know that it has much to do with sex. Parents are too much away from home; parental discipline goes by the wayside. Everyone knows that discipline is gone from the schools; there is not enough time spent with their kids by the parents.

However, to say that the incidence of extramarital sex may not have increased is not to say that there is not a substantial amount of it going on in Middletown. One-fourth of the husbands and wives we interviewed in the family dynamics survey had been married before their present marriages, and sexual infidelity was often mentioned as a factor in the preceding divorce. Three working-class people made these comments.

In my first marriage, it was a woman involved with my wife. . . . I was told that, and I went to work and came back, and my wife was in here [in bed] with another woman. I tried to kill both of them and that's when I got my divorce.

He was on a trucking trip to Florida. I wasn't supposed to call him. He would always call me. And so I had to stay home to receive his calls, if he would call home to check back with me. This one time I called him in Florida. When I asked for him, the hotel people told me that "Mr. and Mrs. _____ just checked out."

[In my first marriage] I wasn't allowed to go anywhere, especially without the kids. If I wanted to go somewhere and I took the kids, that was okay, provided he knew where I was going and when I'd be back and I was back when I said I would be back. But to go even somewhere with my mother, and be gone more than a half-hour to go shopping—you can imagine trying to go shopping with your mother or anyone in a half-hour—if I wasn't back, if I was 10 or 20 minutes late, it was just ridiculous. He was terribly jealous of me going anywhere or doing anything. And he wouldn't keep the kids and let me go someplace to do something. 'Cause if I wanted to go, then they went along. It was sort of like an insurance policy. . . . And, of course, I've heard it said a lot of times, the more jealous a man is, the more he's up to, which I found out to be true. I guess he was afraid I was going to be doing what he was doing when he was away from the house. . . . I had what I considered to be my best friend, the first time I was married, and I found out she was not *my* best friend, but she was my husband's best friend, and since then I have never really formed a close relationship with another girl.

Some clues about attitudes toward extramarital sex can also be found in people's reports about other married people they know or in their comments about hypothetical situations. One working-class wife said in an interview:

I have friends who have always been pretty close friends, who are both teachers, and they have young children and everytime we go down there's a different car, or they have 10-speed bicycles, and the next week there are motor-cycles. . . . They just keep saying they don't want to be split apart, and they've gone through things and they've stayed together *because* [of the children], I think, and that bothers me a little bit. They've each had flings on the outside, extramarital affairs, and they know about it, and for some reason it doesn't bother the other one, and that bothers me. I don't see how they can just accept this, "Went out with Suzie last night." "Oh, swell," and go right on about your business. I'd be ready to kill.

And a business-class man said:

The wife has the strain of the responsibility for the kids and worrying about the fidelity of the husband. Men are away more during the day and can be away. Especially in my job as a teacher. It puts a strain on the wife. What do I think about infidelity? It is inexcusable, very damaging. It should be forgiven, but it would shake the foundation.

Contraception and Abortion

In 1976 there were almost a million legal abortions performed in the United States, or almost one abortion for every three live births. The federal Center for Disease Control's annual statistics on abortions reveal a continuous increase in the number and ratio (per 1,000 live births) of abortions in the nation since 1969, when the national abortion ratio was 6.3. Below are the figures for the total number of abortions reported and the abortion ratios for the period between 1969 and 1976 (Center for Disease Control 1978, 15).

Year	Total Number of Abortions	Abortions per 1,000 Live Births
1969	22,670	6.3
1970	193,491	51.9
1971	485,816	136.6
1972	586,760	180.1
1973	615,831	196.3
1974	763,476	241.6
1975	854,853	271.9
1976	988,267	312.0

The Supreme Court's decision nullifying restrictive state abortion laws was handed down in January 1973. Indiana was one of the states that had restrictive abortion laws, and its abortion rate is still well below the national average. The abortion rates for Indiana

Photo by permission of Ted Thai.

*"The single most important fact about
the nuclear family in contemporary Middletown
is that it is not isolated."*

"*A Middletown Rip Van Winkle . . . would have
noticed innumerable changes but would not have had
any trouble finding his way around town.*" Left: "*Only
partly modernized*" *neighborhood of 50 years ago.*
Right: *Mainstreet Middletown today.*

The Lynds found in the Middletown of 1924
"a sharp division of sex roles in the family."

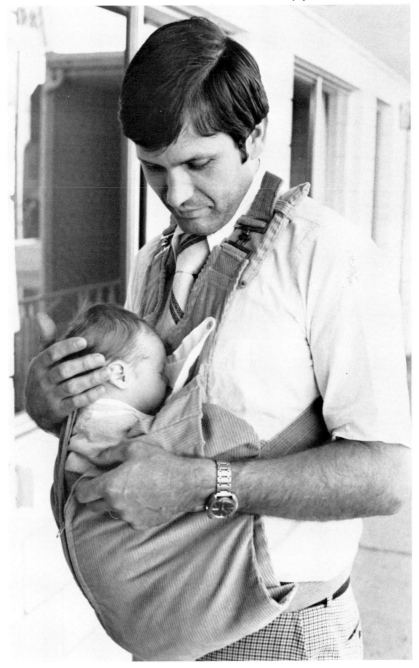

The family in contemporary Middletown
is "a joint, if unequally shared, responsibility."

The Middletown life-style
allows for engaging "in a great deal
of leisure activity together."

Public celebrations and community festivals are "family-oriented."
Above: *Santa arrives by plane.*
Below: *Band performs on a street corner.*

Middletown's "composite families . . .
a safe and comfortable niche
in a hazardous world."

"The importance of earning a living."

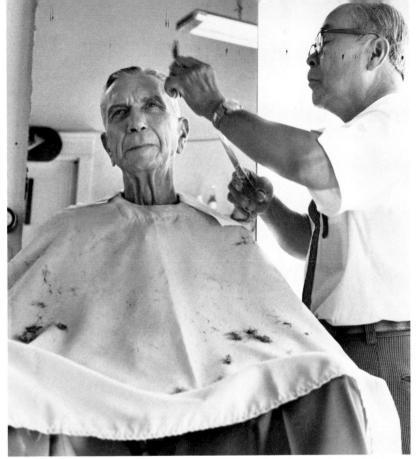

Photo by permission of Ted Thai.

"Today's Middletown is still the same place the Lynds studied in the 1920s."

Photo by permission of Ted Thai.

*"Although its population has changed in some respects, and some
of its customs have been modified by the passage of time, continuity—
not change—has been the keynote of its recent history."*

Photo by permission of Ted Thai.

Photo by permission of Ted Thai.

Kids joking around for the camera: "Reasonably sure Middletown will endure if the world does."

for 1974, 1975, and 1976 were, respectively, 72, 95, and 107 (Center for Disease Control 1976, 15; 1977, 16; 1978, 16).

We do not have information about the Middletown women who obtain abortions, but there is some for the state as a whole. In 1976 there were 32 legal abortions to every 1,000 live births to married women and 601 abortions to every 1,000 live births to unmarried women. In the United States as a whole, the corresponding ratios were 95 for married women and 1,570 for unmarried women. A comparison of abortion ratios in 1976 by age shows that for most age-groups Indiana's abortion ratio was about one-third the national ratio.

The Memorial Hospital in Middletown, as a matter of policy, does not provide abortion facilities. Women who want abortions are referred to clinics or medical facilities located in other cities. A local physician explained, "Middletown women still have to go to _____ [the state capital] for abortions. It is legal in the state but not in X hospital. If they're going to get an abortion, they're going to have an abortion. I send them to a qualified place."

The abortion clinic's brochure distributed by the local Planned Parenthood clinic gives this advice: "If an abortion is on your mind . . . , you are not alone. at the _____ Women's Clinic." The description of the clinic's services seems to aimed at reassuring frightened women and repeats several times the statement that "you are never alone." Part of the brochure's message is this.

Knowing that many persons approach an abortion with some misgivings, the _____ Women's Clinic staff has been trained to anticipate your every question and is prepared to reassure you each step of the way. . . .

Our staff counselors are warm, friendly people. They are experienced in dealing with women who need empathetic support in "going through with it." After the procedure, the same sensitive attention to a woman's innermost feelings is provided. *You are never alone at the* _____ *Women's Clinic.*

In the telephone company's yellow pages for 1978, the first entry was abortion information, followed by the instruction, "See birth control information centers." Under that classification were listed 12 centers, 11 of which explicitly advertised abortion services. The exception was Middletown's own Planned Parenthood clinic. The other 11 were all out-of-city clinics, 3 in Ohio, 3 in Michigan, 4 in the state capital, and 1 in another metropolitan area.

Mentioned in the brief advertisements was the range in the allowed age of fetus, with some clinics advertising "pregnancy termination to 10 weeks" and others saying "termination to 12 weeks" or "abortions up to 22 weeks" or "call collect through 24 weeks."

Despite the legalization of abortion, a large number of Middletowners are still strongly opposed to it. In January 1977, 832 citizens had their names published in a Middletown newspaper as sponsors of a "Celebrate Life" advertisement. The ad, which took up almost a whole page, stated that "today, the unborn child has no protection of his inalienable Right to Life" and urged readers to "join with concerned citizens everywhere in opposing abortion-on-demand and in supporting a Human Life amendment to guarantee the right to life of the unborn child."

For some time after the ad appeared, reactions to it were published in the "Public Letter Box" section of the newspaper, and both advocates and opponents of abortion had their say. The tone of the exchange is illustrated by the following excerpts from letters, the first two from "proabortion" people and the second two from "antiabortion" people.

The opponents of abortion that signed the recent ad "Celebrate Life" are a befuddled lot to say the least. They apparently don't know that there have been 80% less deaths from abortion since the Supreme Court made its wise decision four years ago. Millions of mothers have been spared permanent injury by being allowed the services of competent doctors. When it comes to life and death, I cast my lot with the mothers, rather than the fetus.

The fact that a number of "concerned citizens" have the attitude and/or values against abortion is totally irrelevant to the fact that these types of measures must be taken to control population and insure others of their values.

But that is not my only concern. The world population has doubled since 1930. Our world population is four billion, this total is expected to double again by the year 2000. . . .

The fact that abortion must be kept legal is only one dimension of the problems that lie ahead.

Any person who sees abortion as population control is either selfish or ignorant of the facts. We as Americans have always had a great respect for life. Now we play God and say these unborn babies are a burden to society.

Sure, poverty and food supply are a problem, and always have been. But are we to destroy life by our own selfish means to end this problem? . . .

You know I wasn't alive then, but I heard tell of a man who led many people to their deaths and oppressed many others because he wanted to push his beliefs and feelings on other people. You remember Hitler? Many still do.

With the progress have come the so-called sophisticates who have been brainwashed into thinking abortion is not murder. Whom are they trying to kid? How can girls and women live with themselves after aborting their own flesh and blood? They say these babies are only a fetus. Well, what is a fetus but a dear baby in its earliest stage?

Can't we have "progress" without this wholesale murdering of infants?

The business-class women interviewed by the Lynds in 1925 almost universally favored birth control, and most used what the Lynds described as "relatively efficacious" contraceptive methods. But, among working-class couples, fewer than half had used any form of birth control, and many of those who had, had used relatively unscientific or ineffective methods.[4] In the Middletown of 1925, discussion of both contraception and sexual adjustment in marriage were taboo topics. The Lynds observed that "traditionally, voluntary control of parenthood is strongly tabooed in this culture, as is all discussion of sexual adjustment involved in mating, but this prohibition is beginning to be somewhat lifted, a fact perhaps not unrelated to the increasing secularization of marriage . . ." (Lynd and Lynd 1929, 123). Ten years later, the Lynds found that contraceptives were being discreetly advertised in newspapers and displayed in drugstore windows. There had been a fairly rapid adoption of the "relatively more effective contraceptive practices" among young adults.

The contrast between the attitudes of college authorities in the mid-1930s and at present is instructive. According to the Lynds:

It is of interest in view of Middletown's uneasiness about this whole matter of contraception in relation to its children that the Dean of Women at the local college is said recently to have caused a display of contraceptive materials to be removed from the window of a drugstore near the college (Lynd and Lynd 1937, 167).

In the Middletown of the 1970s, the matter had apparently been fully resolved in favor of contraception. The local university's official sanction was expressed in the establishment of a birth control information center in the campus student center and in frank advertisements, photographs, and feature stories published in the student newspaper. An example of the supportive press coverage now given to birth control and family planning at the university was a special issue of *Capsules*, a weekend supplement of the *X-State Daily News* published in September, devoted entirely to "The Contraceptive Controversy." Presumably, the articles were part of an effort to orient incoming freshmen.

The cover of the eight-page supplement showed photographs of various contraceptive devices and preparations. The articles inside told where the campus birth control information center was located and explained the services available there; they argued against the no-abortion policy of the local hospital; they told how abortions could be obtained in nearby cities and cited the addresses, telephone numbers, and fees of the various clinics; and they described the birth control educational programs and supply services of the local Planned Parenthood office. There was also a coed's account of an abortion and articles entitled "Contraceptives: Ticklish Issue" and "Abortion Claims: Safe? Legal?"

The article in which the student told the story of her abortion contained an explanation of the basis for her decision.

My fiance and I weren't getting married for another year and were unable to support a child let alone ourselves. Besides that, I was unable emotionally to cope with carrying a child for nine months and supporting it afterwards. We also decided it would hurt both of our parents, so it was the quiet and most convenient way.

The staff members at the abortion clinic, she said, ". . . were extremely nice. They did not make you feel like some tramp off the streets. I respected them and they respected me, which relieved any doubts that I might have had." The piece ended with her statement that she would consider another abortion only "if having a child would cause my death"; but, about the abortion she had undergone, she said, "I have no regret."

Planned Parenthood in Middletown keeps records of the method of fertility control selected by its patients. The most popular method of fertility control, the birth control pill, was used by 82 percent of the Planned Parenthood "users" in 1979. Other methods used were: diaphragm (6 percent), intrauterine device (IUD) (4 percent), combination of foam and condom (4 percent), condom (1 percent), and sterilization (2 percent). One-third of 1 percent selected the "rhythm" method.

We must emphasize that the patients of Planned Parenthood are not a representative cross section of women in Middletown. They are much younger (one-third of those selecting a method of fertility control in 1979 were under 20, and most of the remainder were in their twenties), mostly single (over 70 percent of those reported a "family size" of "one"), and poorer (90 percent reported an annual income of $7,800 or less).

The patterns of contraceptive use among all women of childbearing age in Middletown are probably close to the national pattern. National figures on contraceptive use by married couples are available from the National Center for Health Statistics. In 1976, 30 percent of married couples with a wife of childbearing age were sterile, about two-thirds of them because of surgical sterilization. Of the 70 percent who were not sterile, 21 percent were not practicing contraception (almost two-thirds of these wives had just experienced a pregnancy, were seeking a pregnancy, or were pregnant at the time of the survey) and 49 percent were practicing contraception. In this population of "contraceptors," the distribution of methods was as follows: oral contraceptive pill, 46 percent; condom, 15 percent; IUD, 12 percent; rhythm, 7 percent; foam, 6 percent; and other methods, 8 percent (Ford 1978, 2). If we can judge from the national data, there was a significant increase during the 1970s in the proportion of couples selecting surgical sterilization as a method of fertility control. The national population of married couples, and presumably the married population of Middletown, place less reliance on the oral contraceptive pill than do patients of Planned Parenthood in Middletown, although the pill is still by far the most popular method of contraception.

Prostitution, Homosexuality, and Other Variations

In *Middletown in Transition*, the Lynds said that their earlier study of Middletown had been "in error in underestimating the extent of prostitution in the city," and they reported that at one time Middletown had been the center of prostitution in the eastern part of the state. In June of 1935, the city had just "cleaned out" a red-light district occupying five square blocks in the central part of town, and there was some evidence that "informal prostitution" at that time was on the upswing, partly as a result of the increased availability of girls and women due to economic need, the more widespread knowledge of contraception, and the convenience of the automobile as "a house of prostitution on wheels" (Lynd and Lynd 1937, 163-64).

By the 1970s, organized prostitution in Middletown seemed to have fallen on hard times. Said a local police officer who had grown up in the city:

I grew up in the end of the late 1940s, early 1950s. There were several houses of prostitution commonly known. I know firsthand of three or four different houses known by the police at that time. They were left alone. About 1955 some of these closed or just went out of business. Probably it had something to do with change in city administrations, and with madams getting up in age. After that era—about 1955—the only house I know of was down on the _____block of South Liberty, run by a woman named _____. No one bothered her, as far as I know, and I was on the police department at that time.

I don't think there are any houses operating now. The modeling shop on _____, the only thing I can tell you about that place, about 1978 the police department closed that place down. It got a big splash in the paper. . . . As far as I know, it is still closed. We have an intelligence division that is supposed to know about things like that. If it is operating, somebody will soon do something about it. It started out as a massage/modeling-type deal. [The chief] thought there was prostitution going on. . . .

There are probably some hookers operating out of some of the motels, but there's not much problem getting a woman in Middletown if you want one.

The same police officer explained that there was a small population of homosexuals in the city and that the police knew of them but left them alone. "Apart from the public obscenity statutes, there's no particular problem with homosexuals here, nothing we can do. There's a couple of bars identified as homosexual spots, and once in a while another location, such as one where a manager is known to be a homosexual." A university professor said that in the late 1970s there had been an active "gay students organization" but that lately it had been fairly inactive, receiving little public attention. One of the local physicians commented that there had been an increase in the number of homosexuals who came to him for treatment.

I'm seeing more people with deviance problems, such as male homosexuals, worried about VD than I used to. They get VD in so many different locations that you don't know where to look. . . . If it appears to me that their emotions are a problem, I refer them to someone else.

The female homosexuals that I see are generally not discontented. They establish long-term relationships that are quite stable, in contrast to the male homosexual.

The explicit sex magazines available at the university bookstore cater to a homosexual population as well as to heterosexual population. One of the campus counselors explained that "the one thing that the bookstore has tried to draw a line on is the drug-related magazines such as *High Times*, although I did see a copy behind the counter a couple of months ago." Added a sociology professor at the university:

Today's material available at the X State University bookstore is incredibly explicit, including oral sex and group sex, and sometimes female homosexual sex. Ten years ago anyone who sold such magazines would have been arrested and run out of town.

Since pornography is defined by community standards, it is hard to say that what is sold to the university students in the student bookstore is porn. By the community standard definition, if the city wanted to, they could probably shut down all of the adult bookstores.

When the manager of one of the adult bookstores was asked about what his customers were like, he said:

The majority of my customers, I would estimate, are married. Most are between 25 and 50. Almost all are men. I'm lucky if I see five women in here a month. Those that do come in are either with men or they come in in a group. I never see a woman in here alone. . . . I get people in here from every occupation; I get people who work for the city, people who work for CETA, who work in factories. I get some university students, maybe 5 percent of all who come in. People think students come in a lot, but they don't. They'd rather spend their money on the movies. You go to college, you see girls every day, you don't need this.

Some of the magazines for sale on his shelves showed girls who appeared to be in their early teens or younger. When asked whether child pornography was legal, he said that all the models for the sexually explicit photographs were over 18. "They just dress them up to make them look young," he said. "I'm against child pornography; it gives the business a bad name."

The manager firmly rejected the idea that there might be a link between pornography and antisocial behavior. The adult book-stores, he said, exist because they satisfy a human need. They help people.

You mean do I think someone reads this stuff and then goes out and rapes or kills someone? No, I think this gives people a release, it helps people more than anything. I don't think it causes anyone to go out and do anything bad. Not everyone is Robert Redford and can go out and get a date every night.

A sizable proportion of the Middletown population is disturbed by what it sees as a deterioration of moral sentiment in the young. Some Middletowners tie this perceived deterioration specifically to the relaxed sexual standards of the age. Others are more concerned about a "welfare mentality" and an unwillingness to bear the responsibility for one's own actions.

An administrator of the juvenile division of Middletown's police department, who frequently dealt with cases of child abuse and neglect took the view that there had been a decline in family feeling and that it was apparent in the attitudes of many of Middletown's young people.

Parents used to be more devoted to their children. The new generation have lived a little more promiscuously than their parents did. They get mad at the baby, maybe. People live together, then separate, then try a live-in relationship with the parents-in-law. We had an example in a case not too long ago. The [teenaged] mother named the baby a name the father thought was a sissy name, so he stepped on the baby's head. There is more family violence today. There isn't the compassion in the teenager group there used to be. I see this when they come in. Although we do have some very young parents who are very proud of their children. . . . Marriage makes a bond, a tie. Without that there is less compassion and responsibility for the child.

The members of older generations have always seemed to feel that the present generation is "going to the dogs." We might be able to attribute the notion that there has been a decline in moral feeling to this respondent's occupational experience. Whether or not the perception is accurate, it is shared widely enough to be a significant aspect of the contemporary social reality of Middletown. It may not accurately represent how things are, but it is how people think they are.

A related view was expressed by a teacher in the city's Premarital Pregnancy Program.

The girls have a total welfare attitude. They see no expense for the baby beyond having the baby. The state won't pick up the tab for the baby's birth if they marry before the baby is born. . . . They don't seem to resent the boys at all. By the time they get to us, they're very accepting of it. . . . Though they have an ongoing relationship to the father of the child, they remain open to dating other boys. They don't necessarily assume that the boys [the fathers] will marry them. . . . They experience much less stigma than before; they're keeping their babies.

It may be that the benefits to children of the decreased stigma of being born out of wedlock more than compensate for the costs to society of the "total welfare attitude" of the mothers.

One consequence of changing community standards is an inability to understand the conflicts that provide the tension in some of our classical literary works. In the late 1970s, premarital sex among adolescents was "no big deal." In 1979 a Middletown high school teacher questioned her students about the meaning of Hawthorne's *The Scarlet Letter*. "What can we learn from Hester Prynne?" she asked. The response from many of the students was that "people shouldn't get so worked up over nothing."

Summing It Up

Despite a shortage of "hard" data on the sexual attitudes and activities of Middletown in the 1920s, we can make some generalizations about change. Among them are the following, which are supported by the impressionistic evidence from Middletown itself, sometimes buttressed by more quantitative findings of national or regional studies.

1. Middletown people in the 1970s were more tolerant of diversity than they were in the 1920s, and this tolerance extends to different codes of sexual morality and varieties of sexual expression. In a word, Middletown is less "uptight" about sex than it used to be.
2. Middletown adolescents, especially females, are more apt to participate in premarital sex than they were in the 1920s, and they become sexually active at an earlier age.
3. Information about human sexuality, including birth control, is far more widely distributed today.

4. Abortion, the use of contraceptives, and sterilization are more common than they used to be.
5. Pornography is more readily available.

Many Middletown adults, but certainly not a majority of them, express concern about an apparent decline in the "moral fiber" of today's young people. Presumably, such concern about a younger generation is a perpetual consequence of the strain between a rising generation and an established one, but some of the specific issues raised about the personal and social consequences of premarital sexual permissiveness merit much more systematic attention from researchers than they have received.

For example, how compatible is permissive sexuality during adolescence and early adulthood with subsequent marital stability and satisfaction?[5] Is a generation of young people steeped in permissive sexuality different from one raised under stricter normative (although not necessarily behavioral) standards with respect to willingness to sacrifice self-interest for the interests of the collectivity, be it family, community, or nation?

There is evidence that religious people experience more guilt over premarital sex than do the irreligious (Gunderson and McCray, 1979). Our study of religion in Middletown confirms the continued vitality of organized religion there: about half of the city's adults attend church more than once a month, and about a third attend weekly. Apparently, many of these churchgoers, at least many of the teenagers and young adults, are also sexually permissive. Some study of their guilt-reduction techniques or their other modes of coping with personal value conflicts would be very illuminating. Christensen (1969) showed that the negative psychological consequences of premarital intercourse are less common in more permissive societies, and it may be that long-term psychological costs are minimized by involvement in social networks that support the "new morality."

Similarly, the long-term consequences of abortion have received too little attention from researchers, although there has been considerable research on the short-term effects. One author, after reviewing the results of more than 40 studies of the social and psychological effects of abortion, concluded that "abortion itself is often stressful and can be stigmatizing." She called for "continuing research on the negative effects of abortion, and for interventions designed to diminish those negative effects for all concerned" (Adler 1979; see also Bracken et al. 1974 and Smith 1973).

Another neglected topic is the study of the relationship between sexual permissiveness and permissiveness in other aspects of life. More than a century ago, Tocqueville reminded us that religion in the United States was mingled "with all the habits of the nation and all the feelings of patriotism," and he said that "the Americans, having admitted the principal doctrines of the Christian religion without inquiry, are obligated to accept in like manner a great number of moral truths originating in it and connected with it" (Tocqueville 1876, 5-6). Prominent among those moral truths were the Christian standards of sexual purity, the commandments against adultery and fornication. If we accept Tocqueville's idea that the vitality of the American republic was connected to the vitality of its religious life, it follows that changes in sexual morality might have consequences for the public order and for social solidarity generally.

A more recent affirmation that sexual permissiveness is linked to negative personal and social consequences was made by Pitirim Sorokin in his book, *The American Sexual Revolution* (1956). Many of Sorokin's dogmatic assertions about the deleterious consequences of sexual permissiveness were ridiculed or ignored by social scientists, but they have not been tested. It is notable that, 25 years after the appearance of *The American Sexual Revolution*, we remain unable to demonstrate scientifically the effects of premarital and extramarital sex on people's mental health, moral integrity, personal happiness, and altruism.

Therefore, we must conclude this discussion of sex in Middletown with an emphasis on what we are not sure about, rather than what we know. There *have* been some striking changes in sexual attitudes and behavior in Middletown. Unfortunately, we are unable to tell what the individual and social consequences of these changes will be, either in the microcosm of Middletown or in the nation as a whole. But the range of possible scenarios offered by journalists and evangelists is extremely broad, extending from a situation in which premarital sexual permissiveness simply is defined as another stage of growing up that has little long-term relevance to the scenario in which teenage sexuality and other manifestations of an ethic of short-run hedonism corrode the willingness and ability of the citizenry to live together peacefully and to protect themselves from external threats to their safety and freedom. It is time that family researchers set about to document the personal, community, and national consequences of the changes in sexual attitudes and behavior that have been experienced by Americans in the past generation.

Chapter 9

Kinship

It used to be thought that families living in modern cities had little contact with their relatives. This idea was suggested when people compared the apparent individualism of their own family lives with their fondly held, though often misguided, images of the "good old days." During the past two decades, there has been much careful research on kinship ties, and the general findings of these studies are (1) that kinship ties are extremely important in contemporary urban society and (2) that the existence of a vital, all-embracing extended family of the "good old days" was mostly a myth.

As one urban sociologist put it, "Independent nuclear families . . . may be the predominant type of household in all societies. Prior to industrialization, this form may be common mostly because of concrete circumstances; after industrialization, it may also become the culturally preferred pattern" (Abrahamson 1976, 97). Another analysis of family patterns in the United States during the twentieth century arrived at a similar conclusion.

Recent historical studies show the myth of the extended family household to be just that—a myth. The nuclear family, consisting of parents living with their own children and no other adults, has been the predominant family form in America since the earliest period on which historians have data. . . . Relationships among relatives appear to have been historically what they are now: complex patterns of companionship and help that only occasionally involve sharing bed and board. . . . At the same time that historians have been exposing the myth of the extended household, sociologists have been showing that contemporary families have very real kinship networks (Bane 1976, 37).

That obligations to, and cooperation with, relatives persist in modern urban settings has been shown by Ivan Nye (1976) and his associates. From a review of the family literature and from their own research, they concluded that a kinship role is one of eight essential components of the contemporary family (the other seven are providing, housekeeping, child caring, child socializing, sexual, recreational, and therapeutic roles). Their research shows that most people do accept obligations to their kin and that they do disapprove of the nonperformance of kinship duties.

Other studies have found the same strong sense of an obligation to maintain contact with relatives. As many as 85 percent of urban adults recognize an obligation to keep in touch with their parents (Adams 1968, 80). The duty includes telephone conversations as well as face-to-face contact: "Failing to communicate by telephone is as much a breach of kinship obligations as any other failure to interact" (Leichter and Mitchell 1967, 104-5).

A recent, authoritative summary of what is known about relationships between generations of the same family (Troll and Bengtson 1979) concluded that, more often than not, children are similar to their parents. The similarity does not seem to depend on how close to their parents children *feel*. Most parents and children in the United States and in all other highly modernized societies maintain fairly strong relationships throughout life, although the parent-child tie comes under special stress during adolescence. Because kinship obligations are not conditional on agreement in values or opinions ("You can choose your friends, but your relatives are just born"), relationships between close kin are likely to remain strong even when they have little common ground.

Women are generally more active than men in maintaining kinship ties. "Most families around the world seem to be linked through women," Lillian Troll and Vern Bengtson wrote, and "Ties between mother and daughter are closer than those between mother and son, or between father and either daughter or son" (Troll and Bengtson 1979, 153).

Ties to kin are more durable and more flexible than ties to friends. Adults are more likely to turn to relatives than to friends for help during times of trouble. Their relationships with kin persist across time and space, while those with friends are likely to fade after a move to another place or into another social stratum (Troll and Bengtson 1979, 155).

Kinship Ties in Middletown during the 1920s

The nuclear family—parents and their children living together in one household—was the "family" the Lynds studied in *Middletown*. They did not investigate the interrelationships of Middletown's nuclear families, but they did give some tantalizing hints that invited further attention.

From the absence of evidence to the contrary, we infer the suggestion that kinship was not an important force making for community solidarity in Middletown. Kinship ties were not mentioned by the Lynds in their chapter on "things making and unmaking group solidarity"; they considered the effects of class and religion, the Chamber of Commerce and community basketball, patriotism and civic loyalty, but not kinship. Similarly, relatives outside the nuclear family seemed to play no part in "caring for the unable," for the Lynds' chapter on that topic covered person-to-person giving and three types of organizational support for "the unable," but it did not mention relatives.

A second hint about kinship in *Middletown* is that people's values were said to be like their relatives'. "A person's political party is usually determined, like his religion, by his family" (Lynd and Lynd 1929, 415), they wrote, but whether such influence reached beyond the immediate family they did not say. Neither grandparents nor other relatives were mentioned as significant contributors to a child's education in the eight chapters on "training the young" and "making a home."

Another hint: there were some three-generation households in Middletown in 1925. Parents of grown children sometimes provided a home for their divorced children (and presumably for their offspring) (Lynd and Lynd 1929, 127), and the Lynds quoted an advertisement for Go-to-Church Week that included grandparents as part of the family: "Very helpful to every member of the family, from gray-haired Grandpa down to Wee Baby Bessie" (Lynd and Lynd 1929, 369).

Finally, there are numerous details in *Middletown* that suggest that frequency of interaction with relatives in the 1920s was lower than in the earlier decades. Clubs and organized leisure activities were described as having supplanted family gatherings. "Accompanying this incipient decline in home parties is the almost total disappearance of whole-family parties before the specialized parties for each age group and the self-sufficient social system of the high school" (Lynd and Lynd 1929, 280). The introduction of the automobile explains a decline in family get-togethers. "It has done much to render obsolete the leisurely Sunday noon dinner of a generation ago at which extra leaves had to be put in the table for the company of relatives and friends who sat down to the great Sunday roast" (Lynd and Lynd 1929, 153). A deterioration of kinship interaction is also implicit in the response of a working-class woman who had visited her adult daughters only twice during the previous two months, although one of them lived only a block away (Lynd and Lynd 1929, 310).

The Lynds suggested, however, in other places that modernization had increased some types of kinship interaction in Middletown. The automobile facilitated more frequent visits to relatives living some distance away, and at least one respondent told the Lynds that having a car had made family visiting easier. "We used to go to his sister's to visit, but by the time we'd get the children shoed and dressed there wasn't any money for car fare. Now no matter how they look, we just poke 'em in the car and take 'em along" (Lynd and Lynd 1929, 255-56).

The telephone also must have changed the nature and frequency of people's contacts with relatives. The Lynds referred to "the attenuation of visiting to telephone visiting" as one of the changes that had taken place since 1890 (Lynd and Lynd 1929, 275), but not with specific reference to relatives.

Kinship and Community Solidarity Today

Preeminent among the bonds that unite Middletown's families in the 1970s and create community solidarity is the bond of kinship. Its crisscrossing and overlapping sets of mutual obligations and shared identities directly affect at least three-quarters of the city's population. Although most of Middletown's families live in one-family dwellings where the family consists of a married couple, a married couple with children, or a single parent and children, the majority of these two-generation nuclear families are related to members of other families in Middletown.

Much of the "community solidarity" of Middletown is really kinship solidarity. When there are relatives living in town, especially close ones—parents, brothers and sisters, or grown children—they are seen, talked to, and visited more frequently than are friends or neighbors. When Middletown people need assistance or advice, they are apt to turn to their relatives, if there are any available, and usually there are.

While living in Middletown, members of the research staff were repeatedly impressed by the way people's lives were influenced by their relatives. The Middletowners we knew were not isolated urbanites. Rather, they were caught up in complicated patterns of family responsibility. To illustrate the pattern that affects, according to the survey data, most of the city's households, let us mention some of the relationships to kin exhibited by local people who worked for the Middletown III project. A temporary secretary on the project staff, a divorcee, lived with her mother, who tended her children during the day. One research assistant frequently visited her parents, who lived in a local nursing home. Another lived with her parents after going through a divorce. Medical appointments, car trouble, job interviews, and decisions about renting an apartment were all occasions for a mother-daughter visit. One staff member lived in a house her parents owned and provided for her and her roommate. Another's parents lived in Middletown, and, when he visited them, which he often did, he always called on his grandmother, who lived in the same house.

Despite a tendency to take pervasive kinship obligations and activities for granted, there is plenty of information about them in the Middletown press. Embedded in local and regional stories are the names and accomplishments of Middletown citizens and their forebears. Feature stories on prominent local people often include references to their parents, children, and grandchildren, and sometimes even the street addresses of grown children are mentioned.

Stories about festivals, celebrations, and even the occasional "Middletown Is Talking" feature in which a reporter asks a few people to comment on some timely issue, contain references to kin. In a 1979 piece, the writer of the "Our Neighborhood" column (who refers to himself as the OT&T [the Old Trader and Trapper]) talked about a visit to the science complex of the state university in Middletown, where he encountered a biologist, ". . . a pleasant gentleman who hails from the Pennville neighborhood and some of his kinfolk are known to the OT&T." The same day's column contained a relevant comment on politics and kinship in Middletown. "If only the relatives of the candidates for mayor turn out, they may bring quite a number to the polls" (Middletown's morning newspaper, April 5, 1979). A 1977 newspaper article about the eightieth anniversary of the local Catholic church contained an account of reminiscences by the son of the contractor who built the church, listed the grown children of the late contractor and told where they lived, named longtime members of the church who were nephews of the first resident pastor, and named the parents of the pastors and copastors of the church and told where they lived (Middletown's morning newspaper, July 4, 1977).

Of course, kinship ties are especially salient at the high points of the festival cycle. When six persons downtown on December 14 were asked by a newspaper reporter, "Does it seem like Christmastime to you yet?" two of them mentioned relatives in their responses. A young receptionist said, "Yeah, because my nieces are real excited, they talked to Santa Claus. I'm in the mood of Christmas spirit." And a woman who worked in the county courthouse said, "Uh-ha, because of the shops and the cold air. I've got lots of grandkids and you have to get started shopping" (Middletown's evening newspaper, December 14, 1976).

People's family ties are also highlighted in the life-style sections of the newspapers, where there are often long articles about the officers of local organizations or other exemplary citizens. A piece on the president of the alumnae of a local sorority noted that her two daughters lived in Middltown, as did several of the daughters' grown children.

Another way to describe the ties to kin that contribute to community solidarity is to summarize the results of our kinship survey. Take any resident of the city at random. The odds are one in five that he or she has a brother or sister living in the city, one in three that one or both of his or her parents live there, and two in five that he or she has more distant relatives—grandparents, aunts, uncles, cousins—who live in Middletown, also.

We have already said that the Lynds' chapter "Things Making and Unmaking Group Solidarity in Middletown" did not refer to kinship ties. Presumably, the oversight was a matter of perspective; they visualized community solidarity in terms of community organizations—political, religious, educational, and charitable. In retrospect, the oversight is regrettable, for it seems obvious to us that in today's Middletown most families are linked to clusters of families by kinship obligations and affections that are often far stronger than their connections with friends, co-workers, or fellow members of organizations. Middletown's solidarity, in our opinion, is based on crosscutting networks of families. In other words, adults in Middletown families interact not only with members of their own nuclear families but with one or more local families that contain their parents, their grown children, or their brothers and sisters.

Of the 478 respondents in our kinship survey 69 percent said that at least one of their parents was living; and, in almost half of these cases, the parent(s) lived in Middletown. When we add those whose parents lived within 50 miles, we account for 62 percent of those with living parents. Eighty-seven percent of the sample had living brothers or sisters, and nearly half of these had a brother or sister in Middletown. Forty-two percent of the respondents had one or more grown children; of these, 71 percent had a grown child living in Middletown. Besides their "primary kin"—children, siblings, and parents—Middletown adults recognize obligations to more distant relatives. Thirty-eight percent had at least one such relative living in Middletown, and the median number reported was six.

Relatives: How Many and How Far?

One of the studies that showed us that kinship ties are alive and well in American cities was Bert Adams's 1963-1964 survey of 799 young and middle-aged married adults in Greensboro, North Carolina (Adams 1968). Much of Adams's book was devoted to comparisons between families in two main occupational strata (blue-collar and white-collar) with respect to kinship activity. Adams gathered information both about the "objective" dimensions of kinship relations—the number of visits, telephone calls, and letters between his respondents and their relatives and their joint activities—and the "subjective" dimensions—how close people felt to their relatives and whether they identified with them or held similar values. Because we had no kinship items from the Lynd surveys to build upon, it seemed appropriate to replicate, as far as possible, Adams's survey. His blue-collar/white-collar classification is compatible with the Lynds' business-class/working-class dichotomy, which was an essential part of our own analytical scheme. Accordingly, many of the items in our kinship questionnaire were drawn from Adams's interview schedule (adaptation was sometimes necessary to make them suitable for a mailed questionnaire rather than a personal interview), and part of our discussion of kinship in Middletown will parallel Adams's treatment of kinship in Greensboro.

The general purpose of this chapter is to describe the kin relationships of Middletown residents, and that purpose is not served by detailed comparisons between Middletown and Greensboro. Before meaningful comparisons could be made, the historic and demographic differences between the cities would have to be systematically considered, and the effects of the 15-year time difference between the studies would have to be taken into account. There is also a difference in the way the samples were defined. Adams's sample was limited to white adults married 20 years or less; the Middletown sample was a cross section of the entire adult population. It may be that a careful comparison between the two surveys could provide some indication of trends in kinship behavior during the 15-year interval that separates them. Such a comparison, however, would be tangential to our present purpose, which is to determine whether the kinship system observed in Greensboro can also be found in Middletown.

Following Adams, we asked each respondent to enumerate those relatives that he or she would recognize when passing them on the street (Adams called such relatives kin acquaintances.) The respondents were asked how many of the other relatives (we had asked about parents and brothers and sisters earlier, so other relatives referred to those outside the nuclear family) resided in each of five distance categories, which ranged from "in Middletown" to "more than 500 miles away." Then, we asked how many lived in each of eight state or regional categories, beginning with a separate category for Indiana. The two questions provided a useful reliability check for the enumeration of kin; people were less likely to make a rough approximation of the number of their kin when they had to specify where each of them lived. Comparable questions had been asked earlier about the location of parents, brothers and sisters, and grown children.

Adams used the same method, except that his distance and state categories were combined in a single 10-category system. Our use of two separate systems was dictated by the fact that Middletown is not as evenly "embedded" in Indiana as is Greensboro in North Carolina.

Our sample of 478 adults—for specific items, it was slightly smaller because some people did not answer every question—gave us information about 324 parental households, 1,293 siblings, 466 grown children, and 8,530 kin acquaintances. The mean number of kin acquaintances reported by our respondents was 18.1. Respondents listed a total of 2,285 living members of their families of orientation and procreation (excluding children under age 18, but including brothers and sisters of all ages), a mean of 4.8 per respondent.

The distributions of these categories of kin by distance shows a surprising degree of local concentration. Members of the respondents' immediate families were especially concentrated in Middletown. (See Appendix A, Table 9-1.) Fifty-four percent of the grown children, 43 percent of the parents, and 31 percent of the brothers and sisters of our respondents lived right in Middletown.

The data also reveal distinct patterns of localism for parent-child, sibling, and other relationships. Parents and children are most heavily concentrated in the Middletown area. Three-fifths of the surviving parents of the entire sample lived within 50 miles of Middletown. About half of all the respondents' brothers and sisters lived within the same 50-mile radius, as did about one-third of the kin acquaintances.

The state or regional location of these same persons is also of interest. The relatives of Middletown people were heavily concentrated within the state boundaries. Three-fourths of the parents (and the same proportion of grown children), three-fifths of the siblings, and over half of the kin acquaintances of the sample lived in Indiana; most of the remander lived in adjoining states. (See Appendix A, Table 9-2.)

Adams's sample was designed "to guarantee maximum extension of the kin network" (Adams 1968, 9), and so it was not surprising that the total number of kin acquaintances reported by the young and middle-aged married persons in Greensboro was considerably larger than that for the Middletown sample, which included adults of all ages and marital statuses. All of the Greensboro respondents had some kin acquaintances; the range was from 2 to 585. The corresponding range in Middletown was from 0 to 410 kin acquaintances, with a mean of 18 and a median of 8 (versus 39 and 28, respectively, for Greensboro). Even when we adjust our range of variation to correspond roughly to the Greensboro range by excluding Middletown respondents having no kin acquaintances, the mean and median for Middletown are only pushed up to 20 and 10, respectively. Also, there were fewer instances of very large networks of kin in Middletown; over 5 percent of Adams's subjects recorded over 100 kin acquaintances, compared with just 2 percent of Middletown adults.

Do sex and occupation affect the size of the kinship network? Adams argued that, in view of the greater role of women in kin affairs, there ought to be sex differences. Indeed, he found that women reported slightly more kin acquaintances than men (a median of 30, versus 26 for men). He also found that middle-class (white-collar) respondents listed more kin acquaintances than working-class (blue-collar) people, although the differences were affected by respondents' histories of occupational mobility as well as their current class positions. Middle-class women were acquainted with more kin than working-class women; and middle-class men, with slightly more than working-class men (Adams 1968, 19-21).

In Middletown women did not report more extensive kinship networks than men. The mean number of kin acquaintances was 18 for women, 17 for men. However, when we confine the analysis to married women, some sex and class[1] differences appear. Business-class women's greater involvement with kin will be relevant throughout this chapter.

Among young adults in Greensboro, 60 percent of both men and women had parents living within 100 miles, but men were somewhat more likely to have their parents living in the same city. Working-class people were more likely to have their parents living in the city (Adams 1968, 25-26, 99, 148). In Middletown we find a variation in localism by class but not by sex. Sixty-one percent of both males and females had parents living in Middletown or within 50 miles. Fifty percent of the business-class men and 48 percent of the business-class women had parents living within 50 miles, compared to 67 percent of the working-class women and 72 percent of the working-class men. Moreover, the greater localism of working-class respondents was apparent in every category of relative. (Appendix A, Table 9-3, shows the class differences in localism for women. Differences of the same order, or larger, were found for the men.)

Familial Obligations

Almost everyone in Middletown agrees that people ought to keep in touch with their relatives. In answer to a direct question, 86 percent of the respondents in the family role survey said that they recognized an obligation to maintain contact with their close relatives. The question was asked differently in the kinship survey, with opportunities to distinguish between types of obligation and with reference to specific relatives. Still, the obligation to parents and siblings was consistently affirmed.

Middletown people seem to regard keeping in touch with relatives more as a pleasure than as a duty. However, to say that one enjoys seeing one's relatives does not mean that there is no obligation to them. In discussing the relationship between enjoyment and obligation among young adults in Greensboro, Adams made the point that enjoyment may mask obligation. "For him, contact is pleasant, and the attempt to discover whether he would keep in touch out of concern or duty, were his enjoyment to lessen, results in hypothetical fancy" (Adams 1968, 79-80). Despite this presumed effect, most of Adams's respondents mentioned one or another type of obligation as an important reason for maintaining contacts with kin.

Adams identified two types of kinship obligation: a general obligation to keep in touch and a more specific obligation to provide needed assistance. Eighty-five percent of his respondents acknowledged either one or both types of obligation to their parents (Adams 1968). In this respect, our Middletown sample was remarkably like Adams's Greensboro sample; the corresponding figure for Middletown was 87 percent. Adams found the obligation to maintain contact about three times more prevalent than the obligation to help. In Middletown the obligation to help was mentioned more frequently than it was in Greensboro; the obligation to keep in contact was recognized by 73 percent of the Middletown sample, and the obligation to help was recognized by 64 percent. (See Appendix A, Table 9-4.)

Obligations to siblings are less widely recognized than obligations to parents. A general obligation to keep in touch with parents was acknowledged by three-fourths of the Middletown adults. Fifty-eight percent accepted such an obligation for siblings and 36 percent for cousins. The obligation to help showed the same gradient from 64 percent for parents to 44 percent for siblings and 30 percent for cousins. What this seems to mean is that, though the majority accept a responsibility to keep in touch with most of the close relatives, it is only to parents or grown children that they owe material assistance.

Let us see whether we can summarize the norms that govern relations with kin in contemporary Middletown. (1) People should enjoy contacts with their relations. (2) Children and parents and brothers and sisters are mutually obligated to remain in permanent contact. (3) Parents and their grown children are mutually obligated to provide needed help, if at all possible. There is much less obligation of this kind between siblings and practically none between cousins.

The differences in obligation were expressed by one 63-year-old, business-class man.

I tell our kids that they should be decent to each other. That they do not have an inherent obligation to take care of each other; that's my obligation. If they want to help each other that's their option, not mandatory. I know that's unusual, but I make a distinction. Sure, it's nice to have a close-knit family where everybody's responsible for everybody else. . . . Yes, I think they have an obligation to keep in touch.

Although this man thought that his distinction between the obligation to keep in touch and the obligation to take care of each other was an unusual one, Table 9-4 suggests that it is quite common. Parents and children are obligated to keep in touch and to provide material help; brothers and sisters are obligated to keep in touch but not to help.

Even in the parent-child relationship, there are definite limits to the required reciprocal obligation. It will be recalled that three out of four parents and two out of three grown children listed "they need my help" as a reason for contact. But they often took pains to point out the limits. One woman (a 35-year-old, business-class housewife) spoke of a situation 10 years in the future.

I'm trying to give everybody, all the children, a good preparation. And I expect that when they leave home, leave my support, that that'll be the end of it. I know better. It's not going to be. And they'll always have my love and psychological support. But I also don't want anybody hanging around. There won't be a useless kid of 23 leeching off his parents from this house. It will not happen. So on that basis I intend to have as much close and friendly relationships with my children as possible, and as supportive. But I also expect that they won't be living with me.

Sometimes, the intention to keep kinship obligations within reasonable limits does not work out. In our family dynamics survey, one working-class woman (47 years old) said that she had gone out to work chiefly to escape the demands of her grown children and her aged mother. If she had not had a job, she said:

I think I'd be babysitting every day with my grandchildren. I mean my time wouldn't be my own. This way . . . I think I feel better. . . . When I first started working, I couldn't do anything else, so I did housework. . . . My mother . . . used to hint about, "Oh, I wish somebody'd come and clean up my house." I'd say, "Yeah, mine needs to be cleaned up, too."

Despite her defensive strategy, this woman remained deeply involved with her relatives, as shown by her description of a typical evening at home.

Came home, just thought I'd lay down and take me a little rest. Took an Excedrin. Well, I fixed me a hamburger, laid down. My mother called me, talked to me for about an hour. And then I thought about going out to wash dishes, well, I told her I had to. And then one of my daughters came over. She was upset about something in her family. So, there was two of us sitting there, so there I sat until about eleven. Then, my son came by, and he wanted a sandwich. Well, that was my day!

When we compare the reasons men and women give for keeping in touch with relatives, we find that women more often cite enjoyment as the reason. Men are more likely to mention a general obligation, at least with reference to their parents.

The kinship literature suggests that working-class (blue-collar) and business-class (white-collar) people differ in their perceptions of kinship obligations. Adams proposed the theory that working-class people place more emphasis on a general obligation while business-class people have a more contractual orientation (1968, 80-81). His Greensboro data provided only modest support for this notion, and the Middletown data do not support it at all. The proportions of Middletown respondents citing enjoyment, general obligation, or the need for help as reasons for maintaining contact did not vary significantly from one class to the other. And the differences that did appear were in the direction *opposite* from that predicted: 73 percent of business-class women recognized a general obligation to keep in touch with parents, compared to 50 percent of working-class women; and 50 percent of business-class men, compared to 77 percent of working-class men, referred to the parents' need for help. On balance, the class differences in reasons for keeping in touch with parents seem ambiguous and not very important; the sex differences are much sharper.

Contact and Communication

Evidence from earlier research tells us that the major determinants of the amount of interaction between relatives are the distance between their homes and the closeness of their relationship (Reiss 1962, 334 and 337). Frequent interaction is difficult when people live far apart; on the other hand, people who live in the same community may not interact even when they have the opportunity. Proximity creates the opportunity for continual interaction; it is a necessary but not a sufficient condition.

We showed earlier that the relatives of our Middletown sample were a little more likely to live in or near the city than the relatives of Adams's Greensboro sample. Seventy-two percent of our respondents had parents living within 100 miles of Middletown, compared to 60 percent of the Greensboro respondents. Nearest (by age) siblings[2] and best-known cousins were a little closer, too;

the proportions living within 100 miles were 58 and 57 percent, respectively, for Middletown compared to 52 and 49 percent for Greensboro. In both places, the residential distribution of best-known cousins (Adams 1968, 96 and 143), was almost precisely the same as that of near siblings. Inasmuch as best-known cousins are about as available for interaction as near siblings, it follows that any differences we find between interaction with cousins and interaction with siblings can serve as a measure of their relative social distance.

Having noted that living nearby makes it easy to visit relatives, let us ignore that effect for the moment and find out how often relatives see each other or communicate in other ways. According to our kinship survey, 48 percent of the Middletown adults with living parents see them at least weekly and about 80 percent see them at least monthly. Contact with near siblings is about half that frequent; 23 percent saw their closest brother or sister at least weekly and 41 percent at least monthly.

Middletown people get together with their cousins much less often than with their brothers and sisters or parents. Very few (5 percent) see their best-known cousins every week or even every month (15 percent), although these cousins do not live any farther away than the brothers and sisters they see so often.

Our findings about frequency of contact with parents, siblings, and best-known cousins closely parallel those reported by Adams. Where there are differences (only 34 percent of the Greensboro respondents saw their parents every week, for example), they are largely attributable to the greater concentration of the Middletown relatives.

We can look at this matter another way by asking what proportion of Middletown adults seldom or never see their parents, near siblings, and best-known cousins. Asked about the previous two years, only 2 percent indicated that they had seen their parents only once or not at all. Virtually every adult in Middletown who has living parents sees them at least once a year; about 90 percent see their near siblings and 75 percent see their best-known cousins that often.

Some of the constraints imposed by distance can be overcome by other forms of communication. Even when relatives live nearby, visiting is nearly always supplemented by telephone calls. These communications with relatives show much the same pattern as visiting. (See Appendix A, Table 9-5.) Almost everyone talks with his or her primary relatives by telephone, normally more than once a month with parents, about half as often with brothers and sisters, and much less often with cousins. There is much less letter writing than telephoning, but it follows the same gradient as personal visiting and telephoning. About 1 out of 4 adults writes to a parent at least once a month, and 1 out of 10 writes that often to a brother or sister. Almost no one corresponds regularly with cousins; the majority (64 percent) never write letters to cousins, although they may exchange Christmas cards.

In Greensboro, Adams found that men saw their parents as much as women did but that women were more likely to see them *very* often (several times a week) (Adams 1968, 38-39). That difference did not appear in Middletown. Middletown men are as likely as women to see their parents more than once a week (32 and 30 percent, respectively). Similarly, men and women reported about the same amount of visiting with siblings and cousins. The women, however, communicated more often by telephone and letter with their parents and siblings, although not with their cousins.

In another of our surveys, we asked Middletown husbands and wives which spouse ought to be responsible for keeping in touch with the *husband's* relatives. Only 11 percent of the husbands and 7 percent of the wives opined that the wife was primarily responsible for communicating with her husband's relatives. However, when we asked about their actual behavior, it turned out that in about one family out of three the wife took care of communications with the husband's relatives.

The wife's "specialization" in matters of kinship also was evident in answers to a question about role competence. When asked how well they and their spouses kept in touch with relatives, most husbands rated their wives and wives rated themselves above average in that respect. (See Appendix A, Table 9-6.) Practically none of them were rated below average. Husbands, on the other hand, usually rated themselves unfavorably and were so rated by their wives.

Now, let us very briefly consider how interaction between close relatives is affected by sheer proximity. Nearly all those who see their parents often have them living nearby, and vice versa. Most of those whose parents live in Middletown or within an hour's drive of the city see their parents every week. But, when parents live more than 50 miles away, the frequency of visiting drops off sharply. Only a handful of those whose parents live farther than 50 miles away see them every week. Letters seem to substitute for personal contact. The farther away the parents live, the more often they are written to. More than half of the Middletown people whose parents live more than 500 miles away write to them at least monthly. Parents who live in town are telephoned more often than those within 50 miles and much more often than those farther away. Beyond 50 miles, the frequency is level, regardless of distance. (See Appendix A, Table 9-7.)

Brothers and sisters are treated in the same way. When the near sibling lives more than 100 miles away, there is little likelihood that he or she is visited on a weekly basis, and there is little frequent visiting of siblings who live just an hour away. About a fourth of those with near siblings living outside Middletown but less than 50 miles away visit weekly and more often, and the majority of those with near siblings living in town see them at least weekly. The farther away the brother or sister lived, the more letters were written, thus showing again how letters substitute for visits. But telephoning shows the same pattern as visiting; more telephone calls are made to brothers and sisters who live nearby. As with parents, there seems to be a threshold at about 50 miles and siblings who live a little beyond that limit are telephoned no more often than those a thousand miles away.

Activities and Mutual Aid

Knowing how often people see their relatives does not tell us what they do when they get together. To understand how kinship ties affect Middletown people, we must consider the joint activities of kin. In the Middletown III kinship survey, we asked a series of questions about the activities people shared with parents, near siblings, and best-known cousins, and we also inquired about mutual aid between respondents and their close relatives.

Our information about the kinds of things people do with their parents is based on a checklist of 12 activities that followed the question "In the past two years or so . . . how often have you

and your parent(s) engaged in the following types of activities together?'' For each activity, there were four possible answers ranging from "never" to "more than once a month." For the 112 men
and 183 women who answered the question, the percentages reporting a given activity "several times a year" or "more than once
a month"[3] are listed in Table 9-8.

Table 9-8
Activities with Parents

Activities	Men	Women
Commercial recreation	21%	24%
Home recreation, such as picnics, card playing, etc.	47	55
Outdoor recreation, such as fishing, hunting, and camping	16	17
Brief drop-in visits for conversation	66	66
Vacation visits	25	20
Large family reunions (including aunts, uncles, cousins)	20	14
Emergencies of any sort (sickness, death, etc.)	18	21
Working together at the same location or occupation	12	7
Baby-sitting	9	24
Happy occasions, such as birthdays and Christmas	56	68
Attending the same church or religious group	20	23
Shopping together	22	51

Source: Middletown III kinship survey, 1977.

When Middletown people get together with their parents, they
usually do one of three things: they just visit with each other, they
celebrate festive occasions, or they engage in home recreation.
Women have a fourth thing to do; they shop together. Other joint
activities with parents that involve a sizable proportion of the sample are taking part in commercial recreation, going for vacation visits, attending church together, and dealing with emergencies. For 3
of the 12 activities—baby-sitting, festive occasions, and shopping—
the women do more with their parents than the men do. There are

no joint activities in which men are more likely than women to engage.

Only two class differences reached statistical significance. Working-class men more often enlisted their parents as baby-sitters (17 percent versus 2 percent for business-class men) and more often joined their parents on festive occasions (65 percent versus 44 percent for business-class men).

The joint activities with parents reported by Middletown people were about the same as those reported in Greensboro. Adams found, as we did, that "home visits" (he combined brief visits for conversation and home recreation in this single category) and "ritual occasions" (such as Christmas and birthday celebrations) were the leading categories (Adams 1968, 52-53).

Adams discovered that "mutual aid" between generations flowed more from parents to their grown children than in the opposite direction. Fewer men than women received aid from their parents, and slightly more men than women gave aid to their parents (Adams 1968, 57-58).

The mutual aid that passes between Middletown adults and their parents is summarized in Appendix A, Table 9-9. The direction, of course, is affected by the type of aid. The flow of financial assistance is usually from parents to children; more than 40 percent of Middletown adults with living parents reported such assistance. It went both ways, however. About a fourth of the people with living parents had assisted them financially during the previous two years. As in Greensboro, women in Middletown were more likely than men to be helped by their parents, and for three kinds of help (advice on decisions, child care, and handiwork), the differences are statistically significant. The only instance in which men got more help from parents than women was in looking for work. Although women got more help from their parents, they did not give more. Men helped their parents as much as women did.

In Middletown 90 percent of the people with living parents said that they had given gifts to their parents and 80 percent said that they had received gifts from them within the preceding two years. Help during illnesses or emergencies was fairly well balanced between children and parents. Just over half of the sample had given such help to parents during the period, and just under half had received it from parents. Perhaps we can personalize these generalizations and percentages with some excerpts from the interviews. Here are remarks made by four young mothers, all in their early thirties.

My family has been sick. I have been very devoted to them. Now, my husband's parents, if they had sickness, he wouldn't know what to do. He doesn't like sickness. My father eats dinner over here every night. It's an unusual situation. First he had a lung removed, then he had a heart attack. So now he is living next door and he eats all of his meals with us.

My husband is good about helping other people. Any time his brother needs anything, and he lives 10 miles out in the country, he'll take off after work and go to his place and they'll work together. And his brother's just as good about coming back to help him. . . . I think it can be carried too far, people try to take advantage of you, but I am very proud of him that he can do things for people, and is willing to. And he's done so many things for my mom and my dad, even though my dad works at home, he just keeps putting off and putting off and my husband will get disgusted and he'll go down there and do things for Mother and, of course, she's just thrilled to death to have them done and out of the way.

My mom got me this baby-sitting job. She could have had it, and she said, "Well, you need the money, because your husband's laid off," and she gave it to me. . . . When I was little I sort of had a grudge against my father because my mom was divorced. But now I understand it more, I understand why they divorced. . . . Dad was up here only three weeks ago. . . . He called me yesterday, he wanted me to come down. He said he'd send me the money. Well, he's helped me quite a bit; . . . he usually sends me a little extra money each month; he always sends me something. He spoils me. He still treats me like I'm a child, when he's up here. If I go out and I'm gone two hours, he's worried to death. I guess he'll always be like that.

Our family and my sister's and brothers' families do yard cleaning every spring for my mother. It's kind of a family ritual. Also, my sister, mother, and I plant a garden every year on mother's property. Mother buys the seeds, my sister and I plant, and we all share the harvest.

Previous research has consistently shown less mutual aid between brothers and sisters than between parents and children. Adams quoted a 1959 study by Sussman showing that over half of a sample of families in Cleveland, Ohio, had exchanged assistance with siblings in a single month. Adams did not expect to find so high a level of aid in Greensboro because his question referred to the nearest sibling rather than to all siblings. Nevertheless, he was surprised to find that only 16 percent of his respondents reported exchanging assistance with that sibling during the previous two years (Adams 1968, 104-5). That finding puzzles us, too. In Middletown we discovered much more mutual aid between near siblings than that; 39 percent of the women and 30 percent of the men reported assistance to or from their near siblings during the previous two years. Working-class women reported the most assistance (43 percent); and business-class men, the least (27 percent).[4]

The activities Middletown people carry out in the company of their brothers, sisters, and cousins are much the same things they do with their parents, although the average frequency of each activity is lower for brothers and sisters and much lower for cousins. The activities with near siblings most frequently reported were casual visits, mutual festive occasions, and home recreation. The percentages engaging in each of these activities at least several times a year were 60, 51, and 41, respectively, for the women and 50, 41, and 35 for the men. Twenty-four percent of the women with siblings shopped with their near siblings several times a year, compared to only 7 percent of the men.

The most frequent activities involving cousins were exactly the same—casual visits, festive occasions, and home recreation. The percentages for women reporting these activities with their best-known cousins at least several times a year were 33, 24, and 13, respectively; the corresponding percentages for men were 26, 14, and 11. Women were significantly more likely than men to report joining their best-known cousins in festive occasions.

Subjective Dimensions of Kinship

Aside from feelings of obligation, relationships with relatives can be described in terms of affection, agreement, and identification. In Chapter 7, we compared Middletown adolescents and adults in their closeness to their parents and in their agreement with them on attitudes and values. We found a high level of affection and agreement for both groups, although Middletown adults were more likely than Middletown adolescents to want to be like their parents. In this chapter, we will consider some other subjective dimensions of kinship by asking (1) how sentiments of affection, agreement, and identification directed toward parents compare with similar feelings about near siblings and cousins and (2) what the variations in these sentiments by sex and social class are.

"Affection" is defined as being emotionally close to the other person in a relationship; "agreement" refers to similarity in attitudes and values; and "identification" means accepting the other person as a model. These dimensions[5] were measured in Adams's survey of Greensboro (Adams 1968, 5-6, 14-15) and in our Middletown kinship survey by three questions that each respondent answered separately with reference to his or her father, mother, near sibling, and best-known cousin. "How close would you say you are in your feelings toward your _____?"; "Do you and your _____ agree in your ideas and opinions about the things you consider really important in life?"; and "Would you like to be the kind of person your _____ is?" The two most positive response categories to each of these questions ("quite close" and "extremely close" on the first question; "yes, completely" and "yes, to a great extent" on the second question; and "in most ways" and "yes, completely" on the third question) were counted together. Thus, when we counted respondents who expressed affection for their fathers, we combined those who said they were quite close and those who said they were extremely close.

The Middletown women in our sample expressed more affection than the men for every category of relatives. Not only did they express affection more frequently, mothers received more filial affection than fathers. The distribution of affection has three distinct levels: highest for mothers, next highest for fathers and near siblings, lowest for best-known cousins. Thus, in Middletown, as elsewhere, women are the "specialists" in kinship. (See Appendix A, Table 9-10.)

Agreement showed another pattern. Women agreed with all their relatives more than men did, but not significantly more with one parent than the other and no more with parents than with brothers and sisters. Men expressed slightly more agreement with both parents than with siblings, but the difference was not significant. Cousins, again, came in far behind.

The majority of the people in the sample who had living parents idealized one or both of them. Since women were somewhat more likely to idealize their mothers, men were more likely to idealize their fathers, and women were more likely than men to idealize either parent, the net effect is a gradual gradient from the 59 percent of women who idealized their mothers to the 46 percent of men who idealized their mothers. Siblings were idealized much less often, but they were idealized more than cousins.

There were some class differences reported in sentiments toward relatives. Business-class women expressed more positive sentiments than either business-class men or working-class men toward all kin except cousins. Compared to working-class women, they were significantly more likely to express affection for their fathers (65 versus 49 percent) and to agree with either or both of their parents.

The expressions of affection, agreement, and identification in Middletown kin relationships closely paralleled Adams's results in Greensboro. In that earlier study, too, most people expressed affection for their parents, the women more than the men; both men and women showed more affection for their mothers than for their fathers; and white-collar people were closer to their parents than were blue-collar people.[6]

Both the Greensboro and Middletown studies revealed less agreement with parents than affection for them. The Middletown study found more agreement between white-collar people and their parents than between blue-collar people and their parents. In Greensboro, Adams found a similar difference for men but not for women. And, as we did in Middletown, Adams found less affection and agreement between siblings than between children and parents (Adams 1968, 70 and 109).

Both studies show that relationships between cousins are relatively weak compared to those between primary relations, but they are by no means negligible. Fifteen percent of the Greensboro sample reported affection for cousins (21 percent in Middletown); 21 percent of the Greensboro men and 25 percent of the women reported agreement with cousins (23 and 30 percent in Middletown); 11 percent of the Greensboro men and 14 percent of the women idealized their best-known cousins (15 and 16 percent in Middletown). Relationships with cousins did not differ by social class in either place.

Most people in the Middletown sample claimed to be as close or closer to their parents than they had been when they were growing up, but women were much more likely to grow closer to their parents as they grow up. Although 38 percent of the men currently felt closer to one or both parents, no less than 60 percent of the women did. Only 1 woman in 10 and 1 man in 5 reported having less affection for their parents than they had as children. Almost everyone (82 percent of the men and 90 percent of the women) said that they were as close or closer to their parents than they had been when they were growing up. Even when we get all the way out to cousins, the proportion of respondents saying they were as close or closer than when they were growing up remained close to 60 percent.

Taking the respondents' reports at face value, we see that there was a net intensification of relationships with parents and siblings as the respondents grew into maturity. But there was some weakening of relationships with cousins.

After respondents answered the question about how their feelings toward their parents had changed, they were asked, "Why would you say you feel as you do about them now?" This provided an opportunity for people to express themselves outside of the forced-choice categories of the survey. Some of their statements in this part of the questionnaire were as revealing as the quantitative summaries we have considered, with the same recurrent themes.

People attribute their increased closeness to their parents to their own maturity, to their own parental experience, and to the belated recognition of the emotional debt they owe. A few of the statements that made these connections were quoted in Chapter 7. Here are some other nuances.

We have more in common such as how it feels to work every day, raise a family, paying bills, and even some recreational activity.

Due to maturity, I understand their problems better and thus sympathize, but my feelings are not as strong due to a vast difference in values.

I am less inhibited as an adult; we can communicate better.

As I got older, I felt I could express myself more without the risk of punishment or criticism.

We have all grown up a great deal. We are not as afraid of each other. We talk, share, and understand each other more.

These affirmations of maturity and sharing seem to flow from empathy as well as from obligation. Less typical but definitely represented was the perception of a debt owed for earlier parental contributions and sacrifices. This view of parents as moral creditors took various forms.

I realize what they have done for me. In her old age, Mom now needs me.

I see how my parents struggled to raise us. The things they wouldn't get for themselves but got for us children instead.

I realize how hard times must have been for them and what a good job they did of raising their children.

Other recurrent explanations for the closeness of parents and grown children were (1) relaxation of parental authority; (2) increased needs of parents because of sickness, widowhood, or old age; and (3) expectation of bereavement. Here are some of the things that were said about the relaxation of parental authority.

We get along better. They were very over-protective. I hated it growing up.

They are less judgmental and interfering, and I am grateful for their help, favors, gifts, and understanding.

They show me more respect as a person and do not pressure me as much as they once did.

I am more mature and do not see them as much, so have learned to appreciate them more. By only seeing them once a week, it is a real treat to visit them.

And about needs of parents:

I feel closer to my mother because my father is dead.

I have become the one to care for them.

And the expectation of bereavement:

Every day counts. Once they are gone, I won't have the opportunity to enjoy their company.

We are closer mainly because I dread facing the time when I will not have my parents.

Still another positive theme was the affirmation that relationships with parents had not changed, for example, "We've always been close." These responses were less colorful than those alluding to a rapprochement, but they were fairly common (at least a third of the respondents with living parents fell into this category with respect to one or both parents).

Neither they nor I seem to have changed. I still respect them and they treat me as their son, but as an adult.

I felt close to them while growing up; nothing has happened to change my feelings.

In my life, my family is first. My mother and I are on the same wave length, she is my best friend too.

There is much more variety in the comments of the few respondents who reported indifferent or hostile relationships with their parents. For some, the same changes that bring other people closer to their parents—living far apart, illness, death of one parent, knowing parents better, or the child's increased maturity and experience—have had an alienating effect, instead. A few Middletown people blamed their parents for not being better parents and for past or present neglect.

They're not part of our lives. They live far away. They have different values.

Mother makes me very nervous, always telling me what to do. She is a very unhappy person, it rubs off and I resent it.

I have learned too many things they did to my sister. I have lost a lot of feeling.

Having my own family, I see the neglect my father gave me.

But such comments were atypical. Reading over the 259 answers to this question, one cannot help being impressed by the understanding, appreciation, obligation, and love apparent between the generations. Most Middletown people feel good about their parents, love them, and make sacrifices for them when necessary. They see them often and enjoy doing so. Again and again, in various ways, they say about their parents, "I love and respect them" or "We are good friends."

Relatives as Confidants

In the high school survey, adolescents were asked whether they had anyone they trusted enough to confide in and tell their troubles to, someone who understood them. Eighty-six percent said that they had one or more people with whom they maintained such a close personal relationship. Among the 1,324 children who described their confidants, 30 percent mentioned relatives. About half of those mentioning relatives listed one or both of their parents. Mothers were considered to be confidants much more often than their fathers. Indeed, mothers were mentioned more than seven times as often as fathers. Siblings were named as confidants as frequently as parents, and other relatives were mentioned occasionally.

In sum, relatives accounted for more than half of the persons teenagers identified as really knowing and caring about them. The relatives most often selected as confidants were mothers; brothers and sisters were not too far behind. The unimportance of fathers as confidants is striking. When young people mentioned their parents as confidants, most of them meant their mothers, some meant both parents, and only a handful meant their fathers alone. In fact, fathers alone ranked behind cousins and uncles (and were tied with aunts) as confidants.

A question on confidants in the family role questionnaire administered to adults revealed that the use of relatives as confidants declines as people grow out of adolescence. Adults were as likely as adolescents to say that they had a confidant (83 percent and 86 percent), but fewer of them were relatives. Four out of five of the women's confidants and seven out of eight of the men's were unrelated. Fathers were almost as likely as mothers to be the confidant of their grown children. Of 27 respondents who identified parents as their confidants, 13 mentioned their mothers, 9 mentioned their fathers, and 5 mentioned both parents together. The lone parent chosen as confidant was likely to be of the same sex; only one man designated his mother alone and only two women designated their fathers alone.

The Salience of Kinship Ties

In a survey of neighboring in Middletown, we compared activities involving neighbors, friends, and relatives. It turns out that people in this community are in closer contact with their friends than with their neighbors and in closer contact with their relatives than with their friends. Seventy-five percent of the 316 respondents in this survey had relatives or in-laws in Middletown, and 4 out of 5 of these engaged in "mutual visiting and entertaining in each other's houses, drinking or dining" more than once a month, a slightly higher proportion than those reporting the same intensity of interaction with their closest friends. Moreover, visits with relatives were more comprehensive; more often than not, they involved all the adults in both households and very commonly all the children, too.

Kinships and friendships are far more important than organizational memberships in creating some measure of organizational solidarity. Fifty-eight percent of the respondents in the neighboring survey reported no memberships at all, but only 33 percent lacked close contact with a local relative.

In a section entitled "How Important Are Kin?" Adams discussed the responses he obtained to a question on the importance of kinship in people's lives. The question, repeated with slight modification in the Middletown kinship survey, was this.

We have been talking about all sorts of different relatives. Now, *you* know what is really important, or really matters, to you in life. What I want to know is this: Are your relatives one of the most important aspects of your life (excluding your spouse and children), or are they somewhat important, or are they relatively unimportant in your total scheme of things? (Adams 1968, 209-10.)

About 90 percent of the Greensboro people said that their relatives were important parts of their lives. Fifty-eight percent of the women and 37 percent of the men said that they were "very important." With social class taken into account, the highest percentage of "very important" responses was given by white-collar women (59 percent) and the lowest by white-collar men (36 percent) (Adams 1968, 27-29).

In response to a similar question, more than half of the Middletown women and over a third of the men designated kinship ties as being very (quite, most) important parts of their lives. (See Appendix A, Table 9-11.) In Middletown as in Greensboro, kinship ties were most salient for white-collar women, somewhat less so for blue-collar women and men, and least meaningful for white-collar men.

Summary

Kinship ties permeate Middletown. No other affiliative bond directly links as many of the city's people to other people in or near Middletown; and no other affiliative bond, apart from that between a husband and a wife, has the combined power of normative obligation and personal affection to the same extent.

All of the summary statements that we listed from Troll and Bengtson's review (1979) of the literature on kinship apply to Middletown. Grown children are more similar to their parents than to their brothers, sisters, or cousins of their own generation, and most express affection for their parents throughout their lives. Middletown people see more of their closest relatives than of their closest friends, and they do more with them. And, as expected, we can show that Middletown women, especially business-class women, are more involved with their relatives than men are.

The findings of our study on kinship in Middletown closely parallel those reported by Adams for Greensboro 15 years earlier. What differences appear are largely due to differences in survey procedure, but the kinship networks of Middletown do seem to be more locally concentrated and the class differences more muted.

Most Middletown adults recognize an obligation not only to keep in contact with their close relatives but to help them when necessary. Both the amounts of obligation and contact decline rather sharply between primary, secondary, and tertiary relatives.[7] Women in Middletown seem to enjoy the maintenance of kinship ties more than men do; men are more apt to stress the obligations involved. The greater involvement of women in kinship activities appears at every turn.

The major contribution of this chapter, in the context of the Lynds' work and possible future studies of Middletown, is the demonstration that kinship ties are "things making group solidarity" in Middletown. We have also corroborated the Lynds' observation that people's values tend to be like those of their families. In fact, we have found remarkable agreement between parents and children, especially between mothers and daughters. Middletown people show more affection for, agreement with, and identification with their parents than with their brothers or sisters. Most Middletowners admire and respect their parents and share their values. There is less of a "generation gap" than there is a "contemporary gap" between a Middletowner and his or her siblings.

Having examined kinship activity in Middletown in 1976-1977, we can say with assurance that it is the principal focus of social life in Middletown. People's social activities with their relatives who live in or near Middletown are frequent and highly valued. There is no evidence for any weakening of kinship ties during the past 50 years. The sentiments of one young Middletown mother exemplify the euphoric view so many Middletown people take of their extended families.

I'm trying to raise my kids like my father raised us. You have to give kids something to fall back on, which is the family. . . . Relatives are important because you need to know how you were brought up. Keeping in touch with relatives gives you an idea of what you are. You have to know this before you can truly understand yourself. Only then can you begin to understand and help others.

Chapter 10

Family Symbolism in Festivals

Middletown today is a family-oriented community. This fact is evident in its festival symbolism and also when today's festival activities are compared to those of 1890 or 1924. In 1890 Middletown displayed a great deal of patriotic and civic pride, while the "family festivals" as we know them today were relatively undeveloped. In 1924 patriotism was still felt, but its public celebration was much diminished (Lynd and Lynd 1929, 77 and 261). Civic loyalty was both felt and displayed at events such as basketball games and civic club meetings (Lynd and Lynd 1929, 478-95). The Lynds reported an increasing awareness in both men and women of the necessity for spending time with children and family (Lynd and Lynd 1929, 144 ff), but this attachment apparently found little more symbolic expression in 1924 than it had in 1890. The Christmas season especially seems to have been more a time for attending parties and dances than for celebrating family solidarity (Lynd and Lynd 1929, 152 and 460).

Today, national holidays such as Washington's Birthday, Memorial Day, Independence Day, and Labor Day pass almost unnoticed by Middletowners. Expressions of civic loyalty are few and far between, as shown by a general lack of interest in civic ceremonies. Replacing city and country as a focus of festive attention in Middletown is the family. Every widely observed festival in Middletown now celebrates the family and the related ideas of home, mother and child, and feminine roles. There has been a very interesting shift over the past 50 years, and at the end of this discussion we will suggest some reasons for its occurrence.

What we call Middletown's festival cycle is a series of holidays and festive occasions observed throughout the population on specific dates. It does not include private though equally familial observances such as birthdays, weddings, anniversaries, and reunions. The festival cycle is quasi-public in character—everyone knows when it is Christmas, but the celebrations of it in homes, offices, and classrooms are relatively private.

The festival cycle begins with Halloween, followed by Thanksgiving, Christmas, New Year's Day, Valentine's Day, Washington's Birthday, Easter, Mother's Day, Memorial Day, Father's Day, and the Fourth of July. The period between Independence Day and Halloween is relatively barren of holidays (only Labor Day and Columbus Day fall during this period), so the festival year is unbalanced.

A similar imbalance is found in the Christian church calendar, which begins with the first Sunday in Advent and ends with Trinity Sunday, eight weeks after Easter. The summer and autumn calendar in the church consists of Sundays counted after Trinity. Between Halloween and Easter, the secular festivals are primarily associated with the Christian festivals. Thanksgiving, New Year's Day, and Washington's Birthday are exceptions, although Thanksgiving has religious overtones.

The division into religious and nonreligious festivals corresponds almost exactly to a separation into festivals celebrating family solidarity and those celebrating national solidarity. The separation of church and state, and of family and state, suggested by this division is interesting in itself, and we will return to it later.

The American festivals are comparable to the rituals performed in most small-scale, non-Western societies. When anthropologists study such a society, the ritual life of the people and the symbols appearing in those rituals engage their attention most compellingly. Middletown's festival cycle has a good deal in common with ritual cycles in other societies. There are many symbols, ostensibly unrelated but depending on contrasts with each other for their meaning. There is a great deal of prescribed behavior even though Middletown thinks of it as essentially voluntary: giving gifts at Christmas, dressing children in costume at Halloween, cooking large dinners for Thanksgiving, hunting eggs at Easter. The emblems appropriate to one festival must not appear at another. Like other rituals, the festivals must take place in their proper order; they are fixed by a common calendar. It is conceivable that families could get together to celebrate festivals at arbitrary times to suit their own convenience, but no one does this except in extreme cases, such as when a family member cannot be present on the proper day, and even then the celebration is considered irregular or defective. It is important that the festivals be celebrated when they should be, as they should be, and in the appropriate company.

Family Attitudes and Values in Middletown

During the course of the fieldwork for the Middletown III project from 1977 to 1979, 13 surveys of attitude and behavior in contemporary Middletown were carried out. Nearly all of these inform us about some aspect of family life, and together they give us enough information to speak with unusual confidence about typical, or normal, family patterns. This is especially the case with respect to the rituals associated with the festival cycle, since they are celebrated throughout this community with remarkable uniformity, as shown for example by our detailed survey of Christmas-gift exchange and related practices. For information about trends over time, we have relied heavily upon the Middletown III survey of housewives, a general investigation of the life situations of married women living in intact households with their husbands and one or more children under age 18. That survey, an exact replication of a survey administered by the Lynds to a similar population in the same community 54 years earlier, is particularly informative about changes and continuities in local attitudes and values during the past two generations.

It is evident that the family is important in Middletown. Its characteristics may be summarized as follows: the family and home are female concerns, and the mother-child bond is the most important family relationship. There is a contradiction between the obligation to look after helpless children and the duty to encourage their growing independence. The family as a unit is subdivided along generational lines, rather than sex lines. Parents are supposed to give unstintingly to children without any expectation of return. The parent-child, or mother-child, relationship is asymmetrical: parents should provide love, protection, goods, and services;

children need return only moderate obedience and affection. In Middletown's thinking, the family is closely associated with religion. The family is a relatively private sphere opposed to the public spheres of work, politics, and civic activities.

In Middletown the convention that associates home, women, and children is so strong that it would seem impossible to consider one without the others, although there is no inherent necessity for them to be associated. In the literature of anthropology, there are enough negative examples to demonstrate that convention, not "nature," connects them. Some of the comments quoted in previous chapters indicate the strength of Middletown's feeling on this point. One man, speaking of his wife, summed it up this way, "She keeps the home, the place to come home to when I'm through with whatever I'm done with."

Women in Middletown run the households and do most of the child raising. Their moving into the work world has not led, in any significant degree, to their relinquishing these positions to their husbands. It would appear, then, that the association of women with the family is more powerful than the association of men with work; at least, it is more exclusive.

There is a certain ambivalence about the mother-child tie, valued though it is. Caring for children is of great importance, but so too is their maturation and growing independence. The comments of Middletown residents demonstrate that they find both aspects of child rearing of concern. There is evidence, too, that Middletowners fear that one aspect may dominate the other, with the result that the children are either neglected or tied to their mother's apron strings. The two requirements that "children should receive secure and continuous care; they . . . should be initiated into adult society with neither undue haste nor unduly long enforced dependence . . ." (Bane 1976, 3) are clearly at odds. A protected child is not independent; an independent child needs no care. Middletowners have a hard time balancing these demands, and, indeed, the conflict between them cannot be resolved completely. As we will see, the festival cycle attempts a resolution by emphasizing each aspect separately, as if the other did not exist.

The relationship between parents and children in Middletown is unbalanced—the parents give far more to their children than they receive or expect to receive in return. Middletown parents of young children say that their goals for the children are independence, happiness, good jobs, and so on, but they almost never say that they look forward to being supported by those children. Grown children in Middletown acknowledge receiving financial and other help from their parents. There is almost no mention of returns made to the parents, however. The flow of goods and services is clearly one-way.

Middletown tends to think of the church, religion, the family, and women as belonging together. The elaboration of major Christian festivals into family celebrations suggests a close connection, confirmed by survey data, between religion and the family. The two form one kind of experience—which is relatively private and personal—in contrast to the experiences of work and civic activities, which are more public and impersonal. Middletown sees church attendance not as an onerous duty imposed by the church but as a mode of personal gratification: people go to church because they want to and because they enjoy it. Part of the enjoyment comes, as it does in the family, from association with a small group of compatible people. This is shown by such comments as "I enjoy the service and fellowship with friends"; ". . . there is comfort in group worship"; "an opportunity for sharing a quiet and meaningful experience with like-minded individuals." When we compare these comments to those about the home like the one quoted above—the "place to come home to when I'm through with whatever I'm done with"—we see that church and home are valued for the same reasons: they are both intimate, friendly, and comforting; they provide emotional support and peace.

Middletown people regard the family as something private. We have already had some intimation of this in their comments about the value of their home lives. Within the privacy of the family, however, there is an even more private and intimate sphere, that of sex. Unmarried adolescents, as well as husbands and wives, engage in sexual activity, but each generation turns a determinedly blind eye to the sexual activity of the other generation. The sexual activity of parents is legitimate and expected, of course, but no adolescent lists "sexuality" or "sexiness" as desirable characteristics in a parent. The erotic in Middletown is either blatantly public and utterly impersonal (the adult bookstore, the X-rated movie) or so private, because so intimate, as to be officially nonexistent.

Middletown's family is the feminine domain. Women not only cherish the family, they maintain its links to other similar groups. We have noted that women belonging to intact families (husband and wife, children under 18) are twice as likely to attend religious services regularly as women who are single, divorced, and childless, and more likely than men to participate in voluntary church-sponsored activities. Women also maintain the relationships between the family and its friends and relations. Most festivals today are celebrated in part by gift giving; most of the gifts are chosen and given by women. Men have comparatively little to do with gift giving. As we will see, gifts, especially Christmas gifts, symbolize and reinforce every social relationship; thus, the women in Middletown, more than the men, define and maintain social relationships, even those of their husbands. On the whole, women say that they are more willing to help a family member or an acquaintance. When survey respondents were asked whether they would give three days of their time to help an acquaintance in trouble, women consistently offered more help to these hypothetical victims than did men. Women emerge from these responses, as well as from the comments of Middletown householders, as the sympathetic, supporting, cherishing sex.

Middletown's husbands and fathers appear, in fact, to be nearly ciphers in their homes. Their duty is to earn a living. The man of the family links it with the public and impersonal side of life, just as the woman links it with the private, personal side. A man brings in an income, and his wife—to put this very abstractly—turns the impersonal check into social relationships by spending it on meals, greeting cards, gifts, and parties.

The Festival Cycle

We assume for purposes of the following analysis that in each festival the emblems[1] convey one kind of message repeatedly, that each festival produces a different message by being contrasted with the others, and that these messages express different aspects of the same themes: the importance of family and social ties and of women in maintaining both. Since Middletown's festival cycle begins with Halloween, we can usefully begin our analysis there.

Halloween is clearly an antifestival; it is also an antefestival, and this is not just a pun.[2] Following Leach (1961, 132-36) and Ortiz (1972), we assume that the inversion marks the importance of what follows by making a mockery of the serious. The mockery increases the seriousness: for one thing, the mockery suggests what could occur if the serious were no longer taken seriously. At one and the same time, we are allowed to escape normal social bonds and to see, or to infer, the consequences of habitual escape (that is, of not obeying the rules).

Let us start by considering the Halloween witch, a kind of person always described in anthropological writings as a social inversion.[3] The witches of any culture do contrary things, such as walking on their hands, flying, going out at night, killing close relatives, eating babies, trafficking with undesirables, et cetera. Middletown's Halloween witch has been relieved of most of her antecedents' nasty attributes, but a few still remain. She is old, ugly, skinny, warty, hook nosed, snaggletoothed, and wild haired; she dresses in black clothes and a tall, pointy hat; she rides a broomstick; and she has a black spitfire cat for a pet. She lives alone, unmarried and childless, and she emerges on Halloween with malevolent intentions and powers (although no actual harm is ever attributed to her). She is an inversion of several things at once. First, the witch inverts the American Mom, who is usually represented as young, attractive, and cheerfully dressed; who uses a broomstick for sweeping; who lives very much *en famille*; and who has the most benevolent intentions and powers. The only similarity between Mom and the witch is their sex. But the witch also inverts other festival emblems: Santa Claus (with whom she shares age and aerial navigation) by being female, ugly, sexless, and malevolent; the Cupid of Valentine's Day (with whom she shares supernaturality and flight) by being malevolent, female, aged, and heartless; the Easter Bunny (equally asocial) by being among other things human, aged, childless, female, specific, nocturnal, and mean. She demonstrates an evil, selfish femininity, a soured, ungenerous old age, and an aversion to society prompted by hatred rather than shyness. Note that the cat, like the broomstick, is a feminine attribute. The dominant color black is not shared by any of the emblems of the serious holidays following Halloween. The witch thus combines in herself the opposites of characters that will, during the holidays to come (and even to some extent at Halloween itself), be venerated and celebrated.

Inversion explains the jack-o'-lantern, today a less important emblem, as well. An important part of the Thanksgiving meal is the pumpkin pie. The pumpkin, together with cornstalks and gourds, symbolizes the fall harvest. The jack-o'-lantern makes horrific this otherwise innocuous vegetable. The tastiness of the Thanksgiving dessert is emphasized by this perversion of the raw pumpkin.

The newspaper accounts of Halloween parties in Middletown did not mention the witch as an emblem until the mid-1950s. At the beginning of the century, the major emblem was the jack-o'-lantern. The addition of the witch supports the empirical finding mentioned earlier that family and family life have become more important to Middletown since the beginning of the century. Halloween used to be a celebration of harvest and civic pride. Middletown was famous in the region for its unique Halloween celebration, in which the adults dressed in costume and paraded for two or three hours before going to one of the many private Halloween parties.[4]

The other emblems of Halloween are ghosts, skeletons, and haunted houses. The haunted house is a horrible version of home. In contrast to home, the haunted house is cold, dark, and comfortless, and it is inhabited by dreadful beings. These inhabitants, the ghosts and skeletons, prefigure the resurrection celebrated at Easter, the end of the familial phase of the festival cycle.[5] Halloween burlesques Thanksgiving by making commensality impossible; and Christmas by mocking the importance of widespread gift exchanges and the benevolence of mothers and Santa Claus. Because Halloween and Easter stand at ends of the festival cycle, however, the most important aspect of Halloween is its mockery of the resurrection. Easter celebrates the resurrection of body and soul; Halloween displays the horror of either body or soul resurrected without the other.

The practices of Halloween are as revealing as the emblems, and they bear out the hypothesis that Halloween is an antifestival. Since the practices are familiar to us all, I need not describe them in detail. They can be summarized for our purposes: at Halloween, nonpersons imitating nonbeings demand and receive nonmeals from nonrelatives in a nonneighborly way.

Children are not yet persons or social actors. They have no roles beyond being children since they are not tinker, tailor, soldier, sailor, or any other kind of social actor. The costumes they put on represent characters in fiction (Peter Pan), characters no longer in existence (Pocahontas, Robin Hood), characters of the imagination (witches and ghosts), abstractions of persons (a queen, but not Elizabeth II), or nonhuman characters (animals, toys, et cetera). Transvestism is permissible with no stigma attached. A few costumes are not permissible: Santa Claus, the Easter Bunny, and such supernatural beings as God, Christ, the Virgin Mary, and the saints.[6]

The standard treat demanded is candy, but even if it takes another form it must always be something that could never be part of a meal: pretzels, gum, cookies, and so on. (Apples are a partial exception.) The food is usually in small packets—that is, not part of a whole. It would never be proper to hand out pieces of cake or pie at Halloween; these items are sweet, but they are parts of a whole and they are archetypal desserts, parts of a meal. The small packets emphasize a lack of sharing which is, of course, contrary to the spirit of the feasts to follow, beginning with Thanksgiving. The food is presented by unobligated neighbors, rather than by one's own family. The anonymity of the visitors increases the social distance. The treats are given in response to a type of demand that would ordinarily be considered outrageous in Middletown. Hospitality must not be solicited and should appear to be spontaneous. Demands with a threat of violence are contrary to the gift ethos. Here also Halloween is an inversion of the normal order of things.

The two festivals following closely on this antifestival emphasize family solidarity in different ways. Thanksgiving celebrates the family alone, and Christmas celebrates the family within its social network.

The major emblem of Thanksgiving is the turkey, and once again the emblem provides the key for understanding the festival. A roast turkey is an entire undivided animal. Roast beef, ham, and leg of lamb are only parts of animals, the rest being shared by persons unknown; such meats are less suitable for a gathering that denotes unity. Another bird could do as well as the turkey if it were to symbolize unity only, but the bird to be eaten must also suggest abundance by providing more food than even a large family gathering could consume. Among commonly eaten fowl, only the turkey is large enough. The turkey also suggests the mythologized first Thanksgiving in Massachusetts.

Christmas is unquestionably Middletown's most important holiday. Its great variety of activities and symbols conveys two important messages: maintain social ties and nurture the children. These are, as we have seen, the major responsibilities of women in Middletown.

Social ties and gift giving go hand in hand: neither exists without the other (Mauss 1954). The gift affirms the relationship and symbolizes the kind of relationship it is. Each gift must also be "fitting to the character of the recipient" (Needham 1979, 34). Gifts are given on many occasions in Middletown, but only at Christmas is it obligatory to give one to nearly every close relative, friend, and associate. Ideally, each gift given should differ from all the others given by that person. This unwritten (indeed, generally unstated) rule is burdensome, but Middletown people obey it remarkably well. The Christmas present not only reaffirms each relationship, it also specifies what that relationship is, while it flatters, if possible, the recipient's taste and personality. That each gift must convey so much and that overt speculation about the motives for choosing any gift is taboo explain why Christmas shopping is such a problem. Yet it must be done. Social cohesion depends on this annual reaffirmation of relationships.

Within most families, children receive more presents than adults do. This brings us to the other major theme of Christmas: the nurture of children. In this, Christmas stands opposed both to Halloween (when children demand a kind of nurture—not very wholesome—from nonparents) and Easter (when children are urged to be independent). The iconography of Christmas is full of protective images such as firelit interiors, large meals, and warm clothing in agreeable contrast to snowy outdoor scenes.

Santa Claus, the principal emblem of the secular Christmas (we will come to the religious emblems later), symbolizes these same themes. Santa Claus is foremost a gift giver, and a specific gift giver. Each of his gifts is designated for an individual person. Most of his presents are given to children. But while children do give presents to their parents, Santa Claus, a grandparental figure, receives nothing for his generosity (unless the improved behavior of the children is considered a recompense). This relationship exaggerates the predominantly one-way flow of gifts from parents to children. Santa epitomizes the generosity, particularism, and nurturance of Christmas. He also exhibits nurturing in another form: although he lives at the frozen North Pole, he has a warm house full of merry elves and a cheerful, helpful wife. Like the fathers of Middletown's families, he is visualized as bringing good things into the family from the harsh outside world;[7] but, having done so, he plays no further part in the holiday celebration.

Most Christmas preparations are done by women: decorating the house, sending the cards, buying the presents, and above all fixing a lavish Christmas dinner. Christmas is also a time when a women's involvement with housekeeping and her family is dramatized. Usually she keeps the house clean, but at Christmastime she dresses it up. She cooks meals in a relatively humdrum way the rest of the year, but she "puts the big pot in the little one" for Christmas dinner. At other times of the year, she does little things for her family, as well as routine chores; at Christmas she does lavish, showy things for them. The secular Christmas glorifies the hearth and home, and the housekeeper most of all.

That the secular Christmas celebrates the nurturing of children is even more evident when the two minor festivities immediately preceding and following it are considered and when the gospel story of the first Christmas is examined. The minor festivities are the office party and New Year's Eve, the first falling roughly a week before Christmas and the other a week after. Both are aggressively adult in tone, with drinking and some loosening of sexual restraints. Neither of these activities is proper for children or for the celebration of Christmas. The child-oriented nature of Christmas stands out strongly against these two antifestivals that rigorously exclude anything to do with children.

The religious and secular Christmases are usually contrasted, to the disparagement of the secular. "Keep Christ in Christmas!" cries Middletown. "Christmas is too commercialized!" That may be, but we have seen that extensive Christmas gift giving serves an important purpose by maintaining all sorts of personal relationships. The message of secular Christmas is not really different from the message conveyed by the Christmas story. The episodes of the Nativity convey the necessity of looking after a child's, and a family's, welfare. In a sense, we can say that God the Father is caring for His creation, the human race, as parents should care for their own creations, their children. This message is repeated on a smaller scale in the story of the Holy Family itself. Again and again, the family or the Child is threatened, but each time it is rescued. At the beginning, when Joseph was disinclined to marry Mary, an angel ensured the creation of the family and the preservation of the baby by explaining what appeared to be immorality in Mary. The birth of the Christ Child is attended by many nurturing figures from different levels of creation: His own parents, the stable animals, the angels, the shepherds, and, finally, the three kings bearing gifts, each gift symbolizing the nature of the recipient as "king and god and sacrifice." (Here also there is no return made for the gifts.) The Slaughter of the Innocents presents a serious threat to the newborn child; but again, by the intervention of the divine Father and the speedy action of the human one, the Child is saved. The secular and the religious iconographies are analogous in that they use different elements to convey the same meaning: children are helpless, and their parents must help them. They convey also the related message that families must use all possible means to preserve themselves against influences tending to split them apart.

The next family-related festival in the cycle after New Year's is Valentine's Day. This day also has Christian and even older origins. It was once thought to be the day on which birds began their mating season. Today, not much is known of St. Valentine himself; certainly *he* is not celebrated on February 14. Thus Valentine's Day is similar to Halloween in having originally had a part, now only dimly remembered, in the church calendar. Today both holidays are entirely secular.

Valentine's Day, with its dominant colors of red, pink, and white and its emblems of the pierced heart and Cupid, obviously celebrates sentimental attachment. Until recently it was solely concerned with male-female relationships among adults. About three decades ago, children began to be encouraged to send valentines to their friends. In the last few years people in Middletown have been sending valentines to their parents and children of the opposite sex and increasingly even to those of the same sex. Indeed, it is now common for valentines to be sent to participants in any relationship except one between adult males.

The emblems of Valentine's Day express the theme of nonphysical love. Cupid is a small boy, a type of person judged by Middletown to be free of sexual cravings. The convention that represents Cupid in silhouette further removes him from any association with the erotic. The valentine heart is similarly abstract. It does not bleed when pierced but remains as distant from physiological function as the sentimental love it symbolizes. The valentine colors reflect this attitude also. We could say that red symbolizes heat and blood and passion, but these are cooled and rendered acceptable by the purity of white; the lover is passionate but pure minded. Valentine's Day symbolically protects the inviolable privacy of eroticism within the family circle.

The gifts given on Valentine's Day in Middletown suggest that the holiday is primarily a celebration of women. The typical valentine gift is given to a woman by a man and more particularly to a woman as an object of courtship. Flowers, candy, perfume, and jewelry are appropriate. Electric irons, gardening tools, and hair curlers, though sufficiently feminine, are not considered suitable. Women may give cards or small presents to all the members of their families, but in many families men are obligated to give presents to their wives. Again, we see the wife/mother keeping the family together while the husband supports her efforts from outside.

The nonerotic love associated with Valentine's Day, like the pseudohorrors of Halloween and the universal benevolence of Christmas, is related to the secular celebration of Easter, the last major festival of the cycle. After we have investigated Easter in detail, we should be able to see the festival cycle as a whole, with every part related to other parts in opposition or by analogy. The end, Easter, is prefigured in the beginning, Halloween; but Halloween also prefigures the other festivals, and they anticipate, in their various ways, the culmination at Easter. What, then, happens at Easter?

Like Christmas, Easter has both a secular and a religious iconography. The two parallel each other without overlapping. The Easter Bunny never appears at representations of the Crucifixion, nor are the instruments of the Passion ever included in an Easter basket. The symbols of Easter convey a sense of new life, but they also convey, more subtly, the message that the conventional categories of Middletown's culture (especially the social categories) are merely conventional. In this regard, especially, Easter is the opposite of Christmas, when Middletown identifies and reinforces each social relationship. Easter is also, in a different way, the opposite of Halloween. Behavior at Halloween recognizes categories and deliberately goes to the opposite extreme by making nonmothers into mothers nonfood into food, and so on, in a burlesque that depends for its effect on the fact that everyone involved recognizes and accepts the normal categories so perverted. Easter, however, seems to say that particularizing these relationships is unimportant. The symbols do not invert particular categories so much as negate "category" itself. This is especially true in relations between people.

The secular emblem of Easter is the Easter Bunny. An enumeration of the traits of this animal shows him to be an inversion of the great Christmas emblem, Santa Claus.[8] The Easter Bunny is nameless, homeless, without friends or family, dumb, comparatively immature, dubiously charitable, and biologically ambiguous. Santa Claus has a personal name, a known home and family, many friends, speech and literacy, great age, boundless charity, and biological specificity. Santa Claus is specific, the Easter Bunny is general. The presents Santa brings are for individuals and are so designated on the labels, but the Easter Bunny leaves eggs in the garden for anyone who can find them. Because the emblems of these two great festivals are so opposed, we can safely assume that they celebrate opposite things; and, since Christmas emphasizes particularity in social relationships, Easter must emphasize generality, or a blurring of social categories.

The Easter Bunny is an eminently suitable emblem for this kind of celebration, because it is the most ambiguous animal Middletown recognizes.[9] There are many young animals associated with Easter; usually, though, the animals are not those kept as pets but those found in the farmyard (another blurring of conventional distinctions)—chicks, ducklings, lambs (a symbol for the crucified Christ), as well as bunnies. Such animals are consonant with the general theme of renewal of life at that time of the year. Flowers, pale colors, new clothing, and eggs express the same theme. Of such youthful animals, however, only the bunny is ambiguous. The chick, the duckling, and the lamb will grow into adult forms enough unlike the baby forms to be easily distinguishable from them; moreover, in the adult forms, males can easily be distinguished from females. (This is true of all farm animals, not just those associated with Easter.) It is possible to compare a young rabbit with an old one and decide on the basis of size that one is older than the other, but otherwise there is no great difference between them. And, in any case, sexing rabbits without close and expert scrutiny is very difficult (as many have discovered to their chagrin). In these regards, the rabbit is less easily classified than the other young animals of Easter, and, therefore, it makes a better emblem than they would. The ambiguity of rabbits lies in more than their characterless gender and maturity, however. Sheep, chickens, and other such animals are unquestionably part of a class of livestock destined to be eaten as food. As a class, they are differentiated from pets, which are considered inedible, and from wild animals, which are categorized by species as edible or inedible. The important point is that Middletown recognizes four classes of animals and so is able to place any animal into its proper class: domestic and inedible (cats), domestic and edible (cattle), wild and edible (deer), wild and inedible (foxes).[10] Only the rabbit fits all of these categories. Rabbits can be pets, they can be eaten or avoided as food, they can live in the wild, and they can be hunted. The Easter Bunny further exaggerates the ambiguity of rabbits by producing eggs. Not only does he fit into no conventional category, he makes no distinctions himself. His only gifts are eggs, and he gives them to no specific person.

Gift giving at Easter provides as valuable a clue as gift giving at Christmas for the understanding of the festival. Because Christmas gifts must be appropriate to particular relationships, the range of possible gifts is nearly infinite. At Easter, by contrast, only a few kinds of things are appropriate as gifts: eggs, candy (particularly an Eastery kind such as jelly eggs, chocolate bunnies, and marshmallow chicks), and plush or live animals. These may be given by anyone to anyone. The giving recognizes that there is a relationship, but it does not specify the kind of relationship. All relationships become more or less equivalent, because complementary social roles, such as parent and child or teacher and pupil, are blurred or ignored. The theme of these activities is clearly opposed to the theme of Christmas.

Do the secular celebrations at Easter oppose the Christmas emphasis on nurturing children? As we would expect, there is an opposition here, too, and it is evident in the custom of the Easter-egg hunt. At Christmas, the presents are brought into the house, where they can be opened in cozy leisure. At Easter, the eggs are hidden outside and must be hunted competitively by the children. They are urged to go out and do for themselves; they are deprived of overt parental aid and are forced to be independent. Again, the Easter Bunny and his eggs symbolize this idea. Eggs are, in a sense, offspring without parents. The separation from the parent bird is complete because the eggs are brought and hidden by an animal utterly incapable (in the real world) of producing an egg of any kind. Rabbits themselves are famous for the number of offspring they produce, but not much is said about the preliminary activities producing those offspring. Lapine fecundity gives us an image of many young for not much activity. Stretching this, we could say that the Easter Bunny symbolizes children produced asexually. As at Valentine's Day, the element of sexual intercourse is rigorously suppressed, and in this we have a connection between Valentine's Day and Easter. At Valentine's Day, Middletown celebrates women romantically (they are potential sexual partners and, therefore, potential mothers, but these feminine characteristics are never mentioned). Some time later, at Easter, essentially parentless children appear and are celebrated. Obviously, sexual activity of some kind must have taken place during the interval, but it is not even hinted at. The mother and the child are celebrated separately, and the umbilical cord is hidden. Familial sexuality remains intensely private.

As we would expect, the themes of the secular Middletown Easter can also be identified in the religious Easter celebration. Middletown celebrates the confounding of death and the assertion of life; the two concepts are no longer distinguished or, indeed, distinguishable. There are apostles who betray or deny their teacher. The Son gives His Mother to another "son" (St. John the Divine) and considers Himself abandoned by His Father. Conventional distinctions are ignored, and ordinary categories are confused. There is also an emphasis on the independence of children, or offspring. Jesus, the Son, is no longer cherished and protected by all the levels of creation. He is on His own, independent and almost deserted. At Easter itself, we celebrate the Resurrection. The language of the Apostles' Creed demonstrates the shift from dependence at the Nativity to independence at the Resurrection. Whereas Christ was incarnate (that is, by someone else), at Easter He arose (that is, He did this Himself). His subsequent actions—He ascended into heaven and will come again, et cetera—all display an independence in that He is not being looked after as at Christmas but is looking after Himself (and others). As Christ the helpless infant and Christ the willing victim are opposed, so Middletown's offspring as dependent children and as (potentially) independent adults are opposed; each is celebrated at its own festival.

We have seen that Middletown has difficulty balancing the irreconcilable demands of nurturing and liberating children and is afraid to go too far in either direction. The festival cycle eases some of the burden of Middletown's anxiety. Halloween, Christmas, and Easter each treat the problem in their own way. Halloween combines the themes of nurturance and independence (albeit in a topsy-turvey, joking atmosphere) by having children assert to neighboring mothers their dependence by paradoxically demanding care from them. Christmas and Easter try to reduce the conflict by separating the two and concentrating on one at a time.

Easter seems to end Middletown's festival cycle in an anticlimax. It is a celebration of negation. Social categories are ignored; ordinary definitions are made meaningless. Each of the previous festivals has celebrated some particular aspect of family life, but Easter appears to insist on the unimportance of family relationships. Even the independence of children constitutes a kind of negation in that they are represented as being isolated, without any kin or indeed any identity (the eggs, their Easter gifts, being anonymous and essentially uniform). Things can be identified only by their context, and at Easter children are symbolically removed from any context.

But the message conveyed to Middletown by the Easter symbols is not so much that categories do not exist as that things Middletown chooses to separate from other things, and to place in different categories, are ultimately parts of the same whole. The religious Easter celebration proclaims that death can be transformed into life; the secular Easter, that any kind of family relationship is much like all the others. Children, urged to be independent, are the same as adults. Easter reunites everything that the preceding celebrations separated. Without the final celebration of Easter, the festival cycle would celebrate the particulars of Middletown family life without ever relating those particulars to each other. Middletown's festival cycle first celebrates different aspects of family life separately and then suggests that the differences are illusory, since all things are parts of the same order. Once the whole is reassembled at Easter, Middletown is ready to begin the cycle of analysis and synthesis over again.

Why Celebrate the Family?

Having suggested that Middletown's festivals celebrate the family, we come to the question of why the celebration of the family has largely displaced the earlier celebrations of labor, civic, and national solidarity. Current theories about the purpose of ritual in society suggest a possible answer to this question.[11]

We begin by noting that ritual always deals with important matters, such as promoting family solidarity. But there are some important matters in any society that generate no rituals, while others are the focus of much ritual activity. More particularly, though, it has often been observed often that ritual is concentrated on those aspects of a society that are at risk, so to speak, because of conflict or contradiction and loss of credibility.

If we think of society, or culture, as a system of variously interrelated ideas, rather than as a collection of interacting people, we can better understand that what is meant here is not a risk to individual relationships or political credibility but rather the risks created by tension between opposing fundamental cultural ideas. It is impossible for a system of cultural ideas to be free of contradictions, but the acceptability of such a system is diminished by a burden of obvious contradiction. Herein lies the risk. If the tension is so great that the members of the society become aware of it, they will reject as fallacious some or all of the ideas involved, with the result that the society becomes anomic. In an extreme case, its members would hold no common fundamental principles, no "self-evident truths," on which to base their behavior and their judgments. Such a situation clearly would be intolerable. We assume that rituals avert the threat to institutional survival by resolving the dilemmas created by conflicting values and by endowing the entire system with an aura of unimpeachable truth and virtue.[12]

As we have seen, much of the symbolism and activity of the festivals is concerned with child rearing, in which the risk is perceived as being particularly acute. As in every culture, there is some element of risk in raising a child (for example, it may die young, or it may become a murderer). But the chance of a tragic outcome is small compared to the chance that the child will turn out to be a normal, useful member of society. Middletown's concern is more general than this, however. As Middletown worries about the future of the family, it worries especially about child rearing. Neighbors' or relatives' children have behavioral problems that are attributed to their working or unloving mothers. (Such a lack of feeling is often contrasted with the informant's happy involvement with his or her own children.) Middletowners generally disapprove of working mothers, especially those with children under six years old; at the same time, nearly 50% of the married women with children in Middletown hold outside jobs. That outside employment has, on the evidence, little effect on the home lives of employed women (Chadwick and Chappell, forthcoming; Bahr 1979) makes no difference to most Middletown residents. Their perceptions of the situation are different.

There is, however, a much more serious element of risk in the parent-child relationship as it is conceived by Middletowners; this has to do with the insistence that parents give unstintingly to children and expect nothing in return. The unbalanced relationship between the generations in the nuclear family, in which practically all goods and services flow only from parents to children, contradicts the ideal of reciprocity found in all the other social relationships in Middletown. As our study of Christmas gift giving shows,[13] people who give a present (other than to a child) either expect (and receive) a fairly similar one in return, or they are, in effect, tipping the provider of a regular service (the paperboy or the mailman, for example). Even sending a Christmas card to one's boss anticipates, although it does not often get, some sort of equal return.[14] The pattern with regard to children violates the principle of reciprocity in that parents do not ever expect to be repaid by their children.[15] If the child chooses to reciprocate in some manner, the parent is touched and grateful; but, as we have seen, the stated purpose of raising children is to make them independent, not to prepare them as providers for the parents' old age.[16]

Although most gift giving is part of an exchange and can be justified on rational grounds, the justification for looking after children—an inescapable responsibility, demanding and often tiring and frustrating, with only problematic rewards—is much more an emotional than a rational one. Since it is of the greatest importance that children be cared for and taught properly, it is important that parents be convinced, at the emotional level, that they must do their best in these regards. There can be no room for questioning the value of such a crucial activity. We could say that, by glorifying the raising of children and insisting on its importance, the symbols of the festival cycle quell any doubts that parents may have and shore up the emotional conviction that sacrifices for children are worthwhile.

Similarly, we could suggest that Middletown's festival cycle reassures women that their endless giving to their friends and families is worthwhile. Today, the alternative of choosing an outside job, the rewards of which are much more obvious than those of being a wife and mother, is available to every woman who wants it. Although working mothers are considered a threat to their children's welfare in Middletown, the attractions of paid employment as well as the need for a second income might well outweigh the stigma of being thought a bad mother and the risk of having one's children become delinquent. If all of Middletown's women are not to abandon their domestic duties entirely in favor of outside jobs, some counterattraction must be offered. We find it in the messages of the festival cycle. A wife and mother is rewarded, not just with occasional presents and praise from her husband and children and respect from her neighbors for a job well done, but by the extensive celebration of her efforts in every festival.

We suggest, then, that Middletown's festival cycle celebrates family matters because the family is the institution most at risk in the community. It is the institution most dependent on emotions, rather than reason, for its continuance, and in this dependence lies its vulnerability.[17] The ritual of the festival cycle appeals to the emotions, strengthens them by assuring Middletown residents of their rightness, and so ensures the continuity of the family.

Chapter 11

Religion and the Family

The religious beliefs and practices of Middletown were an important element of the original Middletown study. Indeed, that study began as an investigation of the crisis in midwestern Protestantism and became a general community survey as the investigators discovered the close and intricate linkage between religion and the family on the one hand and between the church and other agencies of social improvement on the other. The Lynds' second volume, *Middletown in Transition*, paid less attention to religion but carefully described the effects of the depression on religious behavior in Middletown. Returning to the same site more than 40 years later, in 1976, we resumed the effort to identify the major trends in Middletown's religious practices and to examine the connection between religion and the family.

A superficial reading of the Lynds' two classic volumes is likely to give one the impression that religion was declining in Middletown between the two world wars and that the Lynds anticipated its further decline under secular influences. Indeed, they referred at various points to a process of "secularization," but always obliquely and with some hesitation. For example, when they found that working-class adolescents placed somewhat more importance on "being an active church member" as a desirable trait in a father than did business-class adolescents, they speculated that the difference might signify a varying rate of secularization, on the theory that working-class families lag behind business-class families in responding to social change. But a closer reading of the Lynds' remarkable chapters on the religious beliefs and practices of

Middletown, the leaders and participants in religious rites, and the programming of religious observances shows them to have been hesitant and undecided about what was happening to religion in Middletown. For every trend they identified from their base period of 1890 to their observation period in 1924, and then to their re-study in 1935, some annoying countertrend seemed to pop up. It seemed to them that Middletown people were thinking of Heaven less than they used to and that they did not go as often as they once had to the cemetery to visit the graves of their dead. On the other hand, they noted that the belief in the hereafter was no longer openly challenged by anyone in 1924, as it had been by the local freethinkers of 1890. The Lynds concluded uncertainly that "questioning of the dominant Christian beliefs in public appears to have declined since the nineties, but one infers that doubts and un-easiness among individuals may be greater than a generation ago" (Lynd and Lynd 1929, 331).

They noted a singular stability in church structures and in the activities conducted within them from 1890 to 1924, but they re-cognized also that other buildings under religious auspices, such as those of the YMCA and the YWCA, had been developed to house a wide range of new activities. They pointed out the secularization of Sunday in some families and the intrusion of motoring and golf on Sunday morning, but, at the same time, they remarked that the union meetings and the cockfights that had been regularly sched-uled on Sunday mornings around 1900 would have been unthink-able in 1924. Summarizing the trend in religious observances, they were again forced to hedge. "Like art and music, religious obser-vances appear to be a less spontaneous and pervasive part of the life of the city today, while at the same time this condition is be-ing met by more organized, directed effort to foster and diffuse these values" (Lynd and Lynd 1929, 343). When they examined attendance at religious services, they did find some unmistakable trends. "According to the almost universal testimony of ministers and church members and according to the study of the church-go-ing habits of the forty business-class and 123 working-class families interviewed" (Lynd and Lynd 1929, 359), there had been a con-spicuous decline in church attendance however measured and a conspicuous increase in the number of families, especially in the working class, who avoided church entirely, as well as a decline in

attendance at Sunday evening and weekday services. But, paradoxically, there seemed to have been large increases in Sunday school
attendance from 1890 to 1924.

The Lynds themselves said that they were "puzzled by apparent
contradictions." On the one hand, they saw the tendency in Middletown to measure the results of religion by the same pragmatic
measurements that applied to other activities. On the other hand,
they recorded a tendency for religion to be valued for its very re-
moteness from the routines of everyday life. "In other aspects of
its life " they complained, "Middletown is involved in change. But
it values its religious beliefs in part because it is assured that they
are unchanging" (Lynd and Lynd 1929, 403). And, having said
this they did finally seem to bring in a verdict in favor of secularization, again without mentioning the word.

As changes proceed at accelerating speed in other sections of the city's life,
the lack of dominance of religious beliefs becomes more apparent. The whole
tide of this industrial culture would seem to be set more strongly than in the
leisurely village of thirty-five years ago in the direction of the "go-getter" rather than in that of "Blessed are the meek" of the church; by their religious
teachers Middletown people are told that they are sinners in need of salvation,
by speakers at men's and women's clubs they are assured that their city, their
state, and their country are, if not perfect, at least the best in the world, that
it is they who make them so, and that if they but continue in their present
vigorous course, progress is assured. Meanwhile, secular marriages are increasing, divorce is increasing, wives of both workers and business men would appear to stress loyalty to the church less than did their mothers in training their
children, church attendance is apparently less regular than in 1890, Rotary
which boasts that it includes all the leaders of the city will admit no minister,
social activities are much less centered in the churches, leisure time is increasingly less touched by religious prohibitions in its encroachments upon the
Sabbath, more and more community activities are, as the press points out in
regard to questions of disease and health, being regarded not as "acts of God"
but as subjects for investigation. In theory, religious beliefs dominate all other
activities in Middletown; actually, large regions of Middletown's life appear
uncontrolled by them (Lynd and Lynd 1929, 406).

When the Lynds came back to Middletown to restudy the community in 1935, they were again confronted by apparently contra-
dictory trends in the religious sector. The number of local congregations had grown with the population, and five imposing new
churches had been built, despite the depression. But in the churches

they attended during their brief spring visit, the congregations seemed sparser and older than they had 10 years earlier. They found no change in sermon topics, less interest in revivals, a further decline in interchurch cooperation, a further expansion of religious education, some apparent decline of religious commitment among adolescents, and some evidence of the continued secularization of the Sabbath and the increasing separation of religion and politics. They complained, speaking for themselves, of the churches' refusal to take political positions and their inability to resist the "enveloping instrumentalism" of Middletown's culture. They seem to say that Middletown's religion had not lived up to its responsibility of defining values but that it did continue to provide emotional support for individuals and institutions. Since the institution of the family was changing rapidly in the Middletown of the 1920s and since the church was successfully resisting change, there was some tension between them. The conventional "ideal" family—monogamous, fertile, permanent, and child valuing—was buttressed by prevailing religious values. Divorce, consensual unions, sexual experimentation, and contraception were resisted by fervent but ineffectual appeals to Middletowners' religious values.

The Churches of Middletown

In 1924 Middletown was overwhelmingly Protestant. There was only 1 Catholic for every 15 Protestants. The Jewish community was small. Middletown today retains its Protestant character, 3 out of 4 adult residents named a Protestant denomination when asked for their religious preference in 1978. But the relative proportion of Catholics has increased; 13 percent are Catholics. A few non-Christian groups struggle to survive and together account for about 5 percent of the adult population. Outside the still-modest Jewish community, the non-Christians are concentrated among the students and faculty of the university and are adherents of Buddhism, Islam, Hare Krishna, Scientology, Transcendental Meditation, and the Unification ("Moonie") Church.

An example of the fervor with which the various churches and denominations compete for membership and defend their religious values is the controversy surrounding The Way International's convention held in Middletown. A two-week-long gathering of 3,200 members of The Way International, a sect under the direction of founder and leader Victor Paul Wierwille, was held on the university campus in June 1977. The Way's recruitment of young people and their subsequent total allegiance to The Way provoked parents' accusations that their children had been brainwashed. A group of parents planned to demonstrate at the convention but did not appear. Several local churches protested The Way's presence in Middletown and sought, in their terms, "to win souls back to Christ." The spokesmen for the protest called for a "religious war" fought by a "Christian army" against the "forces of Satan" and issued "calls to repentance" to members of The Way. A local minister was heard to shout at passing Way members, "You are in bondage to the Devil, repent or you will burn in Hell" (Middletown evening newspaper, June 22, 1977). Shouting matches between people from local churches and members of The Way occurred daily, with epithets like "whoremongers" and "adulterers" and admonitions to "go to hell" and "go to heaven" hurled back and forth.

The Way countered these attacks by organizing a Bless Patrol; ostensibly, members of the patrol were to act as guides for convention participants, but they also "provided security." Four Middletown clergymen were arrested for heckling members of The Way. The clergymen proclaimed their willingness to be imprisoned and suffer martyrdom. Eventually, the ministers of several more-ecumenical churches banded together to cool the flames of the conflict. The highly emotional behavior of those involved and the front-page community interest reflect the pervasiveness of religion in Middletown and the care with which all shepherds guard their flocks.

The Church Buildings

All of Middletown's major denominations built houses of worship during the nineteenth century. Several of the church edifices constructed before the turn of the century are still used with pride today, although most have been remodeled or expanded since their original construction.

The attachment of the population to older, traditional church buildings is illustrated by the decisions of the members of the High Street Methodist Church to restore their building after it was badly damaged by an explosion at the height of the Blizzard of 1978, when a nearby gas main ruptured and exploded. The damage was estimated at 4 million dollars. One of the options discussed by the congregation was tearing down the remaining shell and constructing a new building. This idea was rejected, and instead the impressive gothic structure was restored to its original state. Nine stained glass windows destroyed in the explosion were replaced with duplicates of the originals. The dedication of the restored structure was celebrated with enthusiasm.

In the early 1920s, the Lynds counted 42 church buildings serving a community of 36,000 individuals. There was a church building for every 857 citizens. The 1978 phone directory listed 137 regular churches and a score of other religious groups. Their buildings ranged from majestic structures with stained glass windows to modest one- or two-story chapels, converted office buildings, and storefronts. The 137 churches served a population of 80,000 in 1978. There was a church building for every 584 residents. The ratio of churches to people has increased significantly over the past 50 years.

The Religious Beliefs of Middletown

In a sermon delivered before the Middletown Kiwanis Club in 1976, a local minister challenged the notion that people are less believing today than in former times and observed that "many people who once scoffed at old-fashioned ideas concerning religion are now coming to accept and believe them" (Middletown's morning newspaper, December 23, 1976). This statement challenges the belief in the inevitability of secularization that is widely held in Middletown itself and that was widely held there 50 years ago.

The Lynds identified the following dominant religious beliefs in Middletown in 1924 (Lynd and Lynd 1929, 310-31): the sufficiency of Christianity for all mankind, the sacredness of the Bible, the divinity of Jesus, and a personal existence after death. The attitude survey they administered to all of Middletown's high school students in the winter of 1924 included items designed to measure the acceptance of these doctrinal beliefs by the adolescent population. In the winter of 1977, we administered another survey questionnaire to the entire high school population of Middletown. The questionnaire included the Lynds' items verbatim so that the frequency of responses could be directly compared.

With respect to the all sufficiency of Christianity, there was a notable decline. The proportion of respondents agreeing that "Christianity is the one true religion and all people should be converted to it" was 94 percent in 1924 but 38 percent in 1977.

There was a much smaller decline in the acceptance of the sacredness of the Bible. The relevant item read, "The Bible is a sufficient guide to all the problems of modern life." The proportion of respondents agreeing with the statement was 74 percent in 1924 and 50 percent in 1977.

The item regarding the divinity of Jesus was: "Jesus Christ was different from every other man who ever lived in being entirely perfect." The proportion of adolescent respondents agreeing with the statement was 83 percent in 1924 and 68 percent in 1977.

The item that the Lynds used to measure belief in a life after death was: "The purpose of religion is to prepare people for the hereafter." The proportion of adolescent respondents agreeing with the statement was 60 percent in 1924 and 53 percent in 1977—a very modest decline in 53 years.

A more extensive account of these surveys, including a breakdown of the responses by sex, social class, and race, is available elsewhere (Caplow and Bahr 1979 and Bahr 1980).

If the responses are to be trusted, three of Middletown's dominant beliefs of 1924 were still dominant in 1977. The divinity of Christ, the existence of a personal life after death, and the sacredness of the Bible still command a consensus. Only with respect to the all sufficiency of Christianity had there been a shift from acceptance to rejection. Middletown's continued adherence to traditional Christian theology, coupled with its new tolerance for non-Christian religious viewpoints, is confirmed by other data.

The new pattern of tolerance can be discerned not only with respect to strangers and the general community but even within the nuclear family. Although levels of religious observance are not lower in contemporary Middletown than they were in 1924, the pressure exerted by children on parents and parents on children to participate in church activities has been reduced. In 1924, 28 percent of the adolescent respondents identified "being an active church member" as one of the two qualities most desirable in a father, and 25 percent identified it as one of the two qualities most desirable in a mother. In 1977 fewer than 10 percent named "being an active church member" as one of the most desirable qualities in either parent. Similarly, the proportion of students who reported church attendance at religious services as a source of disagreement with their parents declined from 19 percent in 1924 to 13 percent in 1977 (Bahr 1980).

The Lynds attached particular importance to the answers given by 92 of the married women they interviewed to the following three questions.

What are the thoughts and plans that give you courage to go on when thoroughly discouraged?

How often have you thought of Heaven during the past month in this connection?

What difference would it make in your daily life if you became convinced that there was no loving God caring for you?

We repeated the same questions with a very minor change in wording (the phrase "in this connection" was omitted from the second question so that the questions could be asked in a different order) in our 1978 survey of 333 married women living in Middletown with their husbands and children. Of the 73 working-class women who answered the question about what gave them courage in 1924, 27 percent said that it was their religious faith or devotion and 23 percent referred to their families and homes, with the remaining responses widely scattered. Of the 98 working-class housewives who responded to the same question in 1978, 27 percent referred to their religion and 24 percent to their families and 6 percent mentioned both. The remaining responses were scattered among the same themes mentioned by the Lynds: some said that they "never get discouraged," some said that they "just look around and see there's lots of others worse off," some said that they "put their trust in a good cry," and others said that they get involved in work (Lynd and Lynd 1929, 324-25). The curious stability of the percentages is mirrored by the two samples' use of similar language. The following verbatim responses of working-class wives to the question about their sources of courage are from 1924 and 1978. We doubt that many readers would be able to tell them apart without referring to the dates. (The 1924 responses are from Lynd and Lynd 1929, 324.)

I used to cry when I was discouraged, but that didn't help any. Now I just git down on my knees and pray and that gives me strength [1924].

When I'm discouraged, I just read the Bible and think of the coming of the Kingdom [1924].

I pray and think of God. I've lots of faith in prayer. My baby was awfully sick and almost died; a lady came and prayed and folks in church went up and knelt around the altar, and the baby got well and is better than ever. The doctor says it was prayer and nothing else did it [1924].

I rely on the Bible scriptures; there are a lot of promises [1978].

I have the knowledge of a personal Savior there to guide and support me; the knowledge that things will turn our right [1978].

The hope of eternal life and the promise that God will supply my needs [1978].

I know there's a plan for my life. My Heavenly Father is in control. I don't need to worry. If I have a relaxed mental attitude, things will work out according to His plan [1978].

I guess God, really. I think about the beautiful things around me and how there must be a God. My religious beliefs are confused, but when things get really bad, I pray [1978].

Of the 68 working-class women who indicated how often they thought of Heaven in 1924, 46 percent said "often or every day" while 31 percent said they "never or almost never" gave Heaven a thought (Lynd and Lynd 1929, 325). Of the working-class women who answered the same question in 1978, 35 percent said "often or daily" but only 17 percent said "never or almost never."

The trouble is most people just live for today and don't think enough about Heaven. I *know* there's a Heaven and I know there's lots of these people expectin' to be there that'll be fooled [1924].

I often wonder about the future. I study and study over the passages in the Bible that tell about Judgment Day [1924].

My first husband died, leaving me with five children. I'm trying to bring them up to be good Christians, for that's the only way they will ever get to see their father. I just *know* he's up in Heaven now waiting for us! [1924].

On my mind constantly [1978].

Hard to judge. Not a day goes by without my thinking of Heaven. I don't think of myself as being there soon. I play the organ to get in touch. I'm a deep person and I think a lot [1978].

Very often as a friend recently committed suicide. Also, my grandmother is ill [1978].

I think of it when I say my prayers. I don't consciously think of it. It's there. I wonder what it will be like. It makes me feel closer to my parents and grand-parents who are deceased [1978].

As these statements illustrate, a sizable proportion of the married women of Middletown contemplate Heaven on a regular basis. The habit is intensified by the illness or the death of a friend or a rela-tive.

But there are also many people who seldom or never think about Heaven, as the following comments from both surveys show. (The 1924 comments are from Lynd and Lynd 1929, 326.)

Just today and tomorrow are the things I think of [1924].

Never, I guess, but I have the uneasy feeling I ought to [1924].

Almost never. I used to believe in Hell. Now I don't know what to think, but anyway, I don't spend my time worrying about it [1924].

I don't never think of it. What I believe is you get what's coming to you in this life [1924].

None. I don't think I'll ever get there, so I don't think about it [1978].

Zero. If it's there, fine. I'm not going to worry about it [1978].

Really haven't. I have been too busy with the children [1978].

None, I haven't thought about it. Wait, I just thought—I saw the movie *Heaven Can Wait* last month so I'd have to say once [1978].

The responses of the 1978 sample to this question are consistent with their responses to the first question we discussed above. Again, we failed to discover any decline of religious faith since 1924. In-stead, there seems to have been some increase. And, once again, we found no difference between business-class and working-class re-sponses.

In answer to the question "What difference would it make in your daily life if you became convinced that there is no loving God caring for you?" 13 percent of the Lynds' working-class respond-ents rejected the question outright as unthinkable and 58 percent "were so emphatic as to say that life would be intolerable or utter-ly changed" (Lynd and Lynd 1929, 326). When we put the same question to working-class women in 1978, 17 percent of them re-jected the question as unthinkable or outrageous and 51 percent said that life would be intolerable or utterly changed. Their comments were, if anything, a little stronger than those of the 1924 respondents.

It is a sin not to believe in God and His care and anyone who doesn't is just stubborn [1924].

Nobody could make me believe there isn't a God [1924].

I could never become so bitter over things as to doubt God [1924].

I couldn't be convinced. I *know* there is! [1978].

This, to me, is too stupid to even relate to [1978].

I don't believe that would happen. Nothing could convince me of that. God is and always will be [1978].

Eleven percent of the working-class housewives responding in 1924 said that it would make no particular difference to them if they became convinced that there was no loving God; 9 percent expressed that attitude in the 1978 sample.

The comparison of the 1924 and 1978 responses to these questions by business-class women is much less satisfactory. The Lynds' sample of business-class women was excessively small to begin with, and the respondents showed some resistance to these particular questions. Only 5 business-class women responded to the first question about the source of their courage, and their answers were not analyzed. Of the 15 who responded to the query about Heaven, not one woman said that she often thought of it; the modal answer was "never." Of the 19 business-class women responding to the question about how they would respond to a Godless world, the majority said that they would be affected little or not at all if they lost their belief in a loving God; several implied that they had already lost it. The small size of the sample precludes taking these results too seriously. In the 1978 survey, nearly 200 business-class women responded to each of the three questions, and the responses did not differ significantly from those of working-class women, although they were more elaborate and articulate. Of the 187 business-class women who responded to the first question, 27 percent said that they derived their courage from religion, 32 percent from their families, 5 percent from both, and 30 percent from other sources of reassurance (such as self-esteem, the reflection that they were better off than others, or some moral, cyclical, or fatalistic theory), while 5 percent insisted that they were never discouraged. Of the 178 business-class women who responded in 1978 to "How often have you thought of Heaven during the past month?" 29 percent said "often or daily," 24 percent said "never or not at all," and the remainder, for the most part, gave remarkably precise answers ranging from once to 25 times. Whereas some working-class respondents understood "Heaven" to be a general term for religion or God, practically all of the business-class women understood "Heaven" to refer to a personal afterlife, and they answered accordingly. For 3 out of 4 of them, as for a slightly higher proportion of working-class women, Heaven was a fact of life. They thought of it more often after the death of a close relative or a friend, when they were gravely ill, or when they were in church; and they remembered later what they thought when Heaven was on their minds. The 24 percent of the business-class respondents who said that they had not thought of Heaven during the previous month were divided more or less evenly into two dissimilar categories: the nonbelievers who rejected the idea of an afterlife out of intellectual conviction and the religiously inattentive who had other preoccupations. A few answers are difficult to classify. For example:

I'm not even sure that there is a Heaven. I believe in reincarnation but not in a Heaven as they preach in churches.

I don't know how to answer that. My hope is to live eternally on a cleansed earth and my concept of Heaven is that it is a ruling source.

I probably don't think of it at all. I'm too concerned with earth. I will let Heaven take care of itself because I figure my job's down here.

I don't think I'll ever get there, so I don't think about it.

In response to the question "What difference would it make in your daily life if you became convinced that there is no loving God caring for you?" 10 percent of the business-class women found the question unthinkable, 47 percent said that their lives would be intolerable or utterly changed, 22 percent said that it would make a less serious difference (the most frequent response in this category was to the effect that "I would become depressed"), and 21 percent said that it would make no difference (most of them said that they did not believe in a loving God and a minority asserted their own moral strength). The religious commitment implied by these responses is slightly less than that of the working-class women surveyed in 1978 but vastly greater than what the Lynds reported for their tiny sample of business-class women in 1924. Admittedly, the 1924 sample did not provide good statistical evidence, but the Lynds were persuaded on the basis of other evidence that the level of religious faith was higher among the working class than among the business class at that time. Their conclusions on that point cannot be lightly brushed aside. Overall, the 1978 survey suggests that the religious commitment of working-class women has not changed appreciably since 1924, while the religious commitment of business-class women has much increased. Is this finding plausible?

It is possible, of course, that respondents to the 1978 survey were simply giving us what they thought were the expected and socially approved answers to our questions. Certainly, this occurred in some interviews. On the other hand, we would not expect more conventional responses from business-class respondents than from working-class respondents; the former are more familiar with dissenting ideas of all kinds and are more used to expressing them than are working-class women. There is even less reason to suppose that insincere conformity would be more common in 1978 than in 1924; all of our information about Middletown, including some presented here, suggests that the community is much more tolerant of unconventional opinions than it used to be. But what most inclines us to take the religious commitment of the business-class women more or less at face value is the character of their verbatim responses. For the most part, these did not suggest the unthinking repetition of conventional formulas. Here are some of their responses to the question "What difference would it make in your daily life if you became convinced that there is no loving God caring for you?"

I'm afraid I'd become more concerned about acquiring material things, less concerned about people, and my business dealings would be less according to Hoyle.

I would be gone. My whole premise would be torn apart. I couldn't deal with that.

I would see no reason for living if I didn't believe in the afterlife. There'd be no direction or purpose to living. This life stinks.

I'd be afraid to even get up in the morning. I can't really imagine that. No one could convince me that there wasn't a loving God caring for me.

I couldn't handle that, I couldn't.

I'd cut my wrists if no one above loved me as I am. It would be miserable.

You might as well give up and die; if you don't believe in God, you're lost.

I'd give up and sin.

I would wonder what the purpose of trying to teach the children right from wrong would be. I would wonder what was going to become of all of us. It would make all the difference, change all the priorities and motivations.

That the religious attitudes of business-class women and working-class women have moved closer together over the past 50 or so years is not wholly surprising. In the high school surveys previously described, the working-class students of 1924 expressed a significantly higher level of acceptance of the dominant Christian beliefs than their business-class schoolmates. By 1978, those differences had disappeared. Other surveys we conducted in Middletown in 1977 and 1978 showed that, in many ways, the attitudes and habits of the business-class women of 1978 were closer to those of the working-class women of 1924 than to those of the business-class women of 1924 (Caplow and Chadwick 1979).

The suggestion that there has been a resurgence of traditional religion in Middletown is made with caution because of the limited scope of our evidence. But the suggestion is consistent with a variety of indications that Middletown's citizens are more involved in religion today than were their predecessors in the 1920s. In the 1970s, public statements of the religious values held by officials and businesspeople frequently appeared in Middletown's newspapers. For example, in October 1976, a congressman, a superior court judge, a precinct committeeman, a school board member, and a candidate for county judge participated in a panel discussion sponsored by the First Presbyterian Church. Each of the men affirmed their religious commitment and described how their religious beliefs influenced their personal and political lives.

An odd event that occurred during the Christmas holidays of 1977 further illustrates the currency of traditional religious images in the community. On Christmas Eve, a Middletown family posed with several friends for snapshots taken with a Polaroid camera. One photograph emerged with a "large, oddly-shaped image on the wall above the shoulders of two members of the group" (Middletown's evening newspaper, January 1, 1978). The image was immediately identified by those present as Satan's. When the photograph was shown in various churches, it attracted general interest as a snapshot of the devil. Several ministers judged it to be authentic, and a photography expert testified that the photo had not been tampered with. During the ensuing controversy over whether the image was Satan's, copies of the photograph were circulated throughout the factories and assembly plants of Middletown and were extensively discussed.

Attendance at Religious Services

For our present purpose of assessing the long-term trend of religious observance, the Lynds' report of family church attendance (Lynd and Lynd 1929, 530-31) provides the best point of departure. Their report was based on a 1924 sample of 164 Middletown families, all native-born, white, and intact (that is, the husband and the wife were living together with one or more children between 6 and 18); the wife was the principal respondent in every case. They described "Attendance at Religious Services by Business Class and Working Class Families Interviewed in 1924 and by the Wives' Parents' Families in the 90s, as She Reported Retrospectively." The frequency of attendance at Sunday morning and Sunday evening services and Sunday school was given for the entire family and for fathers, mothers, and children. We will limit our initial analysis to attendance at Sunday morning services by various members of business-class and working-class families in 1924 and by the wives' parents' families around 1890. To permit comparison with later data from other sources, we have condensed the six attendance categories given by the Lynds into four attendance categories as follows: regular (attends religious services four times a month or more), intermittent (attends religious services one to three times a month), occasional (attends religious services less often than once a month, and none (never attends religious services). (See Appendix A, Table 11-1.)

The data about church attendance reported by business- and working-class women in Middletown in 1924 for themselves and for their husbands and for their fathers and their mothers around 1890 has interesting implications, some of which the Lynds themselves may have overlooked. If we assume that the respondents' recall of their parents' churchgoing habits was reasonably accurate, there seems to have been a significant decline in regular church attendance from 1890 to 1924 for both sexes and both social classes. The decline was greater for the working class than for the business class and was accompanied in the working class, but not in the business class, by a sharp increase in the proportion *never* attending religious services, from a little over a third in 1980 to two-thirds in 1924. By 1924, the majority of Middletown's working-class adults seem to have entirely given up the habit of going to church.

The business-class wives and husbands of 1924 were twice as likely to attend religious services regularly as their working-class counterparts and much less likely to stay away from church altogether. The proportion of business-class men who never attended church in 1924 was slightly *lower* than the proportion of their fathers-in-law who never attended around 1890, although business-class wives showed a moderate increase in nonattendance compared to their mothers. These figures at first seem to contradict what we have just learned about the greater intensity of religious sentiments and convictions among working-class women in Middletown in 1924. Indeed, they invite question. As noted above, the Lynds were persuaded by their own observations that religious commitment was less fervid in the business class.

The clue to this mystery may be found in the Sunday school attendance of children. It appears that 63 percent of the children in the working-class families of the 1924 sample attended Sunday school regularly and only 12 percent never attended. In other words, in a typical working-class family of 1924, the parents stayed away from church but sent their children to Sunday school. For these people, most of them recent rural migrants to the city, churchgoing was associated with social climbing and a display of respectability, for which they lacked the resources. This condition was to be only temporary.

There is another anomaly in the Lynds' data that calls for explanation. The rates of attendance at religious services reported for husbands and wives in 1924 are virtually identical. This equal participation does not square either with the Lynds' subjective observation of predominantly female congregations or with a questionnaire survey of average weekly attendance at religious services that they distributed to every minister in Middletown in November 1924. The adjusted account of average weekly attendance (Lynd and Lynd 1929, 529) based on the ministers' reports shows 61 percent female attendance at the Sunday morning services during that month. This is not an overwhelming differential, but it is substantial and suggests that, although the rates of attendance of husbands and wives in intact families were practically identical, women in other family situations and other stages of the life cycle attended church services significantly more often than men in those situations. The Lynds did not present any quantitative data about attendance by age, but they mentioned in several places that church attendance increased with age.

The surveys we conducted in Middletown in 1977 and 1978 enabled us to bring some of these trends up to date. Comparing the Lynds' survey of 183 housewives in 1924 and the retrospective information they gave about their parents' habits around 1890 to our survey of 333 housewives in 1978 reveals a grand trend in church attendance for married women in intact, white Middletown families over an interval of about nine decades. (See Appendix A, Table 11-2.) The comparison told us several interesting things. First, the downward trend in church attendance from 1890 to 1924 reversed itself some time between 1935 and 1978. Nearly half of the 1978 respondents reported attending religious services regularly (at least four times a month), more than twice the proportion so reporting in 1924 and not much lower than the figure for 1890. At the other end of the distribution, the proportion of the 1978 respondents who said that they *never* attended religious services was only 17 percent, less than a third of the corresponding proportion in 1924 and significantly lower than in 1890 as well.

In 1890 and 1924, as the Lynds reported, Middletown's two major classes differed sharply in their patterns of church attendance. In 1978 we discovered that business-class and working-class families, although still distinguishable in other respects, were very similar with respect to church attendance, just as we had already found them to be very similar in their religious sentiments. (See Appendix A, Table 11-3.)

A more detailed study of religious attitudes and practices that we undertook by means of another 1978 survey in Middletown led to the same conclusion. In their religious attitudes and practices, Middletown's two major social classes are now culturally homogeneous. The conclusion holds when we examine the relationship between socioeconomic status and religiosity in terms of continuous variables such as income and education, instead of class membership. The correlation of religious behavior with any or all of the basic status indicators is low.

Through our oversight, the question on frequency of attendance at religious services in our 1978 survey of religious attitudes and practices was tied to denominational membership in a way that limited its usefulness. Fortunately, the same question in a more useful form was included in two occupational surveys we conducted in Middletown, one with a sample of 471 female respondents and the other with a sample of 215 male respondents, both in 1978. Based on our current surveys, we calculated the distribution of church attendance by sex. (See Appendix A, Table 11-4.) The proportions of the sexes reporting *no* attendance were similar, but women were somewhat more likely to attend regularly when they attended at all. The contemporary differences between men and women in church attendance are much smaller than those observed in 1924 and in 1935.

Observations made by the researchers while they were attending various Middletown churches in 1977 through 1979 revealed a general pattern of family worship. There were usually a few more women than men in attendance, but the differences were not dramatic.

One reason for the fairly high rate of churchgoing in 1978 was the large number of attendance-promoting activities conducted by the local churches. Revivals are still held in the city and in the surrounding county, especially during the summer. As the term implies, "revivals" are intended to revive church members' religious commitment as well as to "bring new souls to Christ." They generally are well advertised. And a visiting minister conducts a highly emotional service. Those denominations that do not sponsor revivals sometimes bring visiting preachers to Middletown to stimulate interest and increase church attendance.

Campaigns to increase church attendance are often elaborate. For example, during April 1977, one Baptist church attempted to increase its attendance by sponsoring a contest with a church in a neighboring city. Four special services were held during the month in connection with the contest. On the first Sunday, a

200-foot banana split was created in the yard of the church and eaten by the congregation. On Palm Sunday, the congregation flew kites; and, on Easter Sunday, a special program was presented. A "bus appreciation Sunday" concluded the month, and youngsters who rode the bus to church were treated to dinner at MacDonalds (Middletown evening newspaper, April 18, 1977). Activities of this sort help to keep Middletown's churches filled.

Some insight into the persistence of churchgoing is afforded by people's reports about why they attend or stay away from church. The most important reasons reported by married women were (1) that going to church is habitual for them, (2) that they enjoy church services, and (3) that they attend for their children's sake. References to the first and last of these themes from both the 1924 and the 1978 surveys are contrasted below. Once again, they are similar in tone. (The 1924 response is from Lynd and Lynd 1929, 361.)

We were all raised to go to church. It helps you in bringing up a family to do right—and that's hard enough anyway in these days [1924].

It is a habit. It is important to the children. I was raised in the church and enjoy it [1978].

The next comments, again from both surveys, show that there are several kinds of enjoyment Middletown people claimed to obtain from churchgoing: spiritual peace, the pleasure of worship, sociability and fellowship, and the experience of personal improvement. (The 1924 responses are from Lynd and Lynd 1929, 361.)

We like it. It does us good for the whole week, especially Mr. _____'s sermons [1924].

I feel better all week for going and looking forward to it [1924].

I get a lot of good out of it. Real Christians want to hear others' opinions in regard to the future [1924].

I enjoy the music and the peaceful feeling. The minister gives interesting talks and sometimes I need a moral uplifting [1978].

Because I get something out of church service. It renews me in a way and I enjoy seeing people. I sing in the choir and enjoy participating in the service [1978].

I feel it's important. The family needs to go together. A renewal of the spirit. It is a constant reminder of God and Jesus. As we go to church, we try to lead better lives [1978].

Basically I go to make my child religiously aware [1978].

In 1924 habit was the most common motive for church attendance. (See Appendix A, Table 11-5.) By 1978, there had been a very significant decrease in the number of people who said that they went to church primarily out of habit. Middletown people seem to have examined the value of church participation, and those who attend do so because they enjoy the service or expect some benefit from it. Spiritual renewal, instruction, inner peace, and Christian fellowship were repeatedly mentioned as benefits. Compared to the 1924 respondents, the 1978 respondents mentioned benefits to their children somewhat more often and social and business motives somewhat less often.

The reasons given for not attending church were more varied. The six reasons for avoiding church services given most often in 1978 were the same as those given in 1924. (See Appendix A, Table 11-6.) Fatigue was a factor in many cases. (The 1924 responses are from Lynd and Lynd 1929, 362.)

I could pick up and go to church but I just don't—I'm too tired mostly. My husband's a member of the Methodist Church and he don't like to work Sundays but he just has to keep his job [1924].

By the time I get the children ready, it's too late to start and I'm too tired. He works hard all week and rests Sunday. I approve of church all right but just can't scrape up time and energy to go [1924].

I don't attend because I need Sundays to sleep in [1978].

Sundays are our time alone. The children go to church. My husband works long hours and is tired on Sundays [1978].

Other families were habitual nonattenders in the same casual way that some of their neighbors were habitual attenders. (The 1924 responses are from Lynd and Lynd 1929, 362 [the first] and 364 [the second].)

I used to go to evening service pretty regular, but the rest of the family don't want to go so now I stay home. I like the family to be together. Just as good people stay outside the church as in it anyway. My children don't get anything out of Sunday School [1924].

Both he and I are tied down all week and need to get out Sundays. I feel it's better to keep the family all together than for me to go to church Sunday morning and my husband to be at home alone [1924].

Sunday is the only day for the family alone. We both work including some Saturdays. But the church is a great teacher of children [1978].

Sunday is the only time to be with the family and we feel that is more important [1978].

A few people left a particular church in silent resistance to a tithe or a forced contribution. (The 1924 responses are from Lynd and Lynd 1929, 364 [the first] and 365 [the second].)

It cost too much and we just didn't get much out of it. People talk about tithing, but what's a tithe to some ain't a tithe to others. It's all right always to give to others, but when you see other people shiftless and you're saving and scrimping, why ought you to give to them when they get in trouble through not having saved [1924].

I believe in bringing up a child in going to church; it gets him in with a good class of people. We don't have a close church connection any longer, though, because once we couldn't pay our regular contribution, they dropped us from the roll [1924].

Laziness. Plus couldn't keep up with tithing and when the church commented about it, it turned us off [1978].

We left the church when asked for a tithe and we were threatened to be dropped from the membership list [1978].

We don't attend because the church asked for tithing in the form of a bill. They billed me and I didn't like that [1978].

Only 7 percent of the 1924 respondents and 13 percent of the 1978 respondents gave *ideological* reasons for staying away from church. Again, the responses to the two surveys conducted 54 years apart were uncannily similar in tone. (The 1924 responses are from Lynd and Lynd 1929, 365.)

There's too many hypocrites in the churches. They're just all the time asking for money, trying to squeeze it out of you. This church over there is just full of Klan members and I just ain't got any use of the Klan [1924].

After I married, I drifted away from church. Then I began to decide I didn't WANT to attend anyway. There are too many people in church that worship the almighty dollar—too many mean people that oughtn't to be there. People oughta live right, and then it won't matter about church. My girl sometimes wants to go to Sunday School and I won't keep her away—because she MIGHT learn some good. But I won't force any child of mine to go to Sunday school or church, either [1924].

We don't attend because we feel some of the people are hypocrites. We had a bad experience. The minister was dismissed because a major contributor didn't like him and the people didn't have the guts to stand up for what was right [1978].

We are not attending because the church has let down the young people. The people are too social-affluently oriented [1978].

The changes in the pattern from 1924 to 1978 were small. Fatigue is not as important a factor as it used to be. Today's families are more likely to have examined their own feelings about church participation and to have made their decision to attend or not on the basis of what they feel they get out of it.

Financial Contributions

Some Christian denominations, on the authority of the Bible, call on each member family to tithe, that is, to contribute 10 percent of their incomes to the church. In a sample of 100 working-class families, the Lynds found only 1 family that paid a full tithe. The Lynds seemed to suggest, although they did not say so, that the rate of contribution was declining in 1924.

Financial support of the church appears in Middletown at all levels, from the spontaneous giving of the traditional tithe on the part of a few ardent church members, through the stage of giving "because I wouldn't like to live in a land without churches" or because it is "expected," to not giving at all. In the face of increasing financial demands of the individual churches and their denominational boards, "giving of one's substance to the Lord" is meeting with greater competition as community-wide charity is becoming secularized and the outward dominance of the church in the community declining. Meanwhile, according to statements by the ministers and by the treasurers of two business class churches, the increasing money needs of the churches and their denominations and the declining dominance of the "message" of the church with many Middletown people are increasing the relative prominence of the money tie between a church and its members as compared with a generation ago (Lynd and Lynd 1929, 358).

The average percentages of family income contributed to churches by working-class families in 1924 and 1978 were calculated. The competition of private charities has not intensified since 1924; working-class families contributed 0.7 percent of their family income to such charities in 1924 and only 0.8 percent in 1978. Today's families are contributing proportionately *more*, not less, to organized religion. The average family's contribution doubled from 1924 to 1978, from 1.6 percent to 3.3 percent of the family income. Instead of the 1 percent of working-class families who paid a full tithe in 1924, 3.5 percent reported doing so in 1978. The proportions of family income given by working- and business-class families are almost identical.

Middletown and the United States

The use of a specimen community for the study of social change required us to reexamine continually the typicality of that community in order to gauge how well it can serve as a replica of the national society. That issue presents itself with special force in the area of religion, where Middletown's familism and fundamentalism seem to set it a world apart from the image of contemporary America presented in the mass media.

Middletown *is* familistic and fundamentalist, although all sorts of competing beliefs and interests are represented there. But a review of the available survey evidence casts some doubt on the stereotypical image of the United States as an agnostic, alienated country absorbed in following exotic cults. For instance, the level of church attendance in Middletown, which appears so extremely high when viewed in isolation, turns out to be slightly *lower* than the estimated level for the country as a whole. We compared adult church attendance in Middletown in 1978, based on the two occupational surveys described above, with adult church attendance in the United States, based on the careful national sample drawn by the National Opinion Research Center for the 1976 replication of its General Social Survey. (See Appendix A, Table 11-7.) The proportions of respondents reporting regular and occasional church attendance in the Middletown sample and in the national sample were almost identical, but a significantly higher proportion of Middletown respondents *never* attended and a correspondingly lower proportion attended frequently. Other available national data, although scanty, also show reasonable congruence with the data from Middletown.

PART IV Middletown and America

Chapter 12

American Families
during the Twentieth Century

The preoccupation with change in most studies of the family is ironic. Of all social institutions, the family shows least evidence of change. The family in industrial society is amazingly similar to that in primitive society. In fact, in many ways, the modern family is more "primitive," in the sense of being elementary, than the family in primitive societies. Basically, the family varies relatively little from one society to another. It embodies similar principles everywhere, and these principles are so simple that they can be grasped by anyone who thinks about them for a moment. . . .

The central principle of the family is a particular way of assigning responsibility. The family is created by assigning responsibility for children to the couple who physically produces them. The couple is "licensed" to reproduce (marriage); their children are placed and identified with them; each partner's rights and obligations are defined with respect to the other and with respect to the children; and the parents are normatively expected to stay together and provide a stable milieu for the children. Connection through marriage and filiation, thus established, is made the basis for social relationships not only within a particular nuclear family, but also between nuclear families, giving rise to the wider kinship network. This principle is so universal that we take it for granted. . . .

. . . Compared to the complexities of the modern corporation, or a governmental or educational bureaucracy, the family is a remarkably uncomplicated group. It may be "psychologically" complicated, but not organizationally so, and its "psychological" complications seem remarkably similar among societies over time (Davis 1972, 239).

Is Family Life in Middletown a Working Model
for American Family Change?

The story of Middletown's families told in the preceding chapters is one of selective continuity of basic values reinforced by solidarity bonds intergenerationally, but it is also one of selective adaptations to the changing community contexts of the "near environment." From generation to generation, the most dramatic and fundamental contextual changes occurred in the mid-nineteenth century during the lifetimes of the great-grandparents of today's citizens in the transformation from a rural economy based on muscular effort to one dependent on mechanical power. The period studied by the Lynds, 1890-1925-1935, was clearly one of continued community restructuring. Middletown grew from a geographically isolated county trade center of 6,000 souls in 1890 (which was still agrarian in its world orientation and which offered to its families few social amenities and limited ways of making a living) into a fully industrialized city (with a population of 40,000 in 1920).

The phenomena of modernization, urbanization, and specialization continued in Middletown after 1920, but at a much slower pace, with growth leveling off in the 1950s. The problems of family adaptation were, accordingly, less acute than expected by the Middletown III project researchers. Indeed, the continuity of marriage and family patterns from generation to generation seems to have been more characteristic than change during the last 50 years. "Middletown is becoming, for the first time in its history, a place where the present resembles the past and pre-figures the probable future" (Bahr, Caplow, and Leigh 1980).

In this penultimate chapter, we will attempt to discover to what extent family change in the country as a whole, and in selected regions, resembles that observed in Middletown as a specimen community. If social change has slowed down for the country as a whole, has there been a convergence in family patterns among ethnic and regional groups, as there has been between business- and working-class families in Middletown? (See Caplow and Chadwick 1979.) Has diversity in the *timing* of leaving home, taking a job, marrying and having children decreased as the country consolidated its gains in urbanization and industrialization during the twentieth century? Or has the differentiation of life-styles increased with the appearance of nonfamily options that entail the postponement of marriage, parenthood, and settling down to adult family responsibilities? The data required to answer these questions for the country as a whole are incomplete. Moreover, the desired specification by region, ethnic group, and class will be even more difficult to undertake for past historical periods. Let the reader beware!

Theories about the Family and Social Change

Four theories of social change can be invoked to illuminate the empirical data we will shortly present about family trends during the past 200 years. (1) A macrotheory of economic and technological determinism asserts that the family is a relatively powerless reactor, passively accommodating with some time lags to changes in the economy. (2) A macrotheory of cyclic change assumes that family institutions react to historical stimuli but also set limits to the excesses of secularization and the sensate and set in motion counterforces to return the society to a state of equilibrium. According to this theory, the family is not only a reactor to, and a facilitator of, change, but families also act collectively to neutralize and buffer change. (3) A mesotheory of transactional exchanges between families and their "near environments" argues that families initiate actions on, and respond directly to, *proximal forces* of changes in the economy (as in investment opportunities); in the occupational system (as in employment opportunities); in the marketplace (as in increases in living costs); and in the educational, media, health, and transportation systems—rather than to the *distant* and *longer-term* processes of industrialization, urbanization, and modernization. According to this mesotheory, families respond to these last three macroprocesses indirectly and with delays of one or more generations, if they respond at all. (4) A sociohistorical stress theory of family change asserts that families respond adaptively to stressful historical events that create "transitional generations" followed by a resumption of continuity of values and behavioral patterns from generation to generation. We will examine the "closeness of fit" of these theories with the empirical data on the family and social change at the end of the chapter. We will also use them to inform us about findings throughout the discussion.

In arranging our historical data to take advantage of the fourth theory, we found it useful to designate major historical events that represent possible watershed marks for change. Although we have few national statistics about families going back to the antebellum period or the Civil War, these distinct periods should be differentiated in any discussion of the phases in the transformation of American society. By 1890, when most of our Middletown assessments began, the frontiers had closed and transcontinental westward migrations had slowed, not to resume again for 50 years. In the twentieth century, the chief stressful events surely include World War I (1914-1918), the Great Depression (1930-1940), World War II (1941-1945), the Korean conflict (1951-1953), and the period of civil disorder associated with the Vietnam war (1964-1972). Note that these events occurred sequentially, one per decade, producing a cyclical disruption of established patterns that left little time between events for the achievement of a steady state.

Several analysts of social change make World War II the major watershed of change in the twentieth century (Foote 1960 and Modell et al. 1978). Others, drawing on theories of modernization, note that the major social and economic changes in America took place during the period between 1890 and 1920, with change decelerating thereafter (Boulding 1970 and Bahr, Caplow, and Leigh 1980). The Middletown data favor the latter interpretation. (See Chapters 1, 2, and 7.)

There are obvious advantages to using historical markers to punctuate the more global and diffuse processes of urbanization, industrialization, and secularization. Such historical events are stressful for the nation as a whole, as well as for the communities within which families and individuals work out their lives. The dislocations occasioned by the watershed events act both as stimulants to innovation and as constraints on the developmental careers of persons within families.

To "wed biography to history," we should note that individuals experiencing nationwide crises at the same points in their developmental histories become differentiated from those younger and those older as *distinct generations*; for example, we could speak of the depression generation, the World War II generation, and the protest generation. The term "cohort" is used technically to differentiate age-groups in the population born at the same time or those marrying in the same year.

Nelson Foote anticipated our decision to make intercohort and intergenerational comparisons in his explication of the relationship between the historical event as an indicator of change in the making and the behavior of generations as an indicator of the family's collective response to change.

The peculiar mechanism by which generations are differentiated is thus simultaneously *historical* and *biographical*. The historical events which produce the watersheds are economic and political shifts which affect the present and prospective conditions of life in all persons coming to adulthood when they occur. That is, they cause each young person's estimate of what is possible for him to differ from the estimate made by his parents at the same phase in their own life histories. Biographically, membership in a distinctive generation is not so much the result of when one is born as when he becomes an adult, an event far less definitely placed chronologically and which can be substantially hastened or postponed by historical events (Foote 1960, 9-10).

Since Foote's seminal essay was published, a sociology of age differentiation and stratification has developed, summarized by Matilda Riley and her colleagues (1972), which provides both a theoretical orientation and a method for analyzing social change intergenerationally at the level of individual and family. Some of the research on age differentiation will be discussed later in this chapter.

The central issues of family change to which the Middletown investigators have drawn our attention will also be themes for this chapter's assessment of change in the American family in general: getting married and becoming parents, making a home, getting ahead, and holding families together. The first two involve the transition from childhood to adulthood and the power struggle between the families of orientation (old loyalties and blood ties) and the families of procreation (conjugal affection and affinal ties). The third theme involves "life-course management," and the fourth concerns the adequacy of expressive functioning in the realms of marital and parental satisfaction. The chapter concludes with some conjecture about family change in the near future.

Long-Term Changes in the Societal Context

Let us begin with a profile of American society as it stands today: (1) predominantly urban; (2) heterogeneous in its ethnic, racial, religious, and occupational composition; (3) aging, but still young by European standards, with a high ratio of earners to dependents; (4) highly mobile occupationally and residentially; and, as of the 1970s, (5) still favorably disposed toward social change and (6) committed to a mixture of market and administrative allocations. North American society has evolved a distinctive ethos, differentiated sharply both from its European and African origins and from the native American societies. A number of structural and ecological features have encouraged the development of this distinctive society, which has been the beneficiary of continuous innovation and change: (1) a thinly inhabited country with abundant resources; (2) a relatively open opportunity structure, free of vested status and unemcumbered by traditions; (3) several waves of immigration that mingled cultures and encouraged pluralism; and (4) the pragmatic rationalism that has characterized the American approach to new situations, particularly in the realms of technology and private enterprise (Williams 1967, 572).

America today is no longer an adolescent society to be contrasted with long-established adult European and Asian societies. It is relatively cohesive, urbanized, secularized, and stabilized both demographically and economically. It meets all of the criteria for a highly developed modern nation, having low death rates and low birth rates in balance, a high level of education, and one of the highest standards of living in the world.

Although fully exposed to the secularizing influences of education and science, America's citizens remain church and family oriented. Marriage and parenthood are highly valued, with the overwhelming majority of the population living in nuclear families embedded in kinship networks. This is the relatively beneficient context within which contemporary American families are currently pursuing their life goals. Let us turn, now, to the picture of earlier periods in American history.

By 1890, the baseline from which the Lynds assessed family and social change in Middletown, many of the most dramatic changes in American society had already occurred. Two of the three major waves of immigration, 1840 to 1850 and 1870 to 1890, that brought English, Irish, and northern Europeans to America had already occurred. The proportion of the population foreign-born had risen to one-fourth, the level at which it would remain for the next 50 years. The industrial expansion that attracted the European migrants had quintupled the proportion of the population living in urban areas (from 7 percent in 1820 to 35 percent in 1890) and reduced the proportion engaged in farming from nearly 90 percent in 1820 to 42 percent in 1890. Population density had almost quadrupled, from 6 persons per square mile in 1820 to 21 persons per square mile in 1890, and was beginning to level off. The country was filling up.

When we move backward in time to note changes in the family during the nineteenth century, we do not, unfortunately, have much national data to examine. Data on household size, the average number of persons residing in the same dwelling unit (excluding households of public or semipublic character), are available. The census of 1790 shows the average household size as 5.8 persons; the figures ranged from only 4 percent of households with a single person to 36 percent with seven or more persons. Ogburn and Nimkoff (1955, 110) calculated average household size in 1800, also 5.8 persons, to be made up of lodgers, servants, and relatives (10 percent); children (60 percent); and parents (30 percent). One hundred years later, in 1900, household size had dropped to 4.8 persons, with an insignificant increase in the proportion of single-person households (to 5 percent) but a large decline (to 20 percent) in the proportion of households of seven or more persons.

The practice of taking in lodgers involved 15 to 20 percent of urban households throughout the nineteenth century, despite the criticism of middle-class reformers who saw violations of privacy in the practice.

. . . the close quarters often destroy all privacy, and the lodger or boarder becomes practically a member of the family. . . . While such conditions, through custom and long usage, lose the startling effect they would have on one unused to them, they cannot help but blunt a girl's sense of proper relations with the other sex and foster standards which are not acceptable in this country (U.S. Bureau of Labor 1910).

The manuscripts of census enumerations from 1850 onward

reveal that most of the "lodgers" were juveniles, distant relatives, unrelated persons of similar village origins or from the same foreign land, or young men sharing a trade with the household head. The practice was economically adaptive for families in the nineteenth century, which needed added income more than privacy, and especially for families in the later stages of the life cycle (Modell and Hareven 1973).

The analysis of household composition in the nineteenth century reveals very few three-generation households or joint households shared by married siblings. Most couples established separate households when they married rather than doubling up, even when it would have been advantageous to double up. Many families took in strangers as lodgers in preference to boarding their own married children. Reciprocally, young unmarried adults were willing to pay rent to lodge elsewhere, instead of contributing to the family purse and being accountable to parents. The nineteenth-century practice of boarding and lodging in preference to doubling up into extended family households is an adaptive response to the same norm of neo-local residence that prompts twentieth-century households, almost universally, to restrict themselves to nuclear family units. The neo-local residence of nuclear families has been the almost universal pattern in America since colonial times.

But did it imply the isolation of urban families from their kin? Writers in the 1930s and 1940s (Wirth 1938 and Parsons 1943) asserted that the typical American family was urban, isolated, and nuclear. Other forms, they said, might exist within our borders, but they would be found among southern highlanders or unassimilated immagrants and would eventually evolve into the urban, isolated, nuclear structure. Then, in the 1950s, a series of studies of urban communities in most of the regions of the United States and the urbanized provinces of Canada discovered that urban people did have relatives, interacted continually with them, seemed to enjoy it, and turned to their relatives in time of need (Adams 1970).

Estimates of the distribution of three types of nuclear families— (1) the nuclear family embedded in a network of extended kin, (2) the isolated nuclear family, and (3) the mother-child nuclear family, sometimes with matrilineal extensions—were provided by Winch (1971) from his studies of midwestern communities. In a middle-class suburb of Chicago, only 4 percent of Jews, 13 percent of Catholics, and 28 percent of Protestants lived in isolated nuclear families without kin living nearby. At the other end of the scale, 78 percent of Jews, 35 percent of Catholics, and 14 percent of Protestants reported the presence of 12 or more households of kin in the area—very dense kinship networks indeed (Winch 1970, 10). The mother-child nuclear family—usually a result of divorce, widowhood, or unwed motherhood—accounted for about 9 percent of white families and 28 percent of black families, and it was clearly a minority pattern.

More dramatic than the change in household composition during the nineteenth century was the decline in the birth rate, from 55 per 1,000 women in 1800 (one of the highest rates ever recorded anywhere) to 30 per 1,000 in 1900. In terms of completed family size, this meant a drop from 8 to 4 children per mother. Thus, the trend toward smaller families was already well along by the opening of the twentieth century, decades before effective methods of birth control were accessible to the general public.

Popular impressions to the contrary, death rates for adults were not significantly higher in the nineteenth century than they are today (Vinovskis 1978). Infant mortality, to be sure, was high throughout the century, as we know from Massachusetts records, and did not begin to decline until the second decade of the twentieth century. (The rate remained at or above 130 deaths per 1,000 infants from 1850 to 1900 [Historical Statistical Series of the U.S. 1975, Series B-148].) But, if children survived into adolescence, their subsequent life expectancy was high. The life expectancy of 15-year-olds in Massachusetts in 1860 was only 5 years less than their descendants in 1969; by age 30, it was virtually identical (Vinovskis 1978, 553). Life in the nineteenth century was perilous for infants and often uncomfortable for adults, but the prospect of a long life, for those who reached adulthood, was almost as good then as now.

From the scanty information we have about structural changes in the family over the past two centuries, we have shown reductions in household and family size, a sharp reduction of fertility, the paring down of the household to immediate family members, and the persistence of neo-local residence. Virtually no information is as yet available in historical depth for the whole country on such other aspects of family structure as the decision-making patterns within the family, the division of household labor by gender and age, familial authority, and the effectiveness of communication between spouses and between generations. We can get some information about the affectional structure in past eras from novels, but it is vague and unreliable. The assessment of change under these various headings up to World War II is, therefore, a matter of conjecture. Missing from this quick overview of the history of the American family is any mention of how the modal patterns were affected by the racial, ethnic, class, and regional groupings that turn out to be so important when we look at the much-better data of recent decades.

Family historians are just beginning to reconstruct the patterns of black family life in the eighteenth and nineteenth centuries (Gutman 1975, Fogel and Engerman 1974, and Pleck 1978). Enslaved blacks numbered 1.5 million in 1820 and 4 million on the eve of the Civil War. There were about 500,000 free blacks in 1860. Together, the blacks constituted 19 percent of the population. Of equal significance were the distinctive patterns of geographical regions: New England, the Middle Atlantic, the South, the Midwest, the Intermountain West, and the Far West.[1]

Change Versus Continuity in Family Patterns

Sources of data on both majority and minority family patterns are of uneven quality for the historical periods we want to cover in this chapter. To do the task justice, we would need accurate descriptions of regionally distinctive family patterns from at least three significant points in the nineteenth century, perhaps the antebellum period, the postbellum period, and the end of the century. Occasional glimpses of these patterns are provided for New England and the South by regional novelists and by the new family historians, but most historical writing has described events of greater sweep and has paid little attention to the details of courtship, marriage, and family life.

Other sources of data are collections of letters and diaries, generally in too raw a form to be useful; census data that are more valid and reliable but are seldom of direct relevance; and, in more recent decades, surveys of various kinds. Most surveys of family patterns are local rather than regional or national, date from after World War II and, therefore, offer little historical depth. A small number of three-generational surveys using retrospective interviews to gain materials on the older generations do offer some intergenerational comparisons for the first eight decades of the twentieth century. Limited though they are in regional and temporal scope, these surveys are the best sources we have for describing changes in American family patterns from the late nineteenth century to the late twentieth century.

Locating Families in Transition

A major gap in our understanding of the interrelationship between family change and social change is that we have little knowledge about how families traverse the uncertain, uncharted "no-man's-land" between one form of society and another. There is little theory and less information about *families in transition*.

We do have some informed ideas about how families in agrarian societies socialize the incoming generation to perform the same functions as their ancestors. When we turn to fully modernized societies, we can also make sense out of the processes that achieve workable family structures appropriate to the demands of an industrial economy. But societies in transition are more puzzling.

Ideally, we would like to have cohort data gathered during different time periods within the same family lines for the country as a whole. We can only begin to approximate this requirement in the findings to be presented.

We have already shown that America was experiencing a transition from a rural to a predominantly urban society long before the close of the nineteenth century and had largely completed the transition by the early 1900s. Which of the historical markers of the twentieth century help us to locate the heavily stressed generations we call transitional generations? Conceivably, no single cohort of families is *the* transitional generation, but studies of three-generational depth should identify some likely candidates.

The three-generation survey is a research design invented for the specific purpose of assessing less than long-run, but more than intercensal, family change. It was tried out first in Puerto Rico in the 1950s by Reuben Hill and Howard Stanton (Hill 1970a) and used again in Minnesota in the 1960s (Hill 1970b) and in California in the 1970s (Bengtson 1975) to locate the generations that were transitional with respect to norms, values, and practices.

In Puerto Rico from around 1900 to around 1950, there had been enormous changes in the occupational and opportunity structures; the whole industrial revolution had been compressed into 50 years. Hill and Stanton sought in their research with three generations of the same island families to discover how much concurrent change had taken place in family patterns with respect to both the *norms of behavior* and *actual behavior*. Samples of three-generation families were drawn from five communities selected to represent degrees of modernization: a mountain village, a coastal plantation village, an urban slum, a middle-class development of new homes, and an upper-class, walled-in neighborhood. The generations sampled included a grandparent generation married around 1900, at the time of annexation; a parent generation married in the late 1920s, as Puerto Rico achieved control of its schools and obtained self-government; and a married child generation, married in the 1950s, at the height of economic diversification.

What did Hill and Stanton find happening over the more than 50 years spanned by the three generations? Changes in *behavior* had only recently begun (in the third generation of the urban slums, married in the 1950s) and these changes were minimal. But changes in *norms* had been underway for three generations. The changes, moreover, were in the expected directions: less emphasis on marriage and parenthood, preference for fewer children, acceptance of divorce and separation, egalitarian rather than authoritarian relations between the sexes and the generations, less cloistering of girls and more acceptance of women's employment outside the home.

The investigators were unable to confirm from the data obtained by use of the three-generation technique in Puerto Rico the macro-theory of economic determinism, which asserts that economic development is a direct determinant of changes in family norms and behavior. Instead, the findings for Puerto Rico suggest that changes in family norms and behavior lag substantially behind changes in the economy; in Puerto Rico there is a lag of at least two generations, since the third generation was just *beginning to show discontinuities in behavior*. When viewed from within family lines, these effects appear to be retarded by mechanisms that encourage continuity rather than family change.

In a similar three-generation survey in Minnesota in the late 1960s (Hill 1970b), the families studied had departed from the traditional norms and behavior most dramatically between the *first* and *second* generations. They had not maintained continuity into the third generation, as families in Puerto Rico had.

We should note that the background of economic development was quite different for the two regions. Modernization had been under way in Minnesota for much longer than in Puerto Rico. The families studied in Minnesota were drawn from area probability samples of metropolitan Minneapolis-St. Paul, extending 100 miles into its hinterland. The families were widely dispersed by location and socioeconomic level but were somewhat more stable residentially than families without three-generation linkages. Like the Puerto Rican respondents, the Minnesota grandparents (aged 70 to 80) were married in the first decade of the century, the parents (aged 40 to 60) in the 1920s and 1930s, and the married children (aged 20 to 30) in the 1950s.

In the Minnesota sample, there were major differences in education and occupational preparation between the first and second generations. The grandparents were markedly different from the two successive generations in their moral values, their attitudes toward child rearing, their marital roles, and the wives' employment. There was a *marked change from traditional values and practices* between the first and second generations, followed by essential continuity of norms and behavior from the second to the third generations.

The replication of this study in California by Vern Bengtson and his colleagues (Bengtson and Kuypers 1971 and Bengtson 1975) was expected to provide a more rigorous test of the foregoing findings because California is a more heterogeneous and turbulent region than Minnesota and because the youngest cohort sampled was the "protest generation" of the 1960s. Bengtson found considerable continuity of values between generations, but, where differences occurred, the gap was between the grandparent and the parent generations, as it had been in the Minnesota survey performed 10 years earlier. Bengtson added questions about each generation's perception of a "generation gap" to supplement his objective findings on value similarities and differences. He asked, first, how much of a gap respondents perceived in the larger American society and, second, how much of a gap they saw within their own three-generation family.

The findings are interesting. All three generations perceived a gap in each pair of generations in the larger society; the children (the protest generation) and the grandparents (the World War I generation) saw the widest gap and the middle-aged parents (the World War II generation) saw the narrowest gap. But many fewer respondents, regardless of generation, perceived any gap at all in their own lineal families.

The youngest generation saw the widest gap within the larger society and within their own family line between the grandparent generation and their own. The grandparents saw the widest gap between the middle and the youngest generation. All three generations agreed that the closest bonds were between the grandparent generation and the parent generation. The objective findings were quite different! The parents appeared to be much closer to their married children in attitudes and behavior than to their own parents. It is they who must be considered the transitional generation.

Further intergenerational family study is required to understand what constitutes a turning point in family patterns. We are not very clear about how much change in family structure and in the content of family roles actually occurs in any one transitional generation.

The Minnesota and California surveys showed a transitional generation in both regions, the middle generation in each case. A marked discontinuity was found between the norms and the behavior of each grandparent generation and those of the corresponding parent generation, with a resumption of continuity between them and their adult children, the third generation.

The Influence of Historical Events on Three Generations

We now propose to place the three generations of the Minnesota study in relation to major historical events in order to discover how each of them was influenced—or not influenced—by those events. Did the middle generation, for example, encounter the stressful events of depression and war at a particularly vulnerable point in its developmental career, so that it developed differently from the other two generations? We return to Foote's thesis that the timing of entrance into adulthood, that is, of marrying and becoming parents, marks off a generation more than the timing of its members' births. We theorize that the middle generation's marrying during the Great Depression and child raising during World War II will be of high significance in its adaptations.[2]

Figure 12-1 has been constructed to show the relative location of each generation with respect to historical markers that represent watersheds of social changes. The lengths of the bars in Figure 12-1 were derived from actual data about the marital careers of three generations of the same family lines, whose properties we describe further in Figure 12-2. We have had to estimate from actuarial tables the duration of the postparental period for the youngest generation (marital cohort C) in the Minnesota study because this generation still has many years to go before reaching the end of its developmental cycle.

Figure 12-1 represents schematically the developmental careers of three marital cohorts, each consisting of couples married at roughly the same time. The couples within each cohort mature over time while taking on increasing family responsibilities. They pass through a sequence of family role clusters, learning new roles and relinquishing old ones, striving to build an acceptable reputation and identity as a family, accumulating knowledge and social experience, developing increasing competence as spouses and parents, and suffering the cumulative losses to which mortality is heir.

New marital cohorts are continually being formed. Figure 12-1 illustrates only three of many possible cohorts, but these three were selected because they represent generations as well as cohorts, separated as they are by the years required for a new marital cohort to be generated. The time spent in each stage of childbearing, child rearing, and child emancipation varies by marital cohort. Note that the grandparent generation (cohort A) had a more elongated period of childbearing and child rearing than the subsequent generations. Closer spacing of children and an earlier return of wives to the labor force accounts for the shorter period of childbearing for cohort C, but the later entrance into the labor force and later age at marriage of this cohort's children will prolong the child-rearing stage for this generation as they enter middle parenthood.

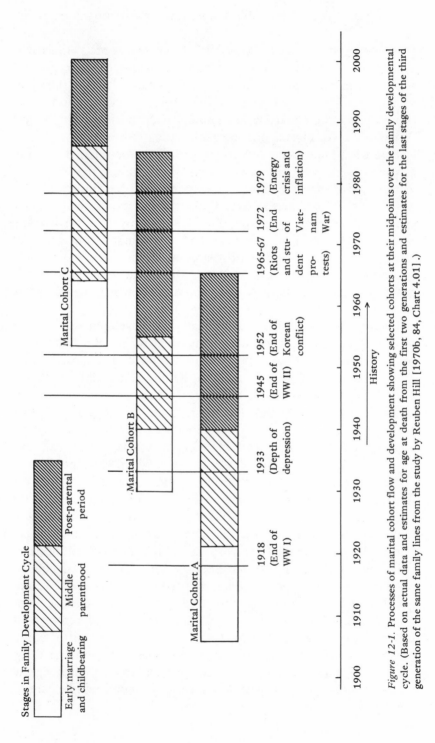

Figure 12-1. Processes of marital cohort flow and development showing selected cohorts at their midpoints over the family developmental cycle. (Based on actual data and estimates for age at death from the first two generations and estimates for the last stages of the third generation of the same family lines from the study by Reuben Hill [1970b, 84, Chart 4.01].)

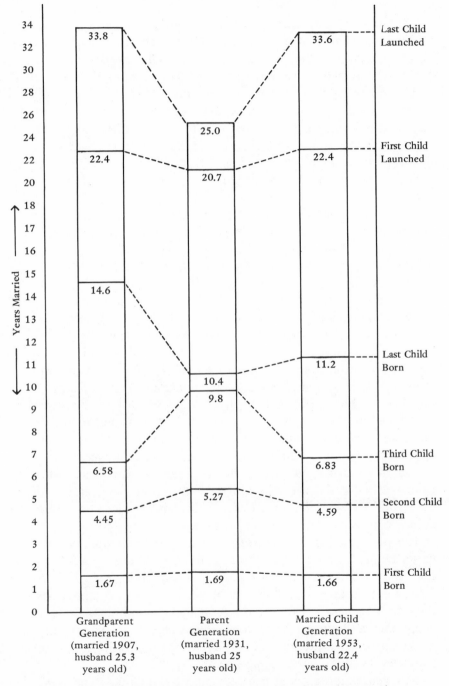

Figure 12-2. Profile of the timing of family composition changes by generation. (Adapted from Hill 1970b, 84, Chart 4.01.)

The major historical events that affected the families described by Figure 12-1 were World War I, the Great Depression, World War II, the Korean conflict, the race riots and civil disturbances of the 1960s, the socially divisive experiences associated with the Vietnam conflict, and the current energy and monetary crises. Each marital cohort encounters a unique sequence of such events. Hence, the developmental patterns of families of different generations work themselves out in different ways. Let us illustrate by delineating the career struggles of cohorts A, B, and C (their historical placement is shown in Figure 12-1 and their developmental careers are summarized in Figure 12-2).

The grandparent generation appears to have settled for the most modest goals, a more cautious development of resources, and a less ambitious occupational career, lagging behind the succeeding generations year by year from early marriage onward. The grandparent generation entered marriage at a later age and, lacking knowledge of family-planning methods, bore more unwanted as well as more planned children at closer intervals over a longer period of time than their successors. (See Figure 12-2.) At the mercy of an unplanned economy and limited occupational opportunities, this generation shifted jobs infrequently and experienced little upward mobility. They acquired property and adequate amenities only after their children were launched. Unprotected by life insurance over most of their careers and prevented from saving for retirement because of the Great Depression, the people of this generation launched their children into marriage later and over a longer period of time and, altogether, spent a long time in childbearing, child rearing, and leave taking. Their educational aspirations for their children were the lowest of the three generations, their children overachieving the goals set for them by their parents.

The parent generation appears to have been the most prudent in its family planning and its development of resources. Having high educational aspirations for its children (more than half set college education as the goal) and having high housing aspirations, the middle generation followed a strategy of family planning, occupational mobility, delayed home ownership, but early acquisition of protective life insurance and retirement equities to achieve a high level of life-course management.

This generation entered marriage during the Great Depression[3] at a prudent age, spaced its children farthest apart, closed its families early with the smallest total number of children, and augmented the family income by the early reentry of the wives into the labor force to take advantage of war-born opportunities for employment. Deferred from military service because of age and family responsibilities, the fathers upgraded their occupational position by shifting jobs frequently. Home ownership was postponed in this generation, but their last children were launched nine years earlier than those of the grandparent generation, thus eventually putting the middle generation in a position to be financially helpful to both the grandparent and the married child generations.[4]

The youngest generation's career strategy showed the most forward planning of any generation. They acquired life insurance and retirement equities more rapidly than their predecessors and were precocious in home ownership. They entered marriage at the beginning of a decade of economic expansion that contrasted sharply with the early married years of their parents. The youngest generation has led the two others in its acquisitions and economic achievements year by year over its shorter career to date, and it has also been the most extended in its utilization of credit. Its strategy of life-course management has been a combination of risk taking in the acquisition of property and prudential hedging by means of heavy investment in insurance and retirement plans.

The couples of this youngest generation entered marriage earliest and had slightly more modest jobs than their parents when they married, but more than half of the wives were working and expected to remain in the labor force. Although they have had the highest aspirations for their children, they have spaced them closer together than the two other generations and have expected to have larger families than their parents. The close spacing may put this generation off phase later in the cycle, since by middle life their closely spaced children will be going to college and getting married within a short period, bringing a pile up of the expenses incurred in educating and marrying off children. The third generation may gain enough margin to overcome this error in life-cycle management, however, since it now leads the generations year by year in its acquisitions of housing amenities and durable goods, in its occupational advancement, and in its rapidly advancing income level (Hill 1970b, 310-11).

The Influence of Historical Events on the Family Cycle

Data from the United States census give us some nationwide information about the marital and birth cohorts corresponding to the three generations of our surveys. Some issues that concerned the Lynds and the team restudying Middletown in the 1970s can be addressed with these cohort data: changes in the timing of marriage, of parenthood, and of closing the family. In addition, they tell us about trends in family dissolution by death and divorce. We turn to work by Paul Glick (1977) and Peter Uhlenberg (1974) for the story.

Table 12-1 shows Glick's findings (1977) about the family cycle —the timing of marriage, first birth, last birth, marriage of last child, and death of one spouse. Glick used the median age of women for comparing the timing of these transition points in the family cycle at successive recent periods.

Table 12-1
Median Ages of Wives at Selected Stages of the Family Life Cycle

Stage of the Life Cycle	Wives Born before 1786 (American Quakers)	American Once-Married Mothers		
		Wives Born 1880-1889	Wives Born 1920-1929	Wives Born 1950-1959
A. Age at first marriage	20.5	21.4	20.7	21.2
B. Age at birth of last child	37.9	32.9	31.5	29.6
C. Age at marriage of last child	60.2	55.4	53.2	52.3
D. Age at death of first spouse to die	50.9	57.0	64.4	65.2

Sources: For wives born before 1786, Wells 1971, 281, Table 1; for other wives, Glick 1977, 6, Table 1.

To provide even greater historical depth, we have added in a separate column alongside Glick's calculations, the calculations made by Robert F. Wells (1971) for Quaker families of the eighteenth century. When the two sets of data are compared, it be-

comes clear that the timing of status changes in the family life cycle varied less within the 80 years covered by Glick than in the
century or so between Wells's cohort and the oldest Glick cohort.
In the early nineteenth century, many more children were born
and childbearing extended over a longer period (the median mother bore her last child when she was nearly 38). The median mother
continued child rearing (based on her last child's age at marriage)
until she was 60, by which time her husband, in the most probable
case, had been dead 10 years.

By the end of the nineteenth century, when Glick's earliest
cohort entered marriage, the probability of a couple surviving into
a postparental period had improved substantially. Childbearing
ended before age 33 for the median mother, and her last child
married when she was 55, only 2 years after the death of her husband. Thereafter, a downward swing in the average number of
children made possible an even longer postparental period. The
number of children declined from 4.0 in 1900 to 3.0 during the
depression years, rose to 3.5 during the 1950s, and fell again to
2.5 in the early 1970s. This trend, combined with an earlier age
of marriage and a modest improvement of life expectancy, further
shortened the period of childbearing and child rearing in the middle years of the century to open up a postparental period of more
than 10 years.

But, overall, Table 12-1 gives an impression of uneventful stability during the twentieth century. The influence of the historical
events that we superimposed on the marital careers of the three
generations described in Figure 12-1 can hardly be discerned in
the changes of life-cycle timing described by Table 12-1.

We have yet to consider the spread, or dispersion, around these
median ages of marriage and parenthood, as well as such departures
from the modal pattern as nonmarriage, postponed marriage, cohabitation outside of marriage, single parenthood, postponed parenthood, and childlessness. The modal nuclear family to which
Glick's figures refer accounted in 1975 for some 84 percent of all
families. We must entertain the possibility that stressful historical
events have generated departures from the modal pattern, but
these departures are as yet too rare to affect the averages very
much.

Peter Uhlenberg (1969 and 1974) has compared the cohorts of

women born in each decade from 1890 to 1930 to determine what proportions have realized the "preferred" life-cycle pattern of getting married, having one or more children, and remaining married through age 50. The events that frustrate the pattern would be early death, spinsterhood, childlessness, widowhood, and divorce. Uhlenberg's analysis treats nonwhite and white women separately. We begin with his findings for white women.

Seventeen percent of the 1890 cohort but only 5 percent of the 1930 cohort died before reaching marriageable age. Ten percent of the 1890 cohort remained in lifelong spinsterhood, compared to 4.5 percent in the 1930 group; 22.5 percent of the 1890 cohort but only 5.5 percent of the women born in 1930 remained childless. Marriages with children disrupted by death or divorce increased from 16.5 percent for the 1890 cohort to 21.5 percent for the 1930 cohort; this was the only form of increasing attrition, and the increase was modest. It is indeed a remarkable achievement for any society to enable almost 80 percent of a birth cohort of women to achieve the preferred modal pattern of marrying, becoming mothers, and having an intact family when they reach the age of 50.

Uhlenberg suggested that the 1930 cohort may well have reached a ceiling in the control of the involuntary life events of death and childlessness and that, from now on, voluntary departures from this pattern may be expected to increase. Indeed, in the 1940 cohort we find a larger percentage still single at ages 25 to 29 and, among those ever married, a larger percentage childless and a smaller percentage with first marriages intact than was the case for the 1930 cohort when they were 25 to 29.

In every cohort, Uhlenberg found proportionately fewer nonwhite women achieving the modal career. Death before reaching age 15 attenuated the nonwhite 1890 cohort drastically, by 39 percent, more than double the loss among white girls. Even in the 1930 cohort, twice as many nonwhite as white girls (10 percent versus 5 percent) died before reaching marriageable age. Spinsterhood among nonwhite women actually increased from 5 percent to 9 percent from the 1890 to the 1930 cohorts, while it was declining for white women. Childlessness, however, declined sharply for both racial groups, so that, by the time the 1930 cohort married in the 1950s, parenthood for married couples had become almost universal. It is to marital instability that the nonwhite women are most vulnerable. In every cohort, death or divorce fractured 35 to 40 percent of nonwhite marriages, virtually double the rates for white marriages, which are also increasing, to be sure. As a consequence, the 1930 cohort of nonwhite women was not much more successful in achieving the modal family life cycle by age 50 than the 1890 cohort had been; the proportion doing so was 29 percent of the 1890 cohort and 33 percent of the 1930 cohort. We have to conclude that for nonwhite women our society has not yet achieved much control over the involuntary life events of premature death, spinsterhood, and marital disruption.

The overall picture of family adaptation in the twentieth century, however, is not a gloomy one. Five cohorts exposed to the disruptions of war, economic depression, and intergenerational conflict, to changes in the status of women, and to competing ideologies of family life have, over their life courses, increased the proportions experiencing marriage, parenthood, and intact marriages to what may be the upper ceiling of achievement.

It is only in the birth cohorts of the 1940s who came of age to marry in the 1960s that we see some turning away from the preferred pattern of marriage and parenthood. It is too early to say much about these cohorts, but as of the late 1970s the rise of nonmarriage, childlessness, cohabitation out of wedlock, and divorce previously reported for them appears to be leveling off. The modal pattern seems to be reappearing with a somewhat later age at marriage, slightly smaller families (Glick 1979), and possibly a higher incidence of celibacy.

The Transition to Adulthood in the Twentieth Century

Marriage as an adult status has been highly prized in America for most of our history. Even during the heavy industrialization of the late nineteenth century, the proportions married in the United States dropped less than in other industrializing countries. Table 12-2 in Appendix A shows the changing proportions of the American population ever married, taking each birth cohort from 1850 to 1970 in its most marriageable decade. The proportion ever married began declining around the middle of the last century and reached a low around World War I, but the decline never amounted to much. Thereafter, the proportion ever married increased again, even during the depression years, and returned to its original level.

It does not appear that family life has lost its attractiveness, the doomsayers of the "future shock" school to the contrary. Very few people in the United States choose, or are forced by circumstances, to forego marriage. We are still the most marrying of modernized societies. Kingsley Davis suggested that in this respect we resemble frontier countries such as Australia and Canada more than Europe (Davis 1972, 242). Let us look more closely at the availability over time of this perhaps overprized status.

The transition from dependency on one's family of orientation to the relative autonomy of adulthood has been of interest to anthropologists, demographers, and family historians, as well as to family sociologists. Four status changes have commonly been linked to the transition: setting up residence apart from the parental family, taking a job to achieve economic independence, getting married, and becoming a parent. John Modell and his colleagues (1976) presented data on three of the above status changes for the seventh decade of the twentieth century. Their measures of variation around aggregate measures[5] complement Glick's analyses of the median ages at which status changes occurred during the past century. The *prevalence* of a status transition is defined as the proportion of a population experiencing it. *Timing* refers to typical points in the life course at which transitions occur (timing may be early or late). *Spread*, or dispersion, is the period of time required for a fixed proportion of a population to undergo a particular transition (for Modell and his colleagues this was the central 80 percent).

Table 12-3 in Appendix A provides measures of the pace of transition to adulthood for males and females in Philadelphia in 1880 and in the whole United States in 1970, according to five indicators: leaving school, entering the work force, leaving the parental family residence, marrying and establishing a household. Looking first at prevalence (the percentage experiencing the status change), Modell and his colleagues (1976) found high prevalence for both 1970 and 1880. Most people finished school, entered the work force, and ultimately left their parents' households to establish their own. But these status changes are more uniformly experienced now than then (with a higher percentage marrying, leaving home, and entering the work force in 1970 than in 1890).

It is commonly but incorrectly supposed that it takes longer to "grow up" today than it did in times past. A calculation of the number of years it took for 80 percent of a cohort to make the transitions provides a partial test of that thesis. Table 12-3 shows that the exit from school (for 80 percent of the cohort) was condensed into a shorter period for the 1880 cohort (4.3 years) than for the 1970 cohort (6.5 years). Entrance into the work force, however, occurred over a longer period for the earlier cohort, as did all of the familial transitions. That is, it takes much less time today for young people to move away from their families, to marry, and to set up their own homes. For both sexes, the period in which 80 percent of the population marry was about half as long for the 1970 cohort as it was for the 1880 cohort, and setting up a separate household required a third less time for the 1970 cohort.[6]

The passage to adulthood has become more determinate, with the whole sequence occurring much more rapidly. In the late twentieth century, more than ever before, there comes a time when one must put away childish things and take on adult responsibilities. The entire schedule is shorter and better marked today.

Now that we have established that the transition to adulthood occupies a shorter time today than formerly, what do the data tell us about the timing of the transition? Do today's youth start later, or are they launched more precociously? Table 12-3 in Appendix A shows that the nonfamilial transitions—leaving school and entering the labor force—occur later now (males in the 1970 cohort left school at age 19.1, compared to 14.4 for 1880, and took a job at age 17.3, compared to 15.3 for 1880). But precocity is the rule in the familial transitions, especially for boys, with departure from home, marriage, and assumption of household headship all occurring earlier for the 1970 cohort. Modell, Furstenberg, and Hesberg offered this interpretation.

Although the pattern of boarding and lodging was quite common, most young people did not leave home until their early 20's, several years later. . . . A fifth of the young people in the nineteenth century remained in the household of their family of origin until their late 20's; this pattern is extremely unusual today. . . . Frequently household formation did not occur until the early 30's for 19th century males, and a delay between marriage and the establishment of a separate household was frequent. During this period, the newlyweds resided in the home of parents or boarded with another family. From the source material we have examined, there is good reason to suspect that many young people did not feel prepared to marry until after they had discharged obligations to their family as well as accumulated some resources to support a family of their own. In that particular sense, the period of preparation for adult responsibility was extensive and often was characterized by a good deal of uncertainty (Modell, Furstenberg, and Hesberg 1976, 18).

After an intricate analysis of their data, Modell, Furstenberg, and Hesberg concluded that there is less segregation of the nonfamilial from the familial transitions in contemporary America. Life-course organization in the nineteenth century was such that most young people took their steps toward adulthood one by one. Their contemporary successors must make more complex decisions because the transition occurs more quickly.

The other side of the coin involves the constraining contexts of formal institutions. Child-labor laws require permits to work before a certain age. Compulsory-attendance laws and the requirement of diplomas and degrees for any but dead-end jobs dictate minimum ages for leaving school. These constraints both delay and shorten the period of leaving school and entering the labor force. By contrast, the nineteenth-century norms allowed for greater latitude in the timing of each step, provided that family obligations were satisfied. "Timely actions to nineteenth century families consisted of helpful response in times of trouble; in the twentieth century, timeliness connotes adherence to a schedule (Modell, Furstenberg, and Hesberg 1976, 30).[7]

The Influence of Historical Events on the Timing of Marriage

Let us conclude this comparison of nineteenth- and twentieth-century patterns of achieving adulthood by looking at the timing of marriage decade by decade. Modell and his colleagues (1978) have provided the necessary information. Table 12-4 in Appendix A summarizes the marriage experiences of American birth cohorts between 1865 and 1934. The first six cohorts showed a very slow decline in age at marriage; from the sixth to the seventh cohort, the decline was more considerable. There was also a marked reduction in the *spread* of age at marriage when the birth cohorts of

1915 to 1924 and 1925 to 1935 married in the late 1940s. To the stimulation of World War II and the affluence of the 1950s must be added the delay of marriage and parenthood for the entire birth cohort that came of age during the Great Depression. The two change-making historical events in tandem (the depression and World War II) constituted a watershed of change in nuptiality patterns that has persisted into the 1970s (Glick 1979).

The foregoing analysis of the "changing of the guard" (the incorporation of new generations into marriages and households of their own) must have made clear that there has been no repudiation of marriage and its accompanying responsibilities in twentieth century America. Indeed, the trends have been toward uniformity in the assumption of the familial statuses of spouse, householder, and breadwinner. A cynic might opine that marriage has been oversold and may not be a suitable vocation for all the novices who take it on. With such a high rate of marrying off among American young people, we must, perhaps, expect a high rate of dissolution. In any case, we get it.

Recent Changes in Family Functions

Highly valued though marriage is in America, the task assignments of families go far beyond the conjugal relation. They include the bearing (and adoption) and rearing of children, the continuation of lineages, the physical maintenance of members, the socialization for roles in the family and elsewhere, the maintenance of motivation, the maintenance of social control within the family and between members and outsiders, and the social placement of maturing members. These roles can be divided between instrumental functions, on the one hand—physical maintenance, socialization, reproduction, and social control—and expressive functions, on the other hand—maintenance of motivation and morale through affection and tension management. We will address the performance of the instrumental functions first in this discussion of twentieth-century changes in ways of making a home and getting ahead and then move to an examination of changes in the expressive functions that hold families together.

During the settlement of America, frontier families were forced to be self-sufficient out of necessity, to assume many functions that, in more-organized communities, would have been assigned to community agents, paid or volunteer.[8] In postindustrial America, with its panoply of institutional services, families have become somewhat more specialized in the performance of services for which there are, as yet, few competitors. It should be noted, however, that even in the most elaborately organized communities of the "welfare state," families continue to provide indispensable *individualized* services to their members that parallel the *bureaucratized* mass services of the social institutions (for example, religious and philosophical orientations, tutoring and help with homework, protection from intruders, and primary medical care). In this sense, families *share* economic, protective, religious, educational, and medical functions with the surrounding bureaucracies (Litwak and Meyer 1966).

The Reproductive Function

Earlier in this chapter we noted the increasing proportion of the population becoming parents. (Of women born in 1890, 22.5 percent remained childless; of those born in 1930, only 5.5 percent did so.) Glick (1977) offered a marital cohort series to which we have added the median interval between marriage and birth of a first child (Table 12-5). This table series offers corroboration of the facts that, in the last two decades, parenthood has become

Table 12-5
Percentage of Ever-Married American Women in Their Forties
Who Remained Childless and Median Interval between
Marriage and Birth of First Child

Year of First Marriage	Percentage Remaining Childless	Interval between Marriage and Birth of First Child
1900	13.9	1.6
1910	14.3	1.7
1920	18.6	1.8
1930	15.1	2.1
1940	9.3	2.0
1950	6.8	1.4
1960	4.4	1.3
1970	4.4	1.5

Source: Adapted from Glick 1977, 6, 8, Table 1 and Table 2.

almost universal for those who marry and that, since 1950, first pregnancies have occurred closer to marriage. If we assume that fewer of the first pregnancies of the later cohorts were unplanned (either unwanted or unscheduled), the short intervals between marriage and pregnancy for these cohorts are impressive.

Two related developments should be noted: first, some standardization of the interval between marriage and first pregnancy; and, second, a trend for late marriers to have children as promptly as early marriers. Prior to 1940, young marriers had children with less delay than those who married at later ages. The convergence took place between 1940 and 1950 and was complete by 1970, another sign that World War II was the major watershed of family change in this century.

Regional Differences in Fertility

Was the decline of fertility over more than a century, and its reversal after the Great Depression and World War II, nationwide, or was it characteristic only of the more populous regions? Were some regions marching to a different drummer? Table 12-6 shows number of children per 1,000 white women aged 20 to 44 from 1800 to 1970, by region (Historical Statistical Series of the U.S., 1975, Tables B-67-98, 54). A quick examination of the range in child-to-woman ratios for the 170-year period shows a steady range of about 700 to 750 between the ratios of the highest and lowest regions from 1800 to 1840 (with an inexplicable jump to 866 in 1830). In 1850, the range fell to 400 to 500 for the 60-year period that witnessed America's most rapid industrial development and the absorption of millions of immigrants. The convergence of the regions from 1920 to 1970 was gradual but steady, even during the postwar baby boom of 1940 to 1960. By 1970, the range extended from the South Atlantic at 469 per 1,000 to the mountain regions at 542 per 1,000, a range of less than 100. The great variations in fertility among the regions of the country have given way to virtual uniformity.

Even as the distinctiveness of regions has blurred over time, the differences in family size between rural and urban families have been reduced. The difference in child-to-woman ratios of 1,319 per 1,000 for rural areas and 845 per 1,000 for urban areas in 1800

Table 12-6

Number of Children under 5 Years Old per 1,000 Women 20 to 44 Years Old, by Race (1850 to 1970) and Residence, by Geographic Divisions (1800 to 1970); and Differences in Child-Woman Ratios between Whites and Blacks (1850 to 1970), between Rural and Urban (1800 to 1850, 1910 to 1970), and between Lowest and Highest Regions (1800 to 1970)

	1970	1960	1950	1940	1930	1920	1910	1900	1890	1880	1870	1860	1850	1840	1830	1820	1810	1800
Adjusted number of children per 1,000 women:																		
White	507	717	580	419	506	604	631	666	685	780	814	905	892	1,085	1,145	1,295	1,358	1,342
Black	689	895	663	513	554	608	736	845	930	1,090	997	1,072	1,087	–	–	–	–	–
Differences in ratios of white and black	182	178	83	94	48	4	105	179	245	310	183	165	195	–	–	–	–	–
Unadjusted number of children per 1,000 white women:																		
United States	503	667	551	400	485	581	609	644	667	754	792	886	877	1,070	1,134	1,236	1,290	1,281
Urban	483	636	479	311	388	471	469	–	–	–	–	–	–	701	708	831	900	845
Rural	558	747	673	551	658	744	782	–	–	–	–	–	–	1,134	1,189	1,276	1,329	1,319
Differences in ratio of urban and rural	75	109	194	240	270	273	313	–	–	–	–	–	–	433	481	445	428	464
United States regions:																		
New England	521	664	516	347	441	518	482	478	440	498	544	622	621	752	812	930	1,052	1,098
Middle Atlantic	486	602	471	320	424	539	533	549	547	624	679	767	763	940	1,036	1,183	1,289	1,279
East north central	530	704	552	388	458	548	555	599	653	757	869	999	1,022	1,270	1,467	1,608	1,702	1,840
West north central	530	743	600	431	495	584	630	710	781	905	990	1,105	1,114	1,445	1,678	1,685	1,810	–
South Atlantic	469	625	572	464	593	694	760	779	777	851	811	918	937	1,140	1,174	1,280	1,325	1,345
East south central	490	656	631	539	655	734	817	834	850	926	903	1,039	1,099	1,408	1,519	1,631	1,700	1,799
West south central	512	695	607	474	584	686	845	925	968	1,043	935	1,084	1,046	1,297	1,359	1,418	1,383	–
Mountain	542	775	663	526	582	664	661	720	757	872	967	1,051	886	–	–	–	–	–
Pacific	482	653	539	339	360	425	460	512	587	775	888	1,026	901	–	–	–	–	–
Range in child-to-woman ratios between lowest and highest region	73	173	192	219	295	309	385	447	528	545	446	483	493	693	866	755	758	742

Source: U.S. Bureau of the Census 1975, 54.

converged by 1970 to 558 per 1,000 and 483 per 1,000, respectively, an almost trivial difference.

Table 12-6 also shows child-to-woman ratios for white and black women, beginning with 1850. The ratios are higher for blacks in every decade, but the differences virtually disappear by 1920, only to increase thereafter into the decade of 1970. Race has been the least differentiating of the three factors (rurality, region, and race) in the past, but it may not remain so in the years ahead.

Changes in Family Size Preferences

What has been happening, meanwhile, in the desire for children and in preferences for various sizes of families? As children have ceased to be economic assets in America, have family size preferences changed? National sample surveys dating back to 1936 demonstrate a rather remarkable stability in the desire for children during recent decades. Men and women show similarity over time in the numbers of children considered ideal for persons in their circumstances.

In her summary of 25 years of such surveys, Judith Blake (1966) found virtually no support for families with no children, except in a single 1936 survey in which a few older respondents checked "no children" as their ideal, reflecting, perhaps, their depression-born hindsights. Neither was the one-child family accepted as an ideal by any appreciable number of respondents. Families of two to four children were preferred by the overwhelming majority, with preferences for three and four children predominating after 1948. The proportions preferring five or more children remained steady at around 10 percent for the 25-year period, with older respondents and male respondents more likely to prefer large families.

Since 1961, preferences have shifted toward smaller families. The majority of couples in a 1976 survey chose two or three children over four or more. But there was no appreciable increase in support for childlessness or for the one-child family.

In the 1970s, only 8 to 10 percent of all married couples were childless; an additional 10 percent had only one child. The expectation of childlessness rose from 2 percent in 1970 to 5 percent in 1975, a small trend overemphasized by the mass media.

The close correspondence in the past between desired and

actual family sizes suggests that most families in the near future will have two or three children. There should be fewer families of five and more, but no increase in one-child families.

So much for the reproductive function. For assessment of other family functions, we turn to a nationwide survey of child-rearing families commissioned by General Mills in 1976-1977 and to Hill and Foote's Minnesota sample survey of three generations of the same family line, the two oldest of which had been exposed to most of the stressful historical events of the twentieth century. We note again that the grandparent generation represents a cohort married at the turn of the century and experienced World War I in middle parenthood; the parent generation was married in the 1920s and 1930s and experienced the depression and World War II in middle parenthood; and the youngest generation entered marriage and parenthood during the boom years of the 1950s.

Making a Living and Managing Family Resources

There was a remarkable upgrading from the grandparent generation to the parent generation to the married child generation in education, occupational achievement, housing and neighborhood quality, durable possessions, and financial security. These all relate to the capacity of families to fulfill the physical maintenance and protective functions.

In average years of schooling completed, each generation surpassed its predecessor by an impressive margin, from a median of under 7 years in the grandparent generation to 9 years in the parent generation to more than 12 years in the married child generation. In each successive generation, husbands and wives became closer in age and in achieved education, making for a more egalitarian family structure and a less-segregated division of labor.

The most significant upgrading in occupational achievement took place between the middle and the youngest generations. The married children started below their parents in less-skilled jobs at the beginning of their careers, but, once they were working in a chosen vocation, they progressed faster than their parents had progressed during the corresponding phase. The grandparent generation had the lowest starting level and the least upward movement during their working lives.

In each successive generation, more wives were gainfully employed during the first years of marriage and more turned to work as their children grew up. In the married child generation, 60 percent of the wives worked during the first years of marriage, compared with 20 percent of the wives in the parent generation who worked and a negligible 7 percent in the grandparent generation who worked at the comparable stage of their own lives. Not until the postparental period did the wives in the oldest generation reach a level at which 20 percent were gainfully employed. Although still in the childbearing period, 40 percent of the wives in the married generation who have been married 6 to 10 years remain in the labor force. For the youngest generation, having working wives has had an enormous effect on the level of family income, on home ownership, and on the acquisition of durable goods.

The income levels of the three generations in 1960 (calculated in 1957-1959 dollars) reflect each generations' stage in its occupational career. The grandparents were in retirement, but their incomes were calculated to have been like those of their last full-time employment (the median was $2,000); the parents were at their peak incomes (the median was $6,000); and the youngest generation were just beginning their careers (the median was $5,000). Asked to assess the adequacy of their family incomes, the grandparents said that they felt the financial squeeze more than the other two generations; half were barely able to afford their necessities. Three-fourths of the youngest generation checked the expression "We have the things we need and a few of the extras." The middle generation was factually better off, and they felt more comfortable, placing themselves at the luxury end of the scale ("We have the things we need and extras and still have money left over to save or invest").

Housing adequacy can best be compared by taking each generation at the same points in their housing careers. Figure 12-3 makes such a comparison, measuring housing adequacy by the percentage of family residences with a bathroom and two or more bedrooms. Each generation improved its housing throughout the life cycle, but the improvement was more dramatic for the two younger generations. The youngest generation started even with parent generation, at 38 percent adequacy, but within 10 years reached 85 percent, a level not reached by the parents until they had been married more than 20 years. The grandparents after 10 years of marriage had advanced only from 10 percent adequacy to 35 percent.

Home ownership shows a similar trend from generation to generation. More than half of the youngest generation had achieved home ownership within the first five years of marriage, five years earlier than their own parents and even farther ahead of their grandparents. These achievements are the more remarkable because the child generation married younger, had less work experience at marriage, and, year for year, had more children to support than its predecessors.

In all economic matters, the child generation seems destined to outstrip the previous generations. In the acquisition of durable goods, the married child generation has already overtaken the grandparent generation and has about the same inventory as its parents had after 35 years of marriage. This was not done at the

Figure 12-3. Adequacy of housing by year of marriage and by generation. (Reproduced from Hill 1970b, 108, Chart 5.05.)

expense of protective insurance or retirement provision, for the married child generation is well along in the acquisition of a portfolio of insurance and investments. Over 50 percent have retirement equities over and beyond social security, and 95 percent have life insurance—more protection than their grandparents ever had and about what their parents had after 30 years of marriage.

The improvement of the physical maintenance and protective functions from the oldest generation to the youngest generation was more than a linear upward movement. Upgrading in education, occupation, income, housing and associated amenities, and financial security occurred at an accelerated rate. Moreover, the people of each generation became more innovative, as indicated by their greater receptiveness to the adoption of new durable goods earlier in their marriages (Hill 1970b, 151-52).

According to one style of home management, the instrumental tasks of families call for the development of expertise in planning and problem solving. The families in each of the three generations were observed over a year's time as they coped with the exigencies of running a household. In each successive generation, the number of plans devised, the number of actions taken, and the proportion of actions that were planned were greater. The supposedly "flighty" youngest generation was the most likely to preplan purchases, residential moves, and other consumer actions. Moreover, the criteria of rational decision making were more faithfully met by the youngest generation. People in that generation were more likely than their elders to search for information outside the immediate family, to weigh alternatives, and to take long-term as well as short-term consequences into account.

Surely these data adequately demonstrate significant improvements in the task performance of these Minnesota families, which, for lack of better data, we have taken as representative. A picture emerges of increasing effectiveness, greater practical competence and material well-being, and more courageous risk taking accompanied by more prudent planning.

Women's Rights and Family Structure

So far in our discussion, we have not considered the vast changes that have occurred in the status of women in and out of the family as they have acquired more education and career opportunities and more personal autonomy. Their increased participation in the labor force has, of course, affected the performance of the family's instrumental tasks, but it has not been neutral with respect to maintaining morale and marital commitment.

The participation of married women in the labor force has been increasing for a long time. in 1890, only 5 percent of married women were employed; that increased threefold over the next 50 years to 17 percent in 1940 and has continued to climb steadily: 25 percent in 1950, 32 percent in 1960, and 47 percent in 1978 (Hayghe 1978). The increase since World War II has been greatest among mothers who had remained out of the labor force earlier. The recent data from Middletown suggest that much of the increase was attributable to the movement of business-class wives into the labor market. Mothers of young children tripled their participation in the labor force from 1948 to 1975. The highest employment rates of all are those of female heads of households.

There has been a substantial lag in arriving at a more equal allocation of housework and child care between spouses when the wife is employed gainfully. In the 1950s, Robert Blood and Donald Wolfe (1960) attempted to show that husbands increased the proportion of home tasks they performed when their wives worked, but this now appears to have been an artifact of the reduction in the time that working wives gave to those tasks.

Several large-scale time-budget studies during the 1960s and 1970s showed husbands' housework and child-care contributions to be very modest, averaging about 1.6 hours per day, compared to a nonemployed wife's 8.1 hours and an employed wife's 4.8 hours (Walker and Woods 1976). Surprisingly, a husband's time contribution did not increase when his wife worked, even though she usually reduced her hours of housework and child care. The husband's workday in families with dual breadwinners averaged 7.9 hours (1.6 hours of family work plus 6.3 hours of paid work), whereas his wife's workday averaged 10.1 hours (4.8 hours of family work plus 5.3 hours of paid work). The "role overload" of working wives was clearly apparent.

Pleck (1979) reported the results of a national survey undertaken in 1977 that assessed the contribution of men to housework and child care in hours per week. Men reported more family work in this later survey, more than half as much as their wives. Moreover, the husbands of employed wives reported 1.8 more hours of housework and 2.7 more hours of child care than other husbands. After 40 years of increasing maternal employment, these findings are the first to suggest some equalization of household responsibilities between men and women. In Pleck's words:

Men are beginning at last to increase their family work when their wives are employed. There is no question, of course, that wives continue to hold the primary responsibility for family work. But even as this reality is acknowledged, it is important to recognize that men's behavior is changing on an important social indicator. The pace of change may seem slow. Yet it should not be dismissed or taken for granted. Change of this magnitude in a national sample actually represents a substantial phenomenon (Pleck 1979, 487).

So far, however, this study and the trend it purports to have discovered must be taken as unconfirmed. The data from a 1978 Middletown survey, presented in Chapter 5, show that employed wives and mothers are still firmly saddled with the main burden of housework and child care and that they are generally content to have it so.

Holding the Family Together: The Expressive Functions

Changes in the family's expressive functions from 1900 to 1970 are much harder to trace than changes in its instrumental functions, like those just discussed. Divorce is one indicator of marital alienation, but the statistics of divorce were of uneven quality prior to World War II; anyway, they tell us nothing about the changes in marital and parent-child adjustment in the large majority of families that did not resort to divorce to settle their differences. There are no statistics at all on "parent-child divorce" because neither parents nor children can legally repudiate their reciprocal obligations. (Disinheritance may once have been a partial equivalent of divorce, but it is rare today.) Parents abandon children and children run away, but little statistical information is generated by these behaviors.

Because the conjugal relation is probably the most valued and the most problematic of the modern family's three subsystems (parent-child, sibling-sibling, and husband-wife), the adequacy of bonding and tension management within that relation has attracted continuous interest in America, dating back to the eighteenth century, when divorces were granted only by legislative decree.

Earlier in this chapter, we noted the very high proportions of both men and women who marry at least once and the relatively precocious age at marriage in the United States. Davis (1972) explained the high propensity to marry, and to marry early, in the United States by pointing out several conditions that make marriage for a young man a less fateful commitment than it had been in other times and places. These conditions include: (1) subsidies from parents at the beginning of marriage, (2) economic support by his wife's working until he completes his training and the continuation afterward of a dual income, (3) the availability of contraceptives to control the number and timing of children, and (4) the accessibility of divorce and remarriage should the first marriage be an unhappy one. Davis concluded, somewhat astringently, "A young man today is simply deciding to get married; he is not deciding to support a wife, have numerous progeny, or enter permanent bondage" (Davis 1972, 246). In a participant-operated mate-selection system in which love is the catalytic agent and through which more than 9 out of 10 (94 to 96 percent) young people are "married off," the pool of married couples subject to dissolution is likely to be larger than in societies that delay marriage to a more mature age and require proof of economic viability and kinship support before nuptials are approved.

Historical Events and Vulnerability to Divorce

Samuel Preston and John McDonald (1979) undertook a revealing analysis of marital cohorts whose divorcing was uniformly above or below expectations for those married between 1910 and 1959. They also linked their findings with the number of children ever born to white women in the same marital cohorts. (See Table 12-7.) Marriages contracted between 1926 and 1944 had divorces uniformly above trend, while the marriages between 1930 and 1934 (at the depth of the depression) eventually had the highest dissolution rate. Marriages contracted between 1945 and 1956, in contrast, have been unusually stable. The congruence between marital cohort divorce and marital cohort fertility is striking.

There are, undoubtedly, some direct causal links between the two historical series shown in Table 12-7. Marital disruption

Table 12-7

Comparison of Divorce and Fertility by Marital Cohorts Married between 1910 and 1959

Year of First Marriage	Average Number of Children Ever Born to White Women by 1970	Difference between Expected Percentage of Marriages Ending in Divorce and Actual Percentage Ending in Divorce: Average of Five-Year Deviations from Trend Line
1955-1959	2.734	0.09
1950-1954	2.984	1.67
1945-1949	2.838	2.10
1940-1944	2.605	−0.88
1935-1939	2.497	−1.63
1930-1934	2.417	−2.29
1925-1929	2.449	−1.00
1929-1924	2.637	−0.16
1915-1919	2.968	−0.19
1910-1914	3.337	0.67

Sources: Adapted from Preston and McDonald 1979, 16, Table 3.

reduces marital fertility by reducing the time of exposure to pregnancy and by reducing the desirability of making marriage-specific investments. Likewise, childless couples have higher divorce rates. But Preston and McDonald attempted to locate factors that were causally prior to both, recognizing that fertility and marital instability are, in a sense, joint outcomes. They cited theoretical formulations and studies (Coombs and Zumeta 1970; Easterlin 1973; Becker, Laudes, and Michael 1976; and Mott and Moore 1977) that suggested that a discrepancy between the level of economic adequacy in the subjects' parental families before they entered marriage and their own economic opportunities and prospects after marriage are antecedent to divorce rates and fertility rates. If the discrepancy is unfavorable, as in the 1926-1944 cohorts, divorce will be high and fertility low; and, if the discrepancy is favorable, as in the marital cohorts of 1945-1956, marriages will be stable and fertility high. This is an ingenious way of connecting the impact of events at early points in a cohort's history with its much later behavior.

At the time this chapter was written, the divorce rate, which had risen steeply between 1965 and 1975 (from 10.6 to 20.3 per 1,000 married women), has slowed its rise. In 1978 it reached 22.0, less than 10 percent above 1975, and in 1979 the advance was even more modest. The most recent data show a tendency toward a slightly longer period between marriage and divorce, with divorces of first marriages averaging seven years of marriage and divorces of remarriages averaging three years of marriage (Glick 1979).

An increasing proportion of divorces and remarriages have involved couples with children, although the majority of divorces were granted to childless couples until the period 1956 to 1960. (See Appendix A, Table 12-8.) Davis (1972) noted that the drop in childlessness at divorce was derived from increased marital fertility and the higher proportion of brides who were pregnant at the time of marriage. The high point of childlessness in divorce was 1940, when 64 percent of divorces were childless and when national fertility was at its lowest ebb. The low point in childlessness in divorce was 1964, when only 37 percent of divorces were childless, after a period of sustained high fertility.

Since remarriage does not occur rapidly enough to keep all children of divorced parents in two-parent households, the number of one-parent households with children has also increased substantially. In 1975, roughly 19 percent of all American children under 18 were living with one parent (up from 9 percent in 1960); 3 percent lived with neither parent; and 78 percent were living with two parents (10 percent in reconstituted families of one natural parent and one stepparent and 68 percent with both of their natural parents). But proportionately three times as many black children as white children were living with only one parent in 1978 (44 percent versus 14 percent, respectively).

Does this recital of increases in divorce, the number of children involved in divorces, one-parent households, and reconstituted families justify the general conclusion that families in the twentieth century have failed in the performance of their expressive functions? It may be worth noting that, as of 1973, more than 85 percent of the child-rearing couples in their middle years were still in their first marriages. Even the marital cohorts of the 1960s are likely to see more than 70 percent of their members reaching the end of the marital span still in their first marriages. Remarriages have nearly as good a record of bonding the marriage pair as first marriages; they are stable environments in which to rear children.

Moreover, it was estimated by Davis (1972) that recent losses of parents by divorce were compensated by decreased losses by desertion and death. Indeed, it was not until 1970 that losses of parents by divorce exceeded losses by death. He pointed out, moreover, that in divorce the lost parent is still living and that children have at least the possibility of having a meaningful relationship with him or her (Davis 1972, 258).

Tension and Solidarity between Generations

Anne Foner (1978) suggested a theory of age stratification to compare the intergenerational tensions experienced in nineteenth- and twentieth-century families. In the Durkheimian tradition, age differentiation is an important source of solidarity because of the interdependence of family members with different functions (Durkheim 1964). The theory of age stratification holds that cohesion and conflict are inherent in the family structure because the family is stratified—not merely differentiated—by age. Not only do family members of different ages have diverse functions, they also receive unequal rewards (Riley and Johnson 1971 and Foner 1978). Age differences in power, prestige, and privilege provoke dissension as power is exercised and resources are distributed within the family.

One source of discord in the nineteenth-century family was the anomalous position of young people in their late teens who remained at home. Entering the labor force before leaving home, they had adult responsibilities in their work roles but remained dependent and subordinate at home (Kett 1971). We showed earlier in this chapter that the transition to adulthood took longer then than it does today (Modell, Furstenberg, and Hesberg 1976) and that it was more dependent on the consent of parents, a situation made to order for intergenerational antagonism. The rapid social change of the period created cultural differences between parents and children, later to be termed "generation gaps." Foner implied that there were both long-term changes associated with industrialization and short-term economic and social shifts that imposed different outlooks on parents and their adult children and even on older and younger siblings. The recognition of these sources of conflict led her to propose that parent-child relationships should be less discordant in the twentieth-century family. This expectation is consonant with our findings cited earlier from the three-generation studies, which showed closer ties between the parent and the married child generations than between the grandparent and the parent generations (Hill 1970b and Bengtson 1975), as well as with the Middletown findings presented earlier, which seem to show some narrowing of the "gaps" between successive generations.

The twentieth-century family displays different patterns. With smaller family size, more frequent and intense interaction encourages solidarity. Economic interdependence has been eroded, however, since parents no longer rely on children's earnings, even when they remain at home. Conflict over inequities of power and reward certainly continues, but some sources of conflict have been blunted over time. The obstacles to early autonomy and the age-cohort differences are less than they used to be (Modell, Furstenberg, and Hesberg 1976).

Foner (1978) made the astute observation that there is more effective socialization of parents by children today. Siblings, sharing the same generational culture, are likely to be allies in supporting each other's attempts to "bring up" their parents. Not only are children in the modern family more effective socializers than their counterparts of the nineteenth century, but the family norms of today enjoin parents to pay attention to children's ideas, as we saw in an earlier chapter.

Family Cohesion from Generation to Generation

We turn back to the Minnesota three-generation survey to see how the family's functions of morale maintenance and tension management have changed during this century. The three Minnesota generations showed some of the differences between the oldest and the youngest generations that Foner noted between nineteenth- and twentieth-century families. The oldest generation was predominanatly fatalistic and present or past oriented, but the youngest generation was much less fatalistic and more oriented to the future.

A second set of values was recorded by asking respondents about what they thought a good mother is, a good father is, and a good child is, a procedure first devised by the Lynds and since followed by many other scholars.[9] The grandparents were clearly the most "traditional" of the three generations; the married child generation was, as might be expected, the most "developmental."

Other marked differences appear in the authority patterns, the division of labor, and the marital integration of families from generation to generation. With respect to authority, the shift to egalitarian patterns is greatest from the grandparent to the parent generation, but the egalitarian pattern holds up into the married child generation. In the division of labor, there is more sharing of tasks and less gender specialization in the married child generation, as well as less adherence to the conventions about what is men's work and what is women's work. Eighty-three percent of couples did some role crossing in the youngest generation, compared to 60 percent (not a negligible fraction) of couples in the grandparent generation.

On a scale of marital role tension, which involves identifying undesirable attributes of the spouse, role tension increased from the grandparent to the married child generation, with grandparents seeing their spouses in a kinder light. On a scale of marital consensus, which involves agreement in the ranking of family values, consensus improved from oldest to youngest. Marital consensus was very low in the grandparent generation despite, or perhaps because of, low role tension. It was highest in the married child generation.

Part of that same survey was a joint interview with husband and wife, in which disagreement between the spouses was deliberately encouraged by posing difficult, ambiguous questions that they were expected to answer as a pair. The interviewers found couples of the youngest generation much readier to enter into conflict. A typical pattern of the youngest generation was to identify differences, engage in argument, and then find a basis for agreement, with one party, usually the husband, undertaking to smooth over the differences and "save face." Altogether, the interviewers found the youngest generation to be the most colorful and interesting, possessing the most flexible family organization and showing the most competence in communication. The couples of this generation were most likely to experience conflict and to express hostility, but they were also most likely to demonstrate skills in conflict management and to conclude their arguments with expressions of consensus and gestures of affection.

The Quality of Family Life during the 1970s

A national family survey commissioned by General Mills, Incorporated, in 1976-1977 confirmed these impressions about the youngest generation of Minnesota families—their effectiveness in fulfilling both the instrumental functions of physical maintenance and protection and the expressive functions of morale maintenance and tension management. The national survey sampled 1,230 intact families with children 6 to 12 years of age. Interviews with the children and with both parents provided multiple perspectives on family problems and achievements. The parents belonged to the baby boom birth cohort of the late 1940s and early 1950s. They had made the transition into adulthood during the era of protest and civil disturbance provoked by the Vietnam war, 10 years later than the youngest Minnesota generation we have already described.

A number of findings from the General Mills survey can be instructively compared with those of the Middletown surveys (1976-1978) and those of the three-generation Minnesota survey (1958-1959). The General Mills survey made the following points.

1. Comparing the state of their families with the state of the country,[10] a remarkable 90 percent reported that their families were in good shape but fewer thought that the country was doing well. They deplored the state of the economy (56 percent), the lack of leadership (47 percent), and the moral climate (24 percent).

2. Three out of four parents (74 percent) believed that the "average American family" was doing a good job of raising its children. In evaluations of their own performance as parents, 63 percent felt good about it, as opposed to 36 percent who worried about the job they were doing as parents and 1 percent who were not sure. Single parents worried more about their adequacy; only 45 percent rated themselves favorably.

3. Some 70 to 80 percent of the parents in the survey were satisfied with "the way the family works together" (80 percent), "amount of time spent with the family" (73 percent), "the way they are handling the problems in their lives" (79 percent), and "the amount of fun and enjoyment derived from family life" (73 percent). Indeed, 90 percent of the married, white parents said that, if they had to do it over again, they would again have

chosen to have children. Single parents (73 percent) and minority parents (72 percent) were somewhat less enthusiastic.

4. Most of the parents perceived their children to be as happy (46 percent) or happier (16 percent) than they were when they were children. Minority parents were more emphatic that their children were better off (36 percent saw them as happier).

5. Three out of four parents (74 percent) wanted their children to be better off than they were in terms of money and success, although college-educated parents (34 percent) had no aspirations for further income advancement for their children.

6. Parents made few long-run claims on their children: "Parents don't count on the future, but expect pleasure from children now" (54 percent); "Parents have no right to count on their children to help them when they are old or in difficulty" (54 percent).

7. Parents appeared to be in transition with respect to questions of discipline. One out of four agreed, one out of four disagreed, and two out of four were undecided about the statement that "strict, old-fashioned discipline is best to raise children." Minority parents were significantly more permissive in scolding less (34 percent versus 52 percent for the total sample) and in spanking less (44 percent versus 50 percent) in the last few months.

8. Most parents agreed that they wished to pass on the following values of the American creed to their children.

Duty before pleasure	90%
Not as important to win as how the game is played	91
Happiness is possible without money	86
Prejudice is morally wrong	84
Everyone should save money even if it means doing without	78
My country, right or wrong	74
Having sex outside marriage is morally wrong	72
People in authority know best	68

9. Two out of three parents agreed that they had trouble communicating with their children, especially on certain sensitive topics, such as homosexuality, death, sex, their own feelings and shortcomings, family problems, and money. Children's complaints about their parents mirrored some of the complaints parents had about their children. (See Table 12-9.)

Table 12-9
Children's Complaints about Parents and Parents Complaints about Children

Complaints	Parents Mentioned as Problem	Children Resented Intervention
Eating habits, snacks, refusing to eat	30%	59%
Television viewing, too much time wasted	23	56
Children with the "gimmes" asking for things advertised	26	–
Parents don't buy what's advertised	–	30
Bad-tempered behavior, temper tantrums	24	–
Parents punish unfairly	–	36

Source: General Mills family survey, 1977, Charts 34 and 55.

The survey also offered this cohort of parents, just a few years removed from the turbulent 1960s, an opportunity to rank the personal values from which they currently derived their greatest satisfactions. Table 12-10 in Appendix A compares their ranking with one from Yankelovich's 1973 survey of university students.

We do not know how much of the difference between the two columns of Table 12-11 in Appendix A is due to developmental effects (being married and a parent and having adult responsibilities may alter a respondent's values) and how much is due to cohort effects. If anything, cohort affiliation should have had an opposite effect, since the college cohorts of the 1960s, to which the parents belonged, were more heavily exposed to a counterculture of anti-familism. What is clear is that family, hard work, religion, having children, and saving money are all ranked more highly by the students of the protesting 1960s, now transformed into parents, than by the students of 1973.

The General Mills survey had the added virtue of having interviewed 469 children in a third of the sample families. From our perspective, this is a fourth generation to be considered; namely, a birth cohort of the late 1960s and early 1970s. Where comparison is possible, we will note the change or continuity in values from the third to the fourth generation. The children's views of parenting, summarized in Appendix A, Table 12-11, were, if anything, more traditional than those of their parents.

Children's perceptions of their parents' expectations varied by race and income, but there appears to be little relaxation of the achievement motive for this fourth generation. (See Appendix A, Table 12-12.) Children of poor and minority families felt more than average pressure to do well in school and to excel in sports. Table 12-12 is further evidence that the family remains an effective socialization agent.

The pressures to excel scholastically and athletically are in line with some of the values the parents said they most wanted to transmit (duty before pleasure, everyone should sacrifice to save) but not with others (happiness is possible without money and it is not as important to win as how the game is played).

Given the currently changing opportunities of women, the differences between boys' and girls' responses to some of these questions merit attention. Girls exceeded boys by several percentage points in valuing home, relatives, friends, teachers, church, school, and self-fulfillment (65 percent versus 47 percent for boys). The stereotypical preferences in school subjects persist in this cohort, with boys preferring science and math (58 percent to 34 percent, 62 percent to 57 percent) and girls preferring art and music (82 percent to 74 percent, 63 percent to 57 percent). But without baseline data for an earlier point in time, we can only conjecture that the stereotypes are blurring but have not yet been erased.

The findings of this survey again affirm the healthy state of the American family suggested by the information about Middletown's contemporary families presented in earlier chapters. Both parents and children seem happy with family life, despite economic pressures and intergenerational differences. Most married people place a high value on their own marriages and the experience of parenthood (9 out of 10 would do it over again). The parents are eager to transmit the American creed to their children, and the children are willing to accept most of it. So far as surveys can inform us, the expressive functions of maintaining morale and managing conflict are being fulfilled in most contemporary families.

The Family and Decelerating Change

None of the theories about the family with which we introduced this chapter turns out to fit the empirical data as closely as we would like. The theory of economic and technological determinism is handicapped in explaining family change when most of the economic and technological changes associated with modernization have already occurred. We have been living through a period of decelerating rather than accelerating change, and modernization theory has little to say about family life in a society approaching equilibrium. What we observe is the steady convergence of distinctive family patterns based on rural-urban, regional, religious, ethnic, and occupational identities, and not a proliferation of new and distinct family patterns.

The cyclic theory of change might be expected to fare a little better since some family phenomena have been clearly cyclical during this century. None of them, however, appear as yet to qualify as the turnarounds that the cyclical theory of family change anticipates, namely, reversals of direction due to having reached the limits of growth, secularization, materialism, or personal freedom. The actual swings in family behavior that we have recorded in the timing of marriage and parenthood do not appear to correspond with political-moral cycles so much as with the business cycle and the changing climates associated with war and peace. Cyclical change theorists would probably treat these as secular variations around a trend line, rather than as fundamental reversals.

The chief defect of our third theory, the otherwise persuasive theory of family-community exchange, is that, being ahistorical, it cannot explain the changes over time encountered by the family in its environment. Without a historical framework, all we can do with this theory is to perform ecological analyses of family behavior for short, nonunitized time spans. But this defect can be remedied by borrowing concepts from the fourth of our theories, the sociohistorical stress theory. That theory has been helpful from the beginning of our presentation in showing how stressful historical events produce transitional generations. It has sensitized us to periods of nationwide turbulence and trouble, which bring together into one highly charged event the cumulated impacts of change in the economic, the political, the military, and the mass psychological dimensions of the society. These powerful *events*, sometimes unifying the society, as did the two world wars, and sometimes disorganizing it, as did the Great Depression and the Vietnam conflict, have punctuated the slowing down of social change in the twentieth century. The utility of the orientation can be seen in the close connections between historical events and cohort behaviors.

Clearly, the watershed of family change in the twentieth century was a combination of two events, the Great Depression and World War II, which, in tandem, deformed the life-course scheduling of millions of individuals (Elder 1977 and Modell et al. 1978). This was evident in the experience of the marital cohorts that began their family careers in the 1930s and early 1940s, with regard to their nuptiality rates, their timing of marriage and parenthood, their spacing of children, and their incidence of divorce.

In closing this chapter, we should emphasize that the deformations of one generation's career patterns in adapting to stressful historical events are visited on the next generation, beneficently as challenges to do better and harmfully in constricted opportunities. According to Richard Easterlin (1973), who first formulated the theory of relative deprivation versus affluence, people in each generation use their parents' economic prospects 20 years earlier as a standard for judging their own career prospects. We have shown that the most recent generations have benefited from such comparisons.

Succession and Renewal: The Secret of Family Adaptation

One explanation for the family's viability over the centuries seems to be its unique renewal in each generation by what anthropologists (Fortes 1963) have called the process of fission, a pattern of succession exhibited by no other institution in society. Foote (1960, 9) felicitously refers to this succession as the determination of each generation not to do unto others exactly what has been done to them. Each generation, in one sense, starts afresh, improvising roles without a script, often profiting from the errors of the past generation to write a new scenario for their own. It is the more remarkable that, given these opportunities to start afresh, there is so much continuity of values, practices, and problem solutions from one generation to the next.

There is a theory of selective continuity and change that ties together some of the inconsistencies in the history of the family in the twentieth century.

Under conditions of social change characterized by higher levels of education, greater range of occupational choice, and greater options for residential location, the bonds of solidarity and interdependence which would normally make for intergenerational continuity do so selectively rather than uniformly. Such bonds tolerate, and even encourage, upgrading and innovation from generation to generation with respect to economic and educational achievements as instrumental to *ends common* to all generations, while maintaining continuity with respect to the expressive patterns of religion and residence proximity. This selective upgrading in instrumental competence has the effect of bringing about change in consumership patterns in one generation, followed by continuity of the new pattern into the third generation. Where higher continuity of behavior three generations in depth occurs, it is predicated on the expressive functioning of linked lineage ties of high cohesion and interdependence (Hill 1970b, 306-7). [Emphasis added.]

If our analysis of family changes in the twentieth century is correct, the continuity from generation to generation and from birth cohort to birth cohort is highly selective, leaving room for adaptability to changes in the near environment. Some generations—the transition generations—undergo more discontinuity in their "renewal" than others. Yet, in a wider perspective, there has been remarkably little change in form and function from generation to generation in the twentieth century.

Two observations made earlier justify repetition as we look forward to the last two decades of this century. Peter Uhlenberg (1974) suggested that we may have reached a ceiling in the control of the involuntary life events of premature death, spinsterhood, and childlessness that thwart the achievement of the modal family cycle. Henceforth, this pattern is likely to be broken by voluntary departures from the modalities: voluntary singleness, voluntary childlessness, and voluntary single parenthood. After noting how little impact the stressful events of the depression and the two world wars had had on the timing of the family cycle, we entertained the possibility that these admittedly powerful change-making events may have enabled new generations to experiment and to innovate novel family forms outside of the stable, unchanging modal pattern. The departures, even in the generation of the counterculture of the 1960s, are statistically unimportant now (in the 1 to 5 percent range), but they may not always be so. Some of the innovations are not really new but are revivals of old novelties, first proposed in the 1840s and 1850s and 1920s, that did not take hold then and may be no more viable today: communal households, trial unions, wife swapping, and polygyny, for example. Some may prove unworkable and even destructive, but other new forms may offer greater potentials for personal growth than conventional patterns do, and they may eventually become part of the "standard package."

The standard family package itself appears to have high survival value since it is the product of the selective continuity and change that renewal in each generation facilitates. Indeed, the future development and elaboration of the family within the relatively affluent and beneficent environment of urban industrial America seems almost assured when viewed against the backdrop of the vicissitudes experienced by families in America's first 300 years. Certainly, American society with its familistic values is far from turning hostile toward marriage and family institutions. I do not think that our successors, in writing about the American family, will mark the 1970s as a watershed of change away from the family as we know it. I think, too, that they will report that the American family of the year 2000 to be minimally changed in form and structure but more successful, especially for women and children, than the family of today.

Chapter 13

The Myth of
the Declining Family

Nearly everyone in Middletown knows about the crisis of the modern family and deplores it. Over and over again, they hear from politicians, educators, and neighbors down the street how serious the situation is. The message is gravely proclaimed in television documentaries and in White House conferences intoned from the pulpit, enshrined in legislative preambles. Any intelligent housewife in Middletown can tick off the degenerative symptoms that make the survival of the family so doubtful: the isolation of the nuclear family, the skyrocketing divorce rate, the widening generation gap, the loss of parental authority, the general dissatisfaction with marriage, and the weakening influence of religion.

The Myth and Its History

No part of the venerable institution, it seems, is immune to the general decay. One widely read guru lamented—of all things—the decline of adolescence.

Recent evidence suggests that American children far from becoming overly dependent on their mothers, form strong attachments to neither parent, acquiring instead, at an early stage in their lives, a cool, detached, and realistic outlook on the world. Adolescence, formerly the tumultuous transition from childhood dependence to the responsibilities of adulthood, has become almost obsolete (Lasch 1979, 74).

A medical authority announced to the readers of a women's magazine that "the cement of static marriages was loosened forever when we became a sexually permissive society" (Gould 1978). An eminent sociologist, who has done good work in many fields, informed us breathlessly that "the American middle-class family, already stripped of most non-essential duties, now faces an attack on its remaining last bastions" (Etzioni 1977, 4). The litany is familiar to everyone. We do not need to illustrate it at greater length, and it would be depressing to do so.

As the first dozen chapters of this book showed, the Middletown family is in exceptionally good condition. Tracing the changes from the 1920s to the 1970s, we discovered increased family solidarity, a smaller generation gap, closer marital communication, more religion, and less mobility. With respect to the major features of family life, the trend of the past two generations has run in the opposite direction from the trend that nearly everyone perceives and talks about. It would be convenient to explain this discrepancy by the peculiarities of Middletown, but, as Reuben Hill showed so clearly in the preceding chapter, Middletown families are reasonably similar to American families in general. What we have discovered about marriage, divorce, child raising, housework, employment of women, home ownership, family festivals, kinship networks, and erotic behavior in Middletown does not diverge greatly from what is known for the country as a whole. Needless to say, however, it is easier to describe the behavior of 80,000 people than the behavior of 200 million.

For Middletown, at any rate, we can show that much of what people think they know about the family as an institution is mistaken. But these errors are not scattered and random. The opinions that Middletown people hold about the family fit together in a coherent way and carry a significant message. They form what we may call a sociological myth.

Ever since the development and the popularization of the sociological perspective in the middle of the nineteenth century, the citizens of complex societies have depended more and more on sociological myths to interpret their collective experience, just as simpler societies turn to narrative myths for the same purpose. The symbolic anthropologists, led by Claude Lévi-Strauss, have shown in loving detail how small societies use narrative myths to develop and preserve their unity in the face of the contradictions and mysteries of their collective experience: nature and culture, male and female, body and spirit, birth and death. The people of complex societies face these same mysteries and resolve them in a similar fashion, as Margaret Holmes Williamson showed us in the chapter on Middletown's festivals. But they must also cope with additional polarities that are less important in tribal villages: common sense and science, tradition and modernity, intimacy and bureaucracy, direct experience and the vicarious experience provided by the media.

In common with the rest of humankind, the people of complex societies must deal with an uncertain future, but for them it is also an unimaginable future, which may turn out to be qualitatively different from any stage of the past because of the unpredictable consequences of technology, the unpredictable vagaries of mass culture, and the unpredictable actions of bureaucracies. They must also learn to make appropriate distinctions between direct and vicarious experience. Sociological myths help with these problems. They establish a connection between one's own experience and the collective experience, and they offer what purports to be reliable information about the future.

Myths do not simply promulgate themselves. The narrative myths of simple societies are often incorporated in seasonal rites. Commonly, there are restrictions on who can recite them and to whom. The myths of complex societies, likewise, are incorporated into ceremonies and festivals and recited on appropriate occasions. Unlike narrative myths, sociological myths can usually be traced to their authors, but the question of who promulgates a myth is usually more interesting than the question of who invented it.

In the People's Republics and other highly centralized states of the contemporary word, sociological myths are promulgated by the state, drilled unceasingly into the population, and revised as necessary to suit the government's convenience. In modern democratic nations, sociological myths are promulgated at every organizational level and by all sorts of "establishments," just as Middletown's Chamber of Commerce promulgated the myth of "Magic Middletown" in the 1920s.

Sociological myths do not achieve wide circulation without organizational backing. Scholars, politicians, and poets provide the raw material, but an accepted sociological myth is a collective product, indeed a collective property. As such, it is anything but inert.

"As men define situations as real, they are real in their consequences," wrote W. I. Thomas the year before *Middletown* was published (Thomas and Thomas 1928, 578). To understand the discrepancy between myth and reality in the changing American family, we must consider both the social origins of the myth and its practical consequences.

The dominant myths of complex societies obsessed with social change are likely to be either myths of inevitable progress or of inevitable decadence. There are few other possibilities: a permanent status quo is implausible; the cyclical trend preferred by the ancient Mayans and Vilfredo Pareto has a poor fit with recent events; irregular trends are dramatically unsatisfying. It is not surprising, then, that myths of progress alternate with myths of decadence in our own society. The myth of decadence, moreover, is particularly attractive when the long downward slide leads to an ultimate, improving transformation. Two of the most important sociological myths in world history—Christian millennialism and historical materialism—share this pattern and weak forms of it are found in some versions of the family decline.

Intellectual fashions and individual preferences play a large part in the choice between myths of progress and myths of decadence, but one's political orientation is equally important. Myths of progress are commonly associated with an acceptance of the status quo, and myths of decadence are associated with social activism of all kinds—revolutionary, reactionary, and reforming.

For the first century or so of the sociological enterprise, from the early nineteenth century to the early twentieth century, the doctrine of social evolution was dominant, and it inspired a myth of progress in the family. It was taken for granted that families in modernizing societies would improve over time, becoming more enlightened, egalitarian, affectionate, and efficient in each generation. It is no accident that the principal figures in this intellectual movement preferred society to the state and saw little need for the intervention of government in private life. This viewpoint prevailed in the United States until after World War I.

The year 1929 saw not only the publication of *Middletown*, but the appointment (by Herbert Hoover) of the President's Research Committee on Social Trends. That committee's report, embodied in 13 monographs and a thick summary volume, *Recent Social*

Trends in the United States which appeared in 1933, coinciding with the launching of the New Deal), marks the approximate point in time when family life was defined as a legitimate interest of the federal government. At that time, the improvement of family life became a normal political goal, like the regulation of interstate commerce. Half a dozen chapters of the summary volume dealt with aspects of the family. One of these, "The Family and Its Functions," by William F. Ogburn assisted by Clark Tibbitts, can be taken to mark the official birth of the myth of the declining family, although its basic themes had been current at the University of Chicago and had appeared in Ogburn's writings and those of his colleague, Ernest W. Burgess, some years earlier. According to Ogburn and Tibbitts:

Two outstanding conclusions are indicated by the data on changes in family life. One is the decline of the institutional functions of the family as for example its economic functions. Thus the family now produces less food and clothing than it did formerly. The teaching functions of the family also have been largely shifted to another institution, the school. Industry and the state have both grown at the family's expense. The significance of this diminution in the activities of the family as a group is far reaching.

The other outstanding conclusion is the resulting predominant importance of the personality functions of the family—that is, those which provide for the mutual adjustments among husbands, wives, parents and children and for the adaptation of each member of the family to the outside world. The family has always been responsible to a large degree for the formation of character. It has furnished social contacts and group life. With the decline of its institutional functions these personality functions have come to be its most important contribution to society. The chief concern over the family nowadays is not how strong it may be as an economic organization but how well it performs services for the personalities of its members (Ogburn 1933, 661-708).

The data they presented for these sweeping conclusions were, by modern standards, remarkably inadequate, starting with an undocumented and idealized description of the colonial family. Past eras were lumped indiscriminately together. One read in the same section about the disappearance of the muzzle-loading gun as a means of procuring food and about an increase of 27 percent in the per capita output of commercial bakeries from 1919 to 1929, from which it was inferred that food production was still being transferred out of the home. Nearly all the empirical data cited were contemporary; changes from the past were described on the basis of common knowledge or no knowledge at all. Citing one contemporary study that showed the time spent on housework to average more than 60 hours a week in both rural and urban homes, the authors remarked that "evidently keeping the home still requires many hours per week although many occupations have left it." The delegation of the protective function from the family to outside institutions was said to be confirmed by the fact that the number of policemen, guards, and firemen increased slightly faster from 1920 to 1930 than the number of families. The decline of the family's religious function was supported by no better evidence than a 1930 survey that showed that family church attendance, Bible study, and grace at meals were about twice as frequent in a rural sample as in an urban sample. The family's loss of religious function was inferred from the consideration "that the farm preceded the city in point of time and the city is often the center of cultural diffusion for the country" (Ogburn 1933, 674).

The protection of collective status was another function the family was alleged to be losing. The authors remarked that "this function is highly developed in China where, it is said, loyalty to family has precedence over loyalty to state. In many countries, marriages are often primarily arrangments between families rather than between young couples . . ." (Ogburn 1933, 678). They presented no information whatever about family status in the United States, merely asserting, "That this family function of determining status is changing is obvious, although it is impossible to find data that can be presented in brief compass to establish a trend" (Ogburn 1933, 702).

The evidence for the growing importance of the personality functions of the family was equally thin. Ogburn and Tibbitts speculated that in small families children may receive more concentrated affection and that parent-child contact may be closer in apartments than in detached houses because of limited play space, but they concluded eventually that "the trends in regard to the personality functions of the family are at present impossible to record" (Ogburn 1933, 702).

I do not mean to suggest that this famous paper is worthless. On the contrary, it is a mine of information about the family in 1930 with respect to matters as diverse as happiness in marriage (a little lower than in 1978), rural-urban differences, the number of relatives living with nuclear families, and family composition and family size by occupational level. Other chapters in the same volume are equally informative. For example, one learns from Hornell Hart's chapter on attitudes that sexual attitudes were more permissive during the period 1924 to 1927 than either before or later (Hart 1933), and from Robert Lynd's remarkable chapter on consumers (Lynd 1933) that the percentage of family income spent for food around 1930 varied from 68 percent in a sample of Kentucky mountain families down to 9 percent among senior faculty members at the University of California. But the evidence for the family's progressive loss of all functions except the affectional rested only on three wobbly legs: the totally speculative description of a patriarchal, self-sufficient colonial family; the assumption that education, protection, or, for that matter, baking must decrease within the family whenever such activities increase outside it; and the method of looking at rural families to see what urban families were like at an earlier time.

So much for the birth of the myth. It has flourished mightily ever since and now seems nearly as indestructible as the American family itself. Its mere persistence suggests that it must have some useful purpose that is not obvious. Any folklorist would take that for granted if he found a narrative myth that had been told again and again around the tribal camp fires and that was still listened to with undiminished interest and alarm.

In an earlier chapter, we touched on the principal advantage that the myth of the declining family confers on those who believe it. When Middletown people compare their own families and their own relationships with spouses, children, and parents with the "average" or the "typical" family's, nearly all of them discover with pleasure that their own families are better than other people's. From a societal standpoint, this nearly universal illusion is an unqualified benefit. At no real cost, most of the people in Middletown have the satisfaction of knowing that their performance as husbands and wives, children and parents, housekeepers and providers, is superior.

At a deeper level, the myth of the declining family offers some comfort for certain frustrations that are built into the Middletown family as an institutional form. These, too, have been mentioned in earlier chapters, especially the asymmetric relationship between generations, whereby parents are expected to provide their children with as many goods and services as possible and to receive very little in return, the abrupt emancipation of adolescents from parental authority, and the inability of marital partners to protect themselves against the risk of divorce at any stage in the family cycle. By defining these harsh structural conditions as part of a social problem, the myth provides a consoling explanation, and it relieves those who are especially afflicted by these arrangements from some of the guilt, shame, and hostility they might otherwise feel.

Other motives impel the promulgators of the myth and those who continually revise and renew it. Ogburn's chapter in *Recent Social Trends in the United States* advocated more parent education, more family clinics, more preparation for marriage, more legislation, more governmental services, and, of course, more research.[1] These suggestions have not gone unheeded since 1933. The decline of the family and the methods taken to stay it provide livelihoods for thousands of scholars, journalists, and social workers and tens of thousands of governmenment employees.[2] When we try to imagine what would happen to this thriving industry without the myth, we can see how important a part it plays.

But this volume has shown no appreciable decline in the Middletown family during the past 50 years. Insofar as changes in the institution can be measured, they seem to reflect a strengthening of the institutional form and increased satisfaction for participants. We have noted the likelihood that the trend for the entire country is similar. These conclusions obviously are contrary to the prevailing belief that the family has been declining for a long time, that its survival past the present generation is in doubt, and that massive intervention is required to save it—so contrary, indeed, that we are likely to be accused of bias no matter how much we insist that the conclusions were forced on us by our data and were as surprising to us as they may be to our readers.

There are several grounds on which our findings could be challenged: (1) that data mostly drawn from questionnaires and interviews administered by strangers do not comprehend the rich tapestry of family life as it is actually lived in Middletown; (2) that the same interviews and questionnaires, addressed to married couples and probably rejected by unconventional couples, scant the importance of the alternative life-styles that are displacing conventional marriage; unmarried cohabitation, swinging, communal marriage, homosexual marriage, and the one-parent family; (3) that the recent increase of child abuse and wife abuse in Middletown, and other places, is plainly a symptom of family disintegration; (4) that, even if existing families are reasonably stable, the loss of demographic vitality in the institution is shown by recent increases in premarital sex, in illegitimate births, and in the number of persons living alone; by the deferral of marriage, the low birth rate, and the continued movement of married women with small children into the labor force. These objections are not trivial. Let us consider each separately.

Some Objections to Our Hopeful View

After reading part of this volume in manuscript, one of our best friends in Middletown wrote:

Where in your text do you indicate an awareness for the complexity of the tapestry of society? . . .

Perhaps it is purely personal bias, or obsession, but the more sociology I know the more I become sensitive to the duopoly in life—the power of our continuities as they are anchored in what we used to call "functional requisites" and the rich tapestry of individual and sub-group interpretations of existence. Any study that puts a thick glaze over that variety is, to my mind, guilty of superficiality or simplistic thinking. Not only is our discipline then properly held in casual or amused contempt, we then have done that which we least of all ever wanted to do—diminish our understanding of the richness of life itself.[3]

This is a valid point, but it applies with equal force to almost any description of social life by means of quantitative data. The weakness is inherent in the sociological method. The ethnographer who lives for several years in a small village and observes its family life at first hand can overcome this limitations, although not without some distortion of the data owing to his own involvement; but the ethnographic method is not really a practical approach to the study of the family in a community as large as Middletown. It is practically impossible to find and hold together a small sample of families that is representative of the entire community. The same objection applies to the use of diaries, letters, personal histories, and case records, which are, besides, hard to come by and of uneven quality. These difficulties are compounded in the study of long-term trends by the difficulty of comparing the subjective experiences of one set of people (in, say, 1924) with those of another set of people (in, say, 1978). Something could be learned, of course, by interviewing elderly people in 1978 about their experiences in 1924. Indeed, Vivian Gordon and Rutledge Dennis are doing just that in their current study of Middletown's black families. But the value of that procedure for tracing social trends is limited by the inevitable distortion that occurs when people are asked to remember the events and emotions of many years before. A better method is to take the personal histories of a sample of informants at a given time and then to go back years later, draw a similar sample from the same population, and ask them similar questions. The oral histories gathered by Gordon and Dennis in 1980 will be enormously more valuable if and when someone goes back to Middletown in the year 2000 or at some later point in time and replicates their procedures.

We have been singularly fortunate at a few points in our own study by being able to compare the extensive answers to certain questions given by the Lynds' 1924 sample of Middletown housewives with the answers our 1978 sample gave to the same questions. If we had more of such material, the Middletown III study would be much better than it is.

A number of investigators have tried to substitute observations obtained from popular fiction for the information about family life in the past that is unobtainable now. Indeed, Hornell Hart's chapter on attitudes in *Recent Social Trends in the United States* attempted to analyze changing social attitudes toward sex between 1900 and 1932 by tabulating the behavior of heroes and heroines in magazine fiction and films. A similar procedure has been used to flesh out our meager knowledge of the American family in colonial times and in the early nineteenth century.[4] The method is a desperate one highly susceptible to error, since we do not know how closely the behavior of characters in any body of fictional literature resembles the behavior of their readers, and since there is no reason for the frequency of a given type of behavior in a body of fictional literature to match its frequency in real life. With respect to both these points, a recent excellent study of television serials during the 1970s (Stein 1979) shows a tendency for that kind of fiction to reverse the patterns of real-life behavior, rather than to follow them; for example, in the world of television fiction, violent crimes are much more likely to be committed by elderly executives than by young, unemployed men, and happily married couples are almost unknown.

A related objection to our view of the Middletown family as a thriving institution is that we seem to take no account of the innumerable family tragedies that appear in the news, in case records, and in local gossip: incest and child abuse; wife beating and conjugal rape; reciprocal infidelity; lost and corrupted adolescents; murder, suicide, and mental breakdown. All of these do occur in Middletown's families, and, when they do, it is customary to attribute them to the demoralization of the family, the loss of religion, and the special wickedness of the age in which we live. This does not take us very far. Most of Middletown's tragedies occur in family situations because most of Middletown's living is done in family situations and most of the significant personages in the lives of Middletown people are their close relatives. But, contrary to the myth, suicide, mental breakdown, and domestic violence appear to be less frequent today than they were two generations ago,[5] while other forms of family trouble show no consistent trend.

Inducements to Change

In an alternative life-style, some combination of persons other than a man and a woman legally married to each other live together in a sexual relationship. Such arrangements were much easier to establish and maintain in the Middletown of the 1970s than ever before in the community's history because of several developments: the introduction in the 1960s of reliable oral contraceptives that made it easy for women to avoid pregnancy while being sexually active, the legalization of abortion by the Supreme Court in 1973, and a series of other judicial decisions that effectively prohibited the social enforcement of sexual norms by public authorities such as the police or by corporate authorities such as college administrators. Such decisions in the early 1970s prohibited job and housing discrimination against unmarried couples and homosexual couples, established the right of adolescent girls to obtain contraceptives and to procure abortions without parental consent, prohibited employers from inquiring into the living arrangements of their employees, restricted the authority of schools and colleges to prescribe the living arrangements of their students, and removed the last vestiges of legal disability from children born out of wedlock.

The general effect of these decisions was to shelter practically all adult sexual behavior, and most adolescent behavior as well, from public and corporate authorities. Adultery continued to be grounds for divorce, but the distinction formerly made in such proceedings between the innocent spouse and the guilty spouse was softened by innumerable judicial rulings and by "no-fault" divorce legislation. By 1980, the plaintiff in a successful divorce action based on adultery could no longer be sure of obtaining child custody or a privileged financial settlement. Prosecutions for fornication—under the Mann Act, for example, or under ordinances prohibiting false registration at hotels—had been abandoned. Other statutes and decisions had removed practically all the disabilities of unmarried couples with respect to obtaining credit, buying homes, traveling together, and raising their own or adopted children. The private legislation of nongovernmental bodies generally followed suit. By 1980, persons "living in sin" were admitted to communion in churches (including the Roman Catholic) that had formerly barred them; and many colleges provided housing for unmarried student couples, who would have been automatically expelled a few years before.

In the 1970s the federal government went well beyond the passive encouragement of alternative life-styles to the active promotion and subsidizing of them. This antifamily policy seemed not to reflect a deliberate intention so much as an accidental result of badly drafted legislation, bureaucratic entrepreneurship, and assorted political pressures. The antifamily policy included three important features unknown in other modernized societies: a tax on marriage, with a special surtax for the poor; bounties for the production of babies out of wedlock; and the systematic promotion of adolescent sexuality.

The tax on marriage, which affected families above the poverty level in rough proportion to their income, was an accidental by-product of the tax reforms of 1978, when the rules for reporting income were revised in such a way that husbands and wives who are both employed paid a substantially heavier tax on their joint income than they would pay if they were unmarried and living together in otherwise identical circumstances.

In 1980, the Internal Revenue Service was trying to get the courts to punish one highly publicized couple—both husband and wife were accountants—who had adopted the habit of obtaining a quick divorce by mutual consent each December and remarrying in January in order to gain the advantage of filing as unmarried.

The marriage tax was abolished by the 1981 tax reform but the two other antifamily measures remained, and one of them was reinforced in 1981 by new restrictions on the earnings of welfare families. Low-income families pay the peculiar, heavy surtax that is the bane of the American welfare system. The core of that system is "aid to families with dependent children"—monthly payments based on the number of children and their special needs. Entitlement to these payments is achieved by having a family income below a set maximum. If the family's income rises above the maximum, the payments cease. In effect, the last few earned dollars that put the family over the limit and make it ineligible for welfare payments are taxed at more than 100 percent; that is, each dollar earned entails the loss of more than a dollar of welfare income.[6] The way this most commonly occurs is for an unemployed father to obtain work or for one employed at low pay to improve his position. The most prudent course, then, is for the father to abandon his wife and children, keeping his own earnings for himself and letting them retain their eligibility for welfare payments. This family-dissolving incentive has been the despair of rational observers for many years.

The bounty for children born out of wedlock is part of the same welfare system and must be presumed to be at least partially responsible for the great increase of the illegitimacy ratio in Middletown and in the United States during the past two decades, when the improvement of contraceptives and the legalization of abortion might have otherwise have been expected to reduce it. The offer the government holds out to adolescent girls is that, if they will produce a child out of wedlock, they will be immediately defined as adults and provided with a sufficient income to set up an independent household. To young girls from disadvantaged minority families and with poor job and marital prospects, the offer is irresistible, as statistics show.[7]

The promotion of adolescent sexuality has been another paradoxical outcome of clumsily designed federal programs. Funds for sex education and contraception are distributed through a network of quasi-public organizations that are almost totally dependent on government funds but have no vested right to receive them. Their grant requests must be rejustified annually on a showing of "cost effectiveness." Practically speaking, this has meant that the survival of these agencies and the jobs of the people who work in them were contingent upon their ability to develop a large case load by delivering contraceptives to as many adolescents as possible. The promotional effectiveness of the program is dramatically evident in Middletown, as we saw in Chapter 7.

Given these powerful inducements for various segments of the population to avoid marriage or to abandon it, the persistence of marriage in Middletown (as reported in Chapter 2) and in the United States generally (as reported in Chapter 12) is as impressive as the large increase in the number of unmarried adults during the past decade. As the same chapters showed, no significant changes have yet been recorded in the lifetime propensity to marry, in the age at marriage, or in family size. The number of persons engaged in pursuing "alternative life-styles," although much larger than it used to be, is too small proportionately to be accurately recorded in a national census or in a community survey, unless we count the female-headed family as an alternative life-style, too. That type of family, produced either by the breakup of an intact family or by the childbearing of unmarried women, accounted for 8 percent of all white families and 29 percent of all black families in the United States in 1980, an overall increase of 32 percent since 1970.

Child Abuse and Wife Abuse

Moral entrepreneurship is a well-established profession in the United States. The moral entrepreneur identifies a social problem that has not previously been recognized, or one that has not been regarded as important, and announces it to the public. If the public is responsive, the launching of the problem is followed by a media barrage. The name of the problem and its supporting arguments are advertised in books, articles, interviews, speeches, films, conferences, and demonstrations. As the problem begins to catch on, new associations are formed to promote it and old associations add it to their causes. Government funds are sought and have often been obtained, and these are used to fund "action programs," "educational programs," "demonstration projects," and eventually research. In the usual case, the problem and its recognized solutions are fixed in the public mind before any serious fact finding is begun. In the early stages of a new social problem, what passes for information consists largely of estimates based on no data.

The problems of "wife abuse" and "child abuse" were introduced in this way in the mid-1970s, and their emergence was—inevitably—interpreted as evidence that wife beating and cruelty to children were increasing in an unprecedented way.[8] One authority on the "battered wife syndrome" estimated the possible number of battered wives in the United States in 1975 as 28 million, a figure equal to 42 percent of all the married women in the country. Nobody blinked an eyelash at this announcement, and it was widely quoted and requoted.

That such movements serve a useful purpose is undeniable. Middletown, like nearly every other sizable community in the country, now has places where a frightened wife can go to be protected from a violent, abusive husband and other places where the neighbors can report a small child left alone in a trailer or severely beaten by his or her parents. But there is no evidence whatever that these ugly behaviors have been increasing. What data we have for Middletown (for example, the number of criminal charges involving domestic violence) suggest a gradual but irregular decline over recent decades, as statistical common sense would anticipate, with increasing levels of education and affluence.

Institutional Vitality

The survival of the Middletown family (or of the American family, for that matter) does not appear to be severely threatened by any of the trends we have been able to establish on empirical evidence. Middletown families compare favorably in most respects with their prototypes of two generations ago, and we have no reason to think that the situation is dramatically different for American families in general. But there are limits to the reassurance that can be drawn from such findings. Social trends, by their nature, are not inexorable, and to show that the institution of the family has not declined over the past 50 years is not to prove that it could not decline during the next 50 years or during the next 10. The extrapolation of past trends is one method of predicting future trends, but it is not the only method and it is highly fallible. In this concluding section, I will try to assess the probable future of the Middletown family by another method, that of examining its institutional vitality.

The survival of the family as an institution would be most directly threatened by any decrease in the marriage rate or the birth rates that carried it out of the historic range, that is, if a large number of people refused to marry or, once married, to have children. Let us begin with marriages. The simplest measure of the propensity to marry is the crude marriage rate, the number of marriages per 1,000 population in a given year. When we examine the trend in this rate from 1910 to 1978 for the United States, we find nothing to arouse concern. The 1910 rate was 10.3 marriages per 1,000 population. The 1978 rate was exactly the same, and the 1980 rate was fractionally higher (U.S. Department of Health and Human Services 1980). The maximum reached during the intervening years was 12.2 in 1945. The minimum was 8.5 in 1960 and 1962. The average for the 1970s was higher than the average for the previous years. That rate, however, is called a crude rate because it does not take account of fluctuations in the size of the eligible population. A much more informative measure is the number of marriages per 1,000 unmarried women of marriageable age (Caplow 1946). When we examine this rate, we find that it declined slowly from 166 in 1950[9] to 140 in 1970 and then more rapidly to 110 in 1977 (U.S. Bureau of the Census 1978, 81, Table 117). The change cannot be attributed to the postponement of marriage, since the median age at marriage has remained constant for many years, at around 23 for men and 21 for women.

The recent increase in the number of single adults in Middletown (which Howard Bahr noted in Chapter 2) is a national phenomenon, but the overwhelming majority of persons still marry eventually. And the decline in the propensity to marry is partially offset by the increasing proportion of married couples who become parents (as Reuben Hill explained in Chapter 12). Still and all, the decline is real and it bears watching.

The American crude birth rate has had an interesting history. After declining from 30 births per 1,000 population in 1910 to 21 in 1930, it fluctuated around that level until the end of the 1960s, when a new decline set in that carried it down to a historic low of 15 in 1973. It has remained at the 1973 level, or slightly higher, ever since. Here again the crude rate is relatively uninformative. It is more useful to know that there were 102 births per 1,000 white women of childbearing age in 1950s and 64 in 1977 and 137 births for the corresponding group of black women in 1950 and 90 in 1977. An even better measure, devised by the Bureau of the Census, is the total fertility rate. It represents the number of children that 1,000 women would bear in their lifetimes at current age-specific rates. Under present conditions, par for this measure is 2,110, which, prolonged over time, would produce zero population growth (not counting immigration). The total fertility rate averaged about 2,700 in the 1940s, 3,500 in the 1950s, 3,000 in the 1960s, and only 1,900 in the 1970s (U.S. Bureau of the Census 1978, 61, Table 82). Combined with the small net immigration that is normal for the United States, fertility at this level should produce an approximately stable population. Indeed, it has already done so; population growth from 1979 to 1980 was only 0.6 percent.

The decline of the birth rate in the early 1970s was exactly concurrent with the legalization of abortion and parallels the experience of other countries, such as Japan, where abortion was suddenly legalized. Any further decline in the birth rate, however, would bring in the prospect of a shrinking population, a situation not previously faced by the United States, which would have unpredictable and perhaps undesirable consequences.

There is less reason for concern about recent changes in the divorce rate. Although the crude rate rose in the 1970s, the more useful rate of divorces per 1,000 married women remains within its historic range and is too low in absolute terms (about 20) to presage any major shift in family attitudes and values. Indeed, given the current tendency for divorced persons to remarry promptly and the fair probability that remarriages will be successful, small rises in the divorce rate are about as likely to contribute to family solidarity as to family disorganization, despite the pain and stress inflicted upon the participants.

Something similar must be said of the well-documented increase in premarital sexual activity. So long as it continues to be perceived by many participants as part of the search for a husband or a wife, its effect on the family as an institution is as likely to be favorable as unfavorable. (This idea is supported by the data presented in previous chapters.) A sharp increase in extramarital activity would be quite another matter, but we found no indication that such has occurred, either in Middletown or in the United States.

We are much more hesitant about assessing the probable effects on family life of the employment of women with young children. In the United States in 1978, 42 percent of married women who lived with their husbands and who had young children and 67 percent of divorced women who had young children were employed full-time. Those proportions have been rising steadily for a century or more, but most of the increase has been concentrated in the past three decades. As recently as 1950, only 12 percent of the married women with young children were in the labor force. The trend has been greatly encouraged by legal changes that restrain employers from discharging or penalizing women employees who become pregnant and that compel them to grant maternity leaves without prejudice to seniority. It also has been affected by the vast expansion of publicly subsidized day-care facilities. Nearly half of the mothers of young children are now in the labor force at any given time, and a much higher proportion are employed at some time during the infancy and early childhood of their children. Based on the evidence gathered so far, the overall results do not seem to have been harmful, for either the mothers or the children. It is still too early, however, to say whether this will continue to be the case as these large cohorts of children grow into adolescence and maturity. Signs of neglect have often been observed in children raised by single, separated, and divorced working mothers. It remains uncertain whether many of the children raised by working mothers in intact families suffer deleterious effects. In our Middletown samples, the majority of working wives with small children were rated by their husbands as doing a superior job of child care. These witnesses may have been biased, but they certainly had ample opportunities for observation.

There is another dimension to this question of institutional vitality, and the data for Middletown show it to be much more important than is generally realized. The habit of visualizing family life in terms of the isolated nuclear family is so strong in our culture that we are always in danger of overlooking or forgetting the emotional, social, and economic importance of those larger kin networks that we may call "composite families," for want of any accepted term. That they do not have a name for the thing shows how much Middletown people underrate the part it plays in their lives. When they refer to the composite family, they call it "my family" or "our family" and rely on the context to distinguish it from the nuclear family that is sometimes included within it and sometimes not. "My family lives right here in Middletown" means that most of a person's close relatives live there; "my family" in this sense does not include a person's own spouse and children. But "Our whole family was together this Christmas" lumps together the speaker's nuclear family and consanguineal relatives with their nuclear families. The single most important fact about the nuclear family in contemporary Middletown is that it is *not* isolated. Most people have relatives in other households nearby with whom they sustain close, continuous, and easy interaction. Indeed, it is the presence of those relatives that accounts for their own presence in the community and keeps them from moving away.

We do not really know how this system compares with the earlier forms from which it evolved, but there is enough scattered information in the Lynds' two volumes, in various historical documents, and in the manuscript censuses for 1850 to 1880, to suggest that what we see does not represent a vestige of an earlier system but a new social form that has developed and strengthened over the years. Although we cannot give an entirely clean bill of health to the nuclear family, the composite family—amorphous and informally organized though it is—is in splendid condition in Middletown.

Christmas in Middletown

We see this clearly in the findings of the very last Middletown III survey, an interview study conducted early in 1979 with a sample of 110 informants who were exhaustively interviewed about how they and their families celebrated the previous Christmas. We recorded among other things the distribution and location of each respondent's primary, secondary, and tertiary relatives; what contact was made with them at Christmas 1978, whether by visiting, telephoning, gift giving, or corresponding; and whether there was gift giving, whether it was one-way or reciprocal, and what items were given.

A primary relative (as here defined) is is a person with whom one's relationship can be precisely described by a single word and with whom one lives or formerly lived in the same nuclear family — father, mother, brother, sister, husband, wife, son, or daughter. A secondary relationship is one that can be precisely described by combining two primary terms; for example, mother's brother, mother's mother, brother's wife, or daughter's son. Three of these terms are needed to describe a tertiary relationship accurately; for example, an aunt by marriage may be a mother's brother's wife or a father's brother's wife; a first cousin may be a father's brother's son, a father's brother's daughter, a father's sister's son, a mother's sister's daughter, et cetera. As contemporary Middletown interprets kinship obligation, one ought to keep in touch with all primary relatives, although the contact need not be close and continuous; and one ought to assist them when called upon, although the obligation is not externally enforced. The maintenance of contact with secondary relatives is expected and approved when they live close by and optional when they live farther away. Contact with tertiary relatives is entirely elective. Most of the people in our sample stayed in touch with a few of them and ignored the others.

Our respondents were asked to tell in considerable detail how they spent the Christmas of 1978, what festive gatherings they attended and with whom, where they had Christmas dinner and what they ate, whether there was a tree there and how it was decorated, what photographs were taken, how gifts were opened, if and where they went to church, how they selected and wrapped the gifts they gave, and how much was spent for them. It is indicative of the importance that Middletown people attach to this annual celebration of family values that they had no difficulty remembering all these details in an interview that took place from several weeks to several months later. Not a single member of our sample — regardless of his or her religion, age, sex, or family situation — abstained entirely from the celebration of Christmas in 1978.

Like the kinship survey reported in an earlier chapter, the

Christmas survey demonstrated the local concentration of the composite family. The women in our sample reported that about 60 percent of their parents, 60 percent of their grandparents, 50 percent of their brothers and sisters, 60 percent of their grown children, and nearly 70 percent of their grandchildren were living within 50 miles of them at Christmas 1978; 71 percent of our respondents had relatives living in other households in Middletown or within 50 miles

The median respondent had 26 primary and secondary relatives, of whom 15 lived within a radius of 50 miles and 11 of those in households other than his own. That Christmas celebrates the composite family as much as the nuclear family is shown by the fact that our respondents attended an average of 3.3 gatherings where gifts were opened. More of these gatherings were in the homes of relatives than in the respondents' own homes.

The ties of Middletown adults with the parents and the grown children from whom they now live apart are so strong as almost to override the estranging effect of distance. The members of our sample saw about 80 percent of their parents and grandparents, nearly 100 percent of their own children, and more than 70 percent of their grandchildren face to face during the Christmas season of 1978. An even higher proportion of these relationships was marked by the reciprocal exchange of gifts. Of all the relatives— primary, secondary, and tertiary—recorded by the respondents, 51 percent were seen face to face, and 23 percent were communicated with remotely, distance playing a much larger part in determining whether contact occurred with aunts and uncles, nephews and nieces. All this is testimony to the strength and cohesion of the composite family in today's Middletown and of how well the moral obligations of kinship are enforced without any visible means of enforcement.

The Christmas survey revealed another feature of the composite family that has seldom been noticed. In contemporary Middletown, the size of the composite family remains relatively constant from cradle to grave. We discovered this when we divided our sample population by decades of age—by separating those in their twenties, thirties, forties, fifties, and older—and tabulated the number of primary and secondary relatives involved in the celebration of Christmas at each age level. The median number fluctuated between 12 and 15 but was scarcely affected by age. As people move through the life cycle, the constellation of relatives keeps shifting, but its size remains about the same. At birth, the constellation consists primarily of parents, grandparents, aunts and uncles, and siblings; in old age, of children, grandchildren, and surviving brothers and sisters, together with the spouses of all of them.

Nieces and nephews, the most numerous class of secondary relatives, play a significant, if unintended, part in maintaining this curious stability. Relationships with nieces and nephews past early childhood are elective. They are likely to be cultivated when there are no children or grandchildren living close by and abandoned when the family circle is already full. This informal but effective system is reminiscent of a classic arrangement found in many tribal societies,[10] whereby the ritual and practical duties of a given relative, like a father's brother—when he is absent, nonexistent, or unable to perform them—fall to a more distant relative "in the same direction," such as a father's father's brother's son. The substitutions that are made in Middletown have a similar effect. They ensure that the moral support and practical assistance expected from relatives often remain available to people who, because of the accidents of birth and death, arrive at a major occasion in their lives without the relatives they need.

An efficient kinship system leaves few people out in the cold and is especially protective in the two helpless phases of the life cycle, infancy and extreme age. An inefficient system produces neglected orphans and lonely old people, as well as isolation and anomie in other phases of the life cycle. Such situations are not unknown in contemporary Middletown, but they are comparatively rare. For most of their members most of the time, Middletown's composite families provide a safe and comfortable niche in a hazardous world.

APPENDIX A

APPENDIX A

Table 2-1
Middletown's Age Distribution, 1920-1970
(in percentages)

Year	Under 5	5-14	15-24	25-44	45-64	65+	Total
1920	8.7%	17.3%	18.3%	31.8%	18.8%	5.1%	100.0%
1930	9.2	16.4	18.4	31.4	19.0	5.5	99.9
1940	8.3	15.2	17.3	32.9	19.6	6.8	100.1
1950	10.7	15.1	16.7	30.1	19.1	8.2	99.9
1960	11.1	18.5	17.2	24.7	19.4	9.1	100.0
1970	8.3	15.6	28.3	19.7	18.6	9.5	100.0

Source: U.S. Bureau of the Census 1922b, vol. 2, p. 317; U.S. Bureau of the Census 1932, vol. 3, part 1, p. 702; U.S. Bureau of the Census 1943, vol. 2, part 2, p. 790; U.S. Bureau of the Census 1952, vol. 2, part 14, p. 14-26; U.S. Bureau of the Census 1961, vol. 1, part 16, p. 16-61; U.S. Bureau of the Census 1972a, vol. 1, part 16, p. 16-100.

Table 2-2
Middletown's Birth Rates, 1920-1975

Year	Births	Births per 1,000 Total Population	Births per 1,000 Women Aged 15-44	U.S. Births per 1,000 Total Population
1920	842	23.1	92.6	27.7
1930	977	21.0	85.0	21.3
1940	1,033	20.8	82.0	19.4
1950	1,651	28.2	116.0	24.1
1960	1,752	25.5	116.1	23.7
1970	1,520	22.0	87.4	18.4
1975	1,221	15.3	60.7*	14.8

Sources: Indiana State Board of Health 1967a, 90, Table 9; U.S. Bureau of the Census 1974, vol. 1, pp. 2-24; Indiana State Board of Health 1976; Lynd and Lynd 1937, 557.

*Estimated.

Table 2-5

Marriages, Divorces, and Divorce Rates for Middletown's County, 1890-1975

Year	Marriages	Divorces	Marriages per 1,000 Population	Divorces per 1,000 Population	Ratio of Divorces to Marriages	Divorces per 1,000 Married Women
1890	283	34	9.4	1.0	0.120	—
1900	570	109	11.5	2.2	0.191	—
1910	557	147	10.8	2.9	0.264	—
1920	798	261	14.2	4.6	0.327	20.9[a]
1930	546	255	8.1	3.8	0.467	15.5
1940	—	287	—	3.8	—	14.6[a]
1945	904	576	10.9	8.6	0.637	26.8[b]
1950	1,110	372	12.3	4.1	0.335	15.9
1960	1,061	432	9.6	3.9	0.407	15.9
1970	1,438	690	11.1	5.3	0.480	22.7
1975	1,300	661	10.1	5.1	0.508	21.7[b]

Sources: Lynd and Lynd 1937, 544-45; Middletown's morning newspaper, January 3, 1946; Indiana State Board of Health 1967b, 5; Indiana State Board of Health 1976, Table 8; Yearbook of the State of Indiana: 1917, 787; Yearbook of the State of Indiana: 1920, 1140; Delaware County Circuit and Superior Court Civil Order Books, 1940-1975; U.S. Bureau of the Census 1908, 796; U.S. Bureau of the Census 1974, vol. 3, p. 1-89; U.S. Bureau of the Census 1908, part 2, p. 715.

Note: The numbers of marriages and divorces for 1890 and 1900 given above differ from the figures in the Lynds' tables. We have checked against original sources and resolved discrepancies between state and federal figures in favor of the latter. (U.S. Bureau of the Census 1908.)

a. The number of married women was estimated by using the 1930 married women/all women proportion.

b. The number of married women was estimated from 1940, 1950, and 1970 enumerations.

Table 2-6

Percentage of Adult[a] Population Divorced by Sex, in Five Indiana Cities of Comparable Size, 1920-1970

| | Total Adult[a] Population | | Percentage Divorced | | | | | | | | | |
| | | | 1920 | | 1930 | | 1950[b] | | 1960 | | 1970 | |
City	1920	1970	Men	Women	Men	Women	Men	Women	Men	Women	Men	Women
Anderson	22,026	51,896	1.1%	1.8%	2.5%	2.9%	4.3%	5.3%	4.3%	6.0%	4.9%	6.9%
East Chicago	22,968	34,087	0.5	0.5	1.5	1.2	3.6	3.2	3.9	3.7	4.5	5.3
Hammond	24,094	79,002	1.0	1.1	1.5	1.7	2.7	2.7	2.5	2.9	3.6	4.4
Middletown	27,042	53,638	2.4	2.6	2.7	2.8	4.2	4.7	3.5	4.8	4.2	5.9
Terre Haute	49,396	55,573	1.5	1.8	2.2	2.5	3.8	4.5	3.2	4.8	3.8	5.8

Source: U.S. Bureau of the Census 1922b, vol. 2, pp. 544, 545; U.S. Bureau of the Census 1932, vol. 3, part 1, pp. 715-17; U.S. Bureau of the Census 1952, vol. 2, part 14, pp. 14-59 through 14-62; U.S. Bureau of the Census 1961, vol. 1, part 16, pp. 16-67 through 16-70; U.S. Bureau of the Census 1972a, vol. 1, part 16, p. 16-113.

a. Aged 15+ until 1940, 14+ thereafter; 1940 figures not available.

b. Census reports for 1950 give divorced and widowed combined; number divorced estimated by using the 1960 percentage of divorced persons and widowed persons combined.

Table 2-7

Marital Situation of Parents or Guardians, Middletown High School Students, 1977, and Retrospective Data for a Sample of Middletown Adults, 1977

Persons Lived With	Inferred Marital Status	1977 High School Students	1977 Adults when Age 16
Both mother and father	Married	68%	77%
Father and stepmother	Remarried following divorce or widowhood	3	2
Mother and stepfather	Remarried following divorce or widowhood	9	5
Father only	Divorced, separated, or widowed	2	2
Mother only	Divorced, separated, or widowed	14	9
Other relatives	Other	3	5
Other	Other	2	1
Total		101%	101%
Number of cases (N)		(1,620)	(476)

Source: Middletown III high school survey and family role survey, 1977.

Table 2-8

Percentages of Middletown Housewives Mentioning Various Causes of Increasing Divorce, by Husband's Occupational Class, 1978

Causes of Divorce (Classification of Respondents' Themes)	Total (N = 332)	Business-class Wives (N = 189)	Working-class Wives (N = 143)
Lack of commitment to marriage	18.7%	23.3%	12.6%
The "new morality" (including infidelity, sin, living together)	17.2	20.6	12.6
Today's women too independent (including women's lib)	14.8	19.0	9.1
Inadequate preparation for marriage	12.0	10.6	14.0
Poor communication between husband and wife	11.7	7.9	16.8
Selfishness, materialism	10.2	10.6	9.8
Ease of obtaining a divorce	9.0	9.5	8.4
Financial problems	7.2	7.9	6.3
Family breakdown	6.6	7.9	4.9
Society's acceptance of divorce	6.3	7.4	4.9

Source: Middletown III, housewives' survey, 1978.

Table 3-1

Husbands' and Wives' Opinions about which Spouse Should Perform which Roles
and Their Reports of Actual Role Performance, 1977

(in percentages)

Role	Husbands' Response		Wives' Response	
	Who Should?	Who Does?	Who Should?	Who Does?
Provide income				
Husband entirely or more than wife	81%	85%	76%	82%
Husband-wife equally, or doesn't matter	18	12	23	13
Wife entirely or more than husband	1	3	1	5
Number of Cases (N)	(219)	(216)	(253)	(245)
Keep house				
Husband entirely or more than wife	1	1	0	1
Husband-wife equally, or doesn't matter	25	9	20	10
Wife entirely or more than husband	74	90	80	89
Number of Cases (N)	(220)	(219)	(253)	(250)
Take care of preschool children				
Husband entirely or more than wife	0	1	0	0
Husband-wife equally, or doesn't matter	31	22	26	11
Wife entirely or more than husband	69	77	74	89
Number of Cases (N)	(218)	(95)	(246)	(110)
Discipline older children				
Husband entirely or more than wife	19	16	12	15
Husband-wife equally, or doesn't matter	80	76	86	64
Wife entirely or more than husband	1	8	2	21
Number of Cases (N)	(216)	(128)	(250)	(147)
Keep in touch with husband's relatives				
Husband entirely or more than wife	36	26	28	27
Husband-wife equally, or doesn't matter	53	43	65	44
Wife entirely or more than husband	11	31	7	30
Number of Cases (N)	(218)	(209)	(253)	(236)
Make home repairs				
Husband entirely or more than wife	84	88	70	76
Husband-wife equally, or doesn't matter	15	8	30	17
Wife entirely or more than husband	1	4	0	7
Number of Cases (N)	(212)	(206)	(246)	(222)
Organize family excursions				
Husband entirely or more than wife	6	13	11	14
Husband-wife equally, or doesn't matter	84	71	82	67
Wife entirely or more than husband	10	16	8	18
Number of Cases (N)	(220)	(214)	(207)	(238)

Source: Middletown III family role survey, 1977.

Table 3-2
Sharing the Provider and Housekeeper Roles in Middletown Families, 1977
(in percentages)

Role	Percentage of Middletown Families
Husband earns all of the income/wife does all of the housekeeping	27%
Husband earns most of the income/wife does all of the housekeeping	7
Husband earns most of the income/wife does most of the housekeeping	26
Husband earns all of the income/wife does most of the housekeeping	17
Husband and wife equally earn the income/wife does most of the housekeeping	8
Other patterns	15
Total	100%
Number of Cases (N)	(460)

Source: Middletown III family role survey, 1977.

Table 3-3
Discrepancies between Preferred Division of Labor and Actual Performance of Family Role Activities in Middletown Families, 1977
(in percentages)

| Family Role | No Discrepancy (Who Should = Who Does) | | Direction of Discrepancies | | | | Number of Respondents | |
| | | | Wife Does More Than She Should | | Husband Does More Than He Should | | | |
	Husbands	Wives	Husbands	Wives	Husbands	Wives	Husbands	Wives
Provide income	54%	48%	13%	11%	33%	42%	(215)	(245)
Do housekeeping	62	58	32	36	6	7	(218)	(250)
Care of preschool children	77	61	17	31	6	8	(95)	(108)
Discipline older children	77	67	16	23	8	10	(128)	(147)
Keep in touch with husband's relatives	57	56	32	30	11	14	(208)	(236)
Make home repairs	63	61	16	13	21	26	(203)	(222)
Organize family excursions	77	74	11	16	12	10	(214)	(238)

Source: Middletown III family role survey, 1977.

Table 3-6
Percentages above Average in Self-rated Family Role Enactment,
by Sex and Occupational Class, Middletown, 1977

	Husbands		Wives	
Family Role	Working-class	Business-class	Working-class	Business-class
Doing housekeeping	22%	32%	40%	57%
Number of Cases (N)	(93)	(99)	(93)	(101)
Doing household repairs	48	41	11	19
Number of Cases (N)	(90)	(97)	(88)	(96)
Organizing family excursions	18	37	23	37
Number of Cases (N)	(92)	(100)	(90)	(98)
Keeping in touch with your own relatives	20	25	40	52
Number of Cases (N)	(93)	(102)	(95)	(100)
Being supportive when the other is upset, depressed, or unhappy	31	46	46	58
Number of Cases (N)	(93)	(102)	(95)	(99)
Taking care of preschool children	29	35	74	74
Number of Cases (N)	(52)	(48)	(42)	(46)
Disciplining older children	33	44	32	49
Number of Cases (N)	(64)	(63)	(60)	(59)

Source: Middletown III family role survey, 1977.

Note: The percentage above average includes "much above average" and "above average" responses.

Table 3-7
Self-Rated Competence of Middletown Husbands and Wives
in the Housekeeping Role, 1977

	Wife's Competence			
Husband's Competence	Above Average	Average	Below Average	Total (N)
Above average	32	20	0	52
Average	44	55	3	102
Below average	18	15	4	37
Total (N)	94	90	7	(191)

Source: Middletown III family role survey, 1977.

Table 3-8

Competence in Role Enactment (Self-assessed), for Middletown Couples, 1977
(in percentages)

Family Role	Net Competence Rating (Couple as a Unit)			Total Couples (N)
	High	Moderate	Low	
	Husband or wife, or both above average, and neither below average	Both spouses average, or one above and the other below average	Husband or wife, or both below average, and neither above average	
Doing housekeeping	50%	38%	12%	(191)
Doing household repairs	33	46	21	(182)
Organizing family excursions	38	46	16	(186)
Keeping in touch with own relatives	40	43	17	(195)
Being supportive when the other is upset, depressed, or unhappy	62	29	9	(194)
Taking care of preschool children	67	25	8	(73)
Disciplining older children	55	37	7	(107)

Source: Middletown III family role survey, 1977.

Table 4-1
Distribution of Middletown's Male Labor Force by Major Occupational Categories,
1920 and 1970

Occupational Category	1920		1970		Percentage Change
	Number	Percentage	Number	Percentage	
Business Class					
Professionals	892	6	5,189	14	+ 8
Managers	581	4	1,811	5	+ 1
Clerical workers	1,662	10	7,865	22	+12
Salesmen	1,659	10	2,264	6	− 4
Subtotal	4,794	(30)	17,129	(47)	
Working Class					
Craftsmen	3,404	21	3,232	9	−12
Operators	3,144	20	7,865	22	+ 2
Laborers	3,278	20	1,363	4	−16
Service workers	807	5	6,031	17	+12
Household workers	602	4	840	2	− 2
Subtotal	11,235	(70)	19,331	(54)	
Total	16,029	100	36,460	101	

Sources: U.S. Bureau of the Census 1922a, vol. 2, Table 20; U.S. Bureau of the Census 1971, vol. 16, Table 86.

Table 4-2
Middletown Housewives Reporting Husbands Unemployed during Previous Year,
by Social Class, 1924 and 1978

Social Class	1924		1978	
	Total Number	Percentage	Total Number	Percentage
Business class	40	1	192	4
Working class	165	28	141	25

Sources: Lynd and Lynd 1929, 57; Middletown III, housewives' survey, 1978.

Table 4-3
Job Satisfaction among Employed Men by Social Class,
Middletown, 1978
(in percentages)

Level of Satisfaction	Business Class (N = 104)	Working Class (N = 94)
Very satisfied	47%	23%
Somewhat satisfied	32	37
Mixed feelings	16	34
Somewhat dissatisfied	2	3
Very dissatisfied	3	3
Total	100%	100%

Source: Middletown III men's occupational survey, 1978.

Question: What is the level of satisfaction you derive from your job?

Table 4-4
Money as a Motive to Work, among Employed Men, by Social Class,
Middletown, 1978
(in percentages)

Response	Business Class (N = 104)	Working Class (N = 94)
Strongly agree	5%	16%
Agree	7	18
Neutral	13	20
Disagree	41	36
Strongly disagree	34	10
Total	100%	100%

Source: Middletown III, men's occupational survey, 1978.

Question: To me work is just a way of making money.

Table 4-5
Women 14 Years and Older in Middletown's Labor Force,
by Decade, 1920-1978

Year	Total	Employed	Percentage
1920	13,604	3,410	25%
1930	17,444	3,947	23
1940	19,566	5,386	28
1950	22,980	7,692	34
1960	26,047	9,330	36
1970	28,799	11,339	39
1978	31,299	13,772	44

Sources: U.S. Bureau of the Census 1922b and 1923, vol. 3, p. 287, vol. 4, p. 469; U.S. Bureau of the Census 1932, 1933, vol. 3, part 1, p. 702, vol. 4, p. 491; U.S. Bureau of the Census 1943, vol. 2, part 2, pp. 790, 795; U.S. Bureau of the Census 1952, vol. 2, part 14, pp. 14-56, 14-70; U.S. Bureau of the Census 1961, vol. 1, part 16, pp. 16-22, 16-61; U.S. Bureau of the Census 1972a, vol. 1, part 16, p. 208; U.S. Bureau of the Census 1972b, p. P-1. 1978 estimated from Middletown III surveys.

Table 4-6
Working Wives Reasons for Working, by Social Class,
Middletown, 1924 and 1978
(in percentages)

Reason	Working Class		Business Class
	1924 (N = 55)	1978 (N = 83)	1978 (N = 81)
Husband's unemployment	44%	12%	6%
Children's education	11	—	4
Debts	9	8	6
Always need extra money	7	31	25
Children require money	5	1	3
Other	24	14	24
Support of self and child	—	8	3
Personal satisfaction	—	27	30
Total	100%	101%	101%

Sources: Lynd and Lynd 1929, 27-28; Middletown III, housewives' survey, 1978.

Table 4-7
Distribution of Middletown's Female Labor Force by Major Occupational Categories,
1920 and 1970

Occupational Category	1920		1970		Percentage Change
	Number	Percentage	Number	Percentage	
Business Class					
Professionals	368	11	1,578	15	+ 4
Managers	17	0	297	3	+ 3
Saleswomen	810	24	655	6	−18
Clerical workers	366	11	3,439	33	+22
Subtotal	1,561	(46)	5,969	(57)	
Working Class					
Craftswomen	47	1	163	2	+ 1
Operators	795	23	1,414	14	− 9
Laborers	181	5	92	1	− 4
Service workers	300	9	2,297	22	+13
Household workers	526	15	414	4	−11
Subtotal	1,849	(54)	4,380	(43)	
Total	3,410	100	10,349	100	

Source: U.S. Bureau of the Census 1922b, vol. 2, Table 20; U.S. Bureau of the Census 1971, vol. 16, Table 86.

Table 4-8

General Happiness of Married Men and Women in Middletown, by Wife's Employment and Social Class, 1978
(in percentages)

	Men				Women			
	Business Class		Working Class		Business Class		Working Class	
Level of Happiness	Housewife (N = 34)	Employed (N = 52)	Housewife (N = 86)	Employed (N = 42)	Housewife (N = 40)	Employed (N = 100)	Housewife (N = 38)	Employed (N = 89)
Very happy	47%	17%	28%	23%	35%	41%	32%	27%
Pretty happy	47	77	53	67	60	50	58	66
Not too happy	–	–	–	–	–	–	–	–
Pretty unhappy	6	6	19	9	5	9	11	7
Very unhappy	–	–	–	–	–	–	–	–
Total	100%	100%	100%	99%	100%	100%	101%	100%

Sources: Middletown III women's and men's occupational surveys, 1978.

Question: Taking all things together, how would you say things are these days – would you say that you are . . . ?

Table 4-9

Marital Satisfaction of Married Men and Women in Middletown, by Wife's Employment and Social Class, 1978
(in percentages)

Level of Happiness	Men				Women			
	Business Class		Working Class		Business Class		Working Class	
	Housewife (N = 36)	Employed (N = 52)	Housewife (N = 36)	Employed (N = 42)	Housewife (N = 40)	Employed (N = 98)	Housewife (N = 38)	Employed (N = 89)
Very satisfied	65%	60%	78%	57%	50%	62%	45%	54%
Satisfied	30	33	14	41	45	31	45	38
Neutral	—	—	—	—	—	—	—	—
Dissatisfied	6	8	9	2	5	7	11	8
Very dissatisfied	—	—	—	—	—	—	—	—
Total	101%	101%	101%	100%	100%	100%	101%	100%

Sources: Middletown III men's and women's occupational surveys, 1978.

Question: How do you feel about your relationship with your wife/husband?

Table 4-10
Family Satisfaction of Married Men in Middletown,
by Wife's Employment and Social Class, 1978
(in percentages)

Level of Family Satisfaction	Business Class		Working Class	
	Housewife (N = 33)	Employed Wife (N = 52)	Housewife (N = 36)	Employed Wife (N = 41)
A great deal	85%	54%	75%	53%
Quite a bit	12	33	19	29
Some	—	—	—	—
A little	3	14	6	17
None	—	—	—	—
Total	100%	101%	100%	99%

Source: Middletown III, men's occupational survey, 1978.

Question: How much *satisfaction* do you get from your family life?

Table 4-11
Family Income Expended in Selected Categories, for Working-class Families
in Middletown, 1923 and 1978
(in percentages)

Expenditure	1923		1978	
	Family with Employed Wife (N = 38)	Family with Housewife (N = 61)	Family with Employed Wife (N = 56)	Family with Housewife (N = 85)
Automobile	3.5%	4.3%	10.4%	11.4%
Books, newspapers	1.2	1.0	0.9	0.8
Music, concerts, music lessons, lectures	1.1	0.5	0.6	0.7
Church and charities	2.0	2.1	1.4	2.4
Furniture	3.4	3.0	2.6	3.5
Housing	20.1	15.9	9.8	10.6
Unions, lodges, and clubs	0.8	0.6	0.9	0.8
Vacations and recreation	2.8	2.8	3.8	3.7
Life insurance	3.5	4.3	2.1	1.8
Total	38.4%	34.5%	32.5%	35.7%

Sources: Lynd and Lynd 1929, 514-17; Middletown III housewives' survey, 1978.

Note: These categories represent elective expenses only. The remaining two-thirds or so of the family income is consumed by food, clothing, fuel, health care, and other necessities.

Table 5-1
Occupancy of Single-Family, Two-Story Houses by Middletown Families,
by Social Class, 1924 and 1978
(in percentages)

Class, Year	(Number)	Single-Family, Two-Story Houses	Other Types of Dwellings	Total
Working-class families, 1924	(124)	34%	66%	100%
Business-class families, 1924	(40)	80%	20%	100%
Working-class families, 1978	(141)	30%	70%	100%
Business-class families, 1978	(192)	40%	60%	100%

Sources: Lynd and Lynd 1929, 94; Middletown III housewives' survey, 1978.

Table 5-2
Residential Moves of Middletown Families During the Five-Year Periods
1893-1898, 1920-1924, and 1973-1978
(in percentages)

Number of Moves	1893-1898 (N = 144)	1920-1924 (N = 164)	1923-1978 (N = 333)
None	65%	43%	73%
One	18	34	15
Two	7	10	5
Three	7	5	3
Four	0	3	2
Five	2	4	1
Six or more	1	1	1
Total	100%	100%	100%
Mean	0.7	1.1	0.6

Sources: Lynd and Lynd 1929, 520; Middletown III housewives' survey,
1978.

Table 5-3

Residential Moves of Middletown Families During the Five-Year Periods
1893-1898, 1920-1924, and 1973-1978, by Social Class
(in percentages)

Number of Moves	1893-1898		1920-1924		1973-1978	
	Working Class (N = 106)	Business Class (N = 38)	Working Class (N = 124)	Business Class (N = 40)	Working Class (N = 141)	Business Class (N = 187)
None	64%	66%	40%	55%	85%	64%
One	15	26	33	35	7	21
Two	9	3	10	10	3	6
Three	9	0	6	0	2	5
Four	0	2	4	0	1	1
Five	2	3	5	0	1	2
Six or more	1	0	2	0	1	1
Total	100%	100%	100%	100%	100%	100%
Mean	0.8	0.6	1.2	0.6	0.3	0.7

Sources: Lynd and Lynd 1929, 520; Middletown III housewives' survey, 1978.

Table 5-4
Daily Hours of Housework Reported by Middletown Housewives,
by Social Class, 1924 and 1978
(in percentages)

Class, Year	(Number)	Fewer than 4 Hours	4 to 7 Hours	Over 7 Hours	Total
Working class, 1924	(112)	7%	69%	24%	100%
Business class, 1924	(40)	23%	54%	23%	100%
Working class, 1978	(141)	52%	38%	10%	100%
Business class, 1978	(192)	60%	35%	5%	100%

Sources: Lynd and Lynd 1929, 168; Middletown III housewives' survey, 1978.

Table 5-5
Weekly Hours of Washing and Ironing Reported by Middletown Housewives,
by Social Class, 1890, 1924, and 1978
(in percentages)

Class, Year	(Number)	Fewer than 2 Hours	2 to 4 Hours	5 to 8 Hours	9 or More Hours	Total
Working class, 1890*	(94)	6%	3%	30%	61%	100%
Business class, 1890*	(40)	52%	10%	15%	23%	100%
Working class, 1924	(120)	2%	20%	54%	24%	100%
Business class, 1924	(70)	60%	15%	20%	5%	100%
Working class, 1978	(141)	1%	21%	41%	37%	100%
Business class, 1978	(92)	2%	31%	41%	26%	100%

Sources: Lynd and Lynd 1929, 174; Middletown III housewives' survey, 1978.

*Mothers of the 1924 respondents, as reported by the latter.

Table 5-6
Bread Baking by Middletown Housewives,
by Social Class, 1924 and 1978
(in percentages)

Class, Year	(Number)	Yes	No	Total
Working class, 1924	(119)	32%	68%	100%
Business class, 1924	(39)	13%	87%	100%
Working class, 1978	(141)	82%	18%	100%
Business class, 1978	(192)	81%	19%	100%

Sources: Lynd and Lynd 1929, 155; Middletown III housewives' survey, 1978.

Table 5-7
Weekly Hours of Sewing and Mending Reported by Middletown Housewives,
by Social Class, 1890, 1924, and 1978
(in percentages)

Class, Year	(Number)	2 Hours or Fewer	3 to 6 Hours	Over 6 Hours	Total
Working class, 1890*	(66)	6%	94%		100%
Business class, 1890*	(35)	31%	69%		100%
Working class, 1924	(112)	22%	42%	36%	100%
Business class, 1924	(39)	51%	23%	26%	100%
Working class, 1978	(141)	78%	14%	8%	100%
Business class, 1978	(192)	80%	10%	9%	99%

Sources: Lynd and Lynd 1929, 165; Middletown III housewives' survey, 1978.

*Mothers of the 1924 respondents, as reported by the latter.

Table 5-8

Paid Help in Middletown Households, by Social Class, 1890, 1924, and 1978
(in percentages)

Class, Year	(Number)	Full-time	One or More Days per Week	Less than One Day a Week	No Paid Help	Total
Working class, 1890*	(118)	0%	No data	No data	No data	
Business class, 1890*	(39)	66%				
Working class, 1924	(118)	0%	1%	4%	95%	100%
Business class, 1924	(39)	33%	31%	26%	10%	100%
Working class, 1978	(141)	1%	4%	3%	92%	100%
Business class, 1978	(192)	1%	12%	4%	83%	100%

Sources: Lynd and Lynd 1929, 169-70; Middletown III housewives' survey, 1978.

*Mothers of the 1924 respondents as reported by the latter.

Table 5-9
Preferred Division of Housework Reported for Married Persons
in Middletown, by Social Class, 1978
(in percentages)

Preference	Business Class (N = 203)	Working Class (N = 189)
Wife entirely	11%	27%
Wife more than husband	60	53
Shared equally	21	13
Husband more than wife	0	1
Husband entirely	0	1
No preferences	8	6
Total	100%	101%

Source: Middletown III women's occupational survey, 1978.

Table 5-10
Actual Division of Housework Reported for Married Persons
in Middletown, by Social Class, 1978
(in percentages)

Actual Division	Business Class (N = 159)	Working Class (N = 157)
Wife entirely	45%	45%
Wife more than husband	40	40
Shared equally	7	9
Husband more than wife	3	1
Third person	6	5
Total	101%	100%

Source: Middletown III housewives' survey, 1978.

Table 5-11
Weekly Hours Middletown Mothers Spent with Their Children,
by Social Class, 1924 and 1978
(in percentages)

Class, Year	(Number)	Under 7 Hours	7 to 16 Hours	Over 16 Hours	Total
Working class, 1924	(85)	24%	31%	46%	101%
Business class, 1924	(40)	5%	48%	48%	101%
Working class, 1978	(141)	7%	27%	66%	100%
Business class, 1978	(192)	7%	32%	62%	101%

Sources: Lynd and Lynd 1929, 147; Middletown III housewives' survey, 1978.

Table 5-12
Weekly Hours Middletown Fathers Spent with Their Children,
by Social Class, 1924 and 1978
(in percentages)

Class, Year	(Number)	None	Under 1 Hour	Over 1 Hour	Total
Working class, 1924	(92)	10%	22%	68%	100%
Business class, 1924	(40)	8%	28%	65%	101%
Working class, 1978	(141)	2%	21%	77%	100%
Business class, 1978	(192)	1%	24%	75%	100%

Sources: Lynd and Lynd 1929, 148; Middletown III housewives' survey, 1978.

Note: The 1978 data are based on reports by the husbands' wives. We must repeat the Lynds' caveat that "such answers are highly fallible."

Table 6-1
Weekly Hours Husbands and Wives Watched Television Together
in Middletown, by Social Class, 1978
(in percentages)

Hours per Week	Business Class (N = 187 couples)	Working Class (N = 141 couples)
0	16%	23%
1-3	24	23
4-6	19	19
7-10	29	19
11-20	9	11
21 and over	3	5
Total	100%	100%

Source: Middletown III housewives' survey, 1978.

Question: How much time do you watch TV with your husband, without any children, during an average week?

Table 6-2
Satisfaction with Marital Relationships in Middletown, by Social Class, 1978
(in percentages)

Level of Satisfaction	Husbands		Wives	
	Business Class (N = 87)	Working Class (N = 80)	Business Class (N = 159)	Working Class (N = 159)
Very satisfied	62%	68%	57%	49%
Satisfied	31	28	36	41
Neutral	2	4	4	9
Dissatisfied	5	1	3	1
Total	100%	101%	100%	100%

Source: Middletown III housewives' survey.

Question: How do you feel about your relationship to your wife/husband?

Table 6-3
Marital Happiness in Middletown, by Social Class, 1978
(in percentages)

Level of Happiness	Husbands		Wives	
	Business Class (N = 87)	Working Class (N = 80)	Business Class (N = 159)	Working Class (N = 159)
Very happy	60%	58%	53%	46%
Happy	32	34	37	41
So-so	6	6	8	14
Unhappy	2	2	2	0
Very unhappy	0	0	1	0
Total	100%	100%	101%	101%

Source: Middletown III housewives' survey, 1978.

Question: Everything considered, how happy is your marriage?

Table 7-1
Adolescents Reports of Evenings Spent at Home during the Past Week
by Sex, 1924 and 1977
(in percentages)

Number of Evenings at Home	Males		Females	
	1924	1977	1924	1977
0	19%	24%	5%	18%
1	11	11	9	12
2	12	12	12	16
3	13	15	18	14
4	15	12	18	15
5	14	12	19	10
6	9	4	11	6
7	7	10	8	9
Total	100%	100%	100%	100%
Number of Cases (N)	(396)	(422)	(458)	(485)

Sources: Lynd and Lynd 1929, 135; Middletown III high school survey,
1977.

Table 7-2

Hours Adolescents Spent During a Sample Week in the Company
of Both Parents Together, Father Alone, and Mother Alone,
by Sex and Father's Occupational Class, 1977

Hours with Parents	Working Class		Business Class	
	Boys	Girls	Boys	Girls
Both:				
0	18%	19%	11%	17%
1-4	14	13	11	10
5-14	27	29	27	34
15-34	19	23	28	23
35+	21	16	23	16
Total	99%	100%	100%	100%
Number of Cases (N)	(301)	(342)	(243)	(252)
Father Alone:				
0	23%	28%	19%	23%
1-4	28	26	26	32
5-14	24	24	31	27
15+	24	22	24	18
Total	99%	100%	100%	100%
Number of Cases (N)	(278)	(312)	(231)	(253)
Mother Alone:				
0	12%	10%	7%	10%
1-4	26	15	21	24
5-14	30	31	38	30
15+	32	44	35	35
Total	100%	100%	101%	99%
Number of Cases (N)	(283)	(323)	(240)	(260)

Source: Middletown III high school survey, 1977.

Table 7-3
Percentages of Middletown Adolescents Reporting Disagreement with Their Parents,
by Subject and by Sex, 1924 and 1977

Source of Disagreement	Boys		Girls	
	1924	1977	1924	1977
The hours (1924: hour) you get in at night	45%	46%	43%	42%
The number of times you go out on school nights during the week	45	31	48	35
Your grades at school (1924: grades at school)	40	34	31	28
Your spending money	37	38	29	29
Use of the automobile	36	29	30	22
The people (1924: boys or girls) you choose as friends	25	33	27	36
Home duties (yardwork, cooking, helping around the house, etc.) (1924: . . . [tending furnace, cooking, etc.])	19	45	26	46
Church and attendance at religious services (1924: . . . and Sunday School attendance)	19	11	19	13
The way you dress (including hair style, general grooming) (1924: the way you dress)	16	25	25	19
Going to unchaperoned parties	15	27	28	29
Sunday (or Sabbath) observance, aside from attendance at services (1924: Sunday observance, aside from just going to Church and Sunday School)	14	6	14	3
Clubs or societies you belong to	6	6	10	5
Other causes of disagreement (please explain) (1924: state any other causes of disagreement	10	16	8	28
Number of Cases (N)	(348)	(442)	(382)	(488)

Sources: Lynd and Lynd 1929, 522; Middletown III high school survey, 1977.

Table 7-4
Reported Closeness to Parents of Middletown Adolescents and Adults, 1977
(in percentages)

Reported Closeness	To Father		To Mother	
	Adolescents	Adults	Adolescents	Adults
Not at all	17%	15%	6%	6%
Somewhat close	11	8	12	9
Fairly close	22	24	18	21
Quite close	27	33	30	36
Extremely close	23	20	33	28
Total	100%	100%	99%	100%
Number of Cases (N)	(1,621)	(470)	(1,604)	(470)

Sources: Middletown III high school survey and kinship survey, 1977.

Table 7-5
Perceptions of Agreement with Parents "in Your Ideas about the Things You Consider
Really Important in Life," 1977
(in percentages)

Reported Agreement	With Father		With Mother	
	High School Students	Adults	High School Students	Adults
Yes, completely	8%	10%	12%	10%
Yes, to a great extent	21	34	27	39
Yes, to some extent	44	37	46	38
No, very little	16	10	13	8
Little or no contact with father/mother	10	9	3	5
Total	99%	100%	101%	100%
Number of Cases (N)	(1,597)	(461)	(1,590)	(470)

Sources: Middletown III high school survey and kinship survey, 1977.

Table 7-6
Acceptance of Parents as Role Models by Middletown Adolescents and Adults, 1977
(in percentages)

Reported Acceptance	Would Like to Be Like Father		Would Like to Be Like Mother	
	Adolescents	Adults	Adolescents	Adults
Not at all	18%	8%	15%	6%
In just a few ways	32	16	30	16
In several ways	20	22	24	22
In most ways	21	37	23	38
Yes, completely	7	11	7	15
Didn't get to know my father/mother	2	6	1	2
Total	100%	100%	100%	99%
Number of Cases (N)	(1,622)	(467)	(1,585)	(473)

Sources: Middletown III high school survey and kinship survey, 1977.

Table 7-7

Sex and Class Differences in Solidarity with Parents, Middletown Adolescents, 1977
(in percentages)

| | To Father | | | | To Mother | | | |
| | Boys | | Girls | | Boys | | Girls | |
Reported Closeness	Working	Business	Working	Business	Working	Business	Working	Business
Not too close	13%	6%	22%	14%	5%	4%	7%	8%
Somewhat close	13	10	12	11	15	13	9	11
Fairly close	20	26	19	22	20	22	16	15
Quite close	26	36	24	33	26	34	30	36
Extremely close	28	22	23	21	34	27	38	30
Total	100%	100%	100%	100%	100%	100%	100%	100%
Number of Cases (N)	(373)	(291)	(416)	(296)	(362)	(295)	(406)	(293)

Agreement about Important Things	With Father				With Mother			
Yes, completely	11%	8%	5%	5%	14%	9%	11%	8%
Yes, to a great extent	17	30	15	33	20	30	27	37
Yes, to some extent	48	49	49	40	47	46	48	42
No, very little	15	11	19	14	15	15	12	11
Little or no contact with father/mother	9	2	12	8	4	0	3	2
Total	100%	100%	100%	100%	100%	100%	101%	100%
Number of Cases (N)	(367)	(290)	(412)	(291)	(361)	(288)	(405)	(293)

Acceptance as Role Model	Of Father				Of Mother			
Not at all	14%	8%	22%	16%	20%	15%	10%	10%
In just a few ways	33	27	40	28	36	28	28	28
In several ways	18	24	17	27	22	29	24	26
In most ways	23	31	15	23	14	22	29	30
Yes, completely	10	9	5	5	6	5	9	6
Didn't get to know my father/mother	2	1	1	1	1	0	0	0
Total	100%	100%	100%	100%	99%	99%	100%	100%
Number of Cases (N)	(370)	(295)	(410)	(298)	(362)	(286)	(405)	(292)

Source: Middletown III high school survey, 1977.

Table 7-8
Most Desirable Qualities of Mothers and Fathers According to Middletown Adolescents,
by Sex, 1924 and 1977
(in percentages)

Qualities Most Desirable	Boys		Girls	
	1924	1977	1924	1977
In a Father:				
Spending time with his children, reading, talking, playing, etc.	62%	64%	67%	71%
Respecting his children's opinions	34	62	42	76
Being an active church member	27	7	30	7
Being a college graduate	23	4	13	4
Never nagging his children about what they do	12	13	12	12
Making plenty of money	12	17	11	10
Being well-dressed	6	6	5	4
Being prominent in social life	5	8	2	7
Having a love of music and poetry	4	1	6	2
Owning a good-looking car	3	5	2	2
Number of Cases (*N*)	(369)	(472)	(415)	(506)
In a Mother:				
Being a good cook and housekeeper	57%	41%	52%	24%
Spending time with her children, reading, talking, playing, etc.	34	58	41	66
Being an active church member	25	8	25	9
Respecting her children's opinions	24	57	22	72
Never nagging her children about what they did	23	14	34	13
Being a college graduate	7	2	4	2
Being well-dressed	8	6	3	6
Having a love of music and poetry	6	2	3	1
Being a good hostess	4	2	4	2
Being prominent in social life	4	9	4	7
Number of Cases (*N*)	(369)	(462)	(423)	(506)

Sources: Lynd and Lynd 1929, 524; Middletown III high school survey, 1977.

Table 8-1

Percentages of White American Teenage Girls Who
Have Ever Had Premarital Intercourse, by Age,
1938-1949, 1971, and 1976

Age	1938-1949	1971	1976
14		2.1	2.6
15	1.0	4.3	7.0
16	2.0	8.8	16.4
17	8.0	18.1	29.1
18	14.0	28.7	42.2
19	18.0	42.6	55.8

Sources: Kinsey, Pomeroy, and Martin 1953, 286 (the
data are taken from a figure, which limits the precise-
ness of the percentages); Zelnik, Young, and Kantner
1979.

Table 8-2

Out-of-Wedlock Births per 1,000 Live Births, Middletown, 1957-1975

Year	Out-of-Wedlock Births	Total Live Births	Out-of Wedlock Births per 1,000 Live Births
1957	106	1,838	57.7
1960	104	1,752	59.4
1962	98	1,667	58.8
1964	110	1,671	65.8
1966	132	1,644	80.3
1968	112	1,615	69.3
1970	156	1,733	90.0
1972	174	1,468	118.5
1974	204	1,379	147.9
1975	178	1,221	145.8

Sources: Figures for out-of wedlock births are from U.S. Census
data; total live births are from Indiana State Board of Health 1976a,
90, and 1966-1975.

Table 8-3
Attitudes about Premarital Sexual Behavior,
Middletown Housewives, 1978
(in percentages)

Perceived Change in Premarital Sexual Behavior	Business Class	Working Class	Total
Increased	76%	82%	78%
Unchanged	0	0	0
Decreased	24	18	22
Total	100%	100%	100%
Number of Cases (N)	(189)	(142)	(331)

Source: Middletown III housewives' survey, 1978.

Question: What is your opinion concerning the reported increase in petting, spooning and sexual freedom?

Note: The differences between business- and working-class respondents are not statistically significant.

Table 9-1
Residential Distribution of Relatives Reported by Middletown Adults, by Distance, 1977
(in percentages)

Distance from Middletown	Parents	Brothers and Sisters	Grown Children	Kin Acquaintances
In Middletown	43%	31%	54%	20%
Within 50 miles	18	16	14	14
50-100 miles	10	13	8	16
100-500 miles	17	21	8	30
500+ miles	12	20	17	20
Total	100%	101%	100%	100%
Total Number of Relatives (N)	(324)	(1,293)	(466)	(8,530)
Total Number of Respondents (N)	(473)	(450)	(471)	(470)

Source: Middletown III kinship survey, 1977.

Note: The 324 units under parents are parental households, representing either a couple living together, the sole surviving parent, or (if both are alive but maintain separate residences) the location of "the one with whom contact is most frequent." These 324 units include 170 couples living together, 32 parents living apart from their spouses, and 122 widows and widowers, or a total of 494 parents. Not included in the 324 parental households are the 32 parents living separately with whom contact by respondents was less frequent. The total number of respondents includes all who answered the question, not merely those having parents, brothers and sisters, or kin acquaintances. For siblings, kin acquaintances, and children, there was some variation in number of respondents by distance category; and these total numbers are means.

Table 9-2
Residential Distribution of Relatives Reported by Middletown Adults,
by State and Region, 1977
(in percentages)

State or Region	Parents	Brothers and Sisters	Grown Children	Kin Acquaintances
In Indiana	74%	59%	75%	54%
Illinois, Ohio, or Michigan	6	11	5	12
Tennesse or Kentucky	6	9	1	9
Another southern state	6	6	9	9
Another midwestern state	1	2	1	3
Northeastern U.S.	3	3	3	4
Far western U.S.	3	8	5	7
Other	1	2	2	1
Total	100%	100%	100%	99%
Total Number of Kin (N)	(319)	(1,286)	(477)	(8,535)
Total Number of Respondents (N)	(470)	(452)	(474)	(471)

Source: Middletown III kinship survey, 1977.

Note: The 319 units under parents are parental households, representing either a couple living together, the sole surviving parent, or (if both are alive but maintain separate residences) the location of "the one with whom contact is most frequent." See the note on Table 9-1.

Table 9-3
Residential Distribution of Relatives Reported by Middletown Women,
by Social Class, 1977
(in percentages)

Distance Away	Parents		Sibling		Cousin	
	Business	Working	Business	Working	Business	Working
In Middletown	27%	47%	18%	38%	18%	37%
Within 50 miles	21	19	11	20	15	19
50-100 miles	12	9	16	7	17	14
100-500 miles	26	12	25	16	31	22
Total Number of Respondents (N)	(82)	(57)	(88)	(69)	(87)	(64)

Source: Middletown III kinship survey, 1977.

Note: Sibling refers to brother or sister closest in age to the respondent. Cousin refers to the cousin known best.

Table 9-4
Reasons for Keeping in Touch with Relatives Reported by Middletown Adults, 1977
(Percentages Saying "Somewhat Important" or "Very Important")

Reason as Stated	Parents	Brother or Sister	Cousin	Grown Children
You simply enjoy keeping in touch	95%	89%	83%	97%
You feel you ought to or have an obligation to	73	58	36	60
They need your help in some way	64	44	30	73
You need their help in some way	53	34	22	54
Number of Cases (N)	(306)	(375)	(305)	(166)

Source: Middletown III kinship survey, 1977.

Note: Brother or sister refers to brother or sister closest in age to the respondent. Cousin refers to the cousin known best.

Table 9-5
Communications with Parents, Near Siblings, and Best-Known Cousins
Reported by Middletown Adults, 1977
(in percentages)

Frequency	By Telephone			By Letter		
	Parents	Near Siblings	Best-known Cousins	Parents	Near Siblings	Best-known Cousins
Once a month or more	65%	36%	9%	23%	9%	3%
Less than once a month	30	53	49	34	47	33
Never	5	11	42	43	44	64
Total	100%	100%	100%	100%	100%	100%
Number (N)	(315)	(413)	(393)	(300)	(405)	(385)

Source: Middletown III kinship survey, 1977.

Note: Responses of those living with their parents were excluded from this table.

Table 9-6
Ratings of Kinship Communication for Self and Spouse
Reported by Middletown Adults, 1977
(in percentages)

	Husbands' Ratings	Wives' Ratings
Yourself:		
Above average or much above average	22%	49%
Average	50	44
Below average or much below average	29	7
Total	101%	100%
Number (*N*)	(215)	(245)
Your Spouse:		
Above average or much above average	51%	24%
Average	39	46
Below average or much below average	10	30
Total	100%	100%
Number (*N*)	(215)	(239)

Source: Middletown III family role survey, 1977.

Question: How well do you and your husband or wife do [at] keeping in touch with your own relatives?

Table 9-7

Frequency of Middletown Adults' Contacts with Parents and Near Siblings,
by Distance, 1977
(in percentages)

Distance	Parents			Near Siblings		
	Visited Weekly	Written Monthly	Called Monthly	Visited Weekly	Written Monthly	Called Monthly
In Middletown	83%	14%	74%	58%	4%	64%
Within 50 miles	60	9	73	24	2	45
50-100 miles	6	30	52	7	16	19
100-500 miles	4	28	56	0	10	15
500+ miles	0	55	47	1	18	19

Source: Middletown III kinship survey, 1977.

Table 9-9

Aid to and from Parents Reported by Middletown Adults, by Sex, 1977
(in percentages)

Type of Aid	Males	Females
Aid Received from Parents in Past Two Years:		
Advice on a decision	52%	64%
Help on special occasions, such as childbirth or sickness	41	52
Help in caring for your children, such as baby-sitting	27	39
Financial assistance, such as money or a loan	43	44
Gifts	81	80
Handwork, such as gardening, sewing, yardwork	34	47
Job placement	15	7
Number of Cases (N)	(116)	(191)
Aid Given to Parents in Past Two Years:		
Help in their home or yard	72%	75%
Taken them to the doctor, or caring for them when sick	47	54
Financial aid	24	23
Gifts	89	91
Number of Cases (N)	(120)	(193)

Source: Middletown III kinship survey, 1977.

Note: Numbers vary slightly because of missing data; these are means.

Table 9-10
Affection, Agreement, and Idealization in Kinship Relations,
Middletown, 1977
(in percentages)

Sentiments Reported	Men	(Number)	Women	(Number)
Affection for				
Mother	56%	(164)	69%	(304)
Father	42	(162)	58	(307)
Brother or sister	39	(146)	56	(270)
Cousin	17	(136)	24	(255)
Agreement with				
Mother	39%	(160)	53%	(309)
Father	40	(159)	47	(300)
Brother or sister	33	(145)	46	(268)
Cousin	23	(125)	30	(235)
Idealization of				
Mother	46%	(159)	59%	(303)
Father	49	(154)	51	(285)
Brother or sister	21	(145)	27	(269)
Cousin	15	(129)	16	(245)

Source: Middletown III kinship survey, 1977.

Table 9-11
General Importance of Relatives in the Lives
of Middletown Adults, by Sex, 1977
(in percentages)

Rating	Men	Women
Most important	10%	13%
Quite important	28	40
Somewhat important	34	30
Not very important	19	10
Unimportant	9	6
Total	100%	100%
Number	(158)	(297)

Sources: Middletown III kinship survey, 1977.

Table 11-1
Church Attendance of Married Couples in Middletown,
by Social Class, 1890 and 1924
(in percentages)

Church Attendance	Business-class Husbands		Working-class Husbands	
	1890 (N = 39)	1924 (N = 40)	1890 (N = 101)	1924 (N = 163)
Regular	69%	40%	44%	21%
Intermittent	3	35	15	8
Occasional	0	0	1	2
Never	28	25	40	69
Total	100%	100%	100%	100%
Church Attendance	Business-class Wives		Working-class Wives	
	1890 (N = 40)	1924 (N = 40)	1890 (N = 119)	1924 (N = 123)
Regular	78%	40%	53%	20%
Intermittent	2	33	11	14
Occasional	0	0	3	2
Never	20	27	33	65
Total	100%	100%	100%	101%

Source: Lynd and Lynd 1929, Table XXI.

Table 11-2
Church Attendance of Married Women in Middletown,
1890, 1924, and 1978
(in percentages)

Church Attendance	1890 (N = 159)	1924 (N = 173)	1978 (N = 333)
Regular	59%	23%	48%
Intermittent	9	23	14
Occasional	2	1	20
Never	30	53	17
Total	100%	100%	99%

Sources: Lynd and Lynd 1929, Table XXI; Middletown III
housewives' survey, 1978.

Table 11-3
Church Attendance of Married Women in Middletown,
by Social Class, 1978
(in percentages)

Church Attendance	Business Class (N = 187)	Working Class (N = 142)
Regular	52%	41%
Intermittent	20	15
Occasional	13	21
Never	15	23
Total	100%	100%

Source: Middletown III housewives' survey, 1978.

Table 11-4
Church Attendance of Middletown Adults,
by Sex, 1977-1978
(in percentages)

Church Attendance	Women (N = 471)	Men (N = 215)
Regular	32%	27%
Intermittent	12	10
Occasional	33	41
Never	23	22
Total	100%	100%

Sources: Middletown III women's and men's occupational surveys, 1978.

Table 11-5
Reasons Given by Middletown Women for
Attending Church, 1924 and 1978
(in percentages)

Reason	1924 (N = 62)	1978 (N = 230)
Habit	44%	15%
Enjoyment	35	65
Benefits to children	8	13
Other	13	7
Total	100%	100%

Sources: Lynd and Lynd 1929; 360-61, 366-67; Middletown III housewives' survey, 1978.

Table 11-6
Reasons Given by Middletown Women for
Not Attending Church, 1924 and 1978
(in percentages)

Reason	1924 (N = 83)	1978 (N = 115)
Work or fatigue	27%	19%
Lack of habit	27	21
Dislike of service	23	31
Competing activities	10	9
Cost	7	7
Ideological reasons	6	13
Total	100%	100%

Sources: Lynd and Lynd 1929, 362-68; Middletown III
housewives' survey, 1978.

Table 11-7
Church Attendance of Adults in Middletown, 1977-1978,
and in the Entire United States, 1976
(in percentages)

Church Attendance	Middletown (N = 686)	Entire U.S. (N = 1,492)
Regular	29%	29%
Intermittent	11	20
Occasional	37	38
Never	23	13
Total	100%	100%

Sources: Middletown III men's and women's occupational
surveys, 1978; National Opinion Research Center, General
Social Survey, 1976.

Table 12-2

Percentages of United States Population Ever Married,
by Year Cohort Was at the Most Marriageable Age,
1850-1970

Year Cohort at the Most Marriageable Age	Percentage Ever Married	
	Males	Females
1850-1860	93.1	94.2
1860-1870	92.8	93.4
1870-1880	92.0	92.9
1880-1890	91.0	91.6
1890-1900	90.1	91.1
1900-1910	89.6	91.0
1910-1920	90.5	92.1
1920-1930	91.8	92.0
1930-1940	92.2	93.6
1940-1950	92.9	95.5
1950-1960	94.1	96.4
1960-1970	92.9	95.1

Sources: Adapted from Davis 1972, 243, Table 1, who
cited U.S. census data.

Table 12-3

Prevalence, Spread, and Timing of Transition to Adulthood for Philadelphia, 1880, and for the United States, 1970, by Sex

	Leaving School		Entering Work Force		Leaving Household of Origin		Marriage		Establishing Own Household	
	1880 Philadelphia	1970 U.S.	1880 Philadelphia	1970 U.S.	1880 Philadelphia	1970 U.S.	1880 Philadelphia	1970 U.S.	1880 Philadelphia	1970 U.S.
Males:										
Prevalence	86.6%	99.7%	NA	95.4%	NA	NA	88.7%	93.7%	86.5%	86.4%
Spread	5.0	7.5	6.9%	8.1	16.0%	12.4%	17.1	7.1	18.1	13.6
Timing: first decile	11.9	16.4	12.4	14.5	17.7	15.8	21.2	19.6	21.6	17.0
Timing: fifth decile	14.4	19.1	15.3	17.3	23.2	20.1	26.0	21.8	25.8	23.9
Females:										
Prevalence	88.0%	99.7%	NA	58.3%	NA	NA	80.3%	93.0%	83.8%	90.1%
Spread	5.8	7.6	6.7%	4.8	19.0%	12.7%	11.7	7.9	17.0	12.4
Timing: first decile	11.3	16.3	11.3	14.3	17.0	16.1	18.5	17.1	19.1	16.8
Timing: fifth decile	14.3	18.6	14.6	17.0	20.1	20.5	22.7	20.2	24.0	22.0

Source: Adapted from Modell, Furstenberg, and Hesberg 1976, Table I, 14.

Note: Prevalences are given in percentages; spread and timing, in years.

Table 12-4
Median, First and Ninth Deciles, and Spread of First Marriages for Cohorts
Born 1865-1874 to 1925-1934, United States
(in years)

Birth Cohort	Midpoint for Those Who Married	First Decile	Ninth Decile	Spread
	Males			
1865-1874	26.2	19.7	38.6	18.9
1875-1884	25.9	19.4	38.9	19.5
1885-1894	25.5	19.1	38.0	18.9
1895-1904	25.0	18.8	37.1	18.3
1905-1914	25.1	18.9	38.2	19.3
1915-1924	24.2	19.0	31.8	12.8
1925-1934	23.4	18.3	31.0	12.7
	Females			
1865-1874	23.8	19.0	31.9	12.9
1875-1884	23.6	18.9	31.9	13.0
1885-1894	22.9	18.8	30.4	11.6
1895-1904	22.6	18.7	30.3	11.6
1905-1914	22.4	18.7	31.6	12.9
1915-1924	22.5	18.8	27.3	8.5
1925-1934	21.0	18.3	26.6	8.3

Source: Adapted from Modell et al., 1978, Table 1, 123.

Table 12-8
Childlessness among Couples Granted
Divorces, 1887-1969
(in percentages)

Year	Percentage Childless
1887-1906	50.2
1922-1925	62.0
1926-1930	61.5
1931-1935	60.1
1936-1940	61.6
1941-1945	62.5
1946-1950	58.7
1951-1955	54.6
1956-1960	45.9
1961-1965	39.0
1965-1969	39.3

Source: Adapted from Davis 1972, 257.

Table 12-10
Ranking of Personal Values by a National Sample of
Parents, 1976-1977, and University Students, 1973
(in percentages)

Values	Parents	University Students
Family	81%	68%
Education	71	76
Self-fulfillment	67	87
Hard work	62	43
Marriage as an institution	60	NA
Religion	52	28
Saving money	50	20
Patriotism	43	19
Having children	43	31

Source: Adapted from General Mills family survey, 1977.

Table 12-11
Parents and Children Supporting Selected Family Norms, 1977
(in percentages)

Family Norm	Parents	Children
Parents should separate if they are not happy	63%	49%
It's the mother's job, not the father's, to cook and clean	70	63
Mothers should go to work if they want	—	76
The man should be the main provider	74	—
It's all right for parents to take vacations without children	—	44
It's important for parents to have their own interests even if it means spending less time with children	66	—
It's all right for parents to spank their children	50	75

Source: General Mills family survey, 1977.

Table 12-12
Perceptions of Parental Expectations by Children, by Ethnicity and Income, 1977
(in percentages)

Expectations	All Children	Minority Children	Children of Families with Income under $12,000	Children of Families with Income over $26,000
Do well in school	75%	90%	85%	65%
Go to college	56	78	NA	NA
Be best in class	30	39	35	23
Be good at sports	24	39	28	21
Win at games	12	16	17	7
Set example for other children	38	44	40	31

Source: General Mills family survey, 1977.

APPENDIX B

The Middletown III Surveys

#1—Kinship Survey

The kinship survey was a mail questionnaire survey of kinship relations among Middletown adults, conducted October 1976 through February 1977. A random sample of 935 households was drawn from the *Middletown City Directory 1976*. The procedure included (1) the mailing of a letter of explanation along with a business-reply envelope and the questionnaire, followed, for persons who did not respond, by (2) a reminder postcard two weeks after the first mailing, (3) followed two weeks later by a second mailing of the complete survey packet, including a new letter of introduction, (4) followed two to four weeks later by another reminder postcard, and (5) followed two or more weeks later by a final follow-up in which a third complete packet containing new letters of explanation was personally delivered to the homes of persons who had not yet responded, or, for a minority of the remaining potential respondents, by a certified mailing (in all, we visited 388 households on the personal follow-up and sent 77 certified letters).

These procedures generated 478 usable questionnaires out of an eligible sample of 835 households (there were 150 ineligible households included in the original 985, including 87 who had moved out of town and 13 who were deceased, underage, senile, or hospitalized), for a completion rate of 57 percent.

The questionnaire was lengthy (19 pages) and fairly complex, with parallel sections about contact with siblings, parents, cousins, and grown children and partial coverage of contact with other relatives.

#2—Family Dynamics Survey

The family dynamics survey was an in-depth interview conducted between December 1976 and June 1977, with most interviews in May and June 1977.

The individual husband or wife, rather than the couple, was the response unit. That is, once a family had been selected, either the husband or the wife was designated as the primary respondent. Potential respondents were married couples listed in the 1976 city directory. To ensure that the main economic strata in the community were represented, couples were stratified by husband's occupation as given in the directory into three categories: (1) professional and managerial/administrative occupations; (2) sales and clerical workers, craftsmen, foremen, and operatives; and (3) laborers, service workers, and private household workers. In practice, names were randomly drawn from the directory, assigned to one of the three occupational strata, and interviewed in roughly the order the names were drawn. Of 52 eligible couples drawn, 27 provided interviews, 14 with husbands and 13 with wives. All couples except 2 had children; 21 of the 27 were in their first marriages.

In view of the high level of cooperation necessary to obtain a very long interview and the need to provide the potential respondents enough information to permit them to make an informed choice about participating, each couple was sent a letter of introduction that described the project and the reasons for it, invited their participation, and said they would be contacted by our interviewers. A few days later, two interviewers made a personal visit to the home, explained the project in greater detail, and, when the person was willing to continue, either conducted the first interview at that time or made an appointment to return.

The research design called for having two interviewers present during each interview. This approach had the advantage of a built-in reliability check, in that there were two observers and two memories functioning rather than just one, and it also made it possible for more comprehensive note taking without sacrificing conversational continuity. The decision to use two interviewers rather than one was also intended to increase the likelihood of establishing good rapport with most respondents—it was hoped that a respondent would get on well with at least one of the interviewers. Also, the fact that interviewers came in pairs was supposed to increase the importance of the study in the eyes of the potential respondents, in that *two* interviewers were devoting themselves solely to obtaining and recording their responses.

Most interviews were at least two hours long, and most respondents participated in at least two interviewing sessions. Where possible, interviews were tape recorded, but, in something over one-fourth of the cases, they were not, either because the respondent demurred or the interviewers felt more comfortable recording the interview manually. Whether or not the interview was taped, interviewers took written notes. The presence of two interviewers meant that, even when the recorder malfunctioned, an interviewer's notes permitted an adequate reconstruction of the session.

The interview sessions included the administration of the kinship and family role questionnaires, whereby respondents provided material directly related to topics for which we had extensive quantitative information from the mail questionnaire surveys. In addition to these standard background and quantitative items, the interview guide contained over two dozen general questions, many with several specific probes. It included queries about marital satisfaction, desirable qualities in husbands and wives, how one's own situation compared with that of other couples, whether it was realistic in today's changing world to expect couples to stay together for a lifetime, attitudes about the various tasks that accompany family life, high points and difficult periods in the marriage, sex-role stereotypes, the quality of the marital bond (including the amount of time spent with spouse), and expectations and hopes for the future.

Two male interviewers were assigned to interview husbands, and two female interviewers interviewed wives. Where it was inconvenient to get a husband or wife alone, portions of the interview were conducted with the other spouse present, but in these situations interviewers avoided asking questions that might create friction between husbands and wives and explained that the standard procedure was to interview spouses separately. Interviewers were also cautioned to remember that the random sampling procedure was merely a selection device in this instance and that there was no urgent need to interview people who were resistant in any way.

#3 – Organization Survey

The organization survey was a mail questionnaire survey of the leaders of Middletown's clubs and organizations conducted in the spring of 1977. Middletown's organizations were surveyed in a replication of the Lynds' 1924 organizational survey. Their brief description of method states that "a questionnaire on club membership and activities was sent to the more than 400 clubs in the city as they were located in the Spring of 1924." Their sampling universe was a list of 458 active clubs; they estimated that it accounted for about four-fifths of such organizations in Middletown (Lynd and Lynd 1929, 285-86, 509). The Lynds did not report how many completed questionnaires they obtained; the Lynd archives at the Library of Congress contain completed questionnaires for 126 organizations.

Our survey of Middletown organizations was conducted in the spring and summer of 1977. The sampling universe was an inventory of organizations drawn from these sources: the local daily newspapers, in particular the sections on "Talk of the Town" and "Metro Mention"; a Chamber of Commerce list of local clubs; the yellow pages of the telephone directory; a "Where to Turn" directory of services for the Middletown community published by Middletown Newspapers, Inc.; a 1977 directory of clubs and organizations compiled by Middletown's Women in Communications, Inc.; a local weekly newspaper; the state university newspaper; the university student program handbook; a YWCA contract book, which listed clubs that held meetings in YWCA facilities; and a high school activity list from the city's secondary schools. Organizations included in the sampling universe had to be local. The final inventory listed clubs at the state university, provided that they were also community organizations, that is, that they were listed in some roster other than the university publications. Sororities and fraternities at the university were not included unless there were community chapters for alumnae. National and regional organizations were counted, provided that there were local chapters. Parent associations affiliated with local schools were counted; as were home demonstration clubs, local 4-H clubs, neighborhood associations, and labor unions. Our inventory contained over 500 organizations, and we estimated that there were at least 100 more that the inventory missed, some of them secret or unwilling to publish information on officers or meetings.

The questionnaire was directed to the president or another appropriate officer of each organization. The accompanying letter explained that it was being sent "to selected resource persons who are officers or otherwise in a position to know about each organization."

The survey process had three stages: an initial mailing included a questionnaire, a prepaid return envelope, and a letter of explanation. Three weeks after the first mailing, we sent a reminder postcard. A month later, a second complete packet containing a new letter of introduction, the questionnaire, and another return envelope was sent to organizations not responding to the earlier mailings.

Among the topics treated in the questionnaire were the size and characteristics of the membership, the organization's history and purposes, the preferred characteristics of candidates for membership, the content of the meetings, the cost of belonging, the intended beneficiaries of activities, and the organization's ties to other organizations.

The final sampling universe—after deletion of organizations ineligible for the survey because they were agencies of local, state, or national governments or had no local chapters—contained 489 organizations. Attempts to contact officers of these units revealed that 6 of them had closed down or moved out of the city, leaving a universe of 483 organizations. Completed questionnaires were obtained from 267 of these, for a completion rate of 55 percent.

#4—Family Role Survey

The family role survey was a mail questionnaire survey conducted in the spring of 1977. A sample of married couples was randomly drawn from the *Middletown City Directory 1976.* The initial mailing in late February went to

548 households and contained a letter of explanation, two blank questionnaires, and two business-reply envelopes so that each spouse could return a
questionnaire separately. There were four subsequent mailings, including a reminder postcard, and a final complete packet. The letters stressed that both
husband and wife were to complete questionnaires, and in the final mailing a
special letter was prepared for households from which only one spouse had
responded.

The response rate ran somewhat lower than we had anticipated; and, in
conjunction with the final mailing, there was a special effort to improve participation. Before the final mailing, those households from which a completed
questionnaire had been received from either the husband or the wife were telephoned to encourage the participation of the "missing" spouse. At the same
time, research assistants made a one-time attempt to visit nonresponding
households and, where appropriate, left new questionnaires and held a brief,
friendly, doorstep conversation to encourage participation in the study.

These extraordinary efforts apparently added only 3 or 4 percentage points
to the completion rate. We were able to obtain completed questionnaires from
only 47 percent of the potential sample of *individuals*. The response rate for
households, that is, the percentage of households from which at least one
spouse responded, was somewhat higher (51 percent).

The questionnaire, entitled "The American Family—1977," was eight
pages long and included questions about who ought to perform selected family roles, who did perform them in the respondent's present situation, how
well each spouse performed the selected roles, whether certain family activities
could be shared with persons or groups outside the family, topics of family
quarrels, and four measures of marital satisfaction.

#5—Neighborhood Survey

The neighborhood survey was an interview survey of neighboring in a sample
of 17 Middletown neighborhoods conducted in May-July 1977. We divided
the 17 census tracts of Middletown (excluding four census tracts that are
mostly open countryside) along ecological boundaries such as railroad tracks,
major highways, open fields, and large fences into 109 smaller districts. Within each census tract a block was drawn randomly. Then, following a standard
set of rules for numbering units, the households on that block, and on contig-
uous blocks as necessary, were numbered sequentially until a cluster of 21 adjoining households had been identified. A map showing the 21 households of
each neighborhood was drawn. Current residents of each household were identified either from information in the city directory or from staff visits to the
neighborhood. Potential respondents were then contacted by postcard and
told that they would be visited by an interviewer.

The interview schedule was brief enough so that it could be completed on the doorstep when admittance to the house was denied. The duration of interviews ranged from 10 minutes to 2 hours, with a mean of 30 minutes. The preferred respondent was the housewife, when she was available. The schedule contained six pages of questions for the respondents plus a half-page to be completed by the interviewer. In addition to a series of items on knowledge of, and interaction with, the 20 other households in the neighborhood cluster, there were questions about the extent of contact with local relatives, involvement in community organizations, and contacts with friends living elsewhere in Middletown. Interviewers carried with them a large map of the city with the 109 districts clearly designated on it, and respondents pointed out the districts where they worked and where their relatives and friends lived.

In 15 of the 17 neighborhoods, the 21 households initially identified and mapped were sufficient to produce between 18 and 20 interviews. In 2 tracts, with a high percentage of black residents, we encountered more resistance and obtained 13 and 16 interviews, respectively. In all, we attempted to contact potential respondents in 375 households. There were 33 refusals and 26 households where the potential respondent was never at home or where the interview could not be completed for other reasons. The completion rate was 84 percent.

#6—High School Survey

The high school survey was an administered questionnaire survey conducted in the winter of 1977. It was a replication of surveys conducted by Robert and Helen Lynd in the Middletown high schools in 1924. The Lynds used two instruments. A questionnaire on the "life of the high school population" was administered in all high school sophomore, junior, and senior English classes. According to the Lynds, the 700 to 800 respondents comprised about three-fourths of the student population in those three grades. The other instrument, a true-false attitude questionnaire, was administered in junior and senior social science classes to about 550 respondents.

The 1977 questionnaire, titled "School Experience, Occupational Plans, Family Background and Attitudes of Middletown High School Youths," was eight pages long and included large portions of both Lynd questionnaires together with additional items about school life, occupational aspirations, and family background. It was designed to fit into a 50-minute-long class period, but in at least one high school less time was allowed and some students had difficulty completing the form. There were three versions of the instrument, each having a slightly different set of attitude and opinion items on the last page.

The survey was conducted in all four of Middletown's high schools, preceded by elaborate negotiations with school officials and a letter to parents informing them of the project and its purposes. The questionnaire was administered by teachers in each school. They received written instructions. It was offered at a given hour to all students then in school; 3,257 completed instruments were obtained from an estimated population of about 4,000. Students in special education classes were included by a decision of school officials. For reasons of economy, a 50 percent random sample of the completed questionnaires (1,673 cases) was coded and is referred to in our writings as "the high school sample."

#7—Ministers' Survey

The ministers' survey was a mail questionnaire survey of the characteristics of Middletown's churches and their ministers conducted in the spring of 1978. The 217 ministers listed in the *Directory of Christian Ministers of Delaware County* were sent a letter of explanation, a questionnaire, and a business-reply envelope in May. Three weeks later, a second letter of explanation was sent to those who had not responded, encouraging them to do so. After another three-week interval, a third letter of explanation and another questionnaire were sent to those who had not responded.

These procedures produced 112 completed questionnaires for a completion rate of 52 percent. The questionnaire requested information about the social characteristics of the congregation, the church's religious activities and rituals, and the role of the minister.

#8—Government Services Survey

The government services survey was a mail questionnaire survey of awareness and utilization of local, state, and federal governmental programs and services in Middletown's county conducted in the spring of 1978. A random sample of 500 households, approximately 4 percent of the county's households, was selected from the *Middletown City Directory 1977*. The questionnaire was mailed with a cover letter in early April. To households headed by married couples, half of the letters were addressed to the husband and half to the wife. The letter asked the recipient to complete the questionnaire and return it in a self-addressed, postpaid envelope. When he or she did not wish to participate in the study, he or she was asked to return the blank questionnaire so that his or her name could be taken off the list for follow-up mailings. Those who did not reply were sent a postcard two weeks later, encouraging them to complete and to return the questionnaire. Those who did not respond to the first two mailings were sent a new packet containing a different cover letter, another copy of the questionnaire, and another return envelope. A final follow-up packet containing cover letter, questionnaire, and return envelope was sent six weeks after the original mailing.

Of the 500 persons addressed, 70 had moved, had died, or were otherwise unlocatable; 107 of the remaining 430 refused to participate by returning the blank questionnaire; and an additional 117 did not respond to any of the four mailings. Two-hundred and six questionnaires were completed; the response rate was 48 percent.

The questionnaire was 12 pages long and assessed the respondents' awareness and utilization of governmental programs and services.

#9—Women's Occupational Survey

The women's occupational survey was a mail questionnaire survey conducted in the spring of 1978. A random sample of 1,006 adult women (7 percent of the population) was drawn from the *Middletown City Directory 1977* and included female heads of households, women living alone, and wives of male heads of household. A cover letter explaining the study and requesting completion of an enclosed questionnaire was sent to each potential respondent. Those who did not wish to participate in the study were asked to return the blank questionnaire. Those who did not reply were sent a postcard two weeks later. Those who did not respond to these first two mailings were sent a new packet containing a different cover letter, another copy of the questionnaire, and another return envelope. A final follow-up packet containing cover letter, questionnaire, and return envelope was sent six weeks after the original mailing.

One-hundred and seventy-two of the women drawn had died or had moved and left no forwarding address. From the 834 eligible respondents, 495 completed questionnaires were obtained. The final response rate was 59 percent.

The questionnaire was 12 pages long and requested a complete marital history together with extensive information about respondent's work experience and its effects on husbands and children.

#10—Men's Occupational Survey

The men's occupational survey was a mail questionnaire conducted in the spring and summer of 1978. A 4 percent systematic random sample of adult men consisting of 651 men was drawn from the *Middletown City Directory 1977*. A cover letter explaining the study and requesting completion of an enclosed questionnaire was sent to each man in the sample. The cover letter asked those who did not wish to participate to return the blank questionnaire. Two weeks later, a postcard was sent to those who had not returned the questionnaire. Four weeks after the original mailing, a second follow-up mailing was sent. A final follow-up mailing was made two months after the initial mailing.

Of the original sample of 651, 94 had died or had moved and left no forwarding address. From the 557 potential respondents, we obtained 215 completed questionnaires. The final response rate was 39 percent.

The questionnaire was 12 pages long and focused on work experience. Information about the influence of work experience on family life was obtained from those respondents who were married.

#11 — Housewives' Survey

The housewives' survey was an interview survey conducted in the summer of 1978. This was a replication of the Lynds' interview survey of married women living with their husbands and with at least one child at home between the ages of 6 and 18 years. A random sample of 2,192 married women was drawn from the *Middletown City Directory 1977*. Each was mailed a letter explaining the purpose of the study. A reply postcard was enclosed for the addressee to indicate whether she had a child of the required age and whether she was willing to be interviewed. Three-hundred and forty-four women returned the postcard and described themselves as ineligible. Two-hundred and sixty-five women reported themselves as eligible, of whom 178 agreed to be interviewed and 87 refused. The 1,583 women who did not return the postcard were telephoned so that the study could be explained, and those who were eligible were again invited to be interviewed. Of those telephoned, 518 were eligible and 155 agreed to be interviewed. The overall response rate was 42 percent: 793 of the sample of 2,193 women were eligible and 333 of these were interviewed.

The interview schedule was a replication almost identical to the Lynds' interview schedule of 1924. Information was sought about the work histories of both husband and wife, their financial arrangements, housekeeping activities, religious beliefs, and child-rearing practices. The average interview took 90 minutes. The interviewing was done by six mature, married women.

#12 — Religion Survey

The religion survey was a mail questionnaire survey of religious beliefs and practices conducted in the summer of 1978. A random sample of 700 households, approximately 7 percent of all households, was selected from the *Middletown City Directory 1977*. The questionnaire, along with a cover letter of instruction, was mailed in late May. To households headed by a married couple, half of the letters were addressed to the husband and half to the wife. The cover letter asked the recipients to complete the questionnaire and return it in a self-addressed, postpaid envelope. When they did not wish to participate, they were asked to return the blank questionnaire. Those who did not reply within two weeks were sent a follow-up postcard. Those who did not respond within another two weeks received a new packet containing a different cover letter, another copy of the questionnaire, and another return envelope. A final follow-up included a cover letter, questionnaire, and return envelope.

Of the 716 persons drawn, 109 had moved, had died, or were otherwise unlocatable. Two-hundred and thirty completed questionnaires were received from the 609 eligible respondents; the response rate was 38 percent.

The questionnaire was 12 pages long and covered religious beliefs and values, religious behavior, attitudes toward various religious groups, and perceptions of religion in relation to family life.

#13 — Christmas Survey

The Christmas survey was an interview survey on the celebration of Christmas 1978 conducted in the spring of 1979. A sample of 250 adults evenly divided by sex was randomly drawn in the usual way. Of 174 apparently eligible respondents, 110 were interviewed for a response rate of 63 percent.

This small survey served as a kind of postscript to the surveys listed above. It was undertaken almost a year and a half after the closing of the project's field office in order to obtain additional information about the composite families whose unexpected significance had been revealed by the analysis of data from surveys #1 and #2.

The interview was conducted by three women interviewers experienced in earlier Middletown III surveys. The interview schedule was long and complex, and the median interview time was just under 60 minutes; many interviews ran much longer. Separate codings elicited from the interviews were established for constructed samples of Christmas gatherings, kin relationships, and Christmas gifts.

Copies of the questionnaires and interview schedules used in these 13 surveys have been placed on permanent file in the Center for Middletown Studies, Bracken Library, Ball State University, Muncie, Indiana 47306, and are available upon written request.

NOTES

Notes

Chapter 1

1. Nearly everybody knows the real name of the place, but it is a form of sociological politeness to respect its collective privacy by using a pseudonym; so, we will talk about Middletown, and never about Muncie, throughout the following pages.

2. For the entire distribution, see Table 3 in Caplow and Bahr 1979.

3. From Table 24 of *Working Papers: Updated Trends*, Middletown III Project, Center for Program Effectiveness Studies, University of Virginia, March 1977.

4. The Middletown III project was able to purchase copies of these photographs from Time-Life, Inc., in 1977.

5. By the end of the 1970s, there were a few signs that Middletown's insatiable appetite for verbal and visual symbols was beginning to peak. Television viewing declined slightly but steady after 1975, and newspaper circulation seemed to be declining, also. But these were only straws in the wind, not a reversal of the trend.

6. For a fuller description of these multiple programs and their purposes, see Austin 1980.

Chapter 2

1. Specifically, census figures on age distribution of the population, number of families, and total persons in families. Number of families does not include "one-person families" (1920-1940) or "unrelated individuals" (1950-1970). The number of one-person families for 1920 was estimated with the use of the 1930 ratio of one-person families to total families. The number of families in 1940 was estimated by subtracting one-person households from total households. The 1920-1940 population of children aged 15 to 17 was estimated by prorating the figures in the published totals for the 15-through-19 age category.

Chapter 3

1. For more than a decade, a group of family scholars under the general leadership of F. Ivan Nye has been exploring the role structure of American families. In a loosely co-ordinated program of research, scholars following Nye's approach have conducted major studies of family roles in two Pacific Northwest cities (Yakima and Seattle) and in the

entire state of Utah. Members of the Middletown III research team were associated with Nye in the early stages of his family-role research program, and the family-role survey conducted in Middletown was an explicit extension of that program. See, for example, Nye and McLaughlin 1976; Nye 1974; Clark, Nye, and Gecas 1978; and Albrecht, Bahr, and Chadwick 1977 and 1979.

2. The survey instrument also included measures of marital satisfaction, standard demographic indicators included in all of the Middletown surveys, opinions about whether activities traditionally assigned to the family might be effectively performed by extrafamilial agencies, and measures of participation in voluntary associations.

3. The questionnaire included a question about respondent's occupation but not one about spouse's occupation. Inasmuch as our social-class comparisons are based on the husband's occupation, only those wives whose husbands also responded could be used in the business-class/working-class comparisons.

4. The Washington and Utah studies of family roles found respondents unwilling to say that certain tasks were "always" or "solely" the responsibility of either spouse. Among the Yakima couples studied by Nye, there was no role that a majority of wives was willing to say belonged solely to either the husband or the wife (the closest candidates were the provider role, which 37 percent assigned solely to husbands, and the housekeeper role, which 42 percent assigned entirely to wives). For most of the other roles, less than 5 percent of the wives assigned sole responsibility to either spouse. Husbands responded in much the same way, except that more husbands said that the men should be solely responsible for providing (57 percent) and fewer (25 percent) said that wives should have all the responsibility for housekeeping. (See Nye 1976, 151.) The Utah survey showed even less sex stereotyping of family roles. Only 32 percent of the men and 19 percent of the women said that husbands ought to be entirely responsible for providing; only 13 and 16 percent, respectively, said that wives should do all the housekeeping.

5. See Adams 1979, 161. Nye and McLaughlin's investigation of family-role performance in Yakima is relevant to the question of whether specialization is necessary or useful in marriage. Interpreting their data, they noted that reciprocity (or role specialization) does occur in family-role performance, but they went on to say that it is not demonstrably essential (Nye and McLaughlin 1976, 200).

Chapter 7

1. The Lynds seem not to have used the term "modernization." They referred, instead, to secularization, social change, change in the technological and mechanical aspects of social life, inventions and the developments of new tools and techniques, adjustment to rapid change, and effects of "machine technology" on Middletown's labor force (1929, 5, 496-97, 500; 1937, 45, 69). All of these changes and many more are implicit in our use of the term "modernization," which we define as the process whereby a contemporary society improves its control of the environment by means of an increasingly competent technology applied by increasingly complex organizations.

2. Unless noted differently, the 1924/1977 comparisons involve part of a 50 percent sample of questionnaires from the 1977 high school survey. Ninth-grade students, not included in the Lynds' sample, were eliminated from ours to make the populations more comparable, as were black students, who were included in the Lynds' sample but not in their tabulations.

3. The two classes identified in Middletown by the Lynds, the business class and the working class, were based on the division between white-collar and blue-collar occupations. We have followed the same procedure. White-collar occupations are those included

in the U.S. census's occupational categories "professional, technical, and kindred," "managers and administrators, except farm," "sales workers," and "clerical and kindred workers." All other occupations are classified as blue-collar.

4. Raymond Fuller's *A Study of Youth Needs and Services in Middletown* was submitted to the American Youth Commission in 1937. Its conclusion, buttressed by 350 pages of evidence, was that Middletown youths were not adequately served by the existing social agencies.

5. Ninth-graders and blacks were included in the tabulation this time, since we were not making direct comparisons with the earlier survey results.

6. The questions were in the kinship survey. The questions had been used previously by Bert Adams in a study of kinship patterns among residents of Greensboro, N.C. See his *Kinship in an Urban Setting* (1968).

7. Dividing the sample into four categories (business-class fathers, business-class mothers, working-class fathers, working-class mothers) and eliminating persons without children of appropriate age leaves fairly small categories (in the range of 40 to 60 cases), so our observations on class differences in these ratings must be considered tentative.

Chapter 8

1. See, for example, Glenn and Weaver 1979 and Udry and Morris 1978.

2. See also Bell 1960. A similar conclusion was reached by Ira Reiss (1966, 125-26).

3. See also Lincoln 1978, where it is asserted that the average age of menstruation has dropped almost 5 years during the last 170 years.

4. "Of the seventy-seven wives of workers for whom information was secured on this subject . . . only twenty used artificial means that might be considered moderately scientific, and only half of these last employed means of the sort utilized by the business class" (Lynd and Lynd 1929, 123).

5. There has not been much research on this topic, and what there is typically derives from analyses of small samples of highly selective populations. See, for example, Jacques and Chason 1979 and Ard 1974. Results from both of these studies suggest that, in the words of Jacques and Chason (p. xxx), "premarital cohabitation may not provide types of learning experiences that significantly alter — in either a positive or negative direction — an individual's success in marriage," but the range of indicators of success is very narrow in both studies and the samples (84 married students, married an average of 13 months in the Jacques and Chason piece, and 161 New England couples who volunteered in 1935-1938 to participate in a longitudinal study of marriage in the Ard article) are unrepresentative enough to dictate great caution in making wide generalizations of these findings.

Chapter 9

1. Throughout this chapter, when we divide Middletown respondents by social class, the categories being compared are business-class males, business-class females, working-class males, and working-class females. Following both the Lynds and Adams, occupational class assignment for women was made on the basis of their husbands' occupations. Thus, only women who were or had been married and who answered a question about the current or former (when husband was unemployed or retired) main occupation of their husbands could be included in the class comparisons. Of the 311 women who returned a kinship questionnaire, 10 percent had never married. An additional 25 percent (76 women) were divorced or widowed and the spouse's occupation item item did not apply to

them. Thirty women did not provide enough occupational information to permit the coding of husband's occupation. In all, there were 174 women, 97 business-class and 77 working-class wives, who qualified on all counts for the class comparisons. The number of cases may be smaller than that because of missing or "does not apply" responses on the variables being studied. The class contrasts for males included all men who recorded a codable occupation, regardless of their marital status. Twenty percent of the male respondents had never married. Maximum subsample size for the males was 69 in the business class and 67 in the working class. There were 29 males for whom there was insufficient occupational information to permit reliable coding.

2. We did not collect data on frequency on contact with all siblings or all cousins but only the sibling closest to the respondent in age and the cousin selected by the respondent as "the cousin whom you know the best." The nearest sibling is very often, but not invariably, the best known. The frequency of interaction with best-known siblings presumably would fall somewhat closer to that with parents.

3. Setting the cutoff point at "several times a year" permits direct comparisons with Adams's findings. Adams (1968, 54-55) maintained that, for activity to be considered as patterned rather than sporadic, it should take place at least three times a year.

4. That difference, combining social class and sex, is statistically significant, but the class and sex differences taken separately are not.

5. Labeled "affectional closeness," "value consensus," and "identification."

6. The shift in terminology is intentional. Adams referred to the "middle class" where we say the "business class"; both terms mean to include men or independent women in white-collar occupations.

7. These terms will be discussed at length in Chapter 13.

Chapter 10

1. "An emblem is a type of symbol that represents a complex but bounded social or cultural phenomenon by means of an easily recognized picture or design which has no more philological relationship to the thing represented." This definition is adapted from Efron 1972, 96. See also Firth 1973 and Leach 1976, who have supplied variant usages. (Caplow and Williamson, 1981, n. 2.)

2. For an illuminating comparison of antifestivals in two other cultural settings, see Abrahams and Bauman 1978, 193-208.

3. For anthropological discussions of witches and witchcraft, see Douglas 1970b, Mair 1969, and Marwick 1970, and, especially, Evans-Pritchard 1937. Compare Needham 1979, 40.

4. Muncie Star, 1907.

5. As mentioned earlier, the holidays following Easter are not as intensely celebrated as those preceding Easter or Easter itself; and, except for Mother's Day and Father's Day, they are not family oriented. Mother's Day and Father's Day are exceptional in having no emblems, no religious associations, and only minimal gift giving.

6. It is, however, perfectly proper to impersonate these being in other contexts: the secular emblems at their proper holidays, the sacred persons at holidays or in passion plays at other times. The mockery, save by the vehicle of the witch, may not be made.

7. Why does Santa come down the chimney? He must enter by an unusual way because he is an unusual person (cf. Van Gennep 1960, 20 ff). He cannot use a window because those are portals for illicit persons—burglars and eloping daughters. What remains but the chimney, situated on top of the house and pointing toward the sky, where Santa travels, and associated with heat, or warmth, which he embodies. How mundane if he were to come in by the front door like an insurance salesman!

8. For a fuller discussion of the Christmas/Easter opposition, see Caplow and Williamson 1981.

9. For an interesting discussion of the possible significance of our "animal categories," see Leach 1964 and Halverston 1976.

10. It must be emphasized that only the *classes* of animals and their attributes are considered, not cases in which dogs and cats have been eaten (as during wartime) or geese, chickens, sheep, and the like have been kept as pets.

11. Many writers have tackled this problem. Those who have most influenced this discussion were Durkheim 1965), Malinowski 1954, Turner 1967, Geertz 1966, Lévi-Strauss 1967, 1969, and Burridge 1969. None of these theorists dealt with a commonly held notion that the festivals are celebrated in their particular ways, or celebrated at all, out of mere habit. It might be possible to account for some kinds of ritualized behavior in this way, but most serious analysts of ritual are unwilling to accept such a simplistic explanation. In any case, force of habit or tradition alone cannot explain modern Middletown's festivals since, as we have seen, these have changed considerably during recent decades and are still changing.

12. There are several theoretical problems left untouched in this discussion, especially the problem of the degree of conscious design in any situation involving symbols. Many believe that symbols achieve their status, and rituals their form, by a primarily unconscious process whereby tradition continues and innovation is accepted only when they are meaningful within the present system of meanings of the culture; that system being, of course, explicated, and so established, by the rituals. But, if we accept the view that rituals evolve unconsciously, how are we to verify the correctness of any symbolic analysis? If, on the other hand, we assume that rituals evolve by conscious design, how are we to justify any analysis that departs from the natives' own interpretations of their rituals? (For proposed resolutions to these problems, see Sapir 1977, 5; Turner 1967, 26; Nadel 1954, 108; and Wilson 1957, 6. Another problem is that there are some societies in which practically no ritual or symbolic activity is reported to exist (e.g., the Basseri [Barth 1961]), although they are presumably no freer from ideological conflicts than other cultures; in others it appears that nothing is too trivial to be incorporated into the symbolic system (e.g., the various Pueblo Indians [Ortiz 1972]), although these societies seem to be no more unstable than other societies. Attempts to explain these variations in terms of language use, ecology, or entropy (Douglas 1970a and Farb 1968) have, unfortunately, not been very successful. A more fundamental problem than any of these is the extent to which order is necessary in society and why people persist in holding values that are mutually incompatible. Why employ ritual to hold such a rickety structure together instead of changing the structure? Is it conceivable that a society could adopt the solution of perpetually changing its fundamental principles in an attempt to resolve contradictions rather than relying on rituals to do so?

13. Such a study is currently being carried out by the Middletown III project.

14. An interesting article on this subject, "Sociology of Xmas Cards," shows that people exchange cards with social equals, send them without reciprocation to superiors whose ranks they wish to join, and receive them without reciprocating from inferiors who wish to join them (Johnson 1975).

15. To American readers this may be no novelty. It becomes remarkable when contrasted with other societies (e.g., the Kwoma of New Guinea, among whom this writer has spent some time) in which parents explicitly state that their reason for looking after their children is so the children will support them in their old age and children say that they support their aging parents as a return for care in childhood.

16. Note the triviality of Mother's Day and Father's Day presents compared to the massive quantity of presents given to children at Christmas.

17. There is some evidence that Christmas celebrations place an unusual strain on family relationships; consequently, the next year's celebrations may be slightly more elaborate to compensate for the seeming failure of the previous celebrations. The greater emphasis may result in greater strain and so a vicious circle continues.

Chapter 12

1. For an assessment of the family types of the southern region, see Hill 1956.

2. For a brilliant analysis of this proposition, see Elder 1974.

3. The most dramatic effects of the Great Depression on this middle generation can be seen by comparing the number of children born to those couples married before (4.1) with couples beginning marriage during the depression (3.0). Child spacing and child launching were both longer for the depression-constrained couples.

4. This generation's kin-keeping contributions are noteworthy. See Hill 1970b, 58-80.

5. They have also timed the completion of schooling and the setting up of a separate household, which, during the nineteenth century, did not necessarily coincide with getting married.

6. See also Bennett and Elder 1979, 157-58, for confirming evidence of compressed transition.

7. See also Hill's (1970b) discussion of the younger generation's greater attention to life-cycle management in his three-generation study in Minnesota.

8. Henretta, describing the decline of communal organization in many New England communities in Colonial America through emigration and immigration, asserted that families assumed functions dropped by the community and spoke of the "rise of the family" in the eighteenth century: "In short, the decline of the community was . . . to some extent offset by the rise of the family. During the eighteenth century, the basic social unit took on more of the tasks of socialization and acculturation. Between the time of the waning of the influence of the church and the emergence of the public school, the family assumed the burden of the education of the young. It was the family, likewise, which became the prime economic institution of the society. With the town lands distributed among the proprietors, it was up to the family to provide for its numerous members" (Henretta 1971,397).

9. See especially Duvall 1946 and Blood 1956, 46-47.

10. See Chapter 6 for Middletown findings.

Chapter 13

1. For a summary of the actual policies advocated by family "professionals" who start from the decline of the family as an article of faith, see Carlson 1980.

2. According to the *Washington Post* (June 11, 1980), more than 100,000 persons were actively involved in planning the 1980 White House Conference on Families.

3. Whitney Gordon, personal communication, October 7, 1979.

4. For example, Furstenberg 1968 and Lantz et al. 1968.

5. An impressive assortment of midwestern family tragedies around the turn of the century is presented in Lesy 1973.

6. This is a highly simplified explanation that leaves out of account the incredibly complex amendments and reforms that have attempted to remedy this situation. They have not done so. The cumulative tax rate for AFDC families frequently reaches 70 percent, and under certain conditions (earnings near the Medicaid "notch," for example) may go above 100 percent. For a summary of recent developments, see Garfinkel 1979.

7. And as Sen. Edward M. Kennedy described eloquently in an address to the NAACP in Detroit, Mich. May 7, 1978: "Look, after all, at what we do. We go to a young girl—a child of 18, or 16, or even younger—and this is what we say. We say, abandon all your hopes. Your schools will not teach you. You will not learn to read or write. You will never have a decent job. You will live in neighborhoods of endless unemployment and poverty, of drugs and violence. And then we say to this child—wait, there is a way, one way, you can be somebody to someone. We will give you an apartment, and furniture to fill it. We will give you a TV set and a telephone. We will give you clothing, and cheap food, and free medical care, and some spending money besides. And in return, you only have to do one thing: just go out and have a baby. And faced with such an offer, it is no surprise that hundreds of thousands have been caught in the trap that our welfare system has become. . . ."

8. In June 1980, a conference was convened in Washington, D.C., to introduce the problem of "elder abuse," that is, the mistreatment of aged persons living with their relatives. The promoters announced in the usual way that millions of victims might be involved and that the problem was increasing rapidly because of the decay of family solidarity.

9. The earliest year for which it can be reliably calculated.

10. For example, the Tikopia studied by Raymond Firth. See especially Firth 1936.

BIBLIOGRAPHY

Bibliography

Abrahams, Roger D., and Richard Bauman. "Ranges of Festival Behavior," pp. 193-208 in Barbara A. Babcock (ed.). *The Reversible World: Symbolic Inversion in Art and Society*. Ithaca, N.Y.: Cornell University Press, 1978.

Abrahamson, Mark. *Urban Sociology*. Englewood Cliffe, N.H.: Prentice-Hall, 1976.

Adams, Bert. *Kinship in an Urban Setting*. Chicago: Markham. 1968.

_____. "Isolation, Function and Beyond: American Kinship in the 1960's," pp. 163-86 in Carlfred Broderick (ed.). *A Decade of Family Research and Action*. Minneapolis: National Council on Family Relations,, 1970.

_____. *The Family: A Sociological Interpretation* (2nd ed.). Chicago: Rand McNally, 1975.

_____. "Mate Selection in the United States: A Theoretical Summarization," in Wesley R. Burr, Reuben Hill, F. Ivan Nye, and Ira L. Reiss (eds.). *Contemporary Theories about the Family: Research-Based Theories* (vol. 1). New York: The Free Press, 1979.

Adelson, Joseph. "Adolescence and the Generation Gap," *Psychology Today* 12 (February 1979), 33.

Adler, Nancy E. "Abortion: A Social-Psychological Perspective," *Journal of Social Issues* 35 (1979), 100-19.

Albrecht, Stan L., Howard M. Bahr, and Bruce A. Chadwick. "Public Stereotyping of Sex Roles, Personality Characteristics, and Occupations," *Sociology and Social Research* 61 (January 1977), 223-40.

_____. "Changing Family and Sex Roles: An Assessment of Age Differences," *Journal of Marriage and the Family* 41 (February 1979), 41-50.

Ard, Ben N., Jr. "Premarital Sexual Experience: A Longitudinal Study," *Journal of Sex Research* 10 (February 1974), 32-39.

Austin, Penelope Canan. "The Federal Presence in Middletown, 1937-1977," *The Tocqueville Review* 2 (Spring-Summer 1980), 93-107.

Axelson, Leland. "The Working Wife: Differences in Perception among Negro and White Males," *Journal of Marriage and the Family* 32 (August 1970), 457-64.

Bahr, Howard M. "Changes in Family Life in Middletown, 1924-77," *Public Opinion Quarterly* 44 (Fall 1979), 35-52.

Bahr, Howard M., Theodore Caplow, and Geoffrey K. Leigh. "The Slowing of Modernization in Middletown," pp. 219-32 in Louis Kriesberg (ed.). *Research in Social Movements, Conflicts and Change* (vol. 3). Greenwich, Conn.: JAI Press, 1980.

Bahr, Stephen J. "Effects of Power and Division of Labor in the Family," pp. 167-85 in Lois Wladis Hoffman and F. Ivan Nye. *Working Mothers.* San Francisco: Jossey-Bass, 1974.

Bane, Mary Jo. *Here to Stay: American Families in the Twentieth Century.* New York, Basic Books, 1976.

Barth, Fredrik. *Nomads of South Persia: The Basseri Tribe of the Khamseh Confederacy.* London: Oslo University Press, 1961.

Becker, Gary, E. M. Landes, and R. T. Michael. *Economics of Marital Instability.* Stanford Calif.: National Bureau of Economic Research, Working Paper no. 153, 1976.

Bell, Robert R. *Premarital Sex in a Changing Society.* Englewood Cliffs, N.J.: Prentice-Hall, 1960.

Bell, Robert R., and Jay B. Chaskes. "Premarital Sexual Experience among Coeds, 1958-1968," *Journal of Marriage and the Family* 32 (1970), 81-84.

Bengtson, Vern L. "Generation and Family Effects in Value Socialization," *American Sociological Review* 40 (June 1975), 352-71.

Bengtson, Vern L., and J. A. Kuypers. "Generational Differences and the Developmental Stake," *Aging and Human Development* 2 (1971), 249-60.

Bennett, Sheila I., and Glen H. Elder, Jr. "Women's Work in the Family Economy: A Study of Depression Hardship in Women's Lives," *Journal of Family History* 4 (Summer 1979), 153-76.

Bird, Caroline. *The Two-Paycheck Marriage.* New York: Rawson, Wade Publishers, 1979.

Blake, Judith. "Ideal Family Size among White Americans: A Quarter Century of Evidence," *Demography* 3 (1966), 154-74.

Blood, Robert O., Jr. *A Teacher's Manual for Use with Anticipating Your Marriage.* Glencoe, Ill.: The Free Press, 1956.

Blood, Robert O., Jr., and Donald M. Wolfe. *Husbands and Wives: The Dynamics of Married Living.* New York: The Free Press, 1960.

Boulding, Kenneth E. "The Family Segment of the National Economy." Address to the American Home Economics Association Annual Meeting, St. Louis, 1970.

Bracken, Alexander Elliott. "Middletown as a Pioneer Community," Middletown III Project Paper no. 10. Charlottesville, Va.: Center for Program Effectiveness Studies, University of Virginia, 1978.

Bracken, Michael B., M. Phil, Moshe Hachamovitch, and Gerald Grossman. "The Decision to Abort and Psychological Sequelae," *Journal of Nervous and Mental Disease* 158 (1974), 154-62.

Burke, Ronald J, and Tamara Weir. "Relationship of Wives' Employment Status to Husband, Wife and Pair Satisfaction," *Journal of Marriage and the Family* 38 (May 1976), 279-87.

Burr, Wesley. "Satisfaction and Various Aspects of Marriage Over the Life Cycle: A Random Middleclass Sample," *Journal of Marriage and the Family* 32 (1970), 29-37.

Burridge, K. O. L. *Tangu Traditions.* London: Oxford University Press, 1969.

Cahen, Alfred. *Statistical Analysis of American Divorce.* New York: Columbia University Press, 1932.

Campbell, Angus. "Women at Home and at Work," in Dorothy G. McGuigan. *New Research on Women and Sex Roles.* Ann Arbor, Mich.: Univeristy of Michigan, 1976.

Caplow, Theodore. "A Critical Study of American Marriage Rates." Ph.D. dissertation, University of Minnesota, 1946.

Caplow, Theodore, and Howard M. Bahr. "Half a Century of Change in Adolescent Attitudes: Replication of a Middletown Survey by the Lynds, " *Public Opinion Quarterly*, 43 (Spring 1979), 1-17.

Caplow, Theodore, and Bruce A. Chadwick. "Inequality and Life Style in Middletown, 1920-78," *Social Science Quarterly* 60 (December 1979), 367-86.

Caplow, Theodore, and Margaret Holmes Williamson. "Decoding Middletown's Easter Bunny: A Study in American Iconography," *Semiotica* 32 (1980), 221-32.

Carlson, Allan C. "Families, Sex, and the Liberal Agenda," *The Public Interest* 58 (1980), 62-75.

Center for Disease Control. *Abortion Surveillance 1974.* Washington, D.C.: U.S. Department of Health, Education, and Welfare, Public Health Service, April 1976.

_____. *Abortion Surveillance 1975.* Washington, D.C.: U.S. Department of Health, Education, and Welfare, Public Health Service, April 1977.

_____. *Abortion Surveillance 1976.* Washington, D.C.: U.S. Department of Health, Education, and Welfare, Public Health Service, August 1978.

Chadwick, Bruce A., Stan L. Albrecht, and Phillip R. Kunz. "Marital and Family Role Satisfaction," *Journal of Marriage and the Family* 38 (1976), 431-42.

Chadwick, Bruce A., and C. Bradford Chappell. "Change in the Two-Income Family in Middletown U.S.A. from 1924 to 1978," in Stephen J. Bahr (ed.). *Economics and the Family.* Lexington, Mass.: Lexington Books, forthcoming.

Christensen, Harold T. "Normative Theory Derived from Cross-Cultural Family Research," *Journal of Marriage and the Family* 31 (1969), 209-22.

Clark, Robert A., F. Ivan Nye, and Viktor Gecas. "Husbands' Work Involvement and Marital Role Performance," *Journal of Marriage and the Family* 40 (February 1978), 9-21.

Coombs, L. C., and Z. Zumeta. "Correlates of Marital Dissolution in a Prospective Fertility Study: A Research Note," *Social Problems* 18 (1970), 92-102.

Cott, Nancy F. "Divorce and the Changing Status of Women in Eighteenth-Century Massachusetts," pp. 115-139 in Michael Gordon (ed.). *The American Family in Social-Historical Perspective* (2nd ed.). New York: St. Martin's Press, 1978.

Crosby, John F. "The Death of the Family—Revisited," *The Humanist* 35 (May/June, 1975), 12-14.

Davis, Kingsley. "The American Family in Relation to Demographic Change," pp. 237-65 in Charles F. Westoff and Robert Parke, Jr. (eds.), Commission on Population Growth and the American Future. *Research Reports: Demographic and Social Aspects of Population Growth* (vol. 1). Washington, D.C.: U.S. Government Printing Office, 1972.

Diepold, John, Jr., and Richard David Young. "Empirical Studies of Adolescent Sexual Behavior: A Critical Review," *Adolescence* 14 (Spring 1979), 45.

Dollard, John. *Caste and Class in a Southern Town.* New Haven, Conn.: Yale University Press, 1937.

Douglas, Mary. *Purity and Danger.* London: Routledge and Kegan Paul, 1966.

_____. *Natural Symbols.* London: Barrie and Rockliff, 1970a.

_____ (ed.). *Witchcraft Confessions and Accusations.* Association of Social Anthropologists (of Great Britain) Monographs, vol. 9. London: Tavistock Publications, 1970b.

_____. *Implicit Meanings.* London: Routledge and Kegan Paul, 1975.

Durkheim, Emile. *The Division of Labor in Society.* New York: The Free Press, 1964.

_____. *The Elementary Forms of the Religious Life.* Glencoe, Ill.: The Free Press, 1965.

Duvall, Evelyn M. "Conceptions of Parenthood," *American Journal of Sociology* 52 (November 1946), 193-203.

Easterlin, Richard. "Relative Economic Status and the American Fertility Swing," pp. 170-223 in Eleanor B. Sheldon (ed.). *Family Economic Behavior: Problems and Prospects.* Philadelphia: Lippincott, 1973.

Efron, David. "Gesture, Race and Culture" (originally published in 1941). Revised ed. in Thomas A. Sebeok (ed.). *Approaches to Semiotics.* The Hague: Mouton, 1972.

Elder, Glen. *Children of the Great Depression.* Chicago: University of Chicago Press, 1974.

——. "Family History and the Life Course," *Journal of Family History* 2 (Winter 1977), 279-305.

Etzioni, Amitai. "The Family: Is It Obsolete?" *Journal of Current Social Issues* 14 (Winter 1977), 4-9.

Evans-Pritchard, E. E. *Witchcraft, Oracles and Magic among the Azande.* Oxford: The Clarendon Press, 1937.

Farb, Peter. *Man's Rise to Civilization, as Shown by the Indians of North America from Primeval Times to the Coming of the Industrial State.* New York: E. P. Dutton and Company, 1968.

Ferree, Myra M. "The Confused American Housewife," *Psychology Today* 10 (1967a), 76-80.

——. "Working Class Jobs: Housework and Paid Work as Sources of Satisfaction," *Social Problems* 23 (April 1976b), 431-41.

Firth, Raymond. *We, the Tikopia: A Sociological Study of Kinship in Primitive Polynesia.* London: Allen and Unwin, 1936.

——. *Symbols: Public and Private.* Ithaca, N.Y.: Cornell University Press, 1973.

Fogel, Robert W., and Stanley Engerman. *Time on the Cross: The Economics of American Negro Slavery* (2 vols.). Boston: Little, Brown and Company, 1974.

Foner, Anne. "Age Stratification and the Changing Family," pp. s340-66 in John Demos and Sarane Spence Boocock (eds.). *Turning Points: Historical and Sociological Essays on the Family.* Supplement to *American Journal of Sociology* 84 (1978).

Foote, Nelson. "The Old Generation and the New," pp. 1-25 in Eli Ginsberg. *The Nation's Children: Problems and Prospects* (vol. 3). New York: Columbia University Press, 1960.

Ford, Kathleen. " Contraceptive Utilization in the United States: 1970 and 1976." Advance Data, U.S. Department of Health, Education, and Welfare, Public Health Service, National Center for Health Statistics, August 18, 1978.

Fortes, Meyer. "Introduction" in Jack Goody (ed.). *Developmental Cycle in Domestic Groups.* Cambridge: Cambridge University Press, 1963.

Francoeur, Robert T. "The Sexual Revolution: Will Hard Times Turn Back the Clock?" *The Futurist* 14 (April 1980), 3-12.

Frank, Carollyle. "Politics in Middletown: A Reconsideration of Municipal Government and Community Power in Muncie, Indiana, 1925-1935." Muncie, Ind.: Ph.D. dissertation, Ball State University.

Fuller, Raymond. *A Study of Youth Needs and Services in Middletown.* Submitted to the American Youth Commission in 1937. Washington, D.C.: American Council on Education.

Furstenberg, Frank F., Jr. "Industrialization and the American Family: A Look Backward," *American Sociological Review* 33 (June 1968), 413-26.

Garfinkel, Irwin. "Welfare Reform: A New and Old View," *Journal of the Institute for Socioeconomic Studies* 4 (1979), 58-72.

Geertz, Clifford. "Religion as a Cultural System," in Michael Banton (ed.). *Anthropological Approaches to the Study of Religion.* Association of Social Anthropologists (of Great Britain) Monographs, vol. 3. London: Tavistock Publications, 1966.

Glenn, Norval D., and Charles N. Weaver. "Attitudes toward Premarital, Extramarital, and Homosexual Relations in the U.S. in the 1970's," *Journal of Sex Research* 15 (May 1979), 108-18.

Glick, Paul C. "Updating the Life Cycle of the Family," *Journal of Marriage and the Family* 39 (February 1977), 3-13.

_____. "Future American Families," *COFO Memo* 2 (Summer/Fall 1979), 2-5.

Gould, Roger. "Coupling, Marriage and Growth," *Cosmopolitan* (May 1978).

Gunderson, Mark Paul, and James Leslie McCray. "Sexual Guilt and Religion," *Family Coordinator* 28 (July 1979), 353-57.

Guterbock, Thomas M. "Social Class and Voting Choices in Middletown," *Social Forces* 58 (June 1980), 1044-56.

Gutman, Herbert G. *The Black Family in Slavery and Freedom, 1750-1925.* New York: Pantheon, 1975.

Halverston, John. "Animal Categories and Terms of Abuse," *Man* (New Series) 2 (1976), 505-16.

Hart, Hornell. "Changing Social Attitudes and Interest," Chapter 8 in *Recent Social Trends in the United States.* New York: McGraw-Hill, 1933.

Hayghe, H. "Marital and Family Characteristics of the Labor Force," *Monthly Labor Review* 101 (March 1978), 51-54.

Henretta, James A. "The Morphology of New England Society in the Colonial Period," *Journal of Interdisciplinary History* 11 (Autumn 1971), 379-98.

Hill, Reuben. "Family Patterns in the Changing South," pp. 127-46 in *Transactions of the Third World Congress of Sociology*, vol. 4. London: International Sociological Association, 1956.

_____. "The Three Generation Research Design: Method for Studying Family and Social Change," pp. 536-51 in Reuben Hill and René Konig (eds.). *Families in East and West.* Paris: Mouton, 1970a.

_____. *Family Development in Three Generations.* Cambridge, Mass.: Schenkman, 1970b.

_____. "Social Theory and Family Development," pp. 9-39 in Jean Cuisenier (ed.). *Le Cycle de la vie familiale dans les sociétés européenes.* Paris: Mouton, 1977.

Hunt, Morton. *Sexual Behavior in the 1970's.* Chicago: Playboy Press, 1974.

Indiana State Board of Health. *Annual Statistical Reports.* Indianapolis: Division of Public Health Statistics, 1966-1975.

_____. *Indiana Births, 1900-1965.* Indianapolis: Division of Public Health Statistics, 1967a.

_____. *Indiana Marriages, 1962-1965.* Indianapolis: Division of Public Health Statistics, 1967b.

_____. *Marriages by County of Marriage and Month of Occurrence.* Indianapolis: Division of Public Health Statistics, 1976.

Jacques, Jeffrey M., and Karen J. Chason. "Cohabitation: Its Impact on Marital Success," *Family Coordinator* 28 (January 1979), 32-39.

Johnson, Sheila K. "Sociology of Xmas Cards," pp. 276-82 in Barry J. Wishart and Louis C. Reichmann (eds.). *Modern Sociological Issues.* New York: Macmillan, 1975. (Reprinted from *Transaction/Society*, 1971.)

Kett, Joseph F. "Growing Up in Rural New England, 1800-1840," pp. 1-17 in Tamara K. Hareven (ed.). *Anonymous Americans: Explorations in Nineteenth-Century Social History.* Englewood Cliffs, N.J.: Prentice-Hall, 1971.

Kinsey, Alfred, Wardell B. Pomeroy, and Clyde E. Martin. *Sexual Behavior in the Human Male.* Philadelphia: W. Saunders Company, 1948.

_____. *Sexual Behavior in the Human Female.* Philadelphia: W. B. Saunders Company, 1953.

Lantz, Herman R., Eloise C. Snyder, Margaret Britton, and Raymond Schmitt. "Pre-industrial Patterns in the Colonial Family in America: A Content Analysis of Colonial Magazines," *American Sociological Review* 33 (June 1968), 413-26.

Lasch, Christopher. *Haven in a Heartless World.* New York: Basic Books, 1979.

Leach, Edmund. *Rethinking Anthropology*. London: Athlone Press, 1961.
———. "Anthropological Aspects of Language: Animal Categories and Verbal Abuse," in E. H. Lenneberg (ed.). *New Directions in the Study of Language*. Cambridge, Mass.: MIT Press, 1964.
———. *Culture and Communication*. Cambridge: Cambridge University Press, 1976.
Leaf, Murray J. *Information and Behavior in a Sikh Village*. Berkeley, Calif.: University of California Press, 1972.
Leichter, Hope Jensen, and William E. Mitchell. *Kinship and Casework*. New York: Russell Sage, 1967.
Lesy, Michael. *Wisconsin Death Trip*. New York: Random House, 1973.
Lévi-Strauss, Claude. "The Study of Asdiwal," in E. R. Leach (ed.). *The Structural Study of Myth and Totemism*. Association of Social Anthropologists (of Great Britain) Monographs, vol. 5. London: Tavistock Publications, 1967.
———. *Structural Anthropology*. London: Allen Lane, 1968.
———. *The Raw and the Cooked* (trans., J. and D. Weightman). London: Jonathan Cape, 1969.
Libby, Roger W., and Robert N. Whitehurst. *Renovating Marriage*. Danville, Calif.: Consensus Publisher, 1975.
Lincoln, Richard. "Is Pregnancy Good for Teenagers?" *USA Today* 107 (July 1978), 35-37.
Litwak, Eugene, and Henry J. Meyer. "A Balance Theory of Coordination between Bureaucratic Organizations and Community Primary Groups," *Administrative Science Quarterly* 11 (June 1966), 31-58.
Long, Larry, and Celia B. Boertlein. "The Geographical Mobility of Americans: An International Comparison," in *Current Population Reports*, Social Studies Series, P-23, no. 64, Bureau of the Census. Washington, D.C.: U.S. Government Printing Office, 1980.
Lynd, Robert S. "The People vs. Consumers," Chapter 17 in *Recent Social Trends in the United States*. New York: McGraw-Hill, 1933.
Lynd, Robert S., and Helen Merrell Lynd. *Middletown: A Study in American Culture*. New York: Harcourt and Brace, 1929.
———. *Middletown in Transition: A Study in Cultural Conflicts*. New York: Harcourt and Brace, 1937.
Mair, Lucy. *Witchcraft*. New York: McGraw-Hill, 1969.
Malinowski, B. *Magic, Science, and Religion*. Garden City, N.Y.: Doubleday, 1954.
Marriage and Divorce Today, 5, 23 (January 21, 1980), 1.
Marwick, Max (ed.). *Witchcraft and Sorcery*. New York: Penguin Books, 1970.
Mauss, Marcel. *The Gift: Forms and Functions of Exchange in Archaic Societies* (trans., Ian Cunnison). London: Cohen and West, 1954.
Modell, John, Frank Furstenberg, and Theodore Hesberg. "Social Change and Transition to Adulthood in Historical Perspective," *Journal of Family History* 1 (August 1976), 7-34.
Modell, John, Frank Furstenberg, Douglas Strong, and Sarane Spence Boocock. "The Timing of Marriage in the Transition to Adulthood, 1860-1975," pp. s120-50 in John Demos and Sarane Spence Boocock (eds.). *Turning Points: Historical and Sociological Essays on the Family*. Supplement to *American Journal of Sociology* 84 (1978).
Modell, John, and Tamara K. Hareven. "Urbanization and the Malleable Household: An Examination of Boarding and Lodging in American Families," *Journal of Marriage and the Family* 35 (August 1973), 467-79.
Mott, Frank L., and Sylvia F. Moore. "The Socioeconomic Determinants and Shortrun

Consequences of Marital Disruption." Paper presented at meetings of the Population Association of America, St. Louis, April 20-22, 1977.

Nadel, S. F. *Nupe Religion.* London: Routledge and Kegan Paul, 1954.

National Opinion Research Center. *General Social Survey.* Chicago: University of Chicago, 1976.

Needham, Rodney. *Symbolic Classification.* Santa Monica, Calif.: Goodyear Publishing Company, 1979.

Nye, F. Ivan. "Emerging and Declining Roles," *Journal of Marriage and the Family* 36 (May 1974), 238-45.

_____. *Role Structure and Analysis of the Family.* Beverly Hills, Calif.: Sage Publications, 1967.

Nye, F. Ivan, and Steven McLaughlin. "Role Competence and Marital Satisfaction," in F. Ivan Nye. *Role Structure and Analysis of the Family.* Beverly Hills, Calif. Sage Publications, 1976.

Ogburn, William F. (with the assistance of Clark Tibbitts). "The Family and Its Functions," Chapter 13 in *Recent Social Trends in the United States.* New York: McGraw-Hill, 1933.

Ogburn, William F., and Meyer F. Nimkoff. *Technology and the Changing Family.* Boston: Houghton-Mifflin, 1955.

O'Neill, William L. *Divorce in the Progressive Era.* New Haven, Conn.: Yale University Press, 1967.

Orden, Susan R., and Norman M. Bradburn. "Working Wives and Marital Happiness," *American Journal of Sociology* 74 (January 1969), 392-407.

Ortiz, Alfonso. "Ritual Drama and the Pueblo World View," in A. Ortis (ed.). *New Perspectives on the Pueblos.* Albuquerque: University of New Mexico Press, 1972.

Parsons, Talcott. "The Kinship System of the Contemporary United States," *American Anthropologist* 45 (1943), 23-28.

Pickett, Robert S. "The American Family: An Embattled Institution," *The Humanist* 35 (May/June 1975), 5-8.

The Playboy Report on American Men. Survey conducted for Playboy Enterprises, by Louis Harris and Associates. New York: Playboy, 1979.

Pleck, Elizabeth. "A Mother's Wages: Income Earnings among Married Italian and Black Women, 1896-1911," pp. 490-511 in Michael Gordon (ed.). *The American Family in Social-Historical Perspective* (2nd ed.). New York: St. Martin's Press, 1978.

Pleck, Joseph H. "Men's Family Work: Three Perspectives and Some New Data," *Family Coordinator* 28 (October 1979), 481-88.

Preston, Samuel H., and John McDonald. "The Incidence of Divorce within Cohorts of American Marriages Contracted Since the Civil War," *Demography* 16 (February 1979), 1-26.

Reiss, Ira L. "The Sexual Renaissance: A Summary and Analyses," *Journal of Social Issues* 22 (1966), 123-37.

Reiss, Paul J. "The Extended Kinship System: Correlates of and Attitudes on Frequency of Interaction," *Marriage and Family Living* 24 (November 1962), 333-39.

Riley, Matilda, and Marilyn Johnson. "Age Stratification of the Society." Paper presented at the annual meeting of the American Sociological Association, Denver, August 28-30, 1971.

Riley, Matilda W., Michael Johnson, and Ann Foner. *Aging and Society: A Sociology of Age Stratification* (vol. 3). New York: Russell Sage, 1972.

Rollins, Boyd, and Harold Feldman. "Marital Satisfaction over the Family Life Cycle," *Journal of Marriage and the Family* 32 (1970), 20-28.

Sapir, J. David. "The Anatomy of Metaphor," in J. D. Sapir and J. C. Crocker (eds.). *The Social Use of Metaphor.* Philadelphia: University of Pennsylvania Press, 1977.

Scharff, Edward E. "The Two-Paycheck Life: A Subtle Revolution," *Money* 8 (1979), 34-39.

Schieffelin, Edward L. *The Sorrow of the Lonely and the Burning of the Dancers.* New York: St. Martin's Press, 1976.

Smith, Elizabeth M. "A Follow-up Study of Women Who Request Abortion," *American Journal of Orthopsychiatry* 43 (July 1973), 574-85.

Snider, Arthur J. "Learn First, Marry Later: One Way to Reduce Divorces?" Salt Lake *Tribune* (February 5, 1975).

Sorokin, Pitirim. *The American Sexual Revolution.* Boston: Porter Sargeant, 1956.

Sperber, Dan. *Rethinking Symbolism.* London: Cambridge University Press, 1975.

Stafford, Rebecca, Elaine Backman, and Pamela Dibona. "The Division of Labor among Cohabiting and Married Couples," *Journal of Marriage and the Family* 39 (February 1977), 54.

Stein, Ben. *The View from Sunset Boulevard.* New York: Basic Books, 1979.

Tanner, J. M. "Growing Up," pp. 17-25 in *Life and Death and Medicine* (a Scientific American Book). San Francisco: W. H. Freeman and Company, 1973.

Terman, Louis H. *Psychological Factors in Marital Happiness.* New York: McGraw-Hill, 1938.

Thomas, W. I., and Dorothy S. Thomas. *The Child in America: Behavior Problems and Programs.* New York: Alfred A. Knopf, 1928.

Tocqueville, Alexis de. *Democracy in America* [1870]. Garden City, N.Y.: Mayer Edition, Doubleday, 1959.

Troll, Lillian, and Vern Bengtson. "Generations in the Family," pp. 127-61 in Wesley R. Burr, Reuben Hill, F. Ivan Nye, and Ira L. Reiss. *Contemporary Theories about the Family: Research-Based Theories* (vol. 1). New York: The Free Press, 1979.

Turner, Victor W. *The Forest of Symbols.* Ithaca, N.Y.: Cornell University Press, 1967.

Udry, J. Richard, and Naomi M. Morris. "Relative Contribution of Male and Female Age to the Frequency of Marital Intercourse," *Social Biology* 25 (Summer 1978), 128-34.

Uhlenberg, Peter R. "A Study of Cohort Life Cycles: Cohorts of Native Born Massachusetts Women, 1830-1920," *Population Studies* 23 (November 1969), 407-420.

——. "Cohort Variations in Family Life Experiences of U.S. Females," *Journal of Marriage and the Family* 36 (1974), 284-89.

U.S. Bureau of the Census. *U.S. Census of the Population: 1900* (vol. 1, part 1; vol. 2, part 2). Washington, D.C.: U.S. Government Printing Office 1901.

——. *Marriage and Divorce: 1867-1907.* Washington, D.C.: U.S. Government Printing Office, 1908.

——. *U.S. Census of the Population: 1910* (vol. 1). Washington, D.C.: U.S. Government Printing Office, 1913.

——. *Fourteenth Census of the United States, 1920, Population, 1920* (vol. 2). Washington, D.C.: U.S. Government Printing Office, 1922a.

——. *U.S. Census of the Population, 1920* (vols. 2, 3, 4). Washington, D.C.: U.S. Government Printing Office, 1922b, 1923.

——. *U.S. Census of the Population, 1930* (vol. 3, part 1; vol. 4). Washington, D.C.: U.S. Government Printing Office, 1932, 1933.

——. *U.S. Census of the Population, 1940* (vol. 2, part 2). Washington, D.C.: U.S. Government Printing Office, 1943.

——. *U.S. Census of the Population, 1950* (vol. 2, part 2). Washington, D.C.: U.S. Government Printing Office, 1952.

_____ . *U.S. Census of the Population, 1950* (vol. 2, part 14). Washington, D.C.: U.S. Government Printing Office, 1952.

_____ . *U.S. Census of the Population, 1960* (vol. 1, part 16). Washington, D.C.: U.S. Government Printing Office, 1961.

_____ . *Census of the Population, 1970. General Social and Economic Characteristics* (vol. 16, Indiana). Washington, D.C.: U.S. Government Printing Office, 1971.

_____ . *U.S. Census of the Population, 1970* (vol. 1, part 16). Washington, D.C.: U.S. Government Printing Office, 1972a.

_____ . *U.S. Census of the Population and Housing, 1970*, Census Tracts PHC (1)-137. Washington, D.C.: U.S. Government Printing Office, 1972b.

_____ . *Vital Statistics of the U.S.: 1970* (vols. 1 and 3). Washington, D.C.: U.S. Government Printing Office, 1974.

_____ . *Historical Statistical Series of the U.S.: Colonial Times to 1970* (Part 1). Washington, D.C.: U.S. Government Printing Office, 1975.

_____ . *Statistical Abstract of the United States, 1978.* Washington, D.C.: U.S. Government Printing Office, 1978.

U.S. Bureau of Labor. *Report on Condition of Women and Child Wage Earners in the United States.* Senate Document 645, 61st Congress, 2nd Session, 1910.

U.S. Department of Health and Human Services. *Monthly Vital Statistics Report*, vol. 29, no. 3 (June 10, 1980). Washington, D.C.: Public Health Service, National Center for Health Statistics.

U.S. Department of Health, Education, and Welfare. *Vital Statistics of the United States: Natality, 1957 through 1975* (vol. 1). Washington, D.C.: Public Health Service, National Center for Health Statistics.

U.S. Department of the Interior, Census Division, *Compendium of the Eleventh Census: 1890* (part 1). Washington, D.C.: U.S. Department of the Interior, 1896.

Van Gennep, Arnold. *The Rites of Passage* (trans. Monika Vizedom and Gabrielle Caffee). London: Routledge and Kegan Paul, 1960.

Vinovskis, Maris A. "Angels' Heads and Weeping Willows: Death in Early America," pp. 546-63 in Michael Gordon (ed.). *The American Family in Social-Historical Perspective* (2nd ed). New York: St. Martin's Press, 1978.

Walker, K. , and M. Woods. *Time Use: A Measure of Household Production of Family Goods and Services.* Washington, D.C.: American Home Economics Association, 1976.

Warner, W. Lloyd, and Paul S. Lunt. *The Status System of a Modern Community.* New Haven, Conn.: Yale University Press, 1942.

Wells, Robert F. "Demographic Change and the Life Cycle of American Families," *Journal of Interdisciplinary History* 2 (Autumn 1971), 273-82.

Wilkes, Paul. "Thoughts on Sex, Love, and Being Single," Middletown's morning newspaper (November 22, 1977).

Williams, Robin. *American Society: A Sociological Interpretation.* New York: Alfred A. Knopf, 1967.

Williamson, Margaret Holmes. "Powhatan Hair," *Man* (New Series) 14 (1979), 392-413.

Wilson, Monica. *Rituals of Kinship among the Nyakyusa.* London: Oxford University Press, for the International African Institute, 1957.

Winch, Robert F. *Mate Selection: A Study of Complementary Needs.* New York: Harper, 1958.

_____ . "Permanence and Change in the History of the American Family and Some Speculations as to Its Future," *Journal of Marriage and the Family* 32 (February 1970), 6-18.

Wirth, Louis. "Urbanism as a Way of Life," *American Journal of Sociology* 44 (1938), 1-24.

Wright, James D. "Are Working Women Really More Satisfied? Evidence from Several National Surveys," *Journal of Marriage and the Family* 40 (May 1978), 301-13.

Yankelovich, Skelly, and White, Inc. *General Mills American Family Report 1976-77: Raising Children in a Changing Society.* Minneapolis: General Mills, 1977.

Yearbook of the State of Indiana: 1917. Indianapolis: The Legislative Bureau, 1918.

Yearbook of the State of Indiana: 1920. Indianapolis: The Legislative Bureau, 1921.

Zelnik, Melvin, Kim J. Young, and John F. Kantner. "Probabilities of Intercourse and Conception among U.S. Teenage Women: 1971 and 1976," *Family Planning Perspectives* 11 (1979), 177-83.

INDEXES

Author Index

Subject Index

of, 25; *Life*, 19. *See also* Mass media
"Magic Middletown," 38, 324
Mann Act, 333
Manufacturing, 11, 13, 60
Marital satisfaction, 16-17, 41, 52-54, 100-103, 116-35, 309
Marital status, differences in between black and white women, 57
Marriage, 116-35; average age at, 19, 296; during the *1970s*, 121-35; during the *1930s*, 120-21; during the *1920s*, 116-20; propensity to enter into, 43-44; rates of, 17, 19, 35, 44, 46, 51, 337; timing of, 296-97. *See also* Marital satisfaction; Marital status
Mass media, 4, 22-23, 74, 98, 112, 128-29; exposure to, 123, 127; intrusion of, 22-25; and sexual revolution, 163. *See also* Magazines; Newspapers; Radio; Television
Massage parlors, 162
Median age, 41, 56
Medicaid, 26
Memorial Day, 225, 226
Memorial Hospital, 183
Middletown County Task Force on Battered Wives, 134
Middletown Psychiatric Clinic, 156
Mobility, 22; geographical, 107; and home ownership, 15; residential, 10, 107-8
Modernization, 274; of the community, 136; effect of on kinship, 198; influence of on the family, 137; as observed by the Lynds, 11; slowing of, 36, 108, 157, 272
Montessori School, 155, 157
Mortgage loans, 13-14, 27, 114
Mothers' Club, 155
Mother's Day, 226
Movie theaters, 24

Narcotics. *See* Drugs
National trusts, 11
Natural gas boom, 11
Negroes. *See* Blacks
New Deal, 22, 26, 326
New morality, 56
New Year's Day, 226, 236
New Year's Eve, 235
Newspapers, 22-23, 83, 173. *See also* Mass media

Nuclear family, 30, 278, 340; death of, 122; definition of, 197; types of, 278-79. *See also* Family

Occupational Safety and Health Administration, 28
Occupations, 12, 20, 34-35, 58, 89-91; effect of on kinship network, 204; of women, 100
Organizations. *See* Associations

Parents: authority of, 33; influence of, 140-44; organized assistance for, 155-57; qualities of good, 149-50; responsibilities of, 137; roles of, 150-55
Parents without Partners, 133
Pensions. *See* Retirement
Pessimism, 37
Planned Parenthood Clinic, 162-63, 169, 170, 174-75, 183, 186-87
Politics, 6, 29
Population: of blacks, 60, 280; density of, 277; differences between black and white in *1920s*, 57; distribution of, 40, 42, 45-46, 87; in *1880s*, 11; of foreign-born people, 277; increase in, 3, 23; median age of, 41, 56; in *1970s*, 22, 60; in *1960s*, 14; in *1920s*, 60, 272; in *1925*, 6, 22; structure of, 41
Pornography, 24, 162, 192; and children, 189
Poverty, 11, 26
Premarital Pregnancy Program, 190
Presbyterian Church, 8. *See also* Churches; Religion
President's Research Committee on Social Trends, 325
Primary relative, definition of, 341
Prohibition, 32
Property: crimes on, 28; ownership of, 10; taxes on, 34
Prostitution, 119, 187-88
Protestant churches, 8, 162, 279. *See also* Churches; Religion
Psychiatric Clinics of Indiana, 156

Quakers, median age at marriage of, 290

Race, 8, 15
Radio, 22, 23, 24. *See also* Mass media
Railroad Retirement Board, 27